C000300769

HNC HND BUSINESS

Optional Units 13-16

Business & Management

Course Book

BPP PUBLISHING

EDEXCEL HNC & HND BUSINESS

First edition January 2001

ISBN 0 7517 7041 8

British Library Cataloguing-in Publication Data

A catalogue record for this book is available from the British Library

Published by

BPP Publishing Limited

Aldine House, Aldine Place

London W12 8AW

www.bpp.com

Printed in Great Britain by Ashford Colour Press

CONTENTS

BPP PUBLISHING

INTRODUCTION

The HNC and HND qualifications in Business are very demanding. The suggested content, set out by Edexcel in guidelines for each unit, includes topics which are normally covered at degree level. Students therefore need books which get straight to the core of these topics, and which build upon their existing knowledge and experience. BPP's series of Course Books have been designed to meet that need.

This book has been written specifically for the optional pathway in Business Management (Units 13 to 16). It covers the Edexcel guidelines and suggested content in full, and includes the following features.

- The Edexcel guidelines
- A study guide explaining the key features of the book and how to get the most from your studies
- An index

In some instances, topics required by the Edexcel Guidelines for these Units have already been covered in the course books published for the HNC/HND Core Units. We cross reference such topics in the Guidelines themselves, so that you can see easily where the information may be found.

Each chapter contains:

- An introduction and study objectives
- Summary diagrams and signposts, to guide you through the chapter
- Numerous activities, topics for discussion, definitions and examples
- A chapter roundup, a quick quiz with answers, answers to activities and an assignment (with answer guidelines at the end of the book)

BPP Publishing are the leading providers of targeted texts for professional qualifications. Our customers need to study effectively. They cannot afford to waste time. They expect clear, concise and highly-focused study material. This series of Course Books for HNC and HND Business has been designed and produced to fulfil those needs.

BPP Publishing
January 2001

Titles in this series:

Core Unit 1	Marketing
Core Unit 2	Managing Financial Resources
Core Unit 3	Organisations and Behaviour
Core Unit 4	Organisations, Competition and Environment
Core Unit 5	Quantitative Techniques for Business
Core Unit 6	Legal and Regulatory Framework
Core Unit 7	Management Information Systems
Core Unit 8	Business Strategy
Option Units 9-12	Business & Finance
Option Units 13-16	Business & Management
Option Units 17-20	Business & Marketing
Option Units 21-24	Business & Personnel

For more information, or to place an order, please call 020 8740 2211, or fill in the order form at the back of this book.

If you would like to send in your comments on this book, please turn to the review form on the last page.

EDEXCEL GUIDELINES FOR UNIT 13 MANAGING ACTIVITIES

Description of the Unit

This unit focuses on the effective and efficient planning and management of work activities. It provides students with the knowledge and skills to design, implement and change operational systems to improve their effectiveness and efficiency.

Summary of outcomes

To achieve this unit a student must:

1 Explain how processes and function inter-relate in the **organisational structure**

2 **Plan work activities** to meet the objectives of the organisation and the needs of the customer

3 **Manage work activities** to achieve organisational objectives

4 Design and monitor appropriate systems to ensure **quality of products and services**

5 Manage **health and safety** in the workplace

6 Make **improvements** to the organisation's systems and activities

Outcomes and assessment criteria

The learning outcomes and the criteria used to assess them are shown in the table below.

Content

		Chapter coverage
1	**Organisational structure**	
	Organisational structure: processes and functions, inter-relationships of functions, mission, aims, objectives and culture	1
2	**Plan work activities**	
	Plan work activities: internal and external customers, communication methods, customer orientation, market research, product development, planning techniques, PERT, critical path analysis, work flow, prioritising workloads, setting work objectives, time management	2
3	**Manage work activities**	
	Manage work activities: product and service specifications and standards, meeting quality, quantity, time and cost objectives, systems eg Just-In-Time, value-added chains, statistical process control, co-ordinating activities, working within organisational constraints and limitations	3
4	**Quality of products and services**	
	Quality of products and services: quality systems, quality circles, ISO9000/EN29000, Total Quality Management (TQM), managing and monitoring quality	4

5 **Health and safety**

Health and safety: legislation and regulations, organisational policies and procedures, risk assessment and monitoring, practical application 5

6 **Improvements**

Improvements: monitoring systems, problem analysis and decision-making, planning, proposing, implementing and evaluating change, identifying wider implications of change within the organisation, Business Process Re-engineering (BPR) 6

Outcomes and assessment criteria

The learning outcomes and the criteria used to assess them are shown in the table below.

Outcomes	Assessment criteria **To achieve each outcome a student must demonstrate the ability to:**
1 Explain how processes and functions inter-relate in the **organisational structure**	• Describe the structure and culture of an organisation • Explain the inter-relationships between the different processes and functions of an organisation • Identify the mission, aims and objectives of an organisation and explain the effect of these on the structure and culture of the organisation
2 **Plan work activities** to meet the objectives of the organisation and the needs of customers	• Identify the internal and external customers of an organisation and select appropriate systems of communication • Select and use appropriate methods of market research to identify customer needs • Plan product development to meet customer needs • Set appropriate work objectives in line with the objectives of the organisation • Plan work activities to meet set objectives • Prioritise workloads in order to meet objectives within appropriate timescales
3 **Manage work activities** to achieve organisational objectives	• Manage work activities to meet appropriate product and service specifications and standards • Implement appropriate systems to meet organisational standards of quality, quantity, time and cost

4 Design and monitor appropriate systems to ensure **quality of products and service**	• Design and implement appropriate systems to manage and monitor quality to standards specified by the organisation
5 Manage **health and safety** in the workplace	• Assess the risks to health and safety in the workplace • Identify health and safety regulations and legislation applicable in specific work situations • Review organisational health and safety policies and procedures in order to ensure that they comply with the appropriate legislation and regulations • Manage the practical application of health and safety policies and procedures in the workplace
6 Make **improvements** to the organisation's systems and activities	• Monitor systems and work activities and identify problems and opportunities for improvement • Recommend solutions to resolve problems and propose changes to improve operations • Identify the wider implications of change within an organisation • Plan, implement and evaluate changes within an organisation

Guidance

Generating evidence

It is recommended that evidence is generated from work-based assignments which should focus on the management of students' own work activities. Examples of effective systems should be drawn from students' own work experience and that of their peers

Links

This unit links with:

- NVQ units in Management at level 4
  - A2 Manage activities to meet requirements
  - A4 Contribute to improvements at work
  - F4 Implement quality assurance systems
- NVQs in Management: personal competencies – acting assertively, building teams, communicating, focusing on results, influencing others, thinking and taking decisions.

Resources

World Wide Web sites can be useful in providing information and case studies (eg www.bized.co.ac.uk which provides business case studies appropriate for educational purposes).

Delivery

The use of case studies enhances students' understanding of the subject matter and skills particularly where workplace situations do not provide appropriate learning opportunities.

Tutors should be aware that there are links between the Higher National management pathway units and other specialist Higher National pathway units. However, the management units should be taught from the viewpoint of general management rather than management of a specialist function.

Suggested reading

There are a large number of textbooks available covering the areas contained within the unit. Examples are:

Johnson R et al – *Cases in Operations Management* (Pitman Publishing, 1993)

Naylor J – *Operations Management* (Pitman Publishing, 1996)

Slack N et al – *Operations Management* (Pitman Publishing, 1995)

EDEXCEL GUIDELINES FOR UNIT 14 MANAGING PEOPLE

Description of the Unit

This unit develops the skills and knowledge that are needed to manage people within an organisation. It recognises that the management of people operates within the internal framework of organisational values, culture, policies and practices and that externally it should meet the requirements of current legislation and ensure ethical and environmentally friendly behaviour.

Summary of outcomes

To achieve this unit a student must:

1 **Select personnel** against specified requirements

2 Analyse the **development** needs of teams and individuals

3 **Allocate work** to teams and individuals agreeing objectives and work plans

4 **Evaluate performance** of teams and individuals

5 Contribute to the implementation of **disciplinary and grievance procedures**

Content

		Chapter coverage
1	**Select personnel**	
	Select personnel: information and documentation needed for clear specifications of personnel required, individual differences and motivation, assessment and selection methods, relevant legislation	7
2	**Development**	
	Development: identifying development needs, learning style and processes, supporting individual learning and encouraging lifelong learning, planning, recording, monitoring and evaluating, group development, processes and behaviour, group roles, conflict, ambiguity	8
3	**Allocate work**	
	Allocate work: planning, work orientation and job design, motivation theories and empowerment techniques, delegation techniques and processes, leadership and management styles, role of performance management systems	9
4	**Evaluate performance**	
	Evaluate performance: monitoring and control, measuring effective performance, feedback approaches, mentoring, coaching and counselling, interpersonal relationships, conflict and conflict resolution	10
5	**Disciplinary and grievance procedures**	
	Disciplinary and grievance procedures: ACAS Codes of Practice, organisational procedures, relevant legislation	11

BPP PUBLISHING

Outcomes and assessment criteria

The learning outcomes and the criteria used to assess them are shown in the table below.

Outcomes	Assessment criteria **To achieve each outcome a student must demonstrate the ability to:**
1 **Select personnel** against specified requirements	• Identify the characteristics of the person(s) required • Suggest suitable methods for selection • Contribute to the selection process
2 Analyse the **development** needs of teams and individuals	• Analyse the development needs of both teams and individuals in order to improve performance • Apply an awareness of how people learn to identify suitable methods for development • Prepare a development plan • Evaluate the effectiveness of one or more of the development activities • Suggest ways in which lifelong learning could be encouraged
3 **Allocate work** to teams and individuals agreeing objectives and work plans	• Plan or analyse a work activity using appropriate objective-setting techniques and processes • Explain how suitable delegation techniques, processes and management and leadership style could/have been used to motivate and enable subordinates • Suggest ways in which a performance management system could/has contributed to this process
4 **Evaluate performance** of teams and individuals	• Evaluate the effectiveness of a team or an individual • Justify the monitoring evaluation and control methods used • Explain how effective performance will be measured • Explain the potential role of coaching, counselling and mentoring in improving performance • Explain how positive relationships can be maintained and potential conflict positively managed

5 Contribute to the implementation of **disciplinary and grievance procedures**	• Contribute to the resolution of a disciplinary and grievance situation using a real work problem or simulation • Explain the stages of the process, the knowledge and the behaviours needed at each stage • Evaluate the effectiveness of each stage using peers or other parties

Guidance

Generating evidence

Where possible, evidence should be generated from real workplace situations. Where real work situations are not practical then students should be encouraged to use a 'host' organisation or a job situation with which they are familiar (or part of) and simulate the role of a manager.

Links

This unit links with:

- NVQ units in Management at level 4
  - C8 Select personnel for activities
  - C10 Develop teams and individuals to enhance performance
  - C13 Manage the performance of teams and individuals
  - C15 Respond to poor performance in the team
- NVQs in Management: personal competencies – acting assertively, behaving ethically, building teams, communicating, focusing on results, influencing others, searching for information, thinking and taking decisions.

Resources

World Wide Web sites can be useful in providing information and case studies (eg www.bized.co.ac.uk which provides business case studies appropriate for educational purposes).

Delivery

The use of case study analysis and role-play would be useful for students to practise skills.

Tutors should be aware that there are links between the Higher National management pathway units and other specialist Higher National pathway units. However, the management units should be taught from the viewpoint of general management rather than management of a specialist function.

Suggested reading

There are a large number of textbooks available covering the areas contained within the unit. Examples are:

Armstrong M – *A Handbook of Personnel Management Practice* (Kogan Page, 1996)

BPP PUBLISHING

Biddle and Evenden – *Human Aspects of Management* – 2nd Ed. (Institute of Personnel and Development, 1990)

Huczynski and Buchanan – *Organisational Behaviour – An Introductory Text* – 2nd/3rd Ed. (Prentice Hall, 1991)

Mullins – *Management and Organisational Behaviour* – 4th Ed. (Pitman Publishing, 1996)

EDEXCEL GUIDELINES FOR UNIT 15 MANAGING INFORMATION

Description of the Unit

This unit enables students to recognise the need for managers to be able to gather, analyse, record, store and disseminate information as part of the management function. The focus of the unit is not on information systems but on the processes. The unit develops the skills and techniques involved in managing information, and students will learn to manage information to inform decision-making.

Summary of outcomes

To achieve this unit a student must:

1 Establish the **type of information** required to manage day-to-day and medium-term operations

2 Use **sources of information** to inform and aid decision-making

3 **Gather information** from different sources to meet information needs

4 **Analyse information** to inform decision-making

5 **Record and store information** to aid understanding and access

6 Use **dissemination channels** to distribute information throughout the organisation

Content

		Chapter coverage
1	**Type of information**	
	Type of information: qualitative, quantitative, marketing, operational, financial, personnel	12
	(Note: This part of the guidelines is covered in depth in Core Unit 7 of the HNC/HND Business qualification, Management Information)	
2	**Sources of information**	
	Sources of information: internal, external, primary, secondary	12
3	**Gather information**	
	Gather information: interviews, networking, questionnaires, meetings, desk research	12
4	**Analyse information**	
	Analyse information: trends, patterns, accuracy, consistency, relevance, sufficiency, reliability, validity	13
5	**Record and store information**	
	Record and store information: manual, computerised, management information, legal constraints, organisational constraints	14
6	**Dissemination channels**	
	Dissemination channels: oral, written, electronic, presentations, meetings, networking, reports	15

Outcomes and assessment criteria

The learning outcomes and the criteria used to assess them are shown in the table below.

Outcomes	Assessment criteria To achieve each outcome a student must demonstrate the ability to:
1 Establish the **type of information** required to manage day-to-day and medium-term operations	• Identify the different uses for types of information in achieving a set objective for a day-to-day or medium-term operation • Establish information required for improvements and management of change in operations
2 Use **sources of information** to inform and aid decision-making	• Identify all the relevant sources of information to aid decision-making for achieving a set objective
3 **Gather information** from different sources to meet information needs	• Use and justify the relevance of information-gathering techniques in identifying the information needed for a set objective
4 **Analyse information** to inform decision-making	• Apply different analytical techniques to gathered data • Explain how using analytical techniques helps to ensure relevant levels of accuracy, consistency, relevance, sufficiency and reliability in outcomes
5 **Record and store information** to aid understanding and access	• Store information in a relevant format taking into consideration legal and organisational constraints • Use integrated software packages to achieve different formats of the information
6 Use **dissemination channels** to distribute information throughout the organisation	• Identify relevant information needs for different audiences • Select and justify the most effective format and channel to disseminate the information to meet organisational objectives.

Guidance

Generating evidence

Evidence should focus on day-to-day or medium-term workplace objectives. For example the implementation of a quality system or improving customer service. Students should use qualitative and quantitative data and recognise how these can work together. Meetings play an important part of both information gathering and dissemination and as such play a significant part in the learning process.

Links

This unit links with 'Management Information Systems' (Unit 7). It also has links with:

- NVQ units in Management
  - D2 Facilitate meetings
  - D4 Provide information to support decision-making
- NVQs in Management: personal competencies – acting assertively, building teams, communicating, focusing on results, influencing others, searching for information, thinking and taking decisions.

Resources

World Wide Web sites can be useful in providing information and case studies (eg www.bized.co.ac.uk which provides business case studies appropriate for educational purposes).

Delivery

The use of case studies, IT workshops and role-play will enhance delivery of this unit. Tutors should note that 'Management Information Systems' (Unit 7) may have implications for the sequence of delivery of this unit.

Tutors should be aware that there are links between the Higher National management pathway units and other specialist Higher National pathway units. However, the management units should be taught from the viewpoint of general management rather than management of a specialist function.

Suggested reading

There are a number of textbooks available covering the areas contained within the unit. Examples are:

Avison D E and Fitzgerald G – *Information Systems Development* (Blackwell Scientific Publisher, 1992)

Gray P, King W R, McLean E R and Watson H J – *Management of Information Systems* (The Dryden Press, 1997)

EDEXCEL GUIDELINES FOR UNIT 16 MANAGING SELF

Description of the Unit

This unit is concerned with personal development and enables students to build on existing skills to enhance current performance and develop new skills for future personal and career development.

The emphasis is on the needs of the individual but within the context of how the development of self-management corresponds with effective team management in meeting objectives.

Summary of outcomes

To achieve this unit a student must:

1 Carry out a personal **skills audit** and self-appraisal

2 Prepare and agree a personal **development plan** with the line manager

3 **Review and monitor progress** in achieving learning objectives and personal targets

4 **Evaluate progress** and achievement of personal development and learning targets and re-set objectives

Content

		Chapter coverage
1	**Skills audit**	
	Skills audit: management skills, leadership skills, personal development, interpersonal skills	16
2	**Development plan**	
	Development plan: career development, personal development, current performance, future needs, aims, objectives, targets, review dates, achievement dates, learning programme/activities	16
3	**Review and monitor progress**	
	Review and monitor progress: against set aims, objectives, targets, dates, self-assessment, feedback from colleagues and line manager	16
4	**Evaluate progress**	
	Evaluate progress: against original aims, objectives, targets, responding to feedback, resetting aims, objectives and targets	16

Outcomes and assessment criteria

The learning outcomes and the criteria used to assess them are shown in the table below.

Outcomes	Assessment criteria **To achieve each outcome a student must demonstrate the ability to:**
1 Carry out a personal **skills audit** and self-appraisal	• Identify, review and assess own performance of current management skills
2 Prepare and agree a personal **development plan** with the line manager	• Set, prioritise and agree personal development targets with the line manager • Devise a personal development plan to achieve personal targets and short- and long-term learning objectives
3 **Review and monitor progress** in achieving learning objectives and personal targets	• Identify relevant sources of information and help • Review and monitor progress against set aims and objectives • Seek and respond to appropriate feedback.
4 **Evaluate progress** and achievement of personal development and learning targets and reset objectives	• Evaluate learning and development with original aims and objectives set in the development plan • Reset objectives in the light of evaluation and feedback

Guidance

Generating evidence

Assessment of this unit could be via a personal journal or skills log complied throughout the programme. It should be based on the student's own personal and career aims and needs.

Links

This unit links with:

- NVQ units in Management
  - C2 Develop you own resources
  - C5 Develop productive working relationships
- NVQs in Management: personal competencies – acting assertively, behaving ethically, building teams, communicating, focusing on results, influencing others, managing self, thinking and taking decisions

Resources

World Wide Web sites can be useful in providing information and case studies (eg www.bized.co.ac.uk which provides business case studies appropriate for educational purposes).

Delivery

This unit would benefit from a series of skills-based workshops or a residential period to facilitate personal development.

Tutors should be aware that there are links between the Higher National management pathway units and other specialist Higher National pathway units. However, the management units should be taught from the viewpoint of general management rather than management of a specialist function.

Suggested reading

There are a large number of textbooks available covering the areas contained within the unit. Examples are:

Adair J – *Effective leadership* (Pan Books, 1987)

Adair J – *Effective Time Management* (Pan Books, 1989)

Hartley P – *Interpersonal Communication* (Routledge, 1993)

Mullins – *Management and Organisational Behaviour* (Pitman Publishing, 1996)

Video

Melrose Learning Resources produce a variety of video resources which many be of use for this unit. Resources can normally be purchased or hired. Some examples are:

- *The Leadership Experience*
- *Managing Yourself*
- *Dealing with Conflict*

Further details and a catalogue are available from:

Video Arts,
Dumbarton House,
68, Oxford Street
London W1D 1LH

Telephone: 020 7637 7288

STUDY GUIDE

This Course Book gives full coverage of the Edexcel guidelines. It also includes features designed specifically to make learning effective and efficient.

(a) Each chapter begins with a summary diagram which maps out the areas covered by the chapter. You can use the diagrams during revision as a basis for your notes.

(b) After the summary diagram there is an introduction, which sets the chapter in context. This is followed by learning objectives, which show you what you will learn as you work through the chapter.

(c) Throughout the book, there are special aids to learning. These are indicated by the following symbols.

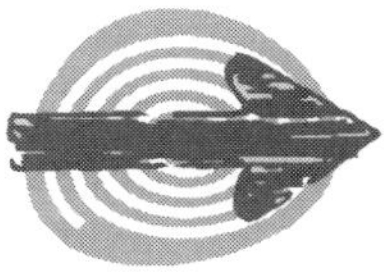

Signposts guide you through the text, showing how each section connects with the next.

Definitions give the meanings of key terms.

Activities help you to test how much you have learnt. An indication of the time you should take on each is given. Answers are given at the end of each chapter.

Topics for discussion are for use in seminars. They give you a chance to share your views with your fellow students. They allow you to highlight holes in your knowledge and to see how others understand concepts. If you have time, try 'teaching' someone the concepts you have learnt in a session. This helps you to remember key points and answering their questions will consolidate your knowledge.

Examples relate what you have learnt to the outside world. Try to think up your own examples as you work through the text.

Chapter roundups present the key information from the chapter in a concise format. Useful for revision.

(d) The wide **margin** on each page is for your notes. You will get the best out of this book if you interact with it. Write down your thoughts and ideas. Record examples, question theories, add references to other pages in the text and rephrase key points in your own words.

(e) At the end of each chapter, there is a **chapter roundup**, and a **quick quiz** with answers. Use these to revise and consolidate your knowledge. The chapter roundup summarises the chapter. The quick quiz tests what you have learnt (the answers refer you back to the chapter so you can look over subjects again).

(f) At the end of the book, you will find two assignments for each unit. Each assignment (with a time guide) allows you to put your knowledge into practice. Answer guidelines for the assignments are after the assignments.

(g) At the end of the book, there is an index.

PART A: UNIT 13

MANAGING ACTIVITIES

Chapter 1 : ORGANISATIONAL STRUCTURES

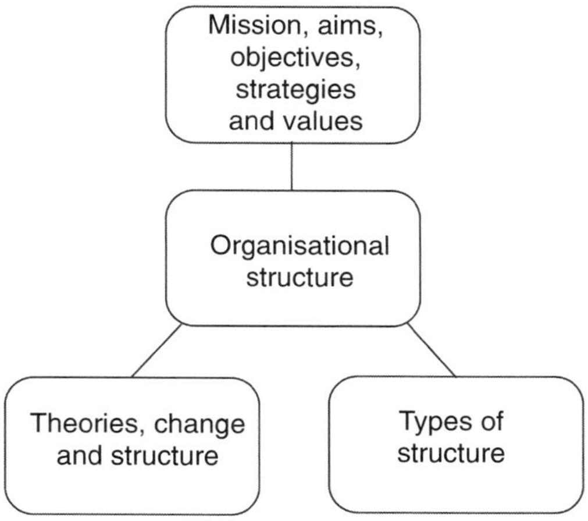

Introduction

Today you want to drive to college. You know that you can call at a BP petrol station and fill the tank, pay with your Visa credit card and go on your way along the district council's well surfaced road. If you break down you can call out the very, very nice man from the AA.

Each of the organisations involved with your drive has **objectives**. The objectives of the organisation and what it does determine the type of structure that it has. An efficient structure for a government department would be effective for an advertising agency. Changes in technology, such as the development of personal computers over the last decade or so, can radically change both the organisation's ways for working and their structures.

Your objectives

In this chapter you will learn about the following.

(a) The hierarchy of organisational objectives

(b) Different organisational structures

(c) How organisations are classified according to various criteria or structure

(d) How changing theories of management have led to different structures

(e) The effects of changes in technology and working practices on the structure of organisations

First we look at the influences that shape organisations.

1 HIERARCHY OF OBJECTIVES

Suppose that none of the organisations involved with your journey to college outlined in the **Introduction** had a formal structure. What would happen? For a start, you could not take it for granted that you could buy petrol at a petrol station. Without having people to take the decisions to drill for oil, extract it, refine it and ship the petrol to the pumps, there is no guarantee at all that it would all happen.

All organisations have some function to perform, some contribution to make. The function of the business organisation may be seen as the creation and/or supply of goods and services. This involves bringing together the factors of production and their successful mix and direction, to provide products or services in order to create value added.

It is the interaction of people, in order to achieve the aims and objectives, which form the basis of an organisation. Some form of structure is needed by which people's interactions are channelled and co-ordinated.

Organisations need:

- objectives
- people
- structure

Most writers agree with the idea that there is a hierarchy of objectives. Mintzberg uses the following:

(a) Mission – 'overriding premise' of the business
(b) Goal – 'general statement of aim or purpose'
(c) Objective – quantification or more precise statement of a goal
(d) Strategies – broad kind of action to achieve objective

Some writers ignore purpose and mission or use aims, goals, objectives and targets interchangeably. However, it is important to be able to clarify the ways in which you are using them.

1.1 Mission

Definition

> **Mission** 'describes the organisation's basic function in society, in terms of the products and services it produces for its clients' (Mintzberg).

One view of the mission is that it is a broad statement of the purpose of an organisation. It is the primary raison d'être, set in advance of strategy. It can define why the company exists or why its managers and employees feel it exists. It outlines who the organisation exists for (eg shareholders, and possibly other stakeholders such as employees and customers). Possible purposes include those below.

- To create wealth for shareholders, who take priority over all other stakeholders.

- To satisfy the needs of all stakeholders (eg including employees and society at large).

- To reach some higher goals ('the advancement of society' and so forth).

1.2 Mission statements

Definition

> **Mission statements** are formal declarations of underlying purpose. They say what an organisation exists to do.

Mission statements might be reproduced in a number of places (eg at the front of an organisation's annual report, on publicity material, in the chairman's office, in communal work areas etc). There is no standard format, but they should have certain qualities

- **Brevity** will make them easier to understand and remember.
- **Flexibility** will enable them to accommodate change.
- They should be **distinctive**, to make the firm stand out.

Scott Adams, creator of Dilbert, defines a mission statement as 'a long awkward sentence that demonstrates management's inability to think clearly'. This illustrates the main problem with mission statements, which is getting people to take them seriously.

FOR DISCUSSION

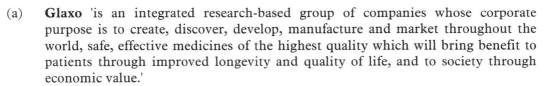

The following statements were taken from annual reports of the organisations concerned. Are they 'mission statements'? If so, are they any good?

(a) **Glaxo** 'is an integrated research-based group of companies whose corporate purpose is to create, discover, develop, manufacture and market throughout the world, safe, effective medicines of the highest quality which will bring benefit to patients through improved longevity and quality of life, and to society through economic value.'

(b) **IBM (UK)**: 'We shall increase the pace of change. Market-driven quality is our aim. It means listening and responding more sensitively to our customers. It means eliminating defects and errors, speeding up all our processes, measuring everything we do against a common standard, and it means involving employees totally in our aims'.

(c) **Matsushita**: 'the duty of the manufacturer is to serve the foundation of man's happiness by making man's life affluent with an inexpensive and inexhaustible supply of life's necessities.'

(d) **Guinness Group**: 'Guinness plc is one of the world's leading drinks companies, producing and marketing an unrivalled portfolio of international best-selling brands, such as Johnnie Walker, Bell's and Dewar's Scotch whiskies, Gordon's and Tanqueray gins, and Guinness stout itself - the world's most distinctive beer. The strategy is to focus resources on the development of the Group's alcoholic drinks businesses. The objectives are to provide superior long-term financial returns for shareholders, to create a working environment in which people can perform to their fullest potential and to be recognised as one of the world's leading consumer brand development companies'.

(e) **British Film Institute**. 'The BFI is the UK national agency with responsibility for encouraging and conserving the arts of film and television. Our aim is to ensure that the many audiences in the UK are offered access to the widest possible choice of cinema and television, so that their enjoyment is enhanced through a deeper understanding of the history and potential of these vital and popular art forms.'

1.3 Aims or goals

Aims or goals are the secondary objectives derived from the mission and also set in advance of strategy.

Organisations have definite aims (or goals); by this we mean they try to make particular things happen. An aim or goal is a future expectation – a desired future state. It is something the organisation is striving to accomplish.

Definition

> **Goals** or **aims** give a sense of direction for the activities of an organisation and are sufficient for the satisfaction of the organisation's mission.

They can be used in a very broad sense to refer to the overall purpose of the organisation, eg to produce washing machines. They may also be used to refer to more specific desired outcomes, eg to produce and sell a given number of washing machines within a given period of time.

The aims of an organisation will determine the nature of the organisation's inputs and outputs, the series of activities through which the outputs are achieved and interactions with its environment. The extent to which an organisation is successful in achieving its aims is a basis for the evaluation of organisational performance and effectiveness.

Aims serve a number of important functions.

- Aims provide a standard of performance. They focus attention on the activities of the organisation and the direction of the efforts of its members.
- Aims provide the basis for planning and management control of the activities of the organisation.
- Aims provide guidelines for decision-making and justification for actions taken.
- Aims influence the structure of the organisation and determine the nature of the technology employed.
- Aims or goals are the basis for objectives and policies of the organisation.

1.4 Objectives

In accordance with its ideology, the aims of the organisation are translated into objectives, which are expressed in a form that can be measured. All the organisation's objectives should be directed towards achieving the organisation's mission. In business organisations, a paramount consideration is profitability. The mission of a business, whether it is stated or not, must be to carry on its activities at a profit.

They should relate to the critical success factors of the organisation, which are typically:

(a) Profitability
(b) Market share
(c) Growth
(d) Cash flow
(e) Customer satisfaction
(f) Quality of the organisation's products

(g) Industrial relations
(h) Added value

Objectives are normally quantified statements of what the organisation actually intends to achieve and should fulfil the SMART criteria outlined below.

Specific
Measurable
Achievable
Results-orientated
Time-bounded

Whereas mission statements describe a value system for the organisation and some indication of the business it is in, objectives are well defined. For example:

(a) mission: deliver a quality service

(b) aim or goal: enhance manufacturing quality

(c) objectives: over the next twelve months, reduce the number of defects to one part per million

Other examples of objectives include:

(a) increasing the number of customers by x% (sales department objective)
(b) reducing the number of rejects by 50% (production department objective)
(c) responding to calls within ten minutes (hospital ambulance service)

Some objectives are more important than others. When there are several key objectives, some might be achieved only at the expense of others. For example, a company's objective of achieving good profits and profit growth might have adverse consequences for the cash flow or good product quality, or to improve market share, might call for some sacrifice of profits. There will be a trade-off between objectives when strategies are formulated, and a choice will have to be made.

1.5 Strategies

A strategy provides the commercial logic for the company and so defines the nature of the firm's business, the markets it competes in and the competencies and competitive advantages by which it hopes to prosper.

Definition

> A **strategy** is a course of action, including the specification of resources required to achieve a specific objective.

Strategy is the organised development of resources (financial manufacturing, marketing, technological, manpower etc) to achieve specific objectives against competition from rival organisations. These perform a series of activities and they are all part of the inter-related sub-system of the organisation.

Resource planning will require answers to the following questions.

- What are the key tasks that have to be completed?
- What control systems exist?
- What changes should be made to resources?

As a result of this planning, organisations may decide to change their structure to meet the strategic requirements more closely.

1.6 Policies and standards of behaviour

Policies provide the basis for decision-making and the course of action to follow to achieve objectives. For example, where the objective is to increase the number of customers by x%, the policy might be to sell to every retail outlet that is credit worthy. Some policy decisions are directly influenced by external factors, eg government legislation on equal opportunities.

Objectives and policy together provide corporate guidelines for the operation and management of the organisation. For example, specific decisions relating to personnel policy could include:

- giving priority to promotion from within the organisation
- enforcing retirement at government pensionable age
- permitting line managers, in consultation with the personnel manager, to appoint staff up to a given salary/wage level

Policies and strategies need to be converted into everyday performance. They are translated into rules, plans and procedures and relate to all activities of the organisation. For example, a service industry that wishes to be the best in its market must aim for standards of service, in all its operations, which are at least as good as those found in its competitors. In service businesses, this includes simple matters such as politeness to customers, speed at which phone calls are answered, and so forth.

Activity 1 **(10 minutes)**

Set out one of your new year's resolutions in terms of:

- mission
- goal (aim)
- objectives
- strategy

1.7 Values

The aims of the organisation will have an ideology based on beliefs, values and attitudes. This ideology is a means of control through shared beliefs and determines the culture of the organisation, providing a set of principles that govern the overall conduct of the organisation's operations, code of behaviour, the management of people and its dealings with other organisations. For example, a firm's moral principles might mean refusing an assignment if it believes the client will not benefit, even though this refusal means lost revenue. A sense of mission, or emotional bond, is where employees' personal values coincide with organisational values.

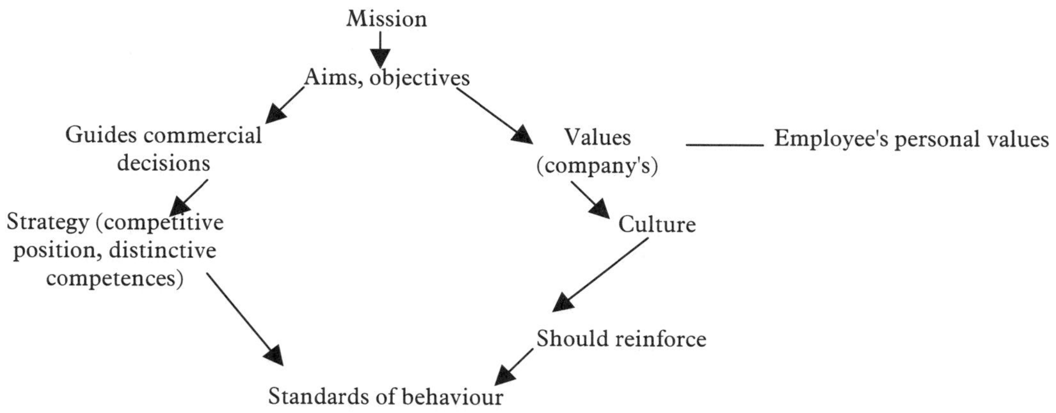

You may feel that philosophical discourse about values and principles is not relevant to organisational performance, and is so much hot air. However, there are several reasons why this scepticism as to the value of mission and aims, because of its emotional content, is misplaced.

- **Values and feelings are integral elements of consumers' buying decisions**, as evidenced by advertising, branding and market research. Therefore there is no reason to exclude them from an organisation's decision-making process.
- **Accountants are a small segment of the population as a whole**, and a respect for numbers that add up and quantifiable information is part of their professional culture and training. This is not necessarily shared by others who hold the issues of value and emotional content, when dealing with customers and doing their job, to be important.
- **Employees are motivated by more than money**, a sense of mission and values can help motivate employees. In some jobs, a sense of vocation and professionalism is bound up with the organisation's mission (eg a hospital).
- Many organisations do take the cultural aspect of mission and aims seriously.

1.8 Organisation structure

Clearly defined and agreed aims and objectives are the first stage in the design of organisation structure and they help facilitate systems of communication between different parts of the organisation. As we have already noted, the aims are related to the input-conversion-output cycle. To achieve its objectives and satisfy its mission and aims the organisation takes inputs from the environment, through a series of activities transforms or converts them into outputs and returns them to the environment as inputs to other systems.

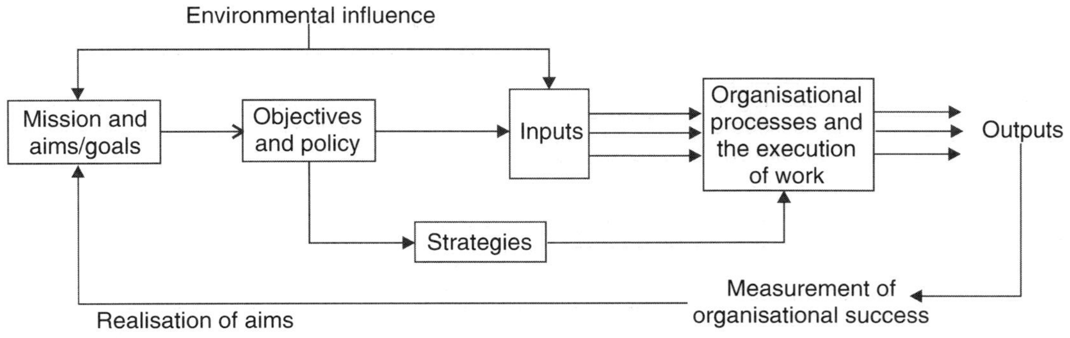

All organisations need lines of direction through the establishment of objectives and the determination of policy.

Other factors also influence the design of the structure. In total, the structure of a business organisation is determined by:

- its mission
- what it does
- its size
- where it operates
- who it deals with
- its culture
- technology
- the complexity of its operations
- its history and future expectations

For example, a hairdresser who provides haircuts to men and women within a two mile radius is clearly going to have a very different market structure to a company providing air travel globally to a global market.

1.9 The public and not-for-profit sectors

Organisations in the public and not-for-profit sectors also have structures determined by the factors listed above. The public services and local government have some additional factors which influence them:

(a) the extent and type of duties and obligations imposed by Parliament, which they must perform;

(b) the changing expectations of society;

(c) changes in government policies and priorities.

Because they are closely associated with government and depend on it for funding, quangos, much of the voluntary sector, many arts and environmental bodies and local clubs and societies that use the facilities of the local authority are all affected by these factors.

FOR DISCUSSION

Consider your college's or university's structure of faculties and departments. Which of the factors listed above have been important in shaping its structure? How do you think that they compare with those that are important for:

(a) a news agent and sub-post office;
(b) the Royal Air Force?

Next we look at the way in which organisations develop hierarchies of authority and specialisation.

2 LEVELS OF ORGANISATION

Organisation structure is the grouping of people into departments or sections and the allocation of responsibility and authority.

Organisation structure implies a framework intended to:

(a) Link individuals in an established network of relationships so that authority, responsibility and communication can be controlled

(b) Allocate the tasks required to fulfil the objectives of the organisation to suitable individuals or groups

(c) Give each individual or group the authority required to perform the allocated tasks, while controlling their behaviour and use of resources in the interests of the organisation as a whole

(d) Co-ordinate the objectives and activities of separate units, so that overall aims are achieved without gaps or overlaps in the flow of work

(e) Facilitate the flow of work, information and other resources through the organisation

2.1 Hierarchy and specialisation

An organisation is a collection of groups joined in a common mission. Each group has its own specific objectives and functions. A group is unlikely to operate successfully without a leader who can take responsibility in seeing that the group performs its tasks. Current changes in management practice are leading to collective responsibility for work being given to groups themselves; however, there must still be an individual who interacts with other groups and with managers of wider groupings.

Many decisions need to be made within an organisation and someone must have the authority to make them at each of the different levels within it. This authority should be given to people who have the appropriate knowledge and experience. Along with the authority goes responsibility, and the need to ensure that decisions are carried out.

Organisations develop layers of authority to ensure that correct decisions are made and implemented. This results in the **organisation pyramid** as shown below. The more important a decision is to an organisation, the fewer are the people entrusted with the authority to make it.

As organisations grow, specialist individuals or groups appear. These have to be co-ordinated, so further layers of management are required. Each department develops its

own pyramid of authority. There can be specialism within a department, requiring more co-ordination. Thus increasing specialisation often leads to more layers of management.

EXAMPLE: BUILDING SOCIETIES

When building societies took deposits and lent funds as mortgages they required only a few specialist departments; deposits, lending, administration, and legal. When they started to offer cheques, make personal loans and offer many types of savings, they had to develop many more specialist departments.

Activity 2 **(20 minutes)**

Think about your local department store (or visit it if you do not know it well).

1 List the departments on all the sales floors.

2 Also list the support departments such as accounts.

3 Now suggest what advantages there are in having this degree of specialisation.

The structure of an organisation depends on how its specialist functions are organised.

2.2 Function and structure

The structure of an organisation arises from the need to delegate authority and responsibility and ensure co-ordination between the specialist functions.

There are three relationships between people in organisations;

(a) line;
(b) staff;
(c) function.

The line relationship

For example, there is a direct line of authority in the manufacturing function in a factory as shown here.

NOTES

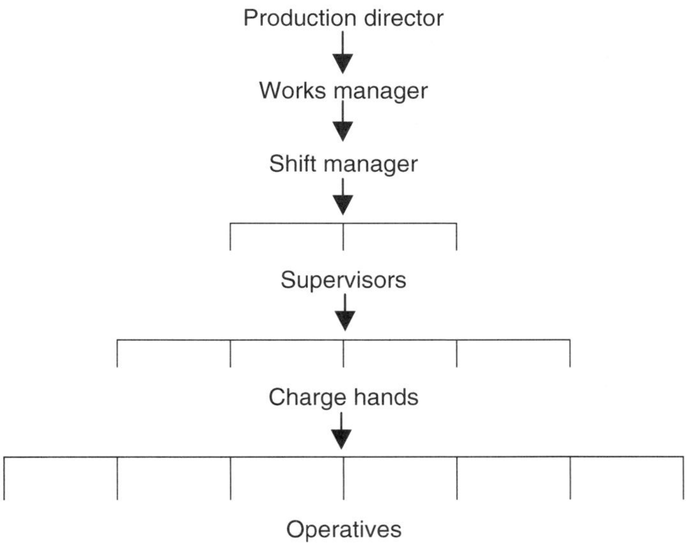

The same could apply in a charity, as shown below. This kind of line of authority applies to business organisations and also those in the public sector.

The staff relationship

The staff relationship refers to the work of support staff and departments. For example, production is supported by purchasing, stores and personnel. Thus production can concentrate on the manufacturing process and the organisation gets the benefit of greater expertise and efficiency through functional specialisation. Staff departments have the right to advise other departments but have no direct say.

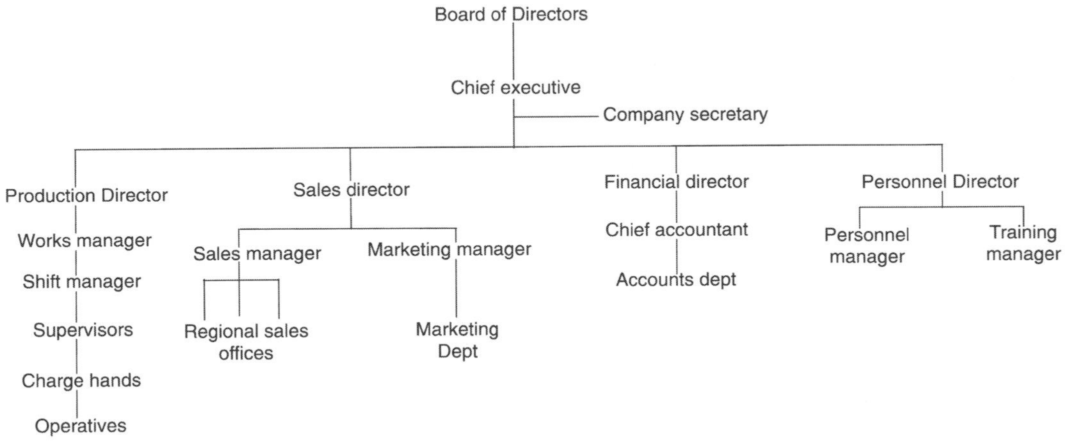

Line and staff structure

The function relationship

Functional authority gives one department the right to specify what goes on in other departments. For example, the personnel department lays down standard procedures for recruitment to which all departments must adhere.

EXAMPLE: FUNCTIONAL AUTHORITY

Banks have compliance officers who ensure that confidentiality is maintained between different areas.

Firms and local authorities may have equal opportunities officers.

Government departments may have security personnel.

All these functions report directly to top management.

Activity 3 **(10 minutes)**

Describe the departments and structures of each of the following:

(a) Your college
(b) Your faculty
(c) The BTEC section

Next we look at how theories of organisations and technical change have influenced the structures of organisations.

3 THEORIES, CHANGE AND STRUCTURE

3.1 Theories and structure

Henri Fayol (1841 – 1925), an industrialist, is generally regarded as the first to analyse management activity. He thought that there should be only one line of command with only one boss for each person to answer to. He also believed that division of labour and specialisation would lead to increased output. He recommended the hierarchical principle of management with clear levels of authority.

Max Weber (1864 – 1920), by contrast, an academic sociologist, analysed authority structures in organisations. He divided them into:

(a) those where power rests in a charismatic leader, such as the founder of a firm; such structures are inherently unstable as the founder's demise leads to conflict. (A striking example would be the effect that Robert Maxwell had on all his group companies.);

(b) traditional organisations where decisions are made in accordance to precedent, and authority is decided by custom and status, often in the case of family firms (for example as has hitherto been the case in Marks and Spencer plc);

(c) the rational-legal organisation with a bureaucratic structure. A bureaucracy is **rational** because it is designed to achieve certain well-defined goals; it is

legal because authority is exercised through a system of rules and procedures.

Bureaucracies

Definition

> **Bureaucracy:** a form of organisation where tasks and duties are allocated to clearly defined positions in a hierarchy of authority which operates on the basis of rules and regulations to ensure uniformity of action.

A major feature of bureaucracy is that it is impersonal: working for the organisation is paramount. Posts are filled on merit based on qualifications.

Today 'bureaucracy' is used almost as a term of abuse to be levelled at hide bound, rigid, unthinking organisations and their managements. Weber saw it as the most technically efficient form of organisation, capable of:

(a) surviving long after its founders are dead

(b) operating efficiently, because personal preferences or out-dated procedures do not divert it from using the best methods to reach its goals.

The bureaucratic structure is a series of steps in which each office's authority embraces all the steps below it. Managerial authority goes with the job, not with the individual who happens to hold it at any one time. Orders are obeyed because the rules say that the office holder can give these commands. This hierarchy is staffed by specialists.

As large-scale business organisations developed they adopted structures designed for efficiency and growth.

3.2 Change and structure

As technology developed and large-scale organisations appeared in business, the principles of specialisation and a rule-based system were widely adopted.

EXAMPLE: THE FIRST RAILWAYS

One hundred and fifty years ago railways were the **only** large-scale industrial organisation. They had to invent a management system almost from scratch, and turned to the only available models – the army and the church, both large bureaucracies. The railways operated single tracks, with trains going in opposite directions on the same line. Strict rules had to be laid down to ensure that the trains ran to time and safely. A hierarchy of authority created powers and responsibilities to see that the rules were obeyed.

Activity 4 **(5 minutes)**

Match the most likely type of authority structure – charismatic, traditional or bureaucratic – to each of the following organisations.

(a) Alanbrooke's Hospital;
(b) New Wave Advertising Ltd;
(c) C H Westlake & Son (Est. 1924).

3.3 The division of labour

In 1776 Adam Smith, a major economic theorist, described the advantages of the division of labour. He looked at the process of pin making: dividing the process into the smallest possible tasks, with specialist workers for each, enabled the workforce to increase the output of pins 250 fold.

The development of this principle reached its peak in 1908 when Henry Ford (1863 – 1947) used the moving assembly line to bring work to operatives who each performed one tiny, specific task in building a car. The car industry later developed the management structure essential for running a large, multi-product firm efficiently, and which enabled it to grow. Alfred Sloan (1875 – 1966), the head of General Motors, divided production and sales among single-model car assembly divisions and centralised all staff functions. Head office could control the production divisions by monitoring their output and financial results. The standard pyramidal organisation allowed for growth by simply employing more workers at the base and adding management layers above them. As firms grew in size and production and administrative work was divided into smaller and smaller tasks, so the number of managers increased. More layers of management meant that senior managers soon become remote from their customers and markets.

3.4 Structures based on the technology of production

Joan Woodward (1916-1971), a professor who surveyed manufacturing organisations in South East Essex, found striking differences in the number of levels of management and in the number of workers supervised. She found that the objectives of a firm – what it wants to make for its chosen markets – determine its technology of production. This leads to differences in organisation structure. She identified three types of structure, ranging from the least to the most complex:

(a) production of units and small batches to customers' requirements – goods are made after the customer has ordered them and it is almost impossible to predict work loads;

(b) large-batch and mass production on assembly lines – every so often a large quantity of an item is made, in advance of use and is stored; there is continual target setting as there are constant adjustments to variations in manufacturing capacity;

(c) process production, as in the oil and gas industries – production is continuous and never-ceasing and uncertainties in production are reduced as the equipment can be set for the desired level of ouptut.

These description can also apply to service industries and public services. For example, unit and small-batch production in advertising or a medical clinic, large-batch cheque processing in banks, and process or flow in an agency providing social security payments.

Unit production has a short hierarchy, with top managers close to production and workers taking a lot of responsibility for output. Mass production has short lines of

NOTES

command within a complex hierarchy of specialist departments. Process production takes place in a continuous flow through the plant and is predictable; it has a tall hierarchy with long lines of command and a high proportion of non-production staff.

3.5 The post-entrepreneurial organisation

Global competition and the need for quick and flexible response to a rapidly changing market have concentrated attention on how the modern corporation can recover the flair and enterprise that make firms into innovative market leaders. Rosabeth Moss Kanter (born 1943), an American professor, has worked as a consultant in many organisations. She proposed that the corporation of the 1990s and early 21st century should be 'post-entrepreneurial' with fewer management levels and able to anticipate change and seize opportunities. Flatter structures make co-operation across divisions and departments easier. The keys are employee empowerment and strategic alliances with suppliers and customers and in joint ventures. The organisation becomes a small head office managing a network of other enterprises.

Definitions

> **Empowerment** – employees are all given the right to take decisions relevant to their sphere of work which would previously have been taken by supervisors; teams are often empowered.
>
> **Strategic alliance** – an arrangement with another organisation to co-operate in some way (for example, in jointly developing a new product).

Other modern thinkers, like Henry Mintzberg, as we shall see later, also see the form of organisations changing as they are forced to adapt to new technology, more competition and better information technology.

FOR DISCUSSION

Business organisations are keen to develop entrepreneurship – the willingness to innovate and take risks – among their managers. They see this quality as the essential element in being competitive and successful in the global market. The effect on the structures of organisations is to make their hierarchies flatter and to create more autonomous units. However, many organisations prefer to remain as bureaucracies, seeing certainty and control as important. They remain structured as hierarchies with clear lines of authority and control.

Consider three organisations you know: a large business, a public service and a voluntary organisation. Discuss how each might find it advantageous or disadvantageous to adopt bureaucracy or entrepreneurship.

Different organisation structures have emerged as managements try to improve co-ordination and control. Next we describe the main ways to classify structures.

BPP PUBLISHING

4 TYPES OF STRUCTURE

You will have encountered the various types of structure in Core Unit 3, Organisations and Behaviour. You should refer back to your notes and course book for more information.

4.1 Specialisation

Specialisation by function leads to line and staff management, as introduced earlier in this chapter. The direct relationship between levels is based on the scalar chain, which shows the extent of authority running downwards and accountability flowing upwards (see the diagram of line and staff structure in Section 2.2). Remember that each staff department has its own line management.

> **Activity 5** **(10 minutes)**
>
> There is often friction between line and staff departments. List three possible sources of conflict between them.

Small organisations do not have all the staff required shown in the diagram in Section 2.7. They buy in specialist services as they are required. As we shall see, modern management thinking is that firms should concentrate on their core businesses and hive off functions such as catering and cleaning to specialists. This leaves senior management free from these time absorbing but non-profit making functions.

All kinds of organisations have line and staff structures. The next diagram shows such a structure for a typical charity.

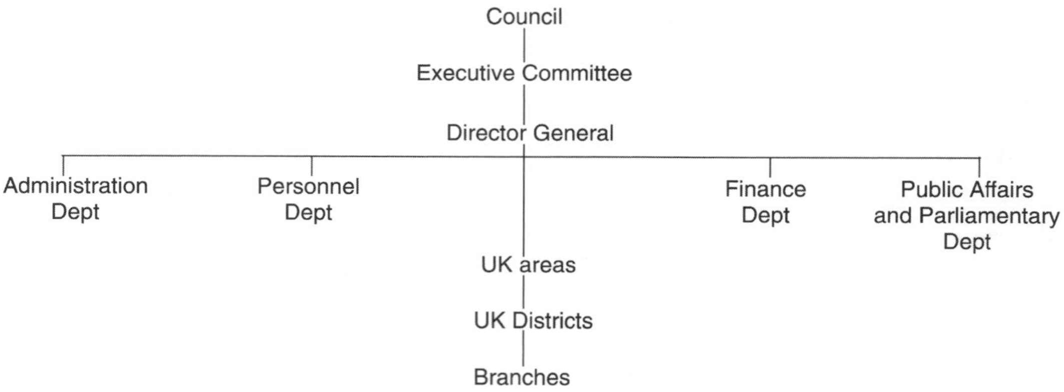

Note. This organisation is also typical for voluntary organisations

Departments can be organised in different ways and this is the next type of structure.

4.2 Departmentation

As organisations grow they are split into divisions and sub-divisions. A division can include many departments. Often it carries out all the line and staff functions except for the strategic direction and control exercised by head-quarters.

The method of departmentation depends on the nature of the organisation and its work and could be as follows.

(a) Functional, where work is divided into specialist areas by primary functions such as production, finance and marketing, each of which is sub-divided into specialist departments. This is line and staff organisation.

(b) Product, where the organisation is divided by product or service. Each division has its own line and staff structure, as shown in the diagram below.

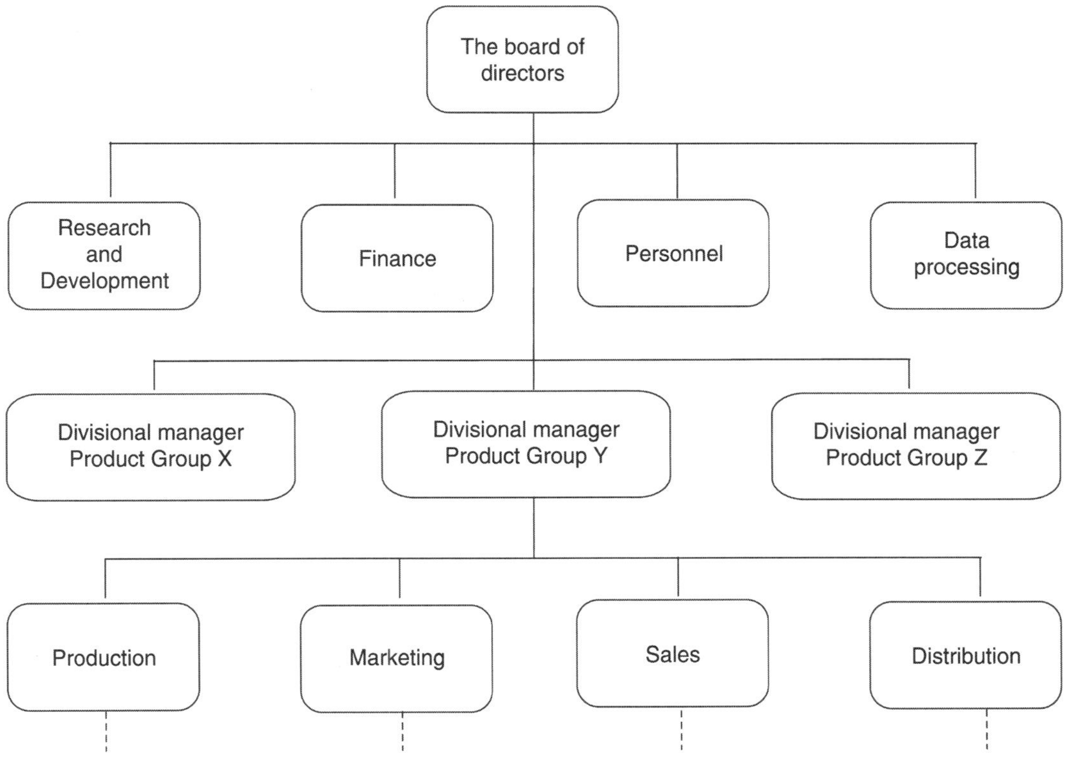

(c) Territorial departmentation is often used by multinational companies, which retain the major staff functions at headquarters and divide their operations geographically. If they are large enough, each regional subsidiary could have its own board of directors supervising a full range of line and staff functions. More often the territorial division will market all the company's products. This is shown in the next diagram.

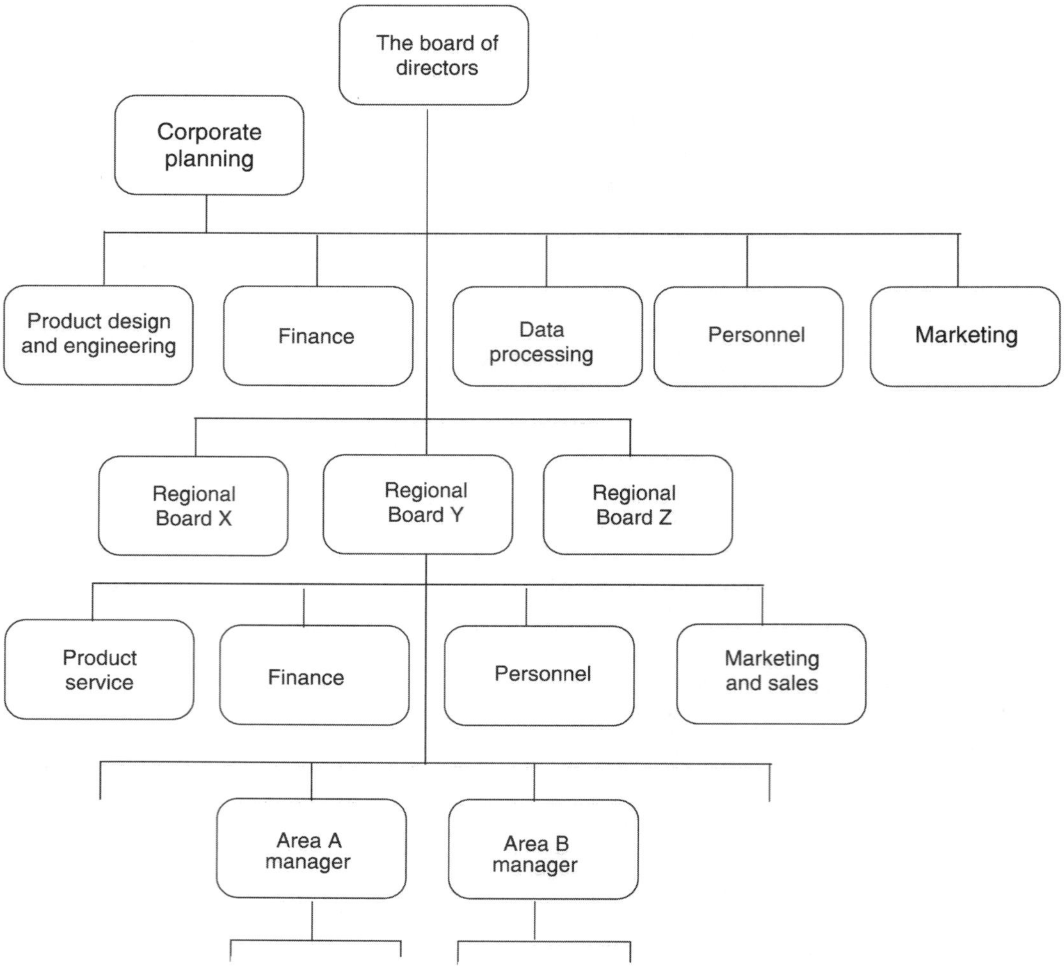

Functional divisions within areas

Multinationals can also divide up their activities by product, with each product division taking responsibility for world wide production and sales, often with a territorial structure that has, in turn, a functional structure.

International charities tend to have territorial structures. For example, the Save the Children Fund has divisions for the UK, Africa, Asia and the Americas and the Pacific.

Activity 6 **(10 minutes)**

What type of departmentation has:

(a) central government?
(b) independent television?
(c) your college?

FOR DISCUSSION

As you can see from these examples, an organisation can use different methods of departmentation at different levels. Why is this so? What advantages are there for a multinational firm in having a territorial structure with regional divisions each structured into product divisions that are organised into functional departments?

Next we examine the matrix organisation – an attempt to overcome the problems of departmentation.

4.3 The matrix structure

Despite its advantages, specialisation by department leads to problems of co-ordination and control. With increasing specialisation no-one may take responsibility, or have authority over *all* aspects of a project. There is a traditional split between line and staff departments. Large complex developments may require the co-ordination of hundreds of production units and suppliers.

Lockheed, the American aircraft manufacturer, first developed the matrix structure in the 1950s. Its previous functional organisation caused its major customer, the US government, to be unable to find a single manager to deal with problems. Project co-ordinators developed from the need to co-ordinate all the line mangers involved in a project to satisfy the government's demand for a project management system. Later the co-ordinators developed functional authority and responsibility for project budgets, design and scheduling. Functional department heads remained responsible for the work of their departments; programme co-ordinators became responsible for all aspects of a project.

With this structure, an employee could expect to receive orders from both the co-ordinator and the department head. This dual command was a significant change in the principle of the single boss. An example of the matrix structure is shown in the diagram below.

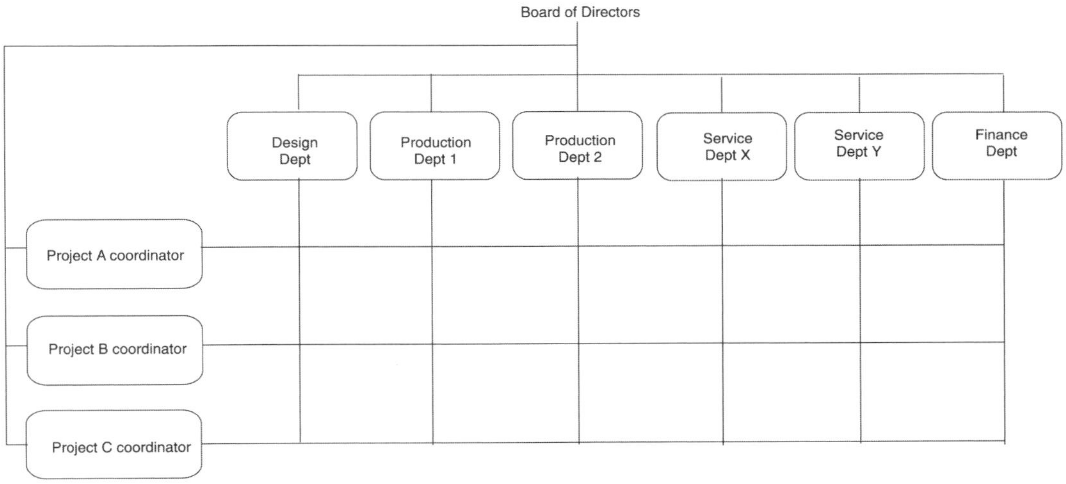

Matrix organisations are primarily found in industries which handle large, complex products, such as the aerospace industry and the construction industry, and in advertising agencies (where a brand manager co-ordinates work across all the specialist functions such as copywriting, design, media buying and research).

It is also possible to have a matrix based on products, as shown in the next diagram. This structure is used in companies where strong brands are important.

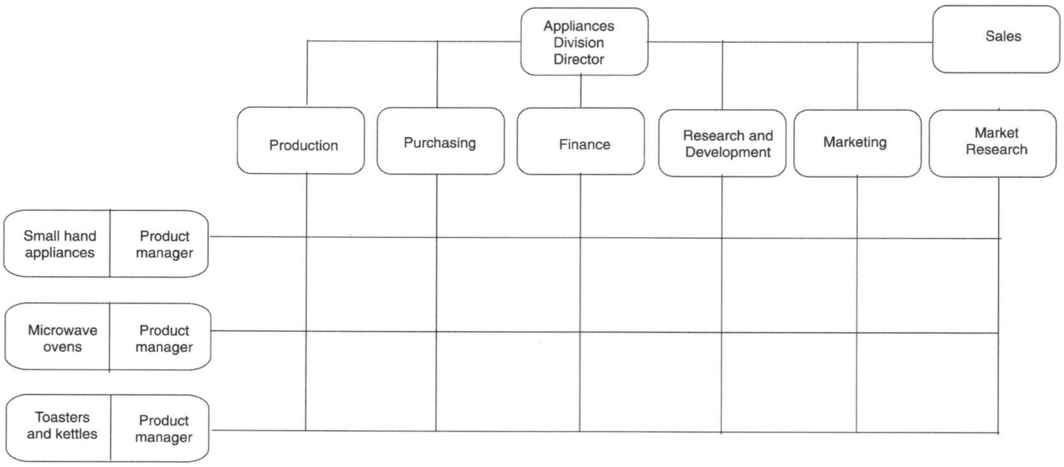

Activity 7 **(15 minutes)**

Could the management of your course be described as part of a matrix organisation? Draw an organisation chart for courses in your department of the college.

Chapter roundup

- The first stage in the design of an organisation's structure is the definition of its mission, aims and objectives.
- The structure of an organisation is determined by influences such as its mission, operations, culture, technology and external factors like changes in government policy.
- Organisations develop the typical pyramid structure because of the need to establish lines of authority and responsibility.
- The typical relationships between people in an organisation are line, staff and function.
- As organisations grow and develop specialist departments they tend to establish a line and staff structure.
- Classical management thinking developed the principles of a hierarchy of authority and bureaucracy with its clearly defined tasks and rules of authority based on the post held, not the person.
- The length of the scalar chain of authority depends on the type of production – unit, mass or process.
- Organisation structures can be classified into the following categories:
  - (a) specialisation – the typical line and staff organisation;
  - (b) departmentation – functional, product or territorial;
  - (c) matrix – authority is shared between the project manager and the line managers in departments.

NOTES

Quick Quiz

1 Objectives should fulfil the SMART criteria. What do the letters stand for?

2 Give two influences which may shape a public service's organisation structure but which may not apply to a business.

3 Why do organisations develop layers of authority?

4 What does a line relationship show?

5 Give three examples of staff departments.

6 What was Fayol's principle of command in organisations?

7 What three types of authority structure did Weber identify?

8 Why did Weber think that bureaucracy is the most efficient form of organisation?

9 What are the differences between the hierarchies of firms engaged in unit, mass and process production?

10 What does a scalar chain show?

11 Draw an outline organisation chart to show a line and staff organisation structure?

12 What are the three types of departmentation?

13 What are the responsibilities of project managers and department heads in a matrix structure?

14 Who is an employee's boss in a matrix structure?

Answers to Quick Quiz

1 Objectives should be: **S**pecific, **M**easurable, **A**chievable, **R**esults-orientated and **T**ime-bounded. (See paragraph 1.4)

2 Public services' structures may be influenced by the duties and obligations imposed by Parliament. These may change because of changes in government policy, for example, reducing defence spending, and because of society's expectations, for example, care for the elderly. (See para 1.9)

3 To ensure that correct decisions are made and implemented at appropriate levels of authority and responsibility. (See para 2.1)

4 It shows the direct line of authority from top management to the lowest level of an organisation. (See para 2.2)

5 You might have listed: purchasing, stores, accounts, transport, marketing, sales, personnel, training and research. (See para 2.2)

6 A single line of command with each worker only having one boss. (See para 3.1)

7 Charismatic, traditional and rational-legal. (See para 3.1)

8 Because posts are filled on merit, not personality, it is impersonal. Working for the organisation is paramount and it uses the best method to reach its goals, uninfluenced by personal preferences or outdated procedures. (See para 3.1)

9 Unit production has a short hierarchy, with the lowest level having a lot of responsibility. Mass production has short lines of command within a

NOTES

complex hierarchy of specialist departments. Process production has a tall hierarchy with long lines of command. (See para 3.4)

10 It shows the levels of authority and responsibility in a hierarchy. (See para 4.1)

11

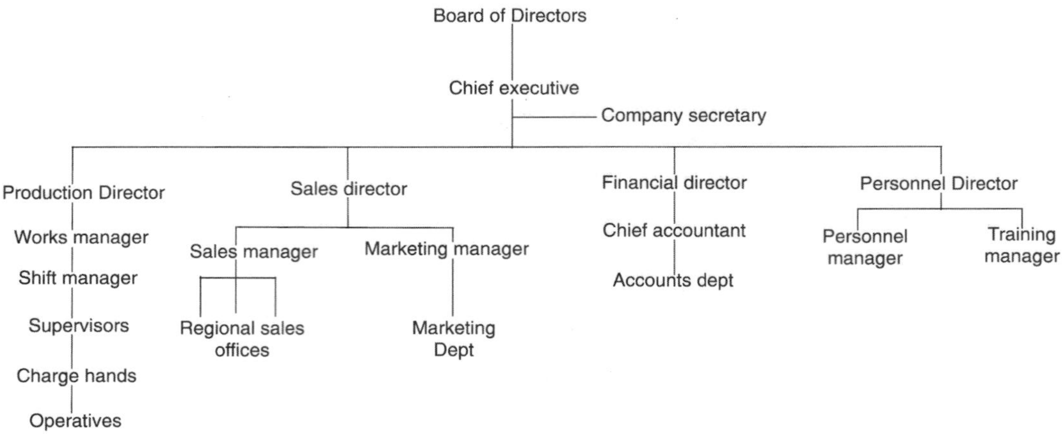

Line and staff structure

(See para 2.2)

12 Functional, product and territorial. (See para 4.2)

13 Project managers are responsible for all aspects of the project, including the schedule and the budget; department managers are responsible for their departments, as line managers. (See para 4.3)

14 Both the project co-ordinator and the department head. Some matrix organisations combine territorial and functional organisation. (See para 4.3)

Answers to activities

1 Mission: have a healthier lifestyle
Aims: get fit and lose weight
Objective: lose a stone by March
Strategies: join local gym and exercise for one hour daily; eat more vegetables, fewer biscuits

2 You will probably have found sales-floor departments such as: ladies' outer wear, gent's outfitting, sports goods, children's clothes, stationery, ladies' shoes, linens, furniture and carpets. Service departments might include: accounts, credit, personnel, transport and warehousing and marketing. The advantages of such specialisation are greater expertise and efficiency.

3 Your answers should be as follows: (a) line and staff'; (b) line and staff if there are support units such as administration and audio-visual, or line if not; (c) line.

4 Your answers should be: (a) bureaucratic; (b); charismatic; (c) traditional.

5 You might have listed: the split of authority that could cause line managers to resent staff 'interference'; line managers regarding staff as inferior; and conflict over resources.

6 The correct answers are (a) functional; (b) territorial; (c) product.

7 You are correct if you said that your course could be described as part of a matrix organisation. See the diagram below for an example organisation chart.

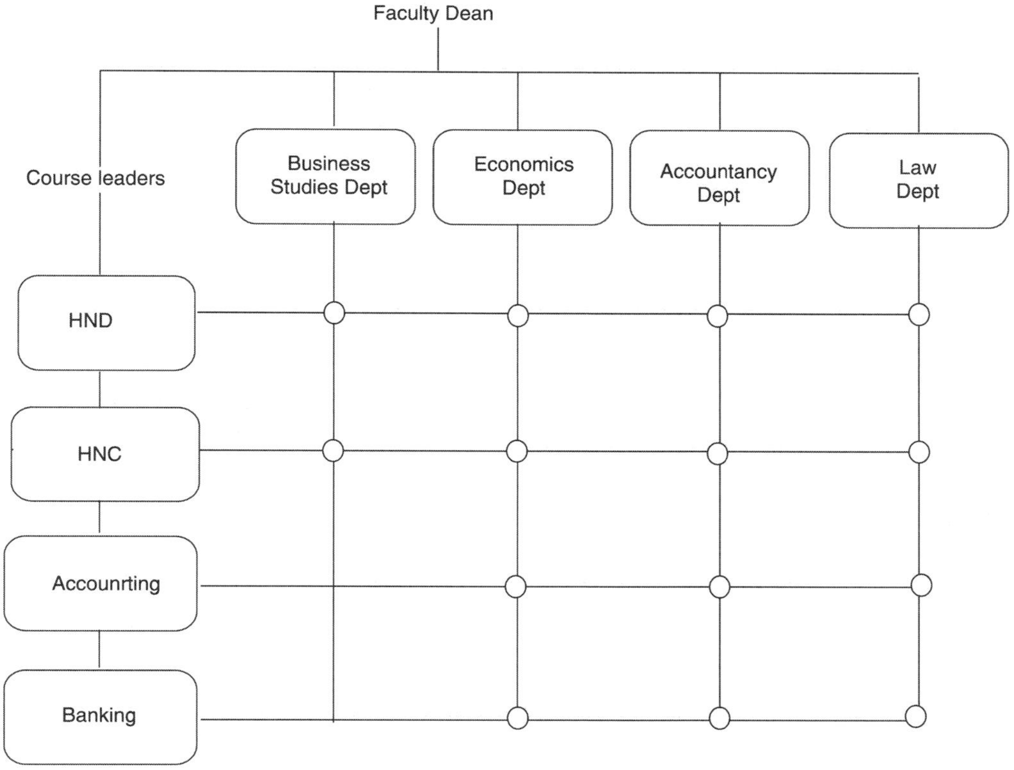

A faculty course matrix

Chapter 2 :
PLANNING WORK ACTIVITIES

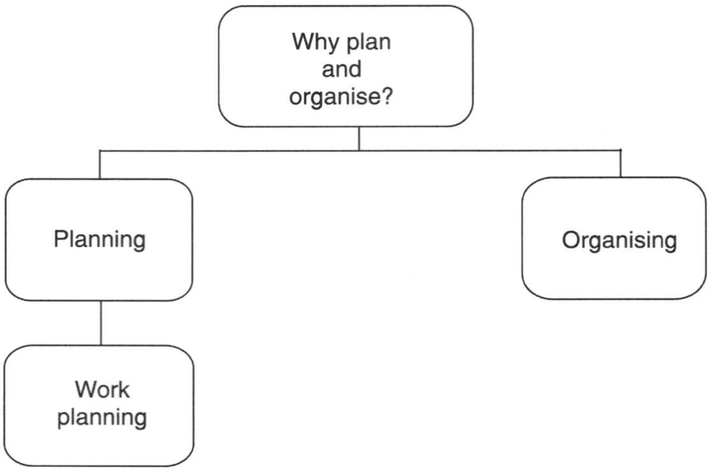

Introduction

Two of the main functions of management are:

- **Planning:** the process of deciding what the 'ends' of activity should be (objective-setting), and determining the most appropriate 'means' of achieving those ends (plans, policies, procedures and so on).
- **Organising**: the process of establishing a framework within which plans can be carried out: determining structures and systems for co-ordinating the human and other resources required.

Your objectives

In this chapter you will learn about the following

(a) The role of planning and organising in achieving controlled performance

(b) Efficiency and effectiveness

(c) The cycle of planning and control

(d) The different types and levels of planning in an organisation and the process of 'work planning'

(e) A simple framework for work planning

(f) The implications of organising for organisational structure, co-ordination and communication, as well as task allocation

1 WHY PLAN AND ORGANISE?

1.1 Purposes of planning and organising

If individuals and groups within an organisation are to be effective in working for the achievement of the organisation's objectives they need to know what it is they are expected to do. Planning allows managers to identify:

(a) the objectives for which they are responsible;
(b) what actions will serve towards achieving those objectives; and
(c) how far they are being successful in achieving those objectives.

Planning and organising are important functions in an organisation for the following reasons.

(a) **Uncertainty**. Organisations cannot deal with things ad hoc, as they occur, without chaos. The future cannot be foreseen with certainty in any case, and even the best-laid plans will go wrong to a greater or lesser degree (which is where 'control' comes in). Nevertheless, plans and structures give some direction and predictability to the work of the organisation: in other words, they are a form of risk management.

(b) **The need for co-ordination**. Organisations are collections of individuals and groups (or sub-systems): each will perceive its own part of the organisation's activity, and work towards its own objectives accordingly. Planning and organising ensures that:

(i) sub units of the organisation know what it is they need to achieve, and when;

(ii) work 'flows' from one process (or department) to another without holdups or clashes, and without idle time or overwork for staff and machinery;

(iii) the resources required for a task are available where and when they are required;

(iv) required work is being done by somebody – but not being duplicated by others, with a waste of effort;

(v) all of the above are achieved in such a way that products/services of the required quality are available to customers at the right place, at the right price and at the right time.

FOR DISCUSSION

Suggest examples of the planning/organising needed in each of the areas given in (i) to (v) above, and what would happen if planning was not carried out.

(c) The need for objectives. Human beings are 'purposive': they like to feel that their actions have a point. If the organisation doesn't set objectives, people will set their own, according to their own interpretation of the situation: chaos ensues. Objectives are also important in learning and motivation, so people can target and adjust their behaviour according to what they want to achieve.

BPP PUBLISHING

Two key aims of business management, and therefore of planning and organising, are:

- efficiency and
- effectiveness.

1.2 Measures of success

Efficiency

Efficiency is a term often used loosely to express the idea of 'doing things well'.

Definition

> **Efficiency** is the relationship between inputs used and outputs achieved. The fewer the inputs used to obtain a given output, the greater the efficiency. Efficiency can be expressed as: $\frac{\text{output}}{\text{input}}$

If a car does 400 miles on 10 gallons of petrol it does $400 \div 10 = 40$ miles per gallon. This is a measure of its efficiency at using fuel.

Efficiency is about avoiding **waste** – of effort, time and material resources – in producing desired outputs, or achieving the organisation's goals. Efficient operation might involve:

(a) producing no less, but no more, than the demand for the product;

(b) avoiding spoiled or unacceptable products, according to the organisation's quality standards;

(c) avoiding overmanning (employing more people than the task requires), or improving productivity: output (or profit, say) per employee;

(d) avoiding unnecessary movements, operations and routines (such as paperwork, task duplications, double-checks and so on) which take time, without adding value in the process;

(e) avoiding expense of finance and resources which add no value and earn no return.

Effectiveness

It has been argued that efficiency focuses too much on controlling the 'inputs' to the organisation's activities, and not enough on the 'outputs'. (You can improve efficiency by cutting costs instead of improving sales ...)

Definition

> **Effectiveness** is the measure of how far an organisation (and its managers) achieve their output requirements, as defined by performance objectives and targets.

In other words, **effectiveness** is about 'doing the right things', not just 'doing things right'. Effectiveness-orientated managers are concerned with fulfilling objectives with regard to:

(a) output quantity;

(b) output quality and customer satisfaction;

(c) added value (the value added to inputs, reflected in the sale price of the output);

(d) innovation, or new products/services/improvements implemented.

Activity 1 **(5 minutes)**

Read through and tick in the relevant columns whether the statements relate to efficiency or effectiveness.

		Efficiency	*Effectiveness*
(a)	A customer is satisfied	☐	☐
(b)	The factory produces more cars	☐	☐
(c)	Waste has been reduced	☐	☐
(d)	Better quality products are produced	☐	☐
(e)	Ten employees were given early retirement packages	☐	☐
(f)	The company increased its dividend payment to shareholders	☐	☐

Efficiency and effectiveness require:

(a) an idea of what outputs the organisation wants from the production system;

(b) an idea of what inputs will be required; and

(c) a way of monitoring and measuring performance, to ensure that it conforms to the organisation's expectations.

In essence, this is the process of planning and control.

2 PLANNING

2.1 Planning and control

Planning is the process of deciding what should be done. **Control** is the process of checking whether it **has** been done, and if not, doing something about it. The combined processes of planning and control are known as a **control cycle**, as shown in this diagram.

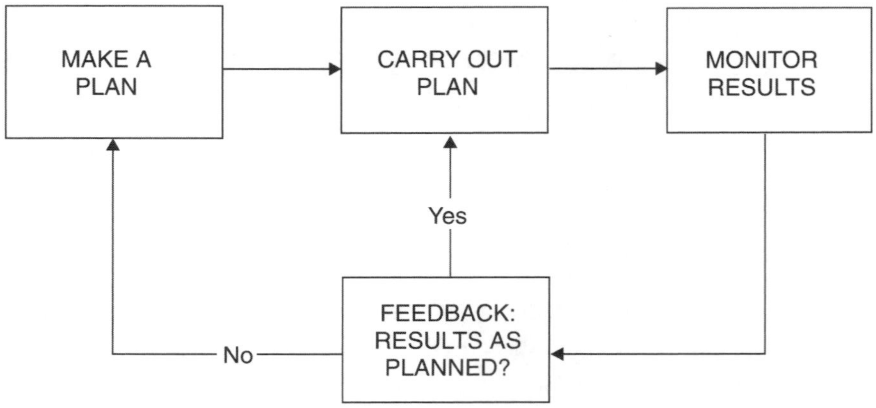

(Figure 1: the control cycle)

In more detail, the control cycle in management has six basic stages.

(a) **Making** a plan: deciding what to do and identifying the desired results. The plan should include:

  (i) **aims**, which dictate;

  (ii) **priorities,** or 'key results' (objectives which must be achieved for the aims to be fulfilled) and 'key tasks' (things that must be done on time and to the required standard if the key results are to be achieved), for which there should be;

  (iii) **performance standards,** the definition of how well key tasks must be performed in order to achieve key results (acceptable quality, cost or amount of output, say); and

  (iv) **specific short-term goals** for key tasks, against which progress can be monitored; so that

  (v) **action plans**, specifying 'what, how, who, when, where and how much' can be formulated.

(b) **Carrying out** the plan, or having it carried out by subordinates.

(c) **Monitoring and measuring** actual results achieved.

(d) **Comparing** feedback on actual results against the plans.

(e) **Evaluating** the comparison, and deciding whether further action is necessary to ensure the plan is achieved. If results are worse than planned (negative feedback), the activity will have to be adjusted to get it back on course. If they are better than planned (positive feedback), it may be desirable to maintain the deviation from the plan, or to adjust the plan itself to take advantage of the situation.

(f) **Implementing corrective action** where necessary.

All managers plan. Some may do more, or more complex, planning than others, but all do some. Let's look briefly at the levels and types of plan used in organisations.

2.2 Levels and types of plan

Planning involves decisions about:

- **what** to do in future
- **how** to do it

- **when** to do it and
- **who** should do it (this is also the area covered by 'organising').

Such questions are relevant at all levels of organisational activity:

(a) at a **strategic** level – deciding what business the organisation should be in, and what its overall objectives should be;

(b) at a **tactical** level – deciding how it should go about achieving its overall objectives: what products it should produce, how it will organise work and so on;

(c) at the **operational** level – deciding what needs to be done from day to day and task to task.

There are therefore a number of different types of plan, which can be categorised as follows.

Objectives

Objectives are the end goals, towards which all the organisation's activities will be directed: to earn a profit, say, or provide a certain service.

Strategies

Strategies are long-term plans for the activities and resources which will achieve the organisation's objectives. (A manpower strategy, for example, is a plan for the number and types of staff to be acquired and maintained in the long term.)

Policies

Policies are general statements or 'understandings' which provide guidelines for management decision making. (It might be company policy, for example, to offer five year guarantees on all products, or to promote managers from within the organisation.) Policy guidelines allow managers to exercise their own discretion and freedom of choice, but within certain acceptable limits.

Procedures

Procedures are chronological sequences of actions required to perform a task: they exist at all levels, but become more extensive lower down in an organisation's hierarchy, where the work is more routine. They have three main advantages.

(a) **Efficiency**. Procedures (ideally) prescribe the most efficient way of doing a job.

(b) **Routine**. Procedures remove the need for the exercise of discretion, where fresh decisions are not necessary.

(c) **Standardisation** of work makes output more predictable and more consistent throughout the organisation.

Rules

A rule (or regulation) prescribes a specific, definite action that must be taken in a given situation. It allows no discretion – unlike a policy. For example:

(a) 'employees in department X are allowed 10 minutes exactly at the end of their shift for clearing up and cleaning their work-bench';

(b) 'employees with access to a telephone must not use the telephone for personal calls'.

Programmes

Programmes are co-ordinated groups or series of plans which together achieve a particular objective; for instance, a company might undertake a programme of expansion, computerisation or customer care, involving different aspects and stages of planning.

Budgets

A budget is a formal statement of expected results set out in numerical terms, usually summarised in money values. It is a plan for carrying out certain activities with specified resources within a given period of time, in order to achieve certain targets.

Activity 2 **(20 minutes)**

Dial-a-Video Limited offers home video rental service to subscribers. Subscribers choose a video from a catalogue, phone Dial-a-Video Limited and the video is delivered by a despatch rider. The Chairman, Rajiv Bharat, says to you: 'I hope to expand the business. I've discovered a market for art movie videos. I've had to knock the directors' heads together to develop plans for building a distribution system: they've agreed a number of stages: for a new catalogue, market research and that sort of thing. We'll charge £4 per video per day including delivery. It is a premium price, but people who like that sort of movie will pay for it. We'll tell the despatch riders not to accept tips though.'

What sort of plans has Rajiv Bharat described to you?

Planning horizons

Planning covers the long-term as well as the short-term. A planning period or time **horizon** is the length of time between making and implementing a planning decision. A decision to build new premises may have a time horizon of many years; a programme to develop a new product might take several years; an operating budget might span a one-year period; a production schedule might be produced weekly.

This has two main consequences.

(a) Long-term objectives might conflict with shorter-term plans, and planners should try to reconcile the two. If a company has a short-term problem with limited funds, for example, it might be tempting to cut costs to maintain profitability – but if spending on research or marketing are ignored, the company's long-term profitability might suffer.

In the short-term, a company might consider profitability as the major objective. In the longer-term, considerations such as social responsibility, employee welfare, corporate image, standards of service and reputation might take on added importance.

(b) Plans, once formulated, should not be rigid, because the future is uncertain: plans might need to be changed if unforeseen circumstances arise. A compromise should be found between the need for flexibility (which suggests keeping plans short-term) and the need for commitment to decisions which have been made (which suggests planning over the whole of a long-term period). The best compromise, perhaps, is regular review of plans, and a willingness to adjust them if necessary.

FOR DISCUSSION

How are you at planning? How did you approach exam-revision, for example, or essay-writing? People must have told you how important it is to 'make a proper plan'. If you didn't do so – why not? Do you think managers suffer from the same difficulties?

3 WORK PLANNING

3.1 What is work planning?

Work planning, as the term implies, is the planning of how work should be done: establishing work methods and schedules to ensure that objectives are efficiently met.

The result has to be a marketable product/service that meets customer needs.

There are four basic elements to work planning.

- **Task sequencing or prioritising:** considering tasks in the order in which they must be completed, either
  - because some tasks depend on the completion of other tasks or
  - because some tasks are more important or urgent than other tasks.
- **Task scheduling:** the decision of when tasks should be started and completed.
- **Resource allocation:** the assessment of a task's human, financial and material requirements, and the availability of appropriate resources at the right place and time.
- **Contingency planning:** allowing for changes of plan to cope with unscheduled events.

We will look at each of the stages briefly. They will be used as a simple framework for classifying planning techniques in the following chapters.

3.2 Task sequence

Some jobs are entirely routine, and can simply be performed one step at a time, but for most people, some kind of judgement will be required: a manager, in particular, may have any number of matters calling for his attention at one time, and will have to decide what to do first, what to delegate and so on. Task sequencing basically involves arranging all the tasks which may face an individual (or unit) at the same time in order of 'preference': because of the individual's *responsibility* to the organisation, it will not just be what he would like to get done first, but what will be most valuable to the attainment of immediate or long-term goals.

Priority

A piece of work will be high priority in the following circumstances.

(a) **If it has to be completed by a certain time (a deadline).** The closer the deadline, the more urgent the work will be. A report due the following day will take precedence over an agenda to be circulated in a week's time. Routine work comes lowest on the list, as it can usually be caught up with later if necessary – but if put off too long it may become urgent!

(b) **If other tasks depend on it.** If the preparation of notes for a meeting depends on a particular file, the first task may be to obtain the file: work can't start unless the file is there. Begin at the beginning!

(c) **If other people depend on it.** An item being given low priority by one individual or department – for example, the retrieval or reproduction of a particular document – may hold up the activities of others for whom the processing of the item is high priority.

(d) **If it is important.** There may be a clash of priorities between two urgent tasks, in which case relative consequences should be considered. If an important decision or action rests on a task, that task should take precedence over an urgent, but less important task.

Routine priorities and regular peak times (such as Christmas for retailers, or the beginning of the academic year for BPP) can be planned ahead of time, and other tasks postponed or redistributed around them. Non-routine priorities occur when unexpected demands are made: events crop up, perhaps at short notice, or errors are discovered and require corrective action. Backup plans for likely contingencies should be made (contacts with temporary employment agencies and additional suppliers, for example).

Deadlines

Definition

A **deadline** is the end of the longest span of time which may be allotted to a task: in other words, the last acceptable date for completion.

It is perfectly possible for every activity to have a deadline (at least a pencilled-in one to aid work planning). The deadline for a long-term job – say building a house – will dictate and depend on a series of shorter-term deadlines right back to the laying of foundations and the ordering of bricks. This pyramid of deadlines must be taken into account in scheduling work and allocation of resources, and is the basis of task sequencing.

Activity 3 **(10 minutes)**

Give three examples of factors that will determine what a task's deadline should be.

Deadlines are important, and we make no apologies for repeating this point. Failure to meet them has a 'knock-on' effect on other parts of the organisation, and on other tasks within an individual's duties. If you are late with one task, you will be late or rushed with the one depending on it.

Once the sequence or order of tasks (or components of a complex activity) has been determined, you can decide when those tasks should be performed. This is scheduling.

NOTES

3.3 Scheduling

Definition

Activity scheduling provides a list of activities, in the order in which they must be completed: we have called this task sequencing.

Time scheduling adds to this the timescale or start and end times/dates for each activity.

Time schedules can be determined by different methods.

(a) **Forward scheduling** can be used, starting with a given start time/date and working through estimated times for each stage of the task (allowing for some which may be undertaken simultaneously, by more than one person or machine) to the estimated **completion** time/date. This method can be used, for example, when producing items for stock, or when completing routine tasks.

(b) **Reverse scheduling** is where you start with a **completion** time/date or deadline, and work backwards through estimated times for each stage of the task, determining **start** times for each stage – and for the task as a whole – which will enable you to meet the deadline. This method can be used in 'make to order' production, where a customer specifies a due date when delivery is required. It can also be used to meet deadlines, for example, for a report to be prepared, for office relocation, product launch and many other projects which have a set completion date.

Activity 4 **(30 minutes)**

You are in charge of organising the annual sales conference of your firm. It will be held in a hotel with a conference room, which will be laid out for your meeting. You will also be the 'secretary' of the meeting, which will involve preparing and circulating the agenda of the meeting to participants, together with briefing information gathered from the sales files, and taking notes for the minutes (written record) of the meeting.

(a) In what order would you sequence your tasks?

(b) What kind of scheduling would you use?

(c) What method would you use to record and to remind yourself of the schedule?

All personnel involved in a task must be given adequate **notice** of work schedules, and the schedules themselves should allow a **realistic** time allocation for each task, if people are to accept the plan without resentment.

3.4 Resource allocation

Resource allocation includes estimates of the task **requirements** with regard to:

(a) 'man hours' (how many people working for how many hours);
(b) machine hours;
(c) raw materials and components (allowing for a certain amount of wastage); and
(d) finance – that is, the cost of all the above.

It also includes estimates of the **availability** of all these resources.

(a) How many people with the required skills or experience are available (inside or outside the organisation)? What is their standard level of productivity, and could it be increased?

(b) What machinery is available, given the demands made on it by the task and by other tasks from other units? What is its standard level of productivity, and could it be increased?

(c) Is there sufficient stock of raw materials or components? If not, can they be bought in or made, and at what cost? Are they of the required specifications and quality? What is the expected usage rate of stock: when will stocks run out and need to be replenished? What is the standard wastage rate in the course of operations, and can this be reduced?

(d) How much money needs to be budgeted or allowed for, to complete the task? Is such an amount available and worth spending, for the expected results?

Activity 5 **(20 minutes)**

Continuing our example of a person organising a sales conference, what kind of resources might (s)he have to plan for?

We have talked about 'estimated' times and resource requirements. Uncertainty is a fact of organisational life. This is where contingency planning comes in.

3.5 Planning for uncertainty

Plans do not give managers control over the future.

(a) The future cannot be forecast with any certainty. You can only anticipate what is **likely** to happen in future, based on what has happened in the past, and any trends or tendencies that you can see in the pattern of past events.

(b) Unexpected, uncontrollable events happen. Computers break down, terrorists blow up buildings, suppliers go bust, transport strikes shut down operations for a day and so on.

Contingencies are unexpected and uncontrollable events which do not feature in the main plan of the organisation. However, some such events can be anticipated: managers do not **expect** them to happen, but acknowledge that they **might** happen, and consider what should be done **if** they do. Contingency plans are those which are prepared in advance to deal with a situation that **may** (or may not) arise.

All plans should be contingency plans to an extent, since planners must make room for:

(a) **margins of error;** time and resource estimates are only estimates;
(b) **changes in the circumstances;**
(c) **slippage** in the schedule which needs to be caught up elsewhere.

Remember that planning is part of the control system: plans may constantly have to be adjusted in order to correct or improve performance.

> **Activity 6** **(20 minutes)**
>
> What kind of contingency plans might you want to make if you were in charge of:
>
> (a) transferring all your transactions onto a new computer system?
>
> (b) accomplishing a project which required all the 'people hours' you have at your disposal?
>
> (c) organising (yet another) sales conference at an external venue?

4 ORGANISING

4.1 Structures and systems

Organising – or organisation – implies the establishment of structures, social arrangements, or systems, for the purposes of:

(a) distributing **authority and responsibility** in such a way as to ensure that each task of the organisation is facilitated and controlled: that someone is both authorised to perform it and accountable for performing it;

(b) **communication** of the information needed for the task and for control feedback;

(c) **co-ordination** of resources – including people's time and effort – towards unified objectives, via a hierarchy of objectives and targets for each sub-unit of the organisation; and

(d) the **grouping and allocation** of tasks in logical ways.

The grouping of organisational activities (into teams, departments or larger divisions) can be done in different ways. The most common are as follows.

(a) **By function**, or specialism. Primary functions in a manufacturing company, for example, might be production, sales, finance, and general administration.

(b) **By territory** or geographical area. This method of organisation occurs when similar activities are carried out in different locations. Water and electricity services, for example, operate region by region. Many sales departments are organised territorially, with regional sales areas.

The main advantage of territorial departmentation is better local decision-making at the point of contact between the organisation (eg a salesman) and its customers.

(c) **By product.** Some organisations group activities on the basis of products or product lines. Functional division of responsibility remains, but under the control of a manager with responsibility for a product, product line or brand, with authority over the personnel of different functions involved in its production, marketing and so on.

NOTES

The main advantages of product departmentation are the development of specialised product knowledge, and the co-ordination of functional activities.

(d) **Matrix organisation.** As we discussed in Chapter 1, the new emphasis on flexibility has created a trend towards task-centred structures, such as multi-disciplinary project teams, which draw people together from different functions. Authority is divided between the members' departmental managers, and the team's product/project manager or co-ordinator.

Having recapped the broader implications of organising for organisation and job design, we will now look briefly at the day-to-day aspects: to whom should a manager allocate or delegate a given task?

4.2 Allocating tasks

Some decisions about division of labour will be pre-programmed by:

(a) **organisational positions and job descriptions**, which dictate who does what (although these are becoming less rigid, in favour of flexibility and empowerment); and

(b) **specialisms**. There may be an obvious expert to whom specialised tasks should be given: a payroll, legal or information technology expert, say.

However, other decisions will require management discretion.

(a) Peak periods in some tasks may necessitate redistribution of staff to cope with the workload: there should be flexibility in who does, and is able to do, non-specialist tasks.

(b) Status and staff attitudes must be considered. Flexibility in reassigning people from one job to another or varying the work they do may be hampered by an employee's perception of his own status: helping out or covering for others may be out of the question: 'I'm a secretary, not a copy typist!' etc. Task allocation must take into account people's experience and seniority – and also the fact that junior employees may want greater challenge and responsibility.

(c) Individual abilities and temperaments differ, and work should be allocated to the best person for the job. Some staff like routine work but crack under pressure, and vice versa; some are good with computers, some with people. Planning should allow for flexibility in the event of an employee proving unfit for a task – or more able than his present tasks indicate.

5 PROJECT MANAGEMENT

5.1 What is project management?

Definition

> A **project** is an undertaking, often cutting across organisational and functional boundaries, and carried out to meet established goals within cost, schedule and quality objectives.

Project management is directed at a particular end: achieving specific objectives within a specific time span. It is not, like general management, directed at maintaining or improving continuous work activities.

> **Activity 7** **(20 minutes)**
>
> See if you can think of an example of a project in each of the following areas.
>
> (a) Building and construction.
> (b) Manufacturing.
> (c) Management.
> (d) Research and development.

Project management therefore requires even closer attention to planning, organising and control, with regard to:

(a) **quality** – the end result should conform to specification; in other words, the project should achieve what it was meant to do;

(b) **cost** – the project should be completed without exceeding authorised expenditure (as specified in a budget) of money and other human and material resources;

(c) **time** – each stage of the project's progress must conform to schedule, so that the end result is achieved when requested or required.

5.2 Project planning

A project plan aims to ensure that the project objective is achieved within the requirements of quality, cost and time. This will involve:

(a) breaking the project down into manageable units of activity, and determining the sequence of, or relationships between, those units or tasks;

(b) estimating the resources (materials, money, time and so on) required for each unit;

(c) sequencing and scheduling each unit in the most appropriate way for co-ordinated performance.

We will now look at techniques and tools used for planning and organising interrelated and interdependent activities.

6 TASK SEQUENCING AND SCHEDULING

6.1 Work breakdown structure (WBS)

Breaking a project down into its component phases or stages is often the best way of:

(a) discovering exactly what work must be accomplished;
(b) determining the resources required; and
(c) sequencing and co-ordinating the work done.

This is called establishing a work breakdown structure (WBS) for the project.

Activity 8 **(30 minutes)**

Suppose you set yourself the project of cooking a dinner party for yourself and five friends.

(a) Define the objectives of the project: devise a three course meal menu.

(b) Estimate (roughly):

(i) the cost and
(ii) the time it will take you to prepare.

(c) Establish a work breakdown structure, in the form of a detailed list of things to do, for preparing your menu.

(d) What does your WBS tell you about your cost and time estimates?

Figure 2 is a simple example of a **diagrammatic** work breakdown structure for a house-building project. We have only broken down two of the component stages to the second level (the foundations and the wiring), but you should get the idea. The breakdown process continues until the smallest sub-unit or task is reached, for which man and machine hours can most easily be calculated and scheduled.

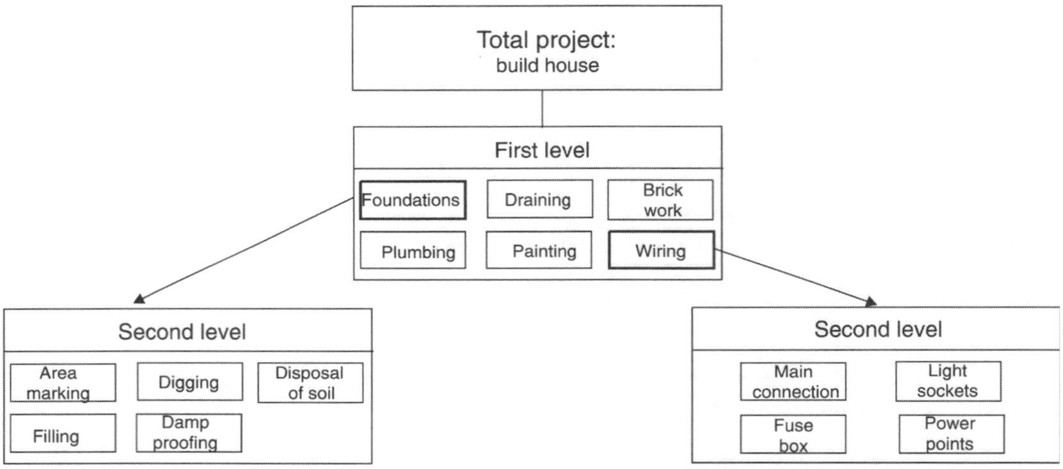

Figure 2 Diagrammatic work breakdown structure

Once the component activities of the project have been determined, they can be sequenced and scheduled. Here, we will show how some of the simple charts can be applied to more complex project planning.

6.2 Using charts

Bar line charts

A simple project plan can be shown on a bar line or Gantt chart. Figure 3 is an example of a chart for a project to build a garage.

NOTES

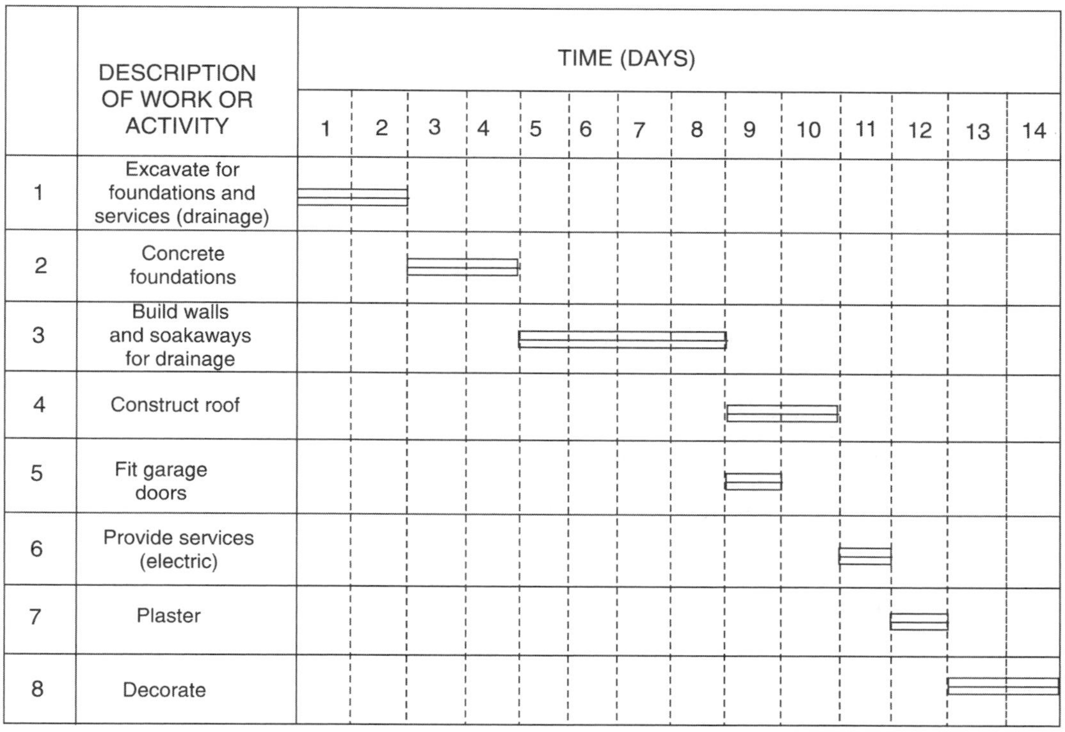
DESCRIPTION OF WORK OR ACTIVITY
TIME (DAYS)
1 2 3 4 5 6 7 8 9 10 11 12 13 14
1 Excavate for foundations and services (drainage)
2 Concrete foundations
3 Build walls and soakaways for drainage
4 Construct roof
5 Fit garage doors
6 Provide services (electric)
7 Plaster
8 Decorate

Figure 3 Gantt chart for building a garage

This chart shows the sequence of activities to be followed, as well as the duration of each activity. You need to excavate before you can put in foundations, before you can build walls: once you've got to that stage, you can do the roof and doors together, if you have the manpower – sheltered from the elements – you can then follow the next sequence.

Activity 9 **(15 minutes)**

How could you, very simply, turn this chart into a work schedule?

This type of chart has the advantage of being very easy to understand. It can also be used as a progress control chart, with the lower section of each bar being completed (eg shaded in) as the activity is completed.

Linked bar charts

In order to show more clearly where the activities are dependent on each other, you might prefer to use a linked bar chart, as in Figure 4.

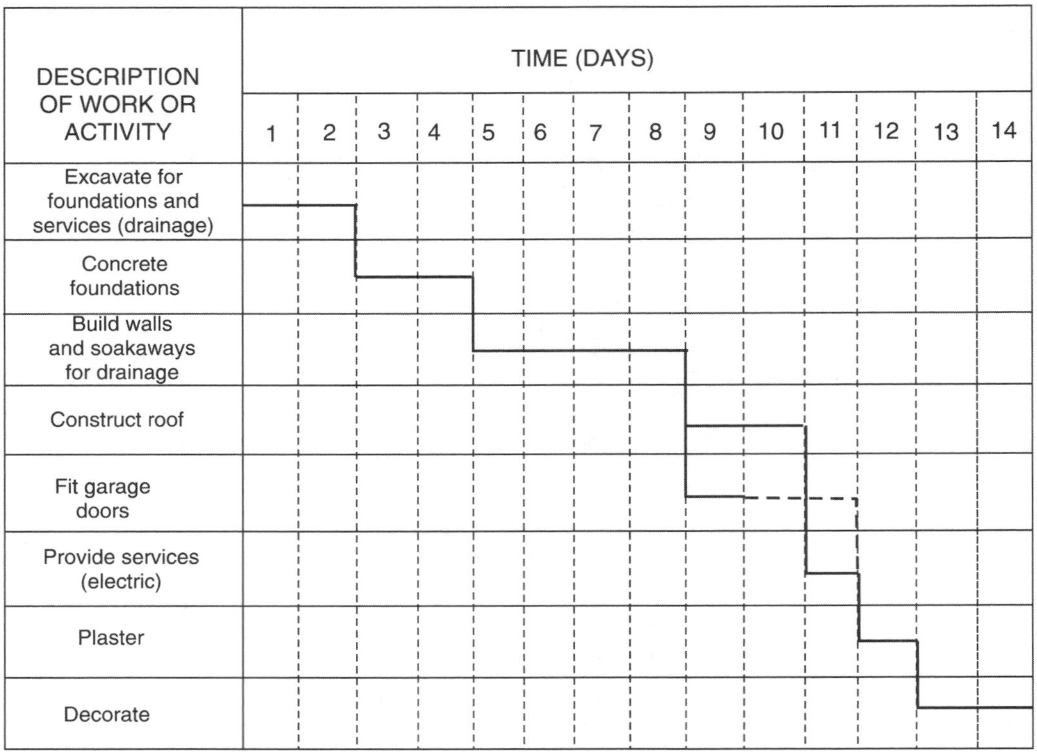

Figure 4 Linked bar chart

This shows the link between activities. In our example, the roofing and door-fitting can be done together, starting on day 9, but the door-fitting only takes one day, while the roofing takes two days – and needs to be finished before electrical wiring can be done, hopefully on day 11. The door-fitting therefore has a certain amount of leeway: it can be started late if necessary, since it does not hold up any other activity until the roofing and electrical installation are finished. This leeway is called float time, and is shown by the dotted line on the chart: the activity can be moved into the dotted area if necessary. Activities that have no float time are called critical activities: they must be completed on time in order to avoid a knock-on effect which will make the project as a whole run over time.

Activity 10 **(20 minutes)**

You are the site manager of the garage construction project. You have drawn up the linked bar chart above as a guide to all your on-site staff as to the order of activities and the speed of progress required to meet the customer's two-week deadline. You decide to use the chart to monitor progress. Using a different-coloured pen, you draw a line beneath the one on your plan chart to show what your team has actually accomplished.

(a) Everything takes the time it was planned to, except that on the Wednesday (day 3) the weather is too bad to work, so that concreting of the foundations actually takes three days.

(b) The door fitting takes one day, and the door-fitter is also qualified to do roofing work. His help will knock a day off the roofing schedule.

Draw the control line onto Figure 4. Has your project run over time?

The big advantage of such charts is that they are easily understood by all levels of staff, and without undue calculation. However they can only display a restricted amount of information, and the links between activities are fairly crude. To overcome these limitations, when planning and organising more complex projects, we use a more sophisticated technique called network analysis.

6.3 Network analysis

Network analysis is a term for project planning techniques which aim to 'map' the activities in a particular project, and the relationship between them, including:

(a) what tasks must be done before others can be started;

(b) what tasks could be done at the same time;

(c) what tasks must be completed on schedule if the completion date for the whole project is not to slip: the critical tasks.

These relationships and sequences are represented in a network diagram, which flows from left to right. The most commonly used form of network is called an **activity-on-arrow** diagram, because activities are represented by an arrowed line, which runs between one event (start or completion of the activity) and another. Events are depicted by a node, or circle.

Hence in the following example we map activity A, which starts at a certain point (event 1) and ends at a certain point (event 2).

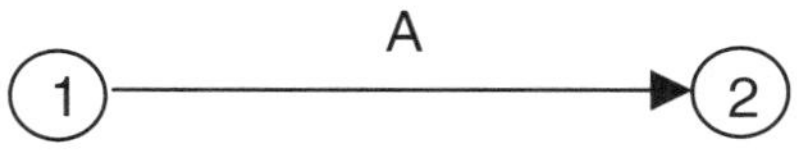

Let us tackle a more complex example. Suppose your work breakdown structure comprises six activities: we will call them activities A–G.

(a) Activities A and B can start together.

(b) You have to have done activity B before you can do activity C.

(c) Once activity A is completed, activities D and E can start, at the same time.

(d) Activity F follows on from activity D.

(e) Activity G will be completed at the same time as activity F, to end the project. However, activities C and E must be completed before G can commence.

Activity 11 **(10 minutes)**

Read (a)–(e) above again. Working from left to right, draw the network diagram showing activities A–G and events 1–6.

One further complication. It is a convention in network analysis that two separate activities should not start and end at the same events. If the real activities **could** start and end at the same event, this is shown on the network by inserting a **dummy activity**, represented by an extra event node with a dotted line joining it to the next event, figure 5.

Incorrect

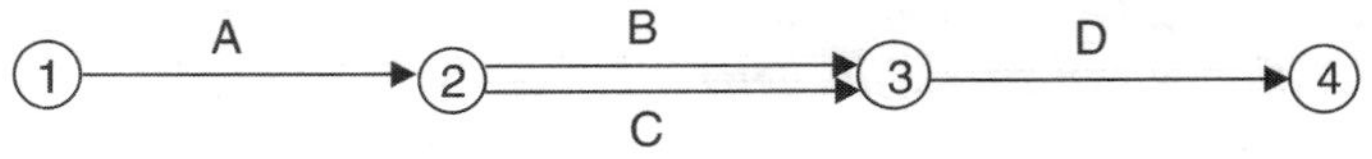

Correct

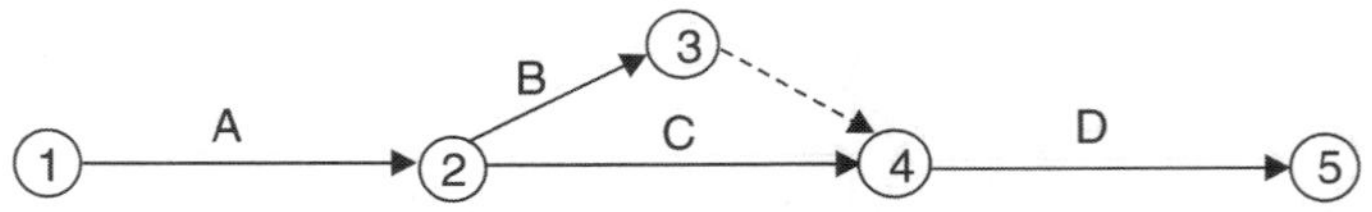

Figure 5 Network diagram with dummy activity

The correct version shows that activities B and C **both** have to be completed before D can begin, and the dotted line indicates that no extra activity is actually done and no extra time is taken between event 3 (completion of B) and event 4 (completion of C). The two activities therefore do start and end at the same points in the sequence, but not at the same nodes on the diagram.

Apart from pure convention, dummy activities may be needed to preserve the basic logic of the network.

Activity 12 **(10 minutes)**

In the network produced in the previous activity, suppose that activity G depended on the completion of activity D, as well as activities C and E. Activity F still depends on activity D alone. There is no extra time or activity involved; all you need to do is to indicate the link between activities D and G. Draw the 'dummy activity' dotted line on our network diagram, to represent this scenario.

Another use of the dummy activity is to ensure that all activities end up at a single completion event, joining in any loose events.

More information can be added to a network diagram, to describe not just what happens next, but when it should happen, and how long the whole project will take if each activity takes as long as it is supposed to. This technique is called CPA, or critical path analysis.

6.4 Critical path analysis (CPA)

If Activity A takes three days, it is shown like this.

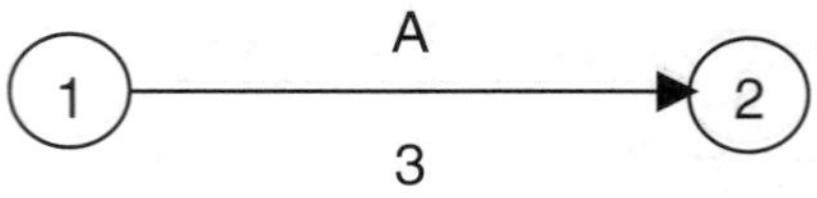

Let us say, building on our original A-G network, that:

Activity A takes 3 days
B takes 5 days
C takes 2 days
D takes 1 day
E takes 6 days
F takes 3 days
G takes 3 days.

Our network would be as in Figure 6.

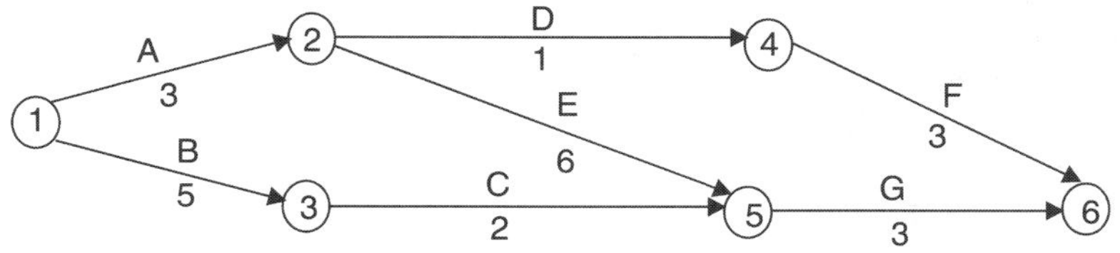

Figure 6 Network diagram with timings

Let us assume that you have all the resources you need to carry out the above project as drawn: in other words, you have enough workers to do activities A and B at the same time, and so on. The shortest possible time in which you can complete the project is 12 days. See if you can work out why, before reading on.

Each of the 'routes' of arrows from the first event to the last event is called a **pathway**, or **path**.

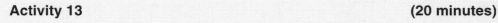

Activity 13 **(20 minutes)**

List all the pathways in Figure 6, and add up how many days each path will take to reach event 6.

The shortest possible duration for the project is 12 days. This is the duration of the longest path (AEG), not the shortest! The activities on the longest path determine the deadline for the whole project, because if one of them runs over time, the whole project will run over time. They are therefore critical activities, and the path on which they sit is called the critical path. We show the critical path on a network by drawing double or thicker lines between the events on that path.

Activity 14 **(30 minutes)**

Draw a network for the following project, and identify the critical path.

Activity	*Depends on activity*	*Duration (weeks)*
A	–	5
B	–	4
C	A	2
D	B	1
E	B	5
F	B	5
G	C, D	4
H	F	3
J	F	2

Hint: all your activities should 'tie up' at event 7.

6.5 Scheduling using the critical path

Once you have estimated activity durations and worked out the total project time, you can start scheduling. First of all, you work forwards from event 1, working out the **earliest start date** of each activity. We show the earliest start date of an activity as follows.

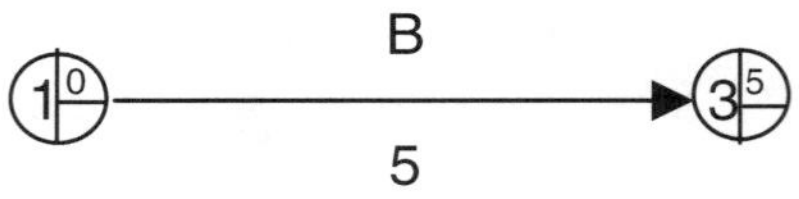

Obviously, event 1 starts at 0 (on day one): the earliest possible time for C to start, given that B takes 5 days, is at the end of day 5. If we do the same exercise with all the activities in our A-G example, we get Figure 7.

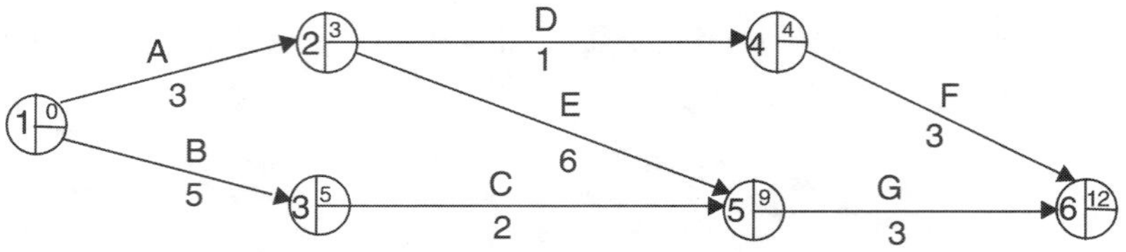

Figure 7 Network diagram showing start times

Note that the earliest start date for G (which has to follow A and E) is 9 days. But B and C only take 7 days: they can take two extra days, if necessary, without affecting the start of G.

We make this clear by next working backwards from event 6 to event 1, identifying the **latest start dates** when activities can start and still keep up with the timing set by the critical path. The earliest deadline of event 6 is 12 days: this is also its **latest** deadline, because it is the end of the critical path, which must not run late. Activity G takes 3 days, so its latest start date is 12 – 3 = 9 days: again, this is the same as its earliest start date, because G is on the critical path. Activity C takes 2 days, so its latest start date (if G is to start on time) is 9 – 2 = 7 days. However, its earliest start date (if B was on time) was 5 days: it has two days' leeway, or **float**. (Remember: activities on the critical path have no float.)

We insert the **latest** start date in the bottom quarter of the circle, as follows.

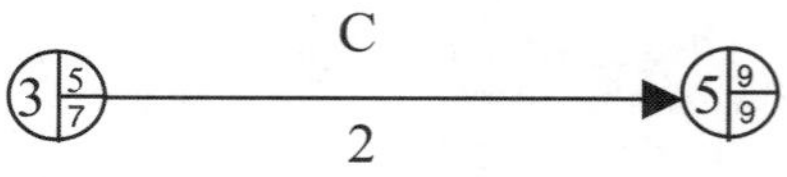

You can see just from this that Activity C can be started any time between days five and seven, giving the project manager a degree of flexibility, but that event 5 is on the critical path and must not run late!

> **Activity 15** **(20 minutes)**
>
> Starting from event 6 and working backwards, fill in the latest start dates in Figure 7. Which activities can afford to start late, and by how much?

Attach actual dates to your days currently numbered 1-12, and you have a detailed and effective schedule.

7 RESOURCE ALLOCATION

7.1 Gantt charts

As well as plotting time to be taken (and actually taken), Gantt charts can be used to estimate the amounts of resources required for a project.

Let us take the example we have been using so far in this section. We will be starting with our final network showing earliest and latest start times for A–G, so you may like to make a clean copy of the solution to activity 15 and keep it by you for reference.

Suppose that, in addition to the information contained on our network, we know the number of workers required to do each job, as follows.

Activity	A	requires	6	workers
	B	"	3	"
	C	"	4	"
	D	"	4	"
	E	"	5	"
	F	"	6	"
	G	"	3	"

Suppose that we have a team of **nine** workers, each of whom is paid a fixed wage, regardless of hours worked in a week (so we want to avoid idle time if possible). Each worker is capable of working on any of the seven activities involved in the project (so we can swap them round freely if required).

Figure 8 shows a Gantt chart, simply plotting the various paths against the 12-day timescale. We have assumed that activities will be started at the **earliest** start times, adding **floats** (where available) as a dotted line.

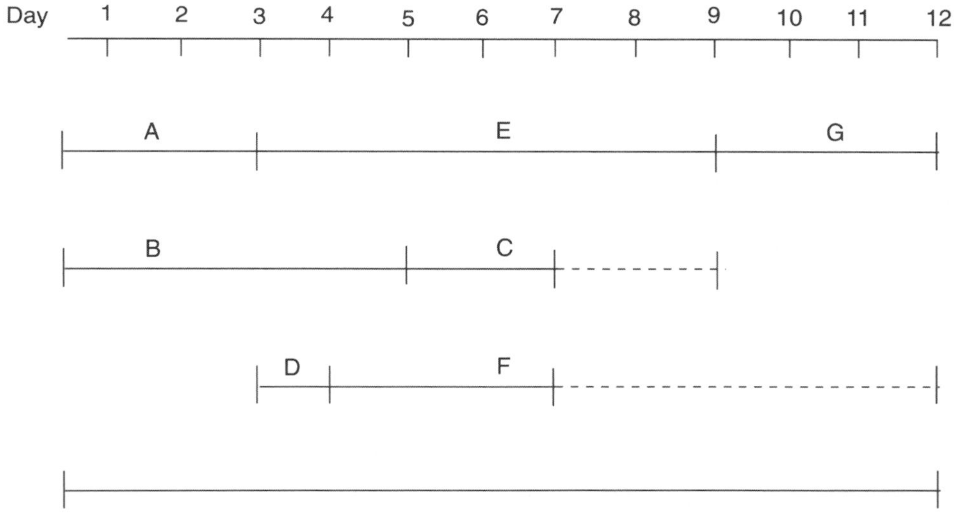

Figure 8 A Gantt chart showing floats

NOTES

EXAMPLE

1 On Figure 8 add the **number** of workers **required**, below the line under the relevant activity letter: $\frac{A}{6}$ and so on.

2 Now, label the line at the bottom of the chart '**Workers required**'.

3 Draw a line vertically through the **start and end of each activity**, from the 'Time' line (days) to the 'Workers required' line. With each activity beginning or ending, the number of workers required will change.

4 In your first section of the 'Workers required' line, which extends from day 0-3, A and B are going on simultaneously. Mark 'AB' above this section of the line.

5 Activities A and B require 6 and 3 workers respectively: that is, 9 workers. Mark '9' below the 'AB' on the 'Workers required' line.

6 Keep going until you have completed all segments of the 'Workers required' line.

ANSWER

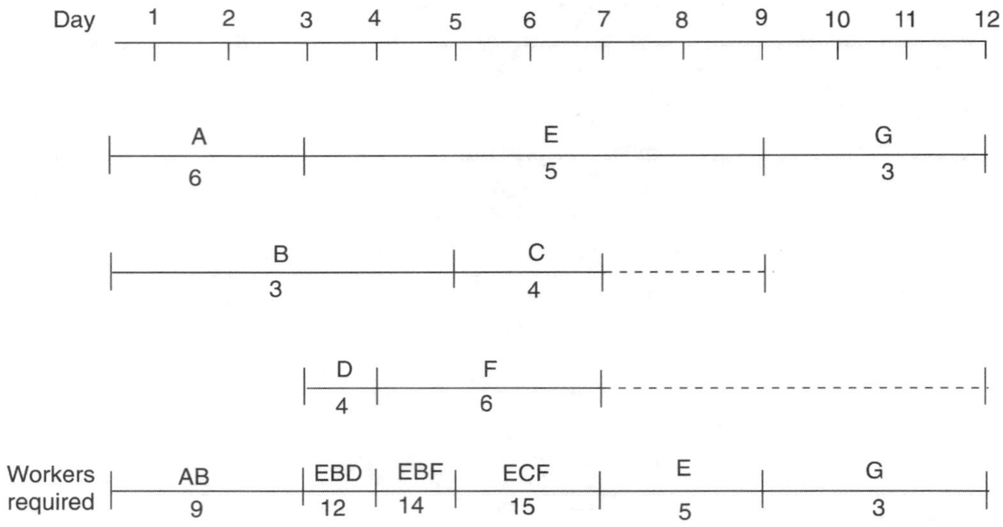

From the answer to the above activity, you may note that on days 6 and 7 you need as many as 15 workers though you only have nine. On days 8–12, you would have most of your team sitting about twiddling their thumbs. What are you going to do?

Let's look at the really busy period of days 4–7. Can you see any activities that **need** not be done during that period? We know that the path DF is **not** on the critical path. It takes four days, and need not finish until day 12: we have a full 5-day float. If we leave DF until its last possible start time (day 9), we are taking pressure off the busy period. Our Gantt chart would be redrawn as in Figure 9.

NOTES

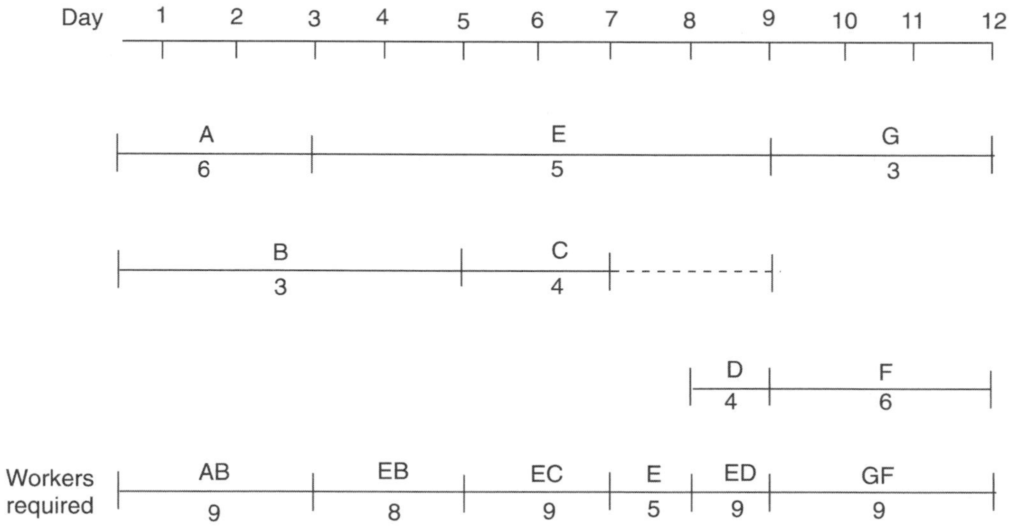

Figure 9 The final Gantt chart

The project can be completed without hiring any additional labour, and without running late. Good job! You can keep shuffling non-critical activities and re-calculating worker requirements like this until you are satisfied you have found the best solution. If there is too little float time at convenient stages to allow you do this, you may have to:

(a) reschedule the project to find the **minimum excess demand for labour**, and hire in extra labour for those times; **or**

(b) move critical activities as well as non-critical ones (thereby lengthening the project) to avoid excess demand for labour. The same method should be used to find the **minimum extension of the project's duration** required.

7.2 Cost scheduling

Cost estimating

It is usually not possible to say with certainty what the costs of a project will be, but some idea will be required in advance so that costs can be monitored and controlled. Estimates of costs can be based on rough guesswork (a 'ballpark' estimate), comparison with similar projects in the past, or the initial plans for the project (a 'feasibility' estimate).

The work breakdown structure will clearly be useful in devising estimates because it enables the project manager to compile a complete list of items that will attract expenditure. **Estimation forms** can be designed, based on the WBS, with columns for labour, materials, components and so on for each of the work units or tasks. This ensures that no items are forgotten, and speeds up the process of estimating, where jobs are routine or similar in type.

Cost scheduling

Costs can be scheduled, in exactly the same way as labour requirements.

(a) Draw a bar chart for the project.

(b) Estimate the cost of each activity.

(c) Divide by the duration of the activity to get the cost of the activity per week (or other appropriate time unit).

(d) Work out the cost of all activities going on in a given week: ie a total cost per week of the project.

For ease of cash flow, the project manager may need to restrict cash outflows in any week. As with labour requirements, he may be able to do this by rescheduling tasks which have a float.

It may, however, be more important simply to keep within the planned amount for the total expense on the project. And even then, it may be preferable to spend extra finance on a project to stop it running over time.

FOR DISCUSSION

In what kinds of project would you consider the time deadlines more important than the expenditure budget? And vice versa? (What projects do you know of which have gone way over budget, or late? Look out for examples in the press.)

Activity 16 **(20 minutes)**

Find your answer to Activity 8 – your WBS for a dinner party menu.

(a) Make up a cost estimate, based on your WBS. Draw a column marked B for budget, down the right hand side of your list, and enter your estimated amounts for each task.

(b) Go out and find out what it would actually cost, and write down each amount in a column marked A for actual, next to your Budget column.

How was your estimating? If you gave your dinner party, you might have written down what you really paid for your ingredients in the Actual column. You could monitor how you were doing, compared to your budget. This is called budgetary control: another useful management technique!

It should be clear from our discussion of 'estimates' that project planning is inexact and uncertain: the project manager does not have a crystal ball to tell him how long an activity will take, how much it will cost or how successful it will be. Finally, in this chapter, we look briefly at this problem of uncertainty, and how it can be planned for.

8 FLEXIBLE PLANNING

8.1 Allowing for delays

As we have already discussed, activities which are not on the critical path are non-critical, and can, within limits, **start later** and/or **take longer**, without holding up the completion time of the project as a whole. This slack time is called the activity's **float.** It allows unexpected delays to be absorbed and resources to be diverted, to avoid the late start of critical activities.

NOTES

What happens if your critical activities are threatened with delays, though, and the final deadline simply cannot be extended?

8.2 Crash times

The crash time is the **minimum** time an activity can take to be completed. Crashing often involves the use of extra resources.

Job X takes one worker $1^1/_2$ days – say, 12 working hours. The worker gets paid £10 per hour, so the cost of the job is £120. If the project manager needs Job X completed at the end of a single day, (s)he might ask the worker to do four hours' overtime to complete the 12 hours work in a single working day. However, the overtime rate of pay is £15 per hour. So the crash cost is (8 hours @ £10) + (4 hours @ £15) = £140.

There would be no point crashing non-critical jobs, because you would not shorten the overall project duration or affect the critical path by doing so. However, crashing can be used to shorten the critical path itself, if necessary, to:

(a) catch up with delays; or
(b) shorten the project duration for any reason.

You may have noted that, in most cases, we are still only talking about estimated job times or durations. What happens if you get those wrong in the first place? One answer is to take account of uncertainty and contingencies at the estimating stage. A well-known technique for doing this is PERT.

8.3 PERT

Programme Evaluation and Review Technique (PERT) recognises that the activity durations in the network are in fact uncertain. Instead of one estimate of each activity time, three estimates are used.

- The **most likely** duration of the activity, given what is known about it (which we will call m)
- The **most optimistic** (shortest) estimate, assuming that all goes well (o)
- The **most pessimistic** (longest) estimate, assuming that things that are likely to go wrong will go wrong (p)

These can be converted into a 'mean' (or middle) estimate, which takes into account the small chance that things will go entirely well or entirely badly. The mean time is calculated using the formula:

$$\frac{o + 4m + p}{6}$$

As an example, here are some more data!

Activity	*Must be preceded by activity*	*Optimistic (o) days*	*Most likely (m) days*	*Pessimistic (p) days*
A	-	5	10	15
B	A	16	18	26
C	-	15	20	31
D	-	8	18	28

PUBLISHING

The mean times for each activity are as follows.

Activity	*(o + 4m + p)*	*÷ 6 =*	*Mean time*
A	5 + 40 + 15 = 60		10 days
B	16 + 72 + 26 = 114		19 days
C	15 + 80 + 31 = 126		21 days
D	8 + 72 + 28 = 108		18 days

Activity 17 **(20 minutes)**

Draw the network for A-D, using the mean times. Include earliest start and latest start times, and show where the critical path is.

Other calculations can be made using PERT, including the probability that a job will overrun by a given time. Because of their complexity, PERT systems are often run on computers, which generate the planning and control data required.

PERT is frequently used where there are a number of possible contingencies which would affect the project duration. Construction projects, for example, need to allow for delays due to unfavourable weather.

Chapter roundup

- Planning is the process of deciding what should be done, by whom, when and how. It is essential for co-ordination and control and for the management of risk and uncertainty.
- Planning precedes all other management functions and is carried out at all levels of the organisation. There is a hierarchy of planning from strategic to operational plans.
- Plans are the basis of the control systems of an organisation, through which performance is monitored, measured against the plan and adjusted where necessary.
- Work planning involves:
  - task sequencing or prioritising;
  - time scheduling;
  - resource allocation; and
  - allowance for adjustments and contingencies.
- Organisation is the process of establishing a framework within which plans can be carried out. It is concerned with the division and co-ordination of labour through:
  - organisation structure and
  - the allocation and delegation of tasks.
- Project management is directed at a particular end: achieving specific objectives within a limited time span.
- Project planning and organisation involves
  - breaking the project into units (work breakdown structure)
  - determining the sequence and/or relationships between those units
  - estimating the resources required for each unit
  - scheduling time and allocating resources for each unit.

- Popular techniques for project planning include:
  - network analysis (including critical path analysis) and
  - Gantt charts.
- Network analysis aims to 'map' the relationships and dependencies of tasks in a project. The critical path is the longest path on the network, representing the shortest possible completion time of the project: if any activity on the critical path runs late, the project will run late. Non-critical activities may have some 'slack' time within which they can be extended without having a knock-on effect on the project duration: this is called a float.
- Estimating costs and job times is not an accurate science. One technique for taking uncertainty into account is Programme Evaluation and Review Technique (PERT) which calculates a mean time for each activity using most likely, optimistic and pessimistic estimates.

Quick quiz

1. How does planning contribute to the flow of work?
2. What are the components of a plan?
3. Why might a task be 'high priority'?
4. What is a deadline?
5. Distinguish between forward scheduling and reverse scheduling.
6. Give three examples of resources that need to be planned and allocated.
7. Outline three different ways of organising work into departments.
8. Suggest three reasons why a manager might allocate a particular task to a particular individual.
9. What is a work breakdown structure, and what can it be used for?
10. What are (a) a critical activity and (b) a float?
11. What is depicted by (a) nodes, (b) arrowed lines and (c) thick arrowed lines, in a network diagram?
12. In what circumstances might you add a 'dummy activity' to a network diagram?
13. Is the critical path the shortest or longest line from start to end of the project network?
14. If you know how many workers are required for each job, and all team members can do all jobs, how might you go about scheduling your manpower in an efficient manner?
15. What is a 'crash time' and why might you not want to 'crash' a non-critical activity?
16. What is the mathematical formula for calculating a mean time for a job whose duration is uncertain?

Answers to quick quiz

1. Planning tries to avoid holdups or clashes and idle time or overwork for people or machines. (See para 1.1)

2 Aims, priorities, performance standards, short-term goals and action plans. (See para 2.1)

3 If a deadline is set, if other tasks or people are dependent on it or if it is important. (See para 3.2)

4 The last acceptable date for completion of a task. (See para 3.2)

5 Forward scheduling means starting with a given **start** time/date. Reverse scheduling means working backwards from a given **completion** time/date. (See para 3.3)

6 People's time, machine time, materials, money. (See para 3.4)

7 By function, territory, product or matrix organisation. (See para 4.1)

8 Work might be allocated on the basis of the individual's specialism, abilities, experience or workload. (See para 4.2)

9 It breaks a project down into its component phases or stages. It can be used to discover what work is needed and what resources are required and for sequencing and co-ordinating. (See para 6.1)

10 (a) One that must be completed on time.
(b) The amount of leeway there is for completion of the activity. (See para 6.4)

11 (a) Events
(b) Activities
(c) Critical activities (See para 6.3)

12 When two activities could start and end at the same event. (See para 6.3)

13 Longest. (See para 6.4)

14 Using a Gantt chart. (See para 7.1)

15 It is the minimum time to complete an activity. Crashing a non-critical activity would not affect the critical path or shorten the overall project time. (See para 8.2)

16 $\frac{o+4m+p}{6}$ (See para 8.3)

Answers to Activities

1 The statements fit the following categories.

Efficiency = b, c, e.

Effectiveness = a, d, f.

Statement (e) is an example of increased efficiency because fewer employees (inputs) are needed. Other interpretations are possible however.

2 The plans Dial-a-Video Limited propose are a strategy to exploit the 'art movie' market segment. A programme for the build-up of the distribution. The £4 charge is a tactic or policy. The 'no-tips' plan is a rule or regulation.

3 Factors involved in deciding a deadline include the following.

(a) Customers' requirements, or promises made to them.

(b) Specific events, such as a conference, before which all preparatory tasks must be completed.

(c) Other tasks, which depend on the task's completion by a time which will preserve the smooth flow of work.

4 Sequencing and scheduling a sales conference would involve:

(a)

Book conference centre/hotel	(perhaps months before)
Specify layout of conference room	(two weeks before)
Retrieve relevant files	(two weeks before)
Prepare agenda/info	(one week before)
Circulate agenda/info	(five days before)
Check layout of conference room	(two days before)
Take minutes of meeting	(day of meeting)

(b) Reverse scheduling – work back from the date of the conference.

(c) You might have suggested a diary, or a timetable, or some kind of chart, a checklist – and so on.

5 Resources for the sales conference will include the conference centre; equipment (overhead projectors etc); staffing of the conference centre; time of speakers; materials such as paper and slides; telephone and fax facilities; refreshments – and so on.

6 Contingency plans for the situations given would include the following.

(a) New systems may have 'bugs', or be unfamiliar to operators. A good contingency plan would be running the old system in parallel with the new one for a trial period.

(b) People get sick, or need holidays, or have problems getting to work during transport strikes, or go on strike themselves. You may have contingency plans to do with pre-notifying holidays, or laid-on transport in the event of transport strikes. A general contingency plan would be a temporary staff agency on standby to provide replacement/overflow staff.

(c) Again, transport may cause unexpected problems, or there could be an upset such as the venue being double-booked, the key speaker falling ill, or overhead projectors not working. Alternative transport/speaker/venue might be pre-planned, and back-up visual aids equipment (such as a flip-chart) on hand. You can't anticipate everything ...

7 You will have come up with your own ideas for different projects: here are some suggestions.

(a) Construction of a motorway extension, say, or the Channel Tunnel.

(b) Limited-edition production of a car, for example, or one-off tailor-made products.

(c) Implementation of a computer system, say, or mounting a trade exhibition or conference.

(d) Ironing out bugs in a system or product, completing a market research survey and so on.

Check that your own examples have a beginning, an end, and goals.

8 The answer will depend on your menu, but your WBS may include stages such as: the purchasing of the various ingredients; washing, peeling and chopping vegetables (if any); mixing ingredients; cooking

NOTES

and/or preparing each dish; laying the table and preparing plates and utensils and so on. Your WBS should give you a fairly clear idea of what ingredients, in what quantities, you will need to buy: a more accurate cost estimate than trying to judge the cost of the meal as a whole. The same is true of the timetable, with the added advantage that it provides the basis for an action checklist and schedule for preparation.

9 To turn figure 3 into a work schedule, you could put the days of the week across the top instead of the number of days given. So the excavations should take up Monday and Tuesday, the foundations start on Wednesday and so on.

10 The control line added to figure 4 yields the result shown here.

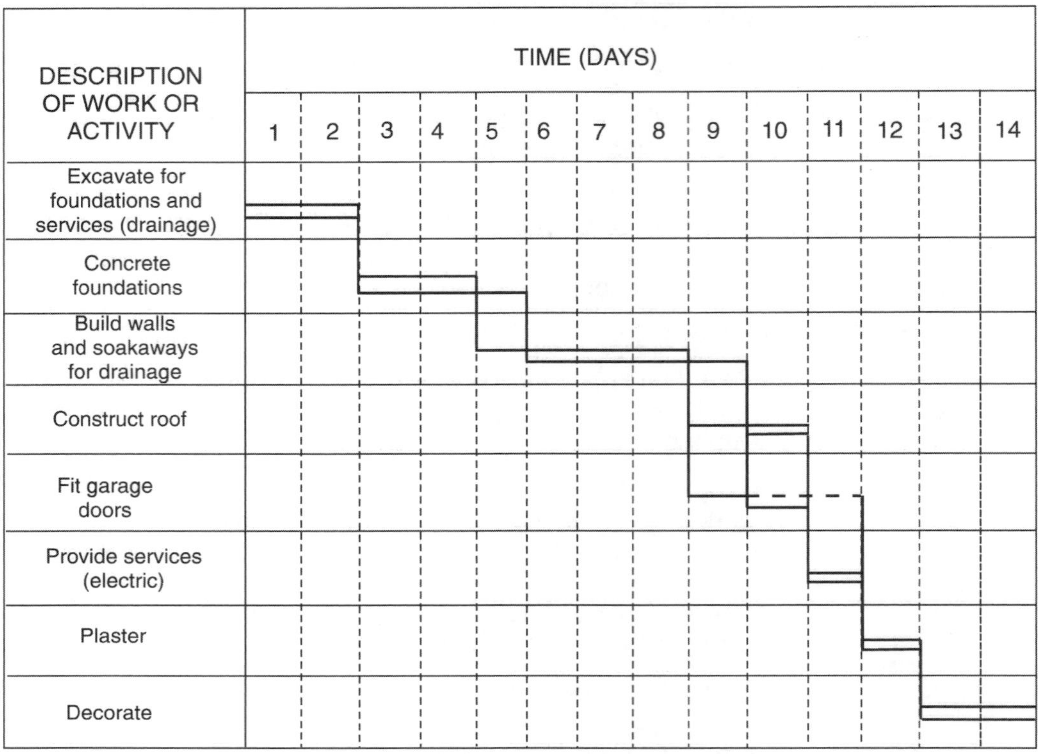

You've made up your lost day of concreting because you had the float time on the door-fitting and were able to divert the door person to the roofing.

11

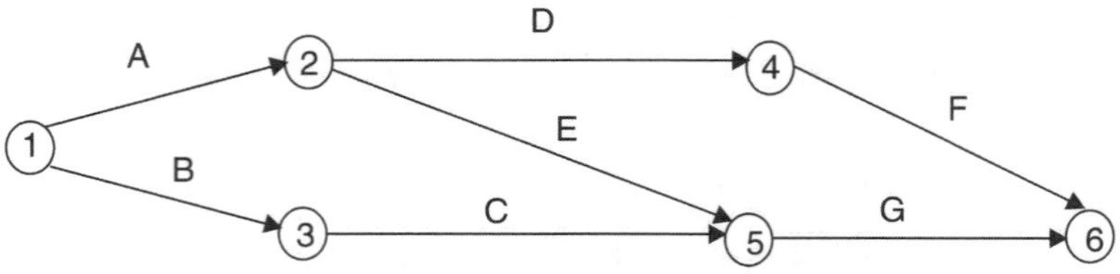

12 You should draw a dotted line from event 4 to 5.

13 There are three paths, as follows.

ADF = 3 + 1 + 3 days = 7 days
AEG = 3 + 6 + 3 days = 12 days
BCG = 5 + 2 + 3 days = 10 days

14

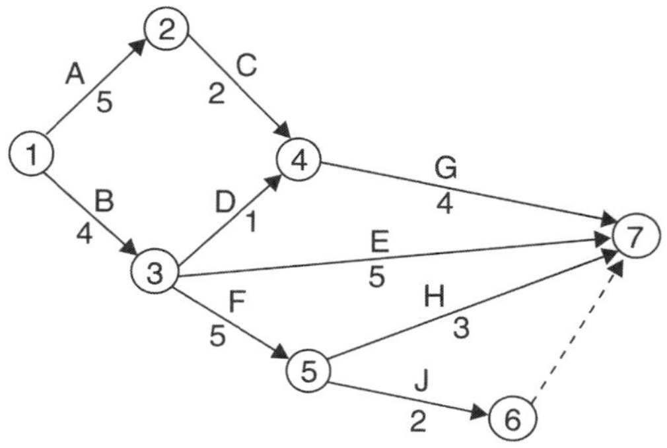

The paths are

ACG	= 5 + 2 + 4	= 11 weeks
BDG	= 4 + 1 + 4	= 9 weeks
BE	= 4 + 5	= 9 weeks
BFH	= 4 + 5 + 3	= 12 weeks
BFJ Dummy	= 4 + 5 + 2 + 0	= 11 weeks

BFH is the longest (and therefore the critical) path: the shortest time in which the project can be completed.

15

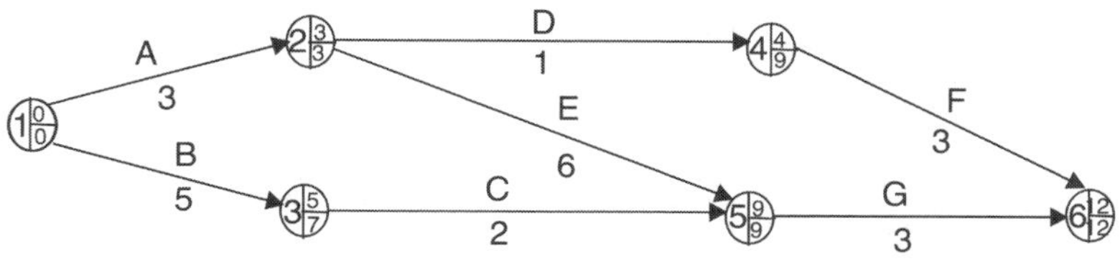

Activity C: anytime between days 5 and 7 (a 2-day float)
Activity F: anytime between days 4 and 9 (a 5-day float)

16 Did you totally underestimate your budget, and have to spend your food allowance for the next three weeks?

17

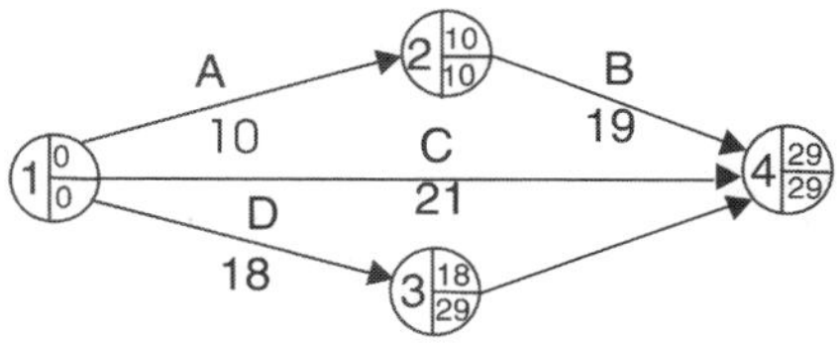

Chapter 3 :
MANAGING WORK ACTIVITIES

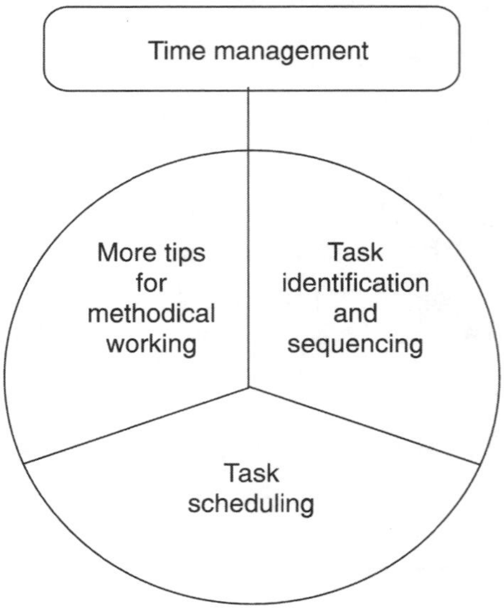

Introduction

Time is a resource, like money and raw materials. You have a finite and fixed amount of it, and various demands in your lifestyle and activities compete for a share of it. It means little in itself, but you can use it - efficiently or otherwise - to accomplish your purposes. Time is an input to every system, with an infinite variety of outputs. If you work in an organisation, your 'time is money': you will be paid for it, or for what you accomplish during it.

Time, like any other resource, needs to be managed, if it is to be used efficiently (without waste) and effectively (productively).

In this chapter, we take a practical look at how planning and organising contribute to efficient time management. We are mainly concerned with issues and techniques you may come across every day in your study or work or the conduct of your personal affairs: coping with a workload or a number of various tasks.

Your objectives

In this chapter, you will learn about the following.

(a) The demands on time and the principles of efficient time management and methodical working

(b) How to formulate personal goals and plans, and work out priorities

(c) How to use lists, action plans, timetables and charts, as appropriate for your activities

(d) How to implement follow-up systems to ensure that you have used your time effectively

1 TIME MANAGEMENT

1.1 Demands on a manager's time

A manager's use of time is affected by a number of factors.

The nature of the job

A manager's job involves regular contact with other people in the organisation: it is important to control the inevitable interruptions which this causes. Other typical causes of wasted time include prolonged or unnecessary meetings, and the preparation of unnecessary paperwork (which could be replaced with a brief oral communication).

The personality of the manager

A confident and assertive manager may be better able to resist interruptions and unnecessarily lengthy contacts than one who is diffident, and finds it difficult to 'say no'. A manager may fail to delegate, and end up with a lot of routine work on his own plate. On the other hand, he may simply be disorganised or lacking in self discipline and so be comparatively idle one minute and extremely busy the next.

The influence and demands of colleagues

There will be extra demands on the manager's time if:

(a) subordinates keep referring to the manager for decisions;

(b) subordinates require either close supervision or a consultative style of management;

(c) the culture of the organisation or department requires lots of communication, informal relationship-building, Management by Walking Around, an 'Open Door' availability policy and so on: this takes time.

Activity 1 **(10 minutes)**

Suggest two ways in which the management style of a superior may make extra demands on a manager's time.

There are two elements to a manager making effective use of time.

(a) Job management – making sure that he or she is knowledgeable about and equipped for his or her job, and that the job, policies and procedures, communication channels and so on are conducive to efficient working.

(b) Time management – allocating time to tasks in the most effective manner.

1.2 Job management

The manager should not waste time wondering what to do next, doing tasks that will not achieve objectives, or doing tasks that might better be done by someone else. He ought to be thoroughly knowledgeable about the policies, systems and procedures of the organisation, and about the structure of authority and responsibility ('proper channels') as well as about his own area of authority or expertise.

Delegation skills will be an important element in job management. Effective use of opportunities for delegation will ensure that the manager is not having unnecessary demands made on him by work inappropriately delegated upwards by subordinates, or downwards by more senior managers.

Communication skills will also be important. Skills in interpersonal relations can be used to get to the purpose of conversations, interviews and meetings with less time wasted. Learning to read faster, write more concise reports and sort out essential from non-essential information will also help efficient management of time.

1.3 Time management

Time management will involve the following.

(a) **Identifying objectives** and the key tasks which are most relevant to achieving them – sorting out what the manager **must** do, from what he **could** do, and from what he would **like** to do.

(b) **Prioritising:** assessing tasks for relative importance, amount of time required, and any deadlines or time-spans.

(c) **Scheduling** – assigning start and end times/dates to tasks (in other words, timetabling).

(d) **Control:** avoiding, where possible, disruption by the unexpected.

Activity 2 **(10 minutes)**

Think about how effectively you manage time by answering these questions.

1 Do you often miss deadlines for activities you are responsible for?

2 Are you often late for meetings or appointments?

3 Do you have to work late regularly to get things done?

4 Do you feel you are constantly trying to beat the clock?

5 Are you too busy to find time to plan?

6 Do you seem to have more work to do than others?

7 Have you got a good balance between time spent on study or work, with family, on yourself?

We will now look in more detail at some practical techniques for time management. Regard what follows as a 'toolbox': take out of it whatever suits you and the particular task you have in hand. But be warned: if you actually do all these things, it may change your life ...

2 TASK IDENTIFICATION AND SEQUENCING

2.1 Goals

If you have no idea what it is you are supposed to accomplish, or only a vague idea, all the time in the world will not be long enough to get it done. You need to set goals for yourself, and to be useful, those goals need to be:

(a) **specific;** and
(b) **measurable**.

So, for example, a daily goal might be: 'to complete all correspondence by 12.00' or 'to interview six people'. A performance goal might be: 'to see that invoices are issued and despatched for all goods sold, on the day of sale'.

On the basis of such goals, you can start making plans.

2.2 Lists

Lists are useful ways of identifying and remembering what needs to be done, and of monitoring how far you've got! You should work from a list of 'Things to do' all the time. If you don't do this already, try it once: you will be hooked, and your daily productivity will shoot up.

(a) Make a list every day before you start work. It is probably best to do this the night before – away from the pressures of work – so long as you don't forget to take your list to work with you the next day!

(b) On the day itself, refuse to do anything that is not on your list. This does not mean that if something more urgent than anything you are currently doing comes up you can ignore it. It means that every new task that arises has to be added to your list.

(c) Every time you finish something on your list, cross it off. This is the really satisfying part of making lists!

(d) At the end of the day take all the items that are still on the list and transfer them to your list for the next day. Don't skip this part and just staple today's unfinished list to tomorrow's unstarted one. The physical act of writing tasks down on paper is an important part of the process.

Do not rely on your memory, even if you think your memory is a fantastically good one. It is highly unlikely to be infallible, and in any case you are not just creating a memory-jogger: the idea is that you should be able to see at a glance **all** the things you have to do so that you can get them into perspective. The items do not need to be in any particular order at this stage: the important thing is that you list down everything that you have to do.

2.3 Checklists

A checklist, or 'tick chart', is simply a list which allows for ticking or 'checking' off each task as it is completed (instead of crossing out). Again, it may or may not reflect the order in which you actually perform the tasks. You may simply have a column to put ticks against each task, or you may want to have a space for times/dates on which you started or finished the activity, or even for stages of the activity (for example, where a particular document is at a given date) – or elements of all of these.

As an example, here is a checklist for an advertising manager preparing deadlines for a number of press advertisements.

Ad	*Due date*	*Writer*	*Designer*	*Photo-grapher*	*Film*	*Print*	*Proofed*	*Sent?*
Times	3/9	21/8	22/8	24/8	30/8	-	2/9	✓
Standard	3/9	22/8	23/8	26/8	30/8	-	2/9	✓
A5 classified	7/9	29/8	30/8	-	-	-	4/9	✓
Leaflet A	12/9	10/8	12/8	15/8	-	2/9		
Leaflet B	13/9	2/9	3/9		-			

Activity 3 **(30 minutes)**

Suppose you are the advertising manager's assistant. She has fallen ill on the 5th September, and has asked you to take over the ad and leaflet production. 'I've left you my work checklist,' she says. 'You can work from that.' You find on her desk the checklist given as our example above.

(a) What can you tell from the checklist?

(b) What does this suggest about the usefulness of checklists?

(c) What tasks that you (as a real person, now) have to perform might benefit from the same approach?

2.4 Priorities

Once you have a list or checklist of tasks, you can decide what order to tackle them in.

Task importance

Remember, a job will be important (or high priority) if:

(a) it has to be completed by a deadline in order to fulfil its objective (particularly if the deadline is close, so the task is also urgent);

(b) other important tasks depend on its completion; or

(c) the potential consequences of **not** doing the task on time are long-term, difficult to reverse, far-reaching and/or costly.

Use your own personal scale to grade activities on your list. For example:

1 – 3 Unimportant
4 – 6 Moderately important
7 – 10 Very important

Another approach that often works well is to imagine that you only have time to do **one** thing on your list: which would it be? That is your first priority. And if you have enough time for one **more** thing? And another? When you have identified your top three or four priorities, tackle them, in order.

Take care to do some important, fairly important **and** routine tasks every day: unimportant, routine tasks (like filing) may become hindrances to doing more important tasks, if they are neglected ...

Task urgency

Note that tasks need not be important just because they are urgent. It is possible to be tyrannised by urgent tasks as their deadlines approach, when in fact they could be delegated, or the deadline could simply be moved back because the task is not otherwise a high priority.

However, if an important task is also urgent, do not put it off, especially if it is large and unpleasant. Today's routine may become tomorrow's emergency – and, worse, today's emergency may become tomorrow's disaster!

In fact, you should try to treat all important tasks as if they were urgent. Procrastination, taking your time (or just plain dithering) is a natural tendency – fewer than 2% of people are reckoned to have a true sense of urgency – but time really does slip away if you don't grab hold of it.

FOR DISCUSSION

'Work expands to fill the time available.' Do you ever feel this: that the more time you have, the less you get done? Why might a manager want to take this phenomenon into account?

Task sequence

Some plans, as we have seen, are already set up as **procedures**, or sequences of tasks, in the order in which they must be performed. In other cases, you may have to put your list of things to do in order, if there is a logical sequence to them. A checklist for an employee in charge of receiving supplies into the stores department, for example, might be as follows.

GOODS INWARDS

1 Receive goods
2 Check goods against order
3 Sign goods received note
4 Inspect goods
5 Retrieve stock record card
6 Record stock details
7 Re-file record card
8 Prepare storage labels.
9 Affix labels
10 Place goods in store

If you haven't done the particular task before, it may not be immediately obvious what the sequence of actions is. A fairly simple approach to working it out is to 'map' it, using what is called a **precedence network**. We discussed network analysis in detail in the previous chapter, as it is particularly useful for planning complex projects. A simple precedence network, however, shows which activities need to be completed before others, Figure 1. The circles or 'nodes' denote activities, and the arrows show logical progression and precedence.

NOTES

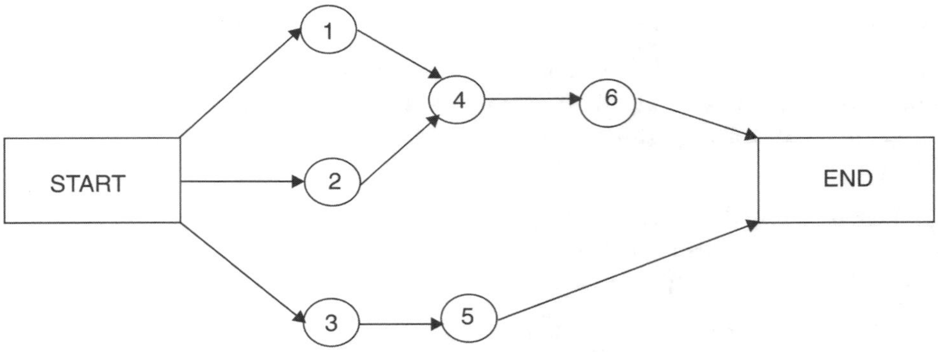

Figure 1 Precedence network

Consider Figure 1 above as a plan for going away on holiday, say.

Activity 1 = Reserving your holiday place by phone

Activity 2 = Booking travel insurance

Activity 3 = Renewing your passport

Activity 4 = Sending in a completed booking form. (This follows a reservation and requires details of insurance cover.)

Activity 5 = Obtaining a travel visa. (This can't be done until you have a valid passport.)

Activity 6 = Collection of tickets (for which you need to have made a written booking).

And you're off! The advantage of such a method is that (unlike a checklist) it allows you to show where a number of activities need to be done at roughly the same time (like activities 1, 2 and 3 above).

Activity 4 **(30 minutes)**

Choose any task you have to complete in the coming week.

(a) Brainstorm a list of the activities it will require, in no particular order.

(b) Put your list into the order in which you will (roughly) have to do the activities.

(c) Convert your checklist into a precedence network. (You could draw one large enough to write the activity into each node box, instead of numbering and listing the activities.)

Now you have planned and prioritised your activities, the next step is to plan and allocate your time.

3 TASK SCHEDULING

You may remember from Chapter 2 that scheduling can be done in two ways.

(a) **Reverse scheduling** – working backwards from a deadline or target completion date. If you know what your end time/date is, and can estimate how long each task will take, you can **subtract** each task time from the due time/date, to get target start times for each task, and for the activity as a whole.

(b) **Forward scheduling** – working forwards from a start date, and **adding** the estimated time of each task to get a total activity duration, and therefore an estimated completion time/date.

Whichever method is used, bear in mind that task times will only be estimates. You may wish to build in some extra 'slack' time, so that:

(a) you are less likely to fall behind; and

(b) if you **do** fall behind on one task, you will have some catch-up time built into the estimate for the following task, so that it can be completed on time.

There are various ways of setting out schedules. Here are some popular ones.

3.1 Action plans

Action plans set out a programme of work or action, including time scheduling. Our example of a checklist for an advertising manager was a kind of action plan.

The following is another example, for the writing of a report.

Activity	*Days before due date*	*Target date*	*Date begun*	*Date completed*
1 Request files	6	3/9		
2 Draft report	5	4/9		
3 Type report	3	6/9		
4 Approve report	1	8/9		
5 Signature	1	8/9		
6 Courier	0	9/9		

3.2 Timetables

The same information could be formatted as a timetable or diary entry. You may already be using such methods to timetable your studies – and/or your social life! Timetables and diaries are designed to:

(a) remind you of key times and dates;

(b) remind you to make necessary advance preparations; and

(c) help you allocate your time effectively – no 25-hour days or clashing appointments.

NOTES

Activity 5 **(15 minutes)**

Here is a timetable/diary page for the week of the 3rd to 9th September. Enter the schedule given in Section 3.1 as an action plan, as you would do a class timetable or appointments diary. Consider how you would highlight the due date.

SATURDAY 3	WEDNESDAY 7
SUNDAY 4	THURSDAY 8
MONDAY 5	FRIDAY 9
TUESDAY 6	Week commencing 3 SEPTEMBER S S M T W T F 3 4 5 6 7 8 9

3.3 Charts

Longer-term schedules may be more conveniently read using charts, peg-boards or year-planners. These can be used to show:

(a) the length of time to be taken for scheduled events or activities;

(b) the relationship between events or tasks – for example, whether they take place at the same time or in sequence. This can be particularly useful for identifying where excessive or clashing demands are being made: you have scheduled two tasks at once, or scheduled a task over a period when you planned a holiday, say;

(c) the relationship between planned and actual task duration or output.

Bar charts and Gantt charts were covered in the previous chapter. They are also effective time management tools.

4 MORE TIPS FOR METHODICAL WORKING

4.1 Concentration

Concentration involves:

- not trying to do two things at the same time;
- avoiding interruptions and distractions;
- attempting to finish tasks once you have started them.

The following tips may be useful.

(a) Make sure that everything that you need is available **before** you start work. If not, one of the things on your list will be to order the supplies, obtain the information or do whatever it is that is holding you up.

(b) Before you start a task clear away everything from your desk that you do **not** need for that particular task. Put irrelevant things where you will be able to retrieve them easily when you come to deal with the tasks that you **do** need them for. If they are not needed by **anyone**, throw them away.

(c) The **half open door**. Do not be available to all comers at all times. Ways of avoiding interruptions include the following.

(i) Being **unavailable**. Use call-diverting facilities on your telephone (and/or ask your secretary, if you have one), or try working somewhere other than your usual desk or office.

(ii) Setting up **surgery hours** during which – and **only** during which – your door is open to visitors.

(iii) Operate **management by exception**. Tell your staff to report to you only when there is a problem or deviation from plan, or important new information.

(d) **Appointments with yourself.** If you need to spend time alone, making plans, reviewing progress – or indeed making sure that you get personal time for rest and relaxation – it is a good idea to treat this as if it were a meeting. Make a time for it in your diary, and stick to it: take it seriously, and do not let other activities encroach on it.

4.2 Organisation

Apart from working to plans, checklists or schedules, your work organisation might be improved by the following.

(a) **An ABCD method of in-tray management**. When a task or piece of paper comes in to your in-tray or 'to do' list, you should never merely look at it and put it back for later. This would mean you would handle it more than once – usually over and over again, if it is a trivial or unpleasant item! Resolve to take one of the following approaches.

Act on the item immediately

Bin it, if you are sure it is worthless, irrelevant and unnecessary

Create a definite plan for coming back to the item: get it on your schedule or timetable

Delegate it to someone else

(b) **Organise your work in batches** of jobs requiring the same activities, files, equipment and so on. Group your filing tasks, copying tasks or word processing tasks, for example, and do them in a session, rather than having to travel to and fro or compete for equipment time for each separate task.

(c) **Take advantage of your natural work patterns**. Self-discipline is aided by developing regular hours or days for certain tasks, like dealing with correspondence first thing or filing at the end of the day. If you are able to plan your own schedules, you might also take into account your personal patterns of energy, concentration, alertness etc. Large or complex tasks might be undertaken in the mornings before you get tired, or perhaps late at night with fewer distractions, while Friday afternoon is not usually a good time to start a demanding task in the office ...

4.3 Control

Control over work must be maintained to ensure that jobs do in fact reach completion, and if those jobs involve various tasks over varying periods, planning will be necessary to keep track of future events, deadlines, results and so on.

Systems which provide for this are called **bring forward** or **bring up** systems. Anything which needs action at a later date (and therefore may get forgotten) should be processed in this way, for example:

(a) checking on progress of an operation;
(b) checking completion when the deadline is reached;
(c) checking payments when they fall due;
(d) retrieving files relevant to future discussions, meetings, correspondence.

Checklists are useful, as we suggested earlier, for monitoring what has been done and what hasn't. Diary systems may also be used. A reminder may be put in the diary or timetable for the relevant day, to check 'task x completed?', 'payment received?', 'response received to letter ref: IO/cw2?', 'one week left for revision' and so on. If you use card index or concertina files, you could slip a card or note into the sequence or appropriate date section, for checking on the day.

FOR DISCUSSION

Examine any timetables, charts or work programmes that relate to your course. How effective are they in communicating information? How useful are they as a plan you can actually work to? What controls or checks do they include, and what other forms of progress monitoring are applied to your work, if any? (You may be able, now, to suggest ways in which your work programme could be improved ...)

---

5 JUST-IN-TIME

Co-ordination of activities is necessary to ensure optimum use of resources. Just In Time (JIT) techniques are an example of long-linked technologies which have the effect of increasing technological interdependence by removing slack from the system.

Definition

> 'A system whose objective is to produce or to procure products or components as they are required by a customer or for use, rather than for stock. A just-in-time system is a "pull" system, which responds to demand, in contrast to a "push" system, in which stocks act as buffers between the different elements of the system, such as purchasing, production and sales.
>
> (a) **Just-in-time production**. A production system which is driven by demand for finished products whereby each component on a production line is produced only when needed for the next stage.
>
> (b) **Just-in-time purchasing**. A purchasing system in which material purchases are contracted so that the receipt and usage of material, to the maximum extent possible, coincide.

5.1 Advantages

JIT emerged from criticisms of traditional responses to the problems of improving manufacturing capacity and reducing unit costs of production. These traditional responses include the techniques given below.

NOTES

- Longer production runs
- Economic batch quantities
- Fewer products in the product range.
- More overtime
- Reduced time spent on preventive maintenance, to keep production flowing

In general terms, longer production runs and large batch sizes should mean less disruption, better capacity utilisation and lower unit costs.

5.2 Differences from traditional means of manufacture

However, JIT techniques and stockless production challenge traditional views of manufacture.

- Its principles include greater flexibility in production, and matching production to meet demand.
- This in turn means shorter batch production runs and a greater product variety.
- There will be much smaller stocks of finished goods, because output is being matched more closely to demand.
- Production systems must therefore be reliable and prompt, without unforeseen delays and breakdowns. Machinery must be kept fully maintained, and so **preventive maintenance** is an important aspect of production.

The most obvious physical manifestation of JIT is a small warehouse. In other words, there are few raw materials stocks, as these are only purchased when needed. There are few finished goods stocks, as effort is not expended on production that is not required. JIT makes a firm vulnerable to disruptions of several types.

- Interruptions in supply
- Poor quality in purchased inputs
- Defective production

CASE EXAMPLES

- JIT makes the organisation far more vulnerable to disruptions in the supply chain. An example of this is given in the case of Renault, the French state-owned car maker. The workforce at Renault's gear-box production plant at Cléon went on strike. The *day afterwards* a British plant had to cease production. Within two weeks Renault was losing 60% of its usual daily output a day. The weaknesses were due to:
  - sourcing components from one plant only;
  - heavy dependence on in-house components;
  - low inventory;
  - the fact '...that Japanese-style management techniques depend on stability in labour relations, something in short supply in the French public sector'.
- A similar effect was seen during the petrol supply crisis in the UK and other European countries in 2000. Prevention of tankers from making deliveries meant that petrol stations ran out of supplies within hours.

BPP PUBLISHING

- JIT, originated by Toyota, was 'designed at a time when all of Toyota's manufacturing was done within a 50 km radius of its headquarters'. Wide geographical spread, however, makes this difficult.

5.3 Impact of JIT

JIT has a significant impact on departmental interdependence, and indeed on the interdependence between different companies in the **supply chain**. This is because there is no slack and no buffer stock. JIT massively increases the need for standardisation of quality, as there is no space for waste, and coordination of deliveries. As a result, firms are establishing long-term relationships with their suppliers.

6 VALUE CHAIN ANALYSIS

In addition to identifying the organisation's resources, it helps to determine how well they are being used, and how much value is added after those resources are acquired. One such technique is **value chain analysis**. Value chain analysis identifies the way in which the firm organises the business's activities. It was developed by Michael Porter in his book *Competitive Advantage*.

6.1 Business activities

Before we go any further, keep in mind that, in Porter's analysis, **business activities** are *not* the same as **business functions**.

- **Functions** are the familiar departments of a business (eg Production function, the Finance function) and reflect the formal organisation structure and the distribution of labour.
- **Activities** are what actually goes on, and the work that is done. A single activity can be performed by a number of functions in sequence. Activities are the means by which a firm creates value in its products. (They are sometimes referred to as *value activities.)* Activities incur costs, and, in combination with other activities, provide a product or service which earns revenue.

Some examples should make this clear. An organisation needs many inputs of resources to function. It needs to secure resources from the environment. This activity can be called procurement. However, procurement will involve more departments than purchasing; accounts will certainly be involved and possibly production and Quantity Assurance.

'Firms create value for their buyers by performing these activities.' The ultimate value a firm creates is measured by the amount customers are willing to pay for its products or services above the cost of carrying out value activities. A firm is profitable if the realised value to customers exceeds the collective cost of performing the activities.

There are two points to note here.

- **Customers purchase value**, which they measure by comparing a firm's products and services with similar offerings by competitors.
- **The business creates value** by carrying out its activities either more efficiently than other businesses, or combined in such a way as to provide a unique product or service.

NOTES

6.2 The value chain

Definition

Value chain. 'The sequence of business activities by which, in the perspective of the end user, value is added to the products or services produced by an organisation.'

Porter analysed the various activities of an organisation into a **value chain**. This is a model of value activities (which procure inputs, process them and add value to them in some way, to generate outputs for customers) and the relationships between them. Here is a diagram of the value chain.

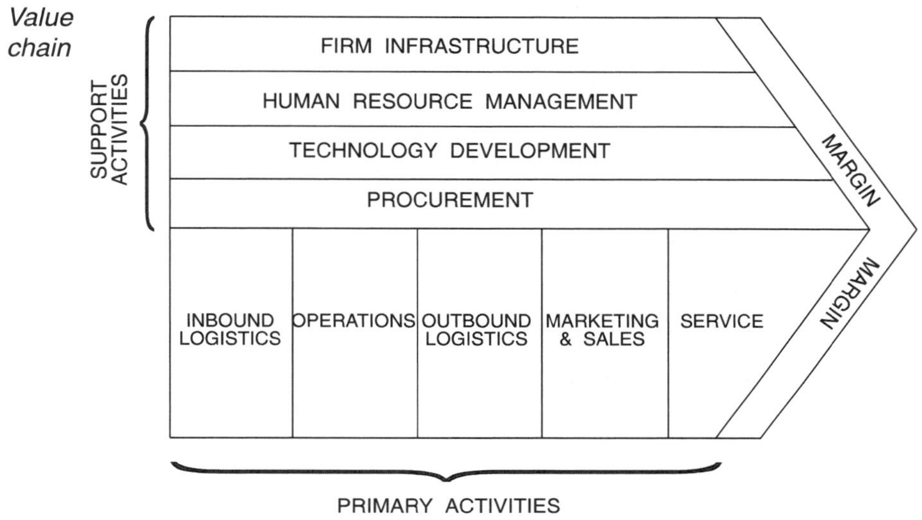

Let us examine some of these elements in turn.

The first distinction which can be made is that between primary activities and support activities.

6.3 Primary activities

Primary activities are those directly related with production, sales, marketing, delivery and services. The diagram shows five primary activities.

(a) **Inbound logistics** are those activities involved with receiving, handling and storing inputs to the production system.

(b) **Operations** are those activities which convert resource inputs into a final product. In a manufacturing firm, this is relatively easy to identify as the factory. In a service company, operations include those activities which make up the basic service.

(c) **Outbound logistics** are those activities relating to storing the product and its distribution to customers.

(d) **Marketing and sales** are those activities that relate to informing customers about the product, persuading them to buy it, and enabling them to do so.

(e) **After sales service** includes activities such as installing products, repairing them and providing spare parts.

6.4 Support activities

Support activities are those which provide purchased inputs, human resources, technology and infrastructural functions to support the primary activities.

(a) **Procurement** refers to those activities which acquire the resource inputs to the primary activities (eg purchase of materials, subcomponents, equipment).

(b) **Technology development** (in the sense of apparatus, techniques and work organisation). These activities are related to both product design and to improving processes and/or resource utilisation.

(c) **Human resource management** is the activities of recruiting, training, developing and rewarding people.

(d) **Firm infrastructure**. The systems of planning, finance, quality control and management are activities which Porter believes are crucially important to an organisation's strategic capability in all primary activities.

6.5 Other activities

Furthermore, in addition to the categories described above, Porter identifies three further types of activity.

- **Direct activities** are concerned with adding value to inputs.
- **Indirect activities** enable direct activities to be performed (eg maintenance, sales force administration).
- **Quality assurance**. This type of activity monitors the quality of other activities, and includes: inspection, review and audit (eg the quality of the financial records)

6.6 Linkages

Linkages connect the interdependent elements of the value chain together. They occur when one element of the value chain affects the costs or effectiveness of another. They require co-ordination.

- More costly product design, or better quality production, might reduce the need for after-sales service.
- To deliver goods on time requires smooth functioning of operations, outbound logistics and service activities such as installation.

6.7 Value systems

Activities that add value do not stop at the organisation's boundaries. For example, when a restaurant serves a meal, the quality of the ingredients - although they are chosen by the cook - is determined by the grower. The grower has also added value, and the grower's success in growing produce of good quality is as important to the customer's ultimate satisfaction as the skills of the chef. Consequently, **a company's value chain is connected to what Porter describes as a value system**.

Value system

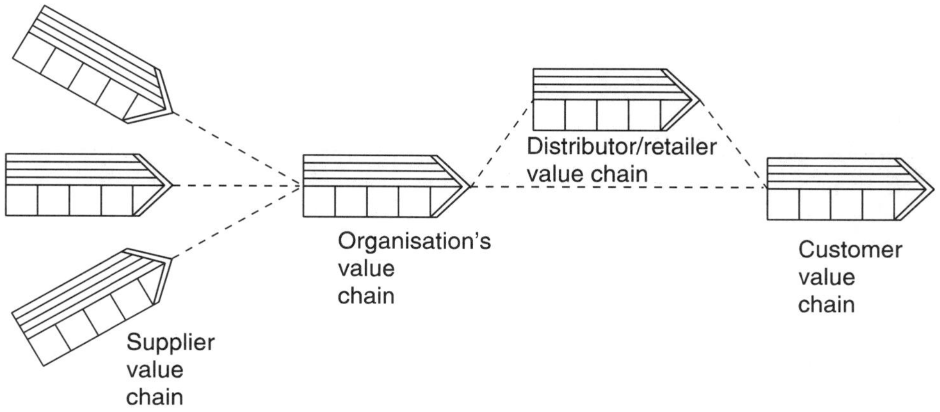

As well as managing its own value chain, a firm can secure competitive advantage by managing the linkages with its suppliers and customers. A company can create competitive advantage by making best use of these links and this means considering the value chains of these suppliers and customers. An example is a just-in-time system where close integration of the firm's operations with those of its suppliers is essential.

Finally, the value chain contains an element for **margin**. This is the excess of the amount that the customer is prepared to pay over the costs of the resource inputs and value activities.

Activity 6 **(15 minutes)**

Sana Sounds is a small record company. Representatives from Sana Sounds scour music clubs for new bands to promote. Once a band has signed a contract (with Sana Sounds) it makes a recording. The recording process is subcontracted to one of a number of recording studio firms which Sana Sounds uses regularly. (At the moment Sana Sounds is not large enough to invest in its own equipment and studios.) Sana Sounds also subcontracts the production of records and CDs to a number of manufacturing companies. Sana Sounds then distributes the disks to selected stores, and engages in any promotional activities required.

What would you say were the activities in Sana Sounds' *value chain?*

7 CO-ORDINATION

7.1 Introduction

We identified co-ordination as one of the functions of management, earlier, defining it broadly as harmonising the activities of individuals and groups toward their common objectives.

You may have noticed that the term 'co-ordination' has also cropped up throughout this section on Managing Activities. Planning, organisation and communication are three of the key factors in maintaining co-ordinated effort and resources.

NOTES

Definition

> To **co-ordinate** is 'to plan, or take action to improve, the inter-relationships (especially of timing and methods of communication) between a number of various activities, which contribute to the achievement of a single objective, so that they do not conflict and the objective is achieved with a minimal expenditure of time and effort.' *(Dictionary of Management)*

7.2 The importance of co-ordination

Remember that we defined the purpose of organisations as 'the controlled performance to achieve collective goals'. This is, in essence, what co-ordination involves. Co-ordination is important because:

(a) the organisation is a collection of individuals and groups, each with their own interests and goals; these must be given a unified, common direction if the organisation as a whole is to achieve its objectives;

(b) the organisation's activities involve a variety of:

(i) people;
(ii) tasks;
(iii) resources; and
(iv) technologies

all of these will have to be at the right place, at the right time, working in the right way, if smooth operations are to be maintained;

(c) some activities of the organisation will be dependent on the successful and timely completion of other activities (as we saw in network analysis): someone needs to ensure that such interrelationships are taken into account in the overall activity of the organisation;

(d) some activities of the organisation will be higher priority than others: someone needs to ensure that there is an overall balance between urgent/high-priority activities and routine activities, on which the organisation nevertheless depends;

(e) resources (human, material and financial) are limited, and possibly scarce. Different units in the organisation are, in effect, in competition for their 'slice' of the resources available. Someone has to balance their demands and the organisation's priorities to ensure that overall, resources are used efficiently and effectively in pursuit of the organisation's goals.

FOR DISCUSSION

Think about a team sport you know well – say, football. What would happen if you had:

(a) no positions for each of the players to adopt?

(b) no team strategy?

(c) no team purpose – if, say, prizes were awarded to individual goal scorers, and there were no such thing as a team win?

(d) nobody in charge of providing kit, the ball, the playing field or the referee on a regular basis?

7.3 What needs co-ordinating?

From the above, we can see that, broadly, managers co-ordinate:

(a) the **timing** of activities, so that their inter-relationships are controlled without wasted time or bottlenecks;

(b) the **direction** or **purpose** of activities, so that sub-units of the organisation pull together towards common objectives, and the relative priority of activities are balanced;

(c) the **resources** (human, financial and material) required for activities, so that each sub-unit of the organisation is able to do what it should, when it should.

Activity 7 **(20 minutes)**

(a) Can you immediately think of some techniques we have already discussed which might help a business in each of these areas?

(b) Give an example of a problem arising from failure to co-ordinate in each of these areas.

7.4 Symptoms of poor co-ordination

A manager might be alerted to problems of co-ordination by the following tell-tale signs.

(a) Complaints from clients, customers and other external parties, indicating that products are not being supplied on time, or that they have been given different information by different departments of the organisation.

(b) Production problems, with alternating overloads and idle time, and associated problems with labour resourcing and production costs. (The equivalent for service organisations might be missed deadlines or commitments to customers, internal paperwork failing to reach the right people at the right time and so on.)

(c) Persistent conflict within and between departments, especially the placing of blame for problems, and empire-building and power games in place of co-operation.

(d) Lack of communication between units of the organisation.

(e) Appeals to rules and red tape in an attempt to give the appearance of integrated activity.

7.5 Causes of poor co-ordination

Some of the major causes of poor co-ordination are as follows.

(a) **Poor communication** – both vertically and horizontally – so that units do not know what they are supposed to be doing, or what other units are doing, or how the two are meant to be related.

(b) **Inadequate planning and control**, so that the objectives of each unit are not clearly understood, or integrated with those of other units, within overall objectives.

(c) **Weak organisation structure,** which does not make the inter-relationships between units clear, or link them via the chain of command. This problem will be particularly acute where the organisation's task requires interdependent input across the boundaries of departments and functions.

(d) **Interpersonal and/or interdepartmental conflict**. Power and resources are limited in organisations, and there is frequently competition, rivalry, jealousies, the guarding of 'territory' and information and so on, to protect the interests of individuals and groups. This kind of activity is known as organisational politics.

(e) **Differences** between the cultures and tasks of different units. These may be differences in:

(i) the time pressures a unit works under;
(ii) the leadership style of the units' managers;
(iii) the technology used by the units;
(iv) the methods of working adopted by the units;
(v) the culture or values of the units;

and so on.

Activity 8 **(20 minutes)**

Give an example of each of the types of difference between cultures and tasks of different units suggested above, which might cause problems of co-ordination.

8 IMPROVING CO-ORDINATION

8.1 Management strategies

The role of the manager in co-ordinating the efforts of his or her team – and in co-ordinating them with other teams in the organisation – will be much along the lines we have already discussed in this section on Managing Activities.

Maintaining and improving communication

Communication is essential for co-ordination, ensuring that:

(a) the inter-relationship of activities and plans is understood;

(b) variations from plan in one activity are notified to, and taken into account by, other units;

(c) conflict and organisational politics are not allowed to develop, to obstruct the common goals of the organisation.

Managers should give attention to horizontal, as well as vertical, communication.

NOTES

Activity 9 **(10 minutes)**

Suggest three ways in which a manager might encourage horizontal communication.

Planning

Systematic planning and control is essential for co-ordination. Tasks need to be sequenced and scheduled in a way that:

(a) balances their relative urgency and priority;

(b) takes into account their inter-relationships and the dependency of one task on another;

(c) allows resources to be rationally allocated on the basis of priorities and overall objectives; and

(d) allows the plans and schedules of each unit to be integrated with those of other units, towards the organisation's overall objectives.

If you need to refresh your memory on planning and associated techniques, briefly review Chapter 2.

Controlling conflict

Managers should try to create conditions in which individuals and departments are able to co-operate instead of conflict.

Direct supervision

The manager occupies a co-ordinating role within his or her own section, as the central person responsible for all the work of the group: issuing instructions, monitoring performance and so on.

8.2 Structures and mechanisms

As well as using the co-ordinating function of managers, an organisation can aid co-ordination through its structures and various formal mechanisms.

Organisation structure

The organisation structure may be designed to provide:

(a) a **co-ordinating level of management**. Just as the individual manager acts as the 'lynchpin' of co-ordination for his own unit, so he has a superior who is responsible for co-ordinating his work with that of other units, see the diagram below;

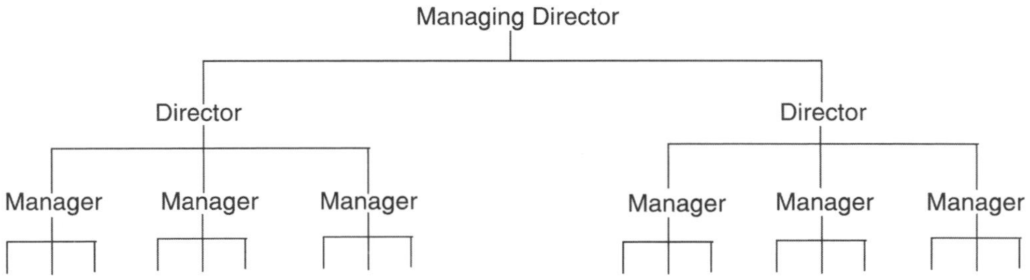

BPP PUBLISHING

(b) **liaison or integration officers** – for example, project co-ordinators, client liaison managers and so on. These posts essentially encourage communication;

(c) **multi-disciplinary teams,** committees, project groups and so on. These are matrix structures, including representation from all departments involved in a given task or activity, with a co-ordinating authority (a project manager, say) crossing functional boundaries.

Standardisation

Standardisation is an important mechanism for co-ordinating work at the operational level: it involves getting people to do things the same way, or with the same results. This adds reliability, or predictability, to work processes, allowing them to be more closely co-ordinated and controlled.

(a) **Standardisation of work processes** is possible for routine tasks, where the actual content of the task is specified or programmed. For example, think about the assembly instructions for a model or piece of furniture, or the operation of a video recorder: the task is designed to be done in the same way, regardless of who is doing it. Standardisation of forms and documents is another important aid to consistency and co-ordination.

(b) **Standardisation of output** is possible for more complex tasks, where discretion is needed in performing the work. The organisation may set standards for design, quality, cost and so on, so that its product or service is consistent, regardless of who does the work and how.

(c) **Standardisation by skill and knowledge** is possible for complex and varied work, which nevertheless requires a certain standard of performance. So, for example, a hospital sets standard requirements for the qualifications of its doctors, as an accountancy firm does for its accountants and so on.

EXAMPLE

McDonald's fast food restaurants are highly standardised in terms of work processes and outputs. This helps them to control consistency of food quality and specification in their outlets spread worldwide. You don't get lettuce in a McDonald's hamburger in the UK, because it is not possible for every hamburger made worldwide to contain lettuce, due to local variations in supply.

FOR DISCUSSION

How well co-ordinated is the course you are on? (Consider how 'smooth' your timetable is: clashes? bottlenecks? idle time? How consistent is the teaching and course material? Is there a course leader or co-ordinator, and what is his or her function?)

---

9 CONSTRAINTS ON MANAGEMENT

9.1 Introduction

In putting forward theories and techniques for managing activities, it is all too easy to give the impression that managers are in a position to make any and all decisions they think necessary to achieve their objectives, bounded only by the scope of their authority within the organisation. Of course, this isn't really so. We have already touched on the uncertainty of forecasting and planning the future; the impossibility of gathering all relevant information; the fact that power and resources are limited; the need for compromise in interpersonal relations and in business decisions alike; the importance – and unpredictability – of human behaviour at work. All these factors act as constraints on the individual manager's right and ability to manage people and activities as (s)he sees fit, or even in the most effective way possible (in an ideal world ...). This section aims to draw together all those threads.

9.2 External stakeholders

Stakeholders are people or groups who have a 'stake' or interest in the activities and performance of an organisation and who impose certain obligations on its management. The external stakeholders of the organisation include:

(a) **its owners or shareholders** – the organisation, and its management, have a primary responsibility to look after the owners' interests and to secure them a return on their financial investment in the organisation; the shareholders of a public company have the right to vote on organisational issues in an Annual General Meeting and any Extraordinary General Meetings that may be called: ultimately, the shareholders have the say in what the organisation does and how it should be managed;

(b) **its customers** – the organisation's customers depend on it for the goods and services they need, and for the safety, value and honest marketing of those goods and services; in a free market economy, however, customers have the choice to accept or reject an organisation's offerings, and this gives them power: organisations need to tailor their products and their image to the values and wants of the market, if they are to survive competition;

Activity 10 **(20 minutes)**

What sort of issues have consumer organisations focused on in the attempt to influence businesses to protect buyers' interests and values? Suggest four examples that you are aware of.

(c) **the community, or society as a whole** – society depends on businesses for employment, investment, social responsibility (eg towards the environment) and so on. It also provides the organisation with labour, with potential customers and with a reputation which may affect the organisation's position in the market, so managers need to consider whether their decisions will be socially acceptable.

In relation to external stakeholders, an organisation has:

(a) obligations or responsibilities, which it may undertake voluntarily, but which do not form a part of its internal guidance or control mechanisms;

for example, value for money, charitable donations, generous wages and so on; and

(b) boundaries or constraints on its managers' freedom to act as they see fit. For example, government legislation (on pollution, health and safety at work, redundancy and so on), regulation (on financial reporting and so on) and agreements with a trade union.

Society as a whole protects its own interests formally, via laws and regulations, designed to ensure that organisations behave morally (or ethically) and responsibly.

9.3 Regulatory control

Regulatory control involves the guidance, monitoring and control of organisational practices through formal mechanisms such as laws, regulations, 'watchdog' bodies and agreed Codes of Practice. These act as constraints on managerial discretion.

Laws

Organisations operate within a framework of laws which is very broad in scope, and deals with such issues as:

(a) **how an organisation does its business:** laws on contracts, selling and advertising practices, safety and labelling of goods, holding personal information on computer files and so on;

(b) **how an organisation treats its employees:** laws on employment protection (dismissal and redundancy), dealing with trade unions, health and safety, pay and benefits, discrimination and so on;

(c) **how an organisation deals with its owners and gives information about its performance:** laws on the duties of directors, reporting of results, constitution of meetings and so on;

(d) **how an organisation complies with criminal law** – on extortion, theft, assault, invasion of privacy and so on;

(e) **how an organisation discharges its responsibilities to government** – to collect and pay taxes, to provide information returns and so on.

In the UK, there is domestic legislation and also, increasingly, the implementation of Directives from the European Union, which are gradually being harmonised with legislation in the member states of the EU.

FOR DISCUSSION

Do you think it is necessary for governments to introduce legislation in areas such as:

(a) health and safety at work (obliging employers to provide a healthy and safe environment and procedures)?

(b) product safety (fire-retardant materials, no asbestos, safety belts in cars, health warnings and so on)?

If so, why? If managers were free to do what they liked or thought best for the organisation, what might standards be like? Do you think that laws encourage people to do only what is required, and not more – perhaps even lowering standards to what can be got away with?

Regulation

In some areas of decision-making, regulation has increased in recent years, where it has been felt to be in the public interest.

(a) Regulatory bodies oversee the activities of privatised utilities like BT, British Gas and the electricity and water companies. They can influence the company's pricing policy, competitive strategy (if they feel it is unfair) and so on.

(b) The financial services industry in the City is more heavily controlled than hitherto, though much of this is self-regulation carried out by the industry itself, with its own regulatory bodies and codes of practice, covering investment advice, 'insider dealing' and so on.

(c) Codes of Practice may be agreed by industry representative bodies, or published by other bodies, like ACAS. They allow monitoring bodies, like the Commission for Racial Equality or the Advertising Standards Authority, to measure the behaviour of organisations against defined standards.

(d) There is a body of regulations and standards covering the reporting of the financial performance of organisations and the verification of reports by auditors. For example, Financial Reporting Standards (FRSs) and other pronouncements by the Accounting Standards Board (ASB) and the Auditing Practices Board (APB).

Activity 11 **(20 minutes)**

What constraints do you think were imposed on employers when the Equal Opportunities legislation was introduced?

Try to think of three main areas which were affected and why.

9.4 PEST factors

A useful acronym, widely used in the UK to describe the external environment of organisations, is PEST: Political-legal, Economic, Socio-cultural and Technological factors.

9.5 The political-legal environment

Political-legal factors which managers must take into account include the following.

(a) Law and regulation, as discussed above.

(b) The power of the government, as the nation's largest supplier, employer, customer and investor. (Consider the effect of a change of government policy on defence for the defence industry, say).

(c) Political events at home and abroad. There may be trading sanctions imposed on states (as was the case with South Africa, Iraq and Serbia) by the international community. A war or change of regime can harm industries (as happened to airlines during the Gulf War) or build them (as in the opening up of commerce in Eastern Europe after the collapse of communism).

(d) Government economic policy – for example, on public spending, borrowing and taxation (**fiscal** policy) and on interest and exchange rates and control of the money supply (**monetary** policy). Businesses are affected by taxation, and by monetary policy: high interest rates, for example, increase the cost of investment and depress consumer spending.

(e) Government industrial policy – for example, encouraging exports (by subsidies or promotion), sponsorship of businesses in depressed regions, protection of domestic industry (duty on imported goods) and so on.

(f) Government social and foreign policy – on education and training of the workforce, trade promotion overseas, obligations towards the EU and so on.

9.6 The economic environment

An organisation is affected by overall economic conditions, as these influence:

(a) the demand for its products; and
(b) the cost of its supplies.

In times of boom and increased demand and consumption, the overall planning problem will be to identify the demand. Conversely, in times of recession, the emphasis will be on cost-effectiveness, continuing profitability, survival and competition.

A company's immediate regional geographical environment is also important. It might be located in a growth area full of modern thriving industry, such as Milton Keynes; or it may be located in an area of urban decay. The economic future of the area will affect wage rates, availability of labour, the disposable income of local consumers, the provision of roads and other services and so on.

9.7 The socio-cultural environment

Social and cultural influences on management decisions include the following.

(a) **Demography**, or demographics: that is, population trends.

Definition

> **Demography** is the analysis of statistics on birth and death rates, sex and age distributions, ethnic groups and geographical movements within a population.

Conditions and changes in the local and/or national population can affect:

(i) the availability of labour of the age and skills required by the organisation in its operating area; and

(ii) the demand for its products and services in particular areas (eg if population is declining or growing) or by particular groups (eg an increasing proportion of the population of a certain ethnic group, or over retirement age).

(b) **Culture:** the beliefs and values, attitudes, customs, language and tastes of a given society or social group.

(i) Organisations need to adapt their products, marketing approach and corporate image to the values of a given group. Language and other cultural barriers may have to be overcome, especially if the organisation is operating internationally. (The custom of giving gifts to business contacts is embedded in some cultures, for example – but would be called bribery in other places!)

EXAMPLE

1 When car-manufacturer Vauxhall launched its Nova in South America, it wondered why the response was poor. Finally, someone realised that 'No va' means 'doesn't go' in Spanish ...

2 In the 1980s, Coca-Cola decided to change its flavour to compete with Pepsi. Market research, taste tests and so forth elicited positive responses to the change, and so the new formulation was introduced. A small group of consumers vociferously opposed the change; and this opposition spread suddenly and rapidly like an epidemic, forcing Coca-Cola to re-introduce the old formula. It seemed that some consumers perceived Coke to symbolise 'American values', so changing the formula appeared to be an assault on them.

(ii) Organisations need to adapt their management styles and practices to the values prevailing in the culture from which they draw their workforce. (Having women in positions of authority is considered inappropriate in some cultures, for example.)

Activity 12 **(15 minutes)**

Give three examples of:

(a) products tailored to a particular cultural market; and
(b) employment and management practice influenced by culture.

9.8 The technological environment

Technology is not just **apparatus** (ie tools and machines), but also **technique** (skills and procedures for the use of tools and machines) and **organisation** (the social and work structure of tasks).

Technological **change** is extremely rapid, and organisations must constantly adapt to it. Technology can affect the management of organisations by:

(a) **presenting opportunities and threats in the market for the organisation's goods and services** – compact discs, satellite dishes and home computers are 'in': records, typewriters and heavy wooden-framed tennis rackets are 'out';

(b) **changing the possibilities for how products are made** – (for example, using computer-aided design and robots) – **and services are provided** (for example, cashpoint machines instead of bank tellers);

(c) **changing the way in which labour is utilised** – technology has facilitated the delayering and downsizing of organisation structures, and created a much more knowledge-based workforce.

In general, managers will be constrained to adopt new technology – especially if the organisation's competitors have done so – in order to cut costs, enhance quality, innovate and so on.

Apart from the PEST factors, which affect all organisations, a business organisation faces competition.

9.9 The competitive environment

Business organisations compete for customers and for labour – and the price of competitive failure may be the collapse of the business. The need to compete may constrain managers to:

(a) maintain or improve the quality of products/services;

(b) control the price charged for products/services;

(c) pay more to secure a reliable supply of high-quality materials from suppliers (particularly in specialised areas);

(d) pay more for selling, advertising, promotion, sponsorship and so on;

(e) pay higher wages, salaries and benefits;

(f) implement attractive human resource practices to attract skilled labour: welfare, training, workplace crèche or whatever.

These constraints will be particularly acute if there is a new or strengthening competitor in the market.

10 INTERNAL ENVIRONMENT

10.1 Internal stakeholders

The internal stakeholders of an organisation are its members or employees.

FOR DISCUSSION

Why do employees have a 'stake' in the organisation? What kind of things do they need or want from it?

The needs, wants and expectations of the employees will act as a constraint on management decision-making because the organisation may be concerned:

(a) to harness the energy and committed co-operation of its employees;

(b) not to lose skilled and experienced employees to competitors;

(c) to maintain a reputation as a responsible or generous employer, to secure a future pool of labour.

NOTES

> **Activity 13** **(20 minutes)**
>
> Give five examples of managerial decisions which might require careful thought because of their potential effects on the morale and attitudes of employees.

10.2 Organisation

The freedom of individual managers to make decisions as they see fit will be constrained by organisational factors such as the following.

(a) **The scope and amount of authority delegated to them:** their 'territory' and power within the organisation. A manager can only manage activities for which (s)he is responsible and has authority.

(b) **Plans, programmes, procedures, rules and so on,** which may already be in place. A manager is rarely able to plan activities and work methods from scratch: systems will have been developed for most routine sequences of activity. Managers often have to stick to plans and expenditure budgets which have been determined (with varying degrees of consultation) by more senior officials.

(c) **The existing organisation structure.** An individual manager is rarely able to organise work and workers from scratch. There may be no experience of multi-disciplinary teamworking to build on, for example, or departmental boundaries and job demarcation lines may be too firmly fixed to change.

(d) **The demand for co-ordination.** As we saw in Chapter 14, some tasks depend on others and have to be scheduled accordingly, and some processes and outputs need standardising in order to maintain co-ordination and consistency. An individual manager cannot make decisions for his or her own unit without reference to the requirements of the organisation system as a whole.

(e) **Organisation culture.** An individual manager is unlikely to be able to choose his or her own style of communication, motivation and management in general, without reference to the culture of the unit or organisation as a whole. A manager who does not 'fit' the organisational 'style' rarely lasts long ...

11 LIMITED RESOURCES

11.1 Money

Money, and the infinite variety of things it represents, is always limited and tightly controlled in organisations. Money allocated to different units represents cost to the organisation, whose financial objectives are likely to be profitability, return on investment and so on: in other words, to **maximise earnings** and **minimise costs.**

Individual unit budgets for expenditure are components of the overall organisational budget – like slices of a cake. A great deal of the politics and conflict within organisations is concerned with competing for bigger slices of the cake!

Limited financial resources therefore constrain managerial decision-making because:

(a) a limited budget can only be stretched so far, and the manager may not be able to obtain or retain all the other resources – quality materials, extra labour, new equipment and so on – that (s)he would want;

(b) a manager may be tempted to spend up to the allocated budget, even though it is not required, so as not to have the allocation reduced next time round.

11.2 Time

You may not have thought about it, but time is a limited resource.

(a) There are only so many working hours available. If these are not sufficient to accomplish everything a manager wishes, (s)he will be constrained to:

   (i) find extra labour or machine capacity, to cover the excess workload in the time available; or

   (ii) eliminate, or simplify, tasks or 'cut corners' in order to get high-priority work done with the existing workforce; or

   (iii) allow work to run late, and adjust the work plan for the knock-on effects.

(b) Deadlines may be imposed by customer requirements or internal co-ordination. Deadlines get closer: they make time both a limited and an increasingly scarce resource. Compromises of cost or quality may have to be made to meet deadlines.

(c) Time for information-gathering and decision-making is also limited. This may constrain managers to make decisions which seem riskier or less informed than they might be, or which have not been subject to as much consultation with team members as the manager's style might otherwise dictate.

11.3 Information

Information is a limited resource for several reasons.

(a) Time and money for gathering it may be limited.

(b) There is a limit to how much a person can take in and use effectively.

(c) Some information is simply not obtainable with any certainty – for example, how people are going to react, or what is going to happen tomorrow!

(d) 'Information is power', and individuals and units in organisations tend to hoard it if they think it will give them extra influence or a competitive edge over others.

Limited information constrains the management of activities because:

(a) decisions have to be taken on the basis of what is known: the full range of possible options can never be known, and a certain degree of uncertainty and inaccuracy remains;

(b) it is not possible to predict the outcome of all decisions and actions, nor the contingencies that might affect them. Changes in the PEST, competitive or physical environment of an organisation cannot always be foreseen and planned for.

NOTES

If **management** information is not made available to a manager – for example, the objectives and results of the organisation, or the attitudes of employees – then the ability of the manager to make effective decisions will clearly be impaired.

Chapter roundup

- Effective time management requires:
  - goals
  - plans
  - priorities
  - schedules
  - concentration
- Tools of time management include:
  - lists and checklists
  - precedence networks
  - action plans
  - timetables
  - charts; and
  - ABCD in-tray management

Quick quiz

1. How can delegation skills improve a manager's use of time?
2. What is a checklist and why might it be useful?
3. When will a task be (a) 'high priority' and (b) 'urgent'?
4. What does a 'precedence network' show?
5. What does 'concentrated' working involve? Suggest a way of achieving it.
6. What is the 'ABCD' method of in-tray management?
7. What is a 'bring forward' system? Give two examples.
8. Give three reasons why co-ordination is necessary.
9. Give three examples of the symptoms of poor co-ordination.
10. Why is (a) communication and (b) planning helpful to co-ordination?
11. What can be 'standardised' in order to co-ordinate activities at an operational level?
12. List the main external stakeholders of an organisation.
13. Give three examples of (a) political and (b) cultural factors.
14. How does (a) organisation structure, (b) co-ordination and (c) organisation culture constrain management discretion?
15. What resources do managers compete for in organisations?

Answers to quick quiz

1. The manager does not waste time doing jobs which would be more effectively completed if delegated. (See para 1.2)

2 A checklist lists all the tasks that need to be done. It helps with both planning and control, because it can be ticked off as tasks are completed. (See para 2.3)

3 (a) When it has to meet a deadline to achieve objective, when other tasks depend on its completion, or when there will be serious problems if it is not completed.

(b) When it is important and the deadline is very close. (See para 2.4)

4 It depicts the order in which tasks should be completed. (See para 2.4)

5 Concentration involves not trying to do more than one thing at a time, avoiding distractions and finishing what you have started. Two ways of achieving this are:

(a) ensuring everything is available for the job;
(b) using the 'half open door' approach. (See para 4.1)

6 A – act on it; B – bin it; C – create a plan; D – delegate it. (See para 4.2)

7 A reminder system. Checklists, diary systems. (See para 4.3)

8 There must be a common direction for the organisation to achieve its goals; co-ordination also helps to maintain smooth operations and to balance high priority work with routine tasks. (See para 7.2)

9 Complaints, production problems, persistent conflict. (See para 7.4)

10 (a) Communication ensures that the inter-relationship of activities and plans is understood, that variations are notified and that conflict is not allowed to develop.

(b) Planning prioritises, understands the dependency of one task on another, allows resources to be rationally allocated and integrates, plans and schedules. (See para 8.1)

11 Work processes, output, design, quality cost, skill and knowledge. (See para 8.2)

12 External stakeholders include owners and shareholders, customers, the community or society as a whole. (See para 9.2)

13 (a) Trading sanctions, war, change of regime.
(b) Beliefs and values, attitudes and customs. (See para 9.5, 9.7)

14 (a) Managers can only manage activities for which they are responsible and have authority.

(b) Decisions are not possible without considering the requirements of the organisation system as a whole.

(c) Decisions must 'fit in' to the organisational 'style'. (See para 10.2)

15 Money, time and information. (See para 11)

Answers to Activities

1 A superior may interfere too much in the manager's job and want constant reports: very disruptive. (Tact in warding off such attention can be a valuable attribute.) On the other hand, if the superior delegates too much, the manager's workload may be excessive.

2 If you answered yes to any of 1-6, and no to question 7, then you need to improve your time management. If you answered more than five of them

this way, then time management must be a priority, particularly whilst you are trying to find time for your HND/HNC studies.

3 (a) Studying the manager's checklist shows that you don't need to worry about the ads: they are finished and sent off. Leaflet A is at the printers, and has been for 3 days: it still needs to be proofed and sent off before the 12th – a week to go. Leaflet B seems to be at the designers – with just over a week to go: it is clearly falling behind and will need watching: in particular, the photography seems to be held up and will have to be dealt with first.

(b) Checklists are particularly helpful in the event that you have to hand a task over to someone else for completion.

(c) You might have suggested shopping lists or things to do in general – or points to be covered in an essay (a very useful planning habit to get into!).

4 The example we have chosen is giving a dinner party.

(a) Brainstorming suggests the following: menu, date, time, people to invite, cooking, table decorations, contacting people, shopping, wines, setting table, shopping list.

(b) We now rearrange these ideas into activity order: people to invite, date, time, contact people, menu, wines, shopping list, shopping, table decorations, setting table, cooking.

(c) This information then converts to the precedence diagram at Figure 4.

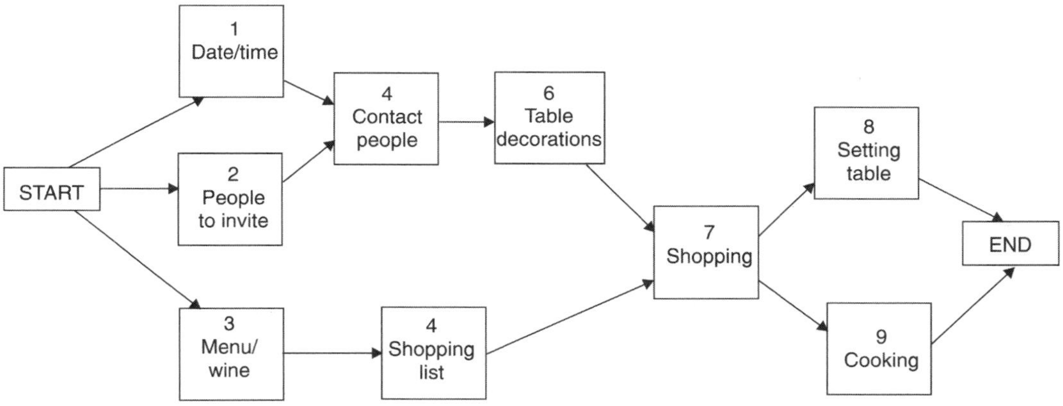

Figure 4 Precedence diagram

5 The action plan for dealing with the tasks identified in activity 3 is as shown in Figure 11.5.

SATURDAY 3	WEDNESDAY 7
SUNDAY 4	THURSDAY 8
MONDAY 5	FRIDAY 9
TUESDAY 6	Week commencing 3 SEPTEMBER S S M T W T F 3 4 5 6 7 8 9

Figure 5 Action plan

6 Sana Sounds is involved in the record industry from start to finish. Although recording and CD manufacture are contracted out to external suppliers, this makes no difference to the fact that these activities are part of Sana Sounds' own value chain. Sana Sounds earns its money by managing the whole set of activities. If the company grows then perhaps it will acquire its own recording studios. The purpose of this exercise has been to drive the point home that a *value chain of activities* is not the same as an *organisation's business functions*.

7 Co-ordination techniques, and problems that might arise if an organisation does not co-ordinate, include the following

(a) Timing: scheduling, network analysis, Gantt charts.

Direction: planning and goal-setting, priority-setting, work breakdown, network analysis.

Resources: network analysis, resource allocation charts, budgets.

(b) Timing: the costing department is 'behind' in its analysis of production employees' time sheets, leaving the payroll department without the information required to prepare and pay the wages.

Direction: the marketing department is trying to sell an 'upmarket' image of the product, while the production department is trying to increase profits by cutting down on 'frills' and packaging.

Resources: the organisation does not have enough trained staff to cope with a peak work period; there are insufficient components in store to complete a given production order on time.

8 Differences between culture and tasks might cause co-ordination problems for the reasons below.

(i) The implementation of a computer system (devised over a period of months or years) by a project group, in an operational department with tight time schedules for ongoing work.

(ii) The manager of one unit may inform his team of decisions, while the manager of the other consults her team, resulting in different approaches. The clash of style may also prevent effective communication between the two managers.

(iii) Incompatible computer systems in two departments, preventing them from sharing information easily.

(iv) Two departments using different forms for the same purpose, making it difficult to share data, and encouraging different approaches (eg different criteria in staff assessment forms), which may become sources of conflict.

(v) One unit dedicated to serving the customer at all costs, another dedicated to saving costs, and never mind the customer!

9 Horizontal communication might be beneficial if a manager encouraged in the following ways.

(a) Not discouraging informal communication at work – even encouraging it, by providing an environment where people can talk during breaks and so on.

(b) Teambuilding and empowerment, so that people do not see themselves as individuals in competition with other individuals, but as teams who must communicate freely in order to do their jobs.

(c) Appointing team members to interdisciplinary or joint team meetings, so that they can exchange information with people at the same level but in different areas of the organisation.

10 Aspects of business activity on which consumer organisations have focused include:

(a) dangerous products and by-products (such as cigarettes and car exhaust emission);

(b) dishonest marketing or promotion; in the UK there is legislation designed to deal with this kind of abuse;

(c) the abuse of political and economic power by organisations (for example, ignoring international sanctions or trading with regimes with poor human rights records);

(d) the availability of information. Consumers are anxious, for example, to be informed of any artificial additives in foodstuffs.

11 Constraints on employers as a result of the Equal Opportunities legislation would involve recruitment and promotion.

In recruitment organisations can no longer specify that they only want, say male applicants (unless exempted for some reason).

In promotion and training the same opportunities have to be offered in both these areas to all employees, regardless of sex, status, race or creed.

12 (a) Cultural products include: kosher food (to the Jewish community); magazines specifically for men, women or gays; low premium car insurance for mature drivers; cosmetics tested without cruelty to animals, for the 'green' market – eg Body Shop.

(b) Employment practices affected by culture include: work hours to allow for religious holidays and observances; separate facilities and offices to differentiate managers and workers (not a cultural norm in Japan, for example); the extension of benefits previously given to 'spouses' of employees to 'partners' (including gay partners) – for example, by British Airways.

13 Managerial decisions requiring special care about morale and employee attitudes include, for example: office relocation; redundancies; change in work practices (eg introducing shiftworking); cut in benefits; cancellation of holidays in busy periods.

Chapter 4 : QUALITY

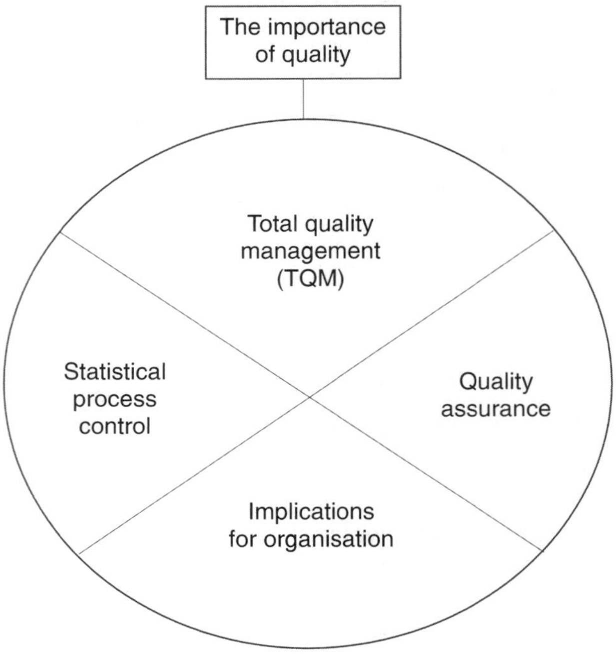

Introduction

In recent years quality has become the key in determining many organisations' positions in respect of their competitive advantage. Unfortunately, quality is difficult to define because it has a wide range of meanings, covering a wide range of businesses and processes.

Quality control is concerned with maintaining quality standards. The process goes through a cycle of establishing standards and procedures, monitoring actual quality and taking control action when actual quality falls below standard. Quality assurance, however, is the term used where a supplier guarantees the quality of goods supplied and allows the customer access while the goods are being manufactured. Total quality management is the term given to programmes that seek to ensure that goods are produced and services are supplied of the highest quality.

Your objectives

In this chapter you will learn about the following:

(a) The importance of quality in a business environment

(b) Total quality management

(c) Quality assurance procedures

(d) Costs of quality

(e) The potential benefits of quality processes

1 THE IMPORTANCE OF QUALITY IN A BUSINESS ENVIRONMENT

The modern business environment is remarkably different from the business environment of a decade or so ago. One change has been the **switch in emphasis away from quantity towards quality**. Consumers and **customers** have become **more sophisticated and discerning** in their requirements. They are no longer satisfied with accepting the late delivery of the same old unreliable products from an organisation which does not appear to care for its customers. They want new products, superior on-time delivery performance and an immediate response to their requests. Many organisations are therefore turning to quality to help them to survive the competitive modern business environment. **By developing new products quickly and supplying them on time at a consistently high level of quality such organisations are likely to become the success stories of the early 21st century.**

Activity 1 **(5 minutes)**

In your opinion, what organisations are likely to become the success stories of the early 2000s? Why?

2 TOTAL QUALITY MANAGEMENT

2.1 Meaning of quality

Quality means 'the **degree of excellence of a thing**' - how well made it is, or how well performed if it is a service, how well it serves its purpose, and how it measures up against its rivals. These criteria imply two things.

(a) That quality is something that **requires care on the part of the provider.**

(b) That quality is largely **subjective** - it is in the eye of the beholder, the **customer**.

2.2 The management of quality

This is the process of:

(a) establishing **standards of quality** for a product or service;

(b) establishing **procedures or production methods** which ought to ensure that these required standards of quality are met in a suitably high proportion of cases;

(c) **monitoring** actual quality;

(d) taking **control action** when actual quality falls below standard.

EXAMPLE

Take the postal service as an example. The postal service might establish a standard that 90% of first class letters will be delivered on the day after they are posted, and 99% will be delivered within two days of posting.

- Procedures would have to be established for ensuring that these standards could be met (attending to such matters as frequency of collections, automated letter sorting, frequency of deliveries and number of staff employed).
- Actual performance could be monitored, perhaps by taking samples from time to time of letters that are posted and delivered.
- If the quality standard is not being achieved, management should take control action (employ more postmen or advertise the use of postcodes again).

Quality management becomes **total (Total Quality Management (TQM)) when it is applied to everything a business does.**

2.3 Get it right, first time

One of the basic principles of TQM is that the **cost of preventing mistakes is less than the cost of correcting them** once they occur. The aim should therefore be **to get things right first time**. Every mistake, delay and misunderstanding, directly costs an organisation money through **wasted time and effort**, including time taken in pacifying customers. The **lost potential for future sales because of poor customer service must also be taken into account.**

2.4 Continuous improvement

A second basic principle of TQM is dissatisfaction with the *status quo*: the belief that it is **always possible to improve** and so the aim should be to '**get it more right next time**'.

2.5 The requirements of quality

Mark Lee Inman usefully lists 'eight requirements of quality' in his article in the May 1995 *ACCA Students' Newsletter.*

- Accept that the only thing that matters is the **customer**.
- Recognise the importance of the **customer-supplier relationship**, where customers include internal customers: passing on sub-standard material is not satisfactory.
- Move away from relying on inspecting to a predetermined level of quality and move towards **preventing the cause of the defect in the first place**.
- Each employee or group of **employees must be personally responsible** for defect-free production or service in their domain.
- There must be a move away from 'acceptable' quality levels. **Any level is unacceptable.**
- **All departments** should try obsessively to get things right first time: this applies to misdirected telephone calls and typing errors as much as to production.
- **Quality certification** programmes should be introduced.
- The **cost of poor quality** should be emphasised: good quality generates savings.

NOTES

Activity 2 **(10 minutes)**

Which of the above 'requirements' has your organisation met? Does your organisation offer a quality product or service? If not, why not?

3 QUALITY ASSURANCE PROCEDURES

Because TQM embraces every activity of a business, quality assurance procedures **cannot be confined to the production process** but must also cover the work of sales, distribution and administration departments, the efforts of external suppliers, and the reaction of external customers.

3.1 Quality assurance of goods inwards

The quality of output depends on the quality of input materials, and so quality control should include **procedures for acceptance and inspection of goods inwards and measurement of rejects**. Each supplier can be given a 'rating' for the quality of the goods they tend to supply, and preference with purchase orders can be given to well-rated suppliers. This method is referred to as 'vendor rating'.

Where a **quality assurance scheme** is in place the supplier guarantees the quality of goods supplied and allows the customers' inspectors access while the items are being manufactured. The **onus is on the supplier to carry out the necessary quality checks**, or face cancellation of the contract.

Suppliers' quality assurance schemes are being used increasingly, particularly where extensive sub-contracting work is carried out, for example in the motor industries. One such scheme is **BS EN ISO 9000** certification. A company that gains registration has a certificate testifying that it is operating to a structure of written policies and procedures which are designed to ensure that it can consistently deliver a product or service to meet customer requirements. This is discussed in greater detail below.

Activity 3 **(10 minutes)**

Does your organisation have BS EN IS0 9000 certification? Do its competitors? Would it be worthwhile for your organisation to gain certification? If not, why not?

3.2 Inspection of output

This will take place at various key stages in the production process and will provide a continual check that the production process is under control. The aim of inspection is *not* really to sort out the bad products from the good ones after the work has been done. The **aim is to satisfy management that quality control in production is being maintained.**

The **inspection of samples** rather than 100% testing of all items will keep inspection costs down, and smaller samples will be less costly to inspect than larger samples. The greater the confidence in the reliability of production methods and process control, the smaller the samples will be.

3.3 Monitoring customer reaction

Some sub-standard items will inevitably be produced. Checks during production will identify some bad output, but other items will reach the customer who is the ultimate judge of quality. **Complaints ought to be monitored** in the form of letters of complaint, returned goods, penalty discounts, claims under guarantee, or requests for visits by service engineers. Some companies actually survey customers on a regular basis.

3.4 Employees and quality

Empowerment

Workers themselves are frequently the best source of information about how (or how not) to improve quality. **Empowerment** therefore has two key aspects.

(a) Allowing workers to have the **freedom to decide how to do** the necessary work, using the skills they possess and acquiring new skills as necessary to be an effective team member.

(b) Making workers **responsible** for achieving production targets and for quality control.

Quality circles

A quality circle is a group of employees who meet regularly to discuss **problems of quality** and **quality control** in their area of work, and perhaps to suggest ways of improving quality.

3.5 Design for quality

A TQM environment aims to get it right first time, and this means that **quality, not faults, must be designed into the organisation's products and operations from the outset.**

Quality control happens at various stages in the process of designing a product or service.

(a) At the **product design stage**, quality control means trying to design a product or service so that its specifications provide a suitable balance between price and quality (of sales and delivery, as well as manufacture) which will make the product or service competitive.

(b) **Production engineering** is the **process of designing the methods for making a product** (or service) **to the design specification.** It sets out to make production methods as efficient as possible, and to avoid the manufacture of sub-standard items.

(c) **Information systems** should be designed to get the required information to the right person at the right time; **distribution systems** should be designed to get the right item to the right person at the right time; and so on.

3.6 Quality control and inspection

A distinction should be made between **quality control** and **inspection.**

(a) **Quality control** involves setting controls for the process of manufacture or service delivery. It is a aimed at **preventing the manufacture of defective items** or the provision of defective services.

(b) **Inspection** is a technique of **identifying when defective items are being produced at an unacceptable level.** Inspection is usually carried out at three main points.

(i) Receiving inspection - for raw materials and purchased components
(ii) Floor or process inspection for WIP
(iii) Final inspection or testing for finished goods

4 QUALITY ASSURANCE: BS EN ISO 9000

4.1 The essentials of quality assurance

The essentials of quality assurance are that the supplier guarantees the quality of goods supplied and allows the customers' inspectors access while the items are being manufactured. Usually, inspection procedures and quality control standards are agreed by the customer and supplier, and checks are made to ensure that they are being adhered to.

- The customer can almost eliminate goods inwards inspection and items can be directed straight to production. This can give large savings in cost and time in flow production, and can facilitate JIT production.
- The supplier produces to the customer's requirement, thereby reducing rejects and the cost of producing substitutes.

Suppliers' quality assurance schemes are being used increasingly, particularly where extensive sub-contracting work is carried out, eg the motor industries. One such scheme is BS EN ISO 9000 (formerly BS 5750) certification. This is a nationally promoted standard, only awarded after **audit and inspection of a company's operations**. In order to gain registration, a company must **obtain independent verification that its quality system meets standards**. The British Standards Institution is the largest of the certification bodies.

EN ISO 9000 is based on BS 5750, first introduced in 1979. A company that gains registration has a certificate testifying that it is operating to a structure of written policies and procedures which are designed to ensure that it can consistently deliver a product or service to meet customer requirements.

4.2 The standard

The standard falls into three parts.

- Part 1 (ISO 9001) covers design, manufacture and installation.
- Part 2 (ISO 9002) covers just manufacture and installation.
- Part 3 (ISO 9003) covers inspection and testing.

The standard does not address the quality of individual goods and services, but aims to ensure that quality management systems of a suitable standard are in place. The British Standards Institution states that the standard 'sets out how you can establish, document and maintain an effective quality system which will demonstrate to your customers that you are committed to quality and are able to satisfy their quality needs'.

There have been some problems with BS EN ISO 9000.

- The standard is complex and particularly onerous for small firms.
- Some feel that it is written in jargon and is incomprehensible to most people apart from management consultants.
- It is inflexible and bureaucratic.

NOTES

5 STATISTICAL PROCESS CONTROL

Statistical process control (SPC) is an aspect of TQM. Statistical quality control charts might be used to record and monitor the accuracy of the physical dimensions of products. A typical control chart is shown below. The horizontal axis on the graph is time, the vertical axis is the physical dimension of the product in appropriate units. Above and below the level of the expected dimension of the product are the control limits. The graph shows inner warning limits and outer action limits although in many cases only one limit is used. The limits are set such a distance from the expected dimension that a value outside the limits is very unlikely to have occurred by chance and consequently the size of the deviation from the expected dimension indicates that something may have gone wrong with the manufacturing process. Normally, the values plotted on the chart would be the mean of a small sample taken at regular points in time.

Quality control chart

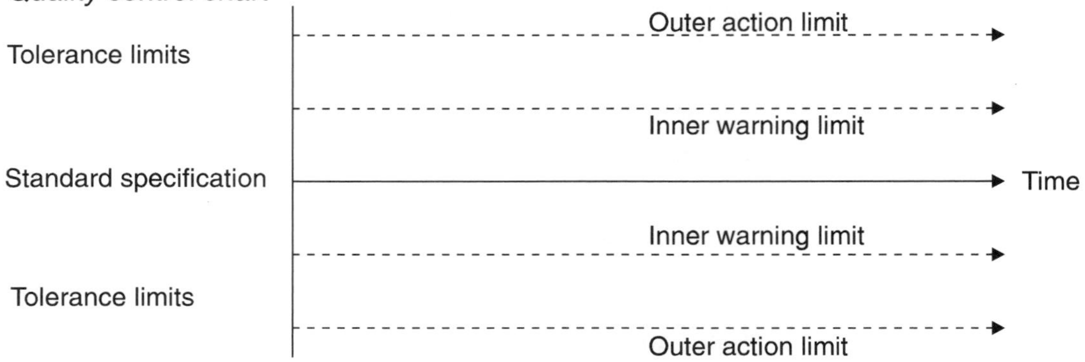

Representational samples of an output manufacturing process may be taken daily or even every hour, and faults in the manufacturing process which are revealed may be fairly simple to correct by adjusting the appropriate machinery. If output exceeds the control limits consistently, more urgent management action would be called for, because this would indicate a systematic fault such as those below.

- Inefficiency in production, by labour or the machines
- Inadequacy in production methods
- Inadequate quality of raw materials and components
- Excessively tight tolerances in the first place

The ultimate goal of SPC is, in accordance with Taguchi's ideas, the reduction of variation.

6 QUALITY FUNCTION DEPLOYMENT (QFD): DESIGN QUALITY

SPC enables the review of the actual production process. However, many of the thinkers quoted earlier refer to the much wider role of quality in the organisation. Quality function deployment (QFD) is a quality technique used to cut across functional boundaries. QFD is aimed at getting design quality right, early in the process.

- QFD starts by 'translating the voice of the customer'. The means applying the marketing concept in assessing in detail the customer's needs and including them in a design specification, so that they are accurately translated into **relevant technical requirements.**

- **Obeying the customer's voice** is the objective. This means translating customer demands (eg that paper will not tear) into quality requirements (it must be of a minimum thickness). There is a matrix of relationships between customer demand and technical requirements.

- Customer demand C has a strong relationship to quality characteristic W but a weak one to X.

Quality characteristics

Customers' demands	V	W	X	Y	Z
A					
B	○				
C		⊙	△		
D					
E					

⊙ = strong relationship

○ = medium relationship

△ = weak relationship

  - This matrix can determine where most effort should be expended
  - Furthermore, certain customer requirements might contradict each other, so the matrix identifies possible trade offs.

- There might be a large number of further refinements before these are translated into accurate product and process plans.

You might note a certain similarity to Taguchi's ideas, in that it concentrates on design issues up front. Also, QFD takes manufacturing issues into account.

Neither SPC nor QFD *in themselves* are TQM, which many authors believe is a **culture as much as a set of techniques**. This is why **continuous improvement is at the heart of TQM**.

7 CONTINUOUS IMPROVEMENT

Quality management is not a one-off process, but is the continual examination and improvement of existing processes. The idea of continuous improvement might appear to go against the law of diminishing returns, in that it might be arguable that there is a limit beyond which there is no point in pursuing any further improvements.

Advocates of continuous improvement, however, believe that this 'law' does not always apply. Remember, that continuous improvement does not only apply to the finished product, but also to the processes which give rise to it.

- It is not easy to determine where diminishing returns set in.
- A philosophy of continuous improvement ensures that management are not *complacent*, which can be a cultural disaster.
- Customer needs change, so a philosophy of continuous improvement enables these changes to be taken into account in the normal course of events.
- New technologies or materials might be developed, enabling cost savings or design improvements.
- Rarely do businesses know every possible fact about the production process. Continuous improvement encourages experimentation and a scientific approach to production.
- It is a way of tapping employees' knowledge.

- Reducing *variability* is a key issue for quality, if this is assessed on Taguchi's quality-cost model. It often requires improving the process itself, rather than changing the machines or adjusting them.
- Improvement on a continual, step by step basis is more prudent in some cases than changing things all at once.

Holmes proposes an eight stage model for improving quality.

Step 1. **Find out the problems** (eg from customers and employees).

Step 2. **Select action targets** from the number of improvement projects identified in *Step 1*, on the basis of cost, safety, importance, feasibility (with current resources).

Step 3. **Collect data** about the problem.

Step 4. **Analyse data** by a variety of techniques to assess common factors behind the data, to tease out any hidden messages the data might contain.

Step 5. **Identify possible causes** (eg using brainstorming sessions). No ideas are ruled out of order.

Step 6. **Plan improvement action**. Significant help might be required.

Step 7. **Monitor the effects of the improvement**.

Step 8. **Communicate the result**.

Activity 4 **(15 minutes)**

You have just overheard the following conversation. The Board of a company are in a meeting and they are having a 'full and frank exchange of views' (ie a blazing row).

Chairman : Ladies and gentlemen, *please....*

Marketing director: No, he's said quite enough. Customers are *our* department, and all this TQM nonsense is just another, yes *another* example of those jargon-spouting boffins and bodgers in production trying to encroach on my turf! I *do* need resources. I don't need white-coated robots criticising the angles at which I fix the paper clips on to my reports!

Chairman: Ladies and gentlemen, *please.....*

Production director: No, she's said quite enough. Marketing people couldn't give *one* hoot, let alone two, about quality and we all know it's quality that sells the goods. Remember, when we had to abandon our solar powered torch? State of the art, state of *the art* that was, and did they try and sell it? Did they?

Chairman: Ladies and gentlemen, *please.....*'

Finance director: '*No*, they've both said quite enough. If all we get out of TQM is pointless rows like this, I might as well go back and count some more beans. At least it's *meaningful* and relaxing.

Chairman: Ladies and gentlemen! No, you've all said *quite* enough. Not one of you has grasped the point. I'd better get another management consultant in with a better flipchart.

What insights do each of the above characters have into TQM?

8 ORGANISATIONAL IMPLICATIONS

Introducing TQM involves a significant shake up.

- TQM is associated with giving employees a say in the process (eg in the *quality survey*) and in getting them to suggest improvements.
- TQM implies a greater discipline to the process of production and the establishment of better linkages between the business functions.
- TQM involves new relationships with suppliers, which requires them to improve their output quality so that less effort is spent rectifying poor input. Long-term relationships with a small number of suppliers might be preferable to choosing material and sub-components on price.
- It requires both work standardisation and employee commitment.

8.1 Participation

Participation is important in TQM, especially in the process of continuous improvement, where workforce views are valued. The management task is to encourage everybody to contribute. **Barriers to participation** are numerous.

- An autocratic chief executive, who believes he or she is the sole key to the process.
- Individualism, in which people 'possess' ideas in order to take credit for them rather than share them for mutual benefit.
- Ideas of managers as leaders and directors rather than facilitators and supporters.
- Middle managers who feel their authority is threatened.

8.2 Difficulties

Managers find some aspects particularly hard to accept.

- Social and status barriers are removed with the removal of office partitions.
- Administrative functions must now be seen as **supporting the shop floor**.
- The **shop floor** is the most important area.
- Managers are judged by their contribution to team spirit, not 'the virility of their decisions'.
- Meetings are used to gather information, not to take decisions.
- New personal skills are needed (eg the ability to listen and communicate).
- A manager's role is in supporting and training, not disciplining and restricting.

Holmes believes that managers most suited for a TQM culture will 'understand how people motivate themselves and direct this motivation towards good team results. They are concerned with achieving the goals of the team, supporting the individual members of the team, and keeping the team together'. They will 'ensure time is spent setting objectives, planning, briefing. controlling, evaluating. These activities will be conducted in a participatory or controllable way'.

8.3 Service quality

As well as physical products, quality also applies to **service businesses** such as banks and restaurants. Quality issues arise in a number of areas.

- Customer expectations
- The process by which the service is delivered
- The attitudes and demeanour of the people giving the service
- The environment of the service encounter

9 COSTS OF QUALITY

When we talk about quality-related costs you should remember that a concern for **good quality saves money**; it is **poor quality that costs money.**

Definitions

Prevention costs are the costs of any action taken to investigate, prevent or reduce defects and failures.

Appraisal costs are the costs of assessing the quality achieved.

Internal failure costs are the costs arising within the organisation of failing to achieve the required level of quality.

External failure costs are the costs arising outside the organisation of failing to achieve the required level of quality (after transfer of ownership to the customer).

EXAMPLES

Quality-related cost	Example
Prevention costs	Quality engineering Design/development of quality control/inspection equipment Maintenance of quality control/inspection equipment Administration of quality control Training in quality control
Appraisal costs	Acceptance testing Inspection of goods inwards Inspection costs of in-house processing Performance testing
Internal failure costs	Failure analysis Re-inspection costs Losses from failure of purchased items Losses due to lower selling prices for sub-quality goods Costs of reviewing product specifications after failures
External failure costs	Administration of customer complaints section Costs of customer service section Product liability costs Cost of repairing products returned from customers Cost of replacing items due to sub-standard products/marketing errors

NOTES

EXAMPLE: COST OF POOR QUALITY

A manufacturer's inspection procedures indicate that one faulty item out of every 1,000 good items produced is sent to a customer. The management regards this as acceptable, as a replacement will be supplied free of charge. Unit sales are 10,000,000 per year, and each unit costs £20 to manufacture and makes a profit of £5. It is probable that every customer who buys a faulty product will return it, and will thenceforth buy a similar product from another company. The average customer buys two units a year. Marketing costs per new customer are £10 per year.

(a) What is your best estimate of the net cost of this policy for a year?
(b) What name(s) would you give to quality-related costs of this type?
(c) Could the situation be improved by incurring other types of quality-related cost?

ANSWER

(a) Presumed number of bad units delivered a year = 10,000,000/1,000= 10,000

	£
Cost of defects 10,000 × £20	200,000
Cost of free replacement 10,000 × £20	200,000
Manufacturing cost	400,000
Marketing costs for replacement customers £10 × 10,000	100,000
Gross cost of poor quality	500,000
Less income from original sale	250,000
Net cost of poor quality	250,000

Although the cost of the original defective item is recovered, the company **does not get it right first time**. The company has still suffered the cost of the replacement and the cost of replacing the customer by marketing to new customers.

(b) The cost of replacements is an external failure cost; the cost of defects and the new marketing costs are internal failure costs.

(c) It appears that the manufacturer already incurs *appraisal* costs, since there are inspection procedures for goods about to be despatched. The reason(s) for the fault should be established (a further *internal failure* cost) and the extent of the problem should be more precisely ascertained (further *appraisal* costs), since it is not certain that all dissatisfied customers return their goods, though it is highly likely that their business is lost. Once this has been done it will be possible to decide whether, by spending more on *prevention*, the overall cost of poor quality can be reduced.

9.1 Traditional accounting systems and the cost of quality

Traditionally, the **costs** of **scrapped units, wasted materials and reworking** have been **subsumed within the costs of production** by assigning the costs of an expected level of loss (a normal loss) to the costs of good production, while **accounting for other costs of poor quality within production or marketing overheads.** So such costs are not only **considered as inevitable** but are not highlighted for management attention.

Traditional accounting reports **tend also to ignore the hidden but real costs of excessive stock levels** (held to enable faulty material to be replaced without hindering production) **and the facilities necessary for storing that stock**. The introduction of a system of **just-in-time** purchasing and manufacturing should eradicate such costs, however. A just-in-time production system is driven by demand from customers for finished products so that components on a production line are only produced when needed for the next stage of production, thereby eradicating stocks of work in progress and finished goods. In a just-in-time purchasing system, materials are not delivered until they are needed in production, thereby eradicating stock of raw materials.

To **implement a TQM programme, costs of quality** must be **highlighted separately** within accounting reports so that *all* employees are aware of the cost of poor quality.

9.2 Explicit and implicit costs of quality

Explicit costs of quality are those that are recorded in accounting records, to be separately highlighted with the implementation of a TQM programme.

Implicit costs of quality are not recorded in accounting records. They tend to be of two forms.

- **Opportunity costs** such as the loss of future sales to a customer dissatisfied with faulty goods
- **Costs which tend to be subsumed** within other account headings such as costs which result from the disruptions caused by stockouts due to faulty purchases

10 THE POTENTIAL BENEFITS OF QUALITY PROCESSES

Glyn Thomas in *Accounting Technician* provides a useful summary of the benefits of TQM.

'It makes quality the central concern of the business. Too often, quality is either confused with addressing customer complaints with inevitably leads to it being viewed negatively, or is viewed as a direct measure of the product or service itself. Instead, all activities that are involved should be considered. Quality should be inherent in every facet of the business and not just a "bolt-on extra".

A key factor of [TQM] is that it can apply to all or parts of your business, so there may be scope for partially introducing it and then expanding at a later date. Applied to the whole business however, it will allow a holistic approach to quality throughout the whole company and have an effect from shop floor through to ordering, sales and management.

It **reduces wastage and mistakes**, and therefore **leads to contracts being completed on time without unnecessary remedial work**. In addition, due to built-in fault-logging procedures, it is **unlikely that problems will be duplicated in the future**.'

Activity 5 **(10 minutes)**

(a) What are the potential benefits of training for quality?

(b) What are the potential benefits of quality control?

Activity 6 **(10 minutes)**

Read the following extract from an article in the *Financial Times* in April 1993, and then explain how the bank could monitor the impact of the initiative.

'If you telephone a branch of Lloyds Bank and it rings five times before there is a reply; if the person who answers does not introduce him or herself by name during the conversation; if you are standing in a queue with more people in it than the number of tills, then something is wrong.'

'If any of these things happen then the branch is breaching standards of customer service set by the bank since last July ... the "service challenge" was launched in the bank's 1,888 branches last summer after being tested in 55 branches in 1990 ...'

'Lloyds already has evidence of the impact. Customers were more satisfied with pilot branches in 1991 than with others.'

Chapter roundup

- **Total quality management (TQM)** is the process of applying a zero defect philosophy to the management of all resources and relationships within an organisation as a means of developing and sustaining a culture of continuous improvement which focuses on meeting customer expectations.
- **Quality assurance procedures** should not be confined to the production process but must also cover the work of sales, distribution and administration departments, the efforts of external suppliers and the reaction of external customers.
- **Quality control** happens at various stages in the process of designing a product or service.
- **Quality control** is aimed at preventing the manufacture of defective items or the provision of defective services. **Inspection** is a technique for identifying when defective items are being produced at an unacceptable level.
- The costs associated with a concern for quality are **prevention costs, appraisal costs, internal failure costs** and **external failure costs.**
- **Explicit costs** of quality are those that are recorded in accounting records, to be separately highlighted. **Implicit costs** of quality are not recorded in accounting records.

Quick quiz

1. What are the four aspects of the process of managing quality?
2. What are the two basic principles of TQM?
3. The aim of TQM is for a process to go out of control less than 10% of the time. True of false?
4. What are the three main points at which inspection is usually carried out?
5. What are internal failure costs?
6. Provide two examples of external failure costs.

Answers to quick quiz

1
- Establishing standards of quality for a product or service
- Establishing procedures or production methods which ought to ensure that these required standards of quality are met in a suitably high proportion of cases
- Monitoring actual quality
- Taking control action when actual quality falls below standard (See para 2.2)

2 'Get it right first time' and 'Get it more right next time' (See paras 2.3, 2.4)

3 False. The aim of TQM is for a process never to go out of control. (See para 2.5)

4
- Receiving inspection for raw materials and purchased components
- Floor or process inspection for WIP
- Final inspection or testing for finished goods (See para 3)

5 The costs arising within the organisation of failure to achieve the quality specified. (See para 9)

6 Administration of customer complaints section

Costs of customer service section

Product liability costs

Cost of repairing products returned from customers

Cost of providing replacement items due to sub-standard product or marketing errors. (See para 9)

Answers to activities

1 One of the companies that responds to consumer demands with new, high-quality products is Iceland. The management at Iceland listened to their customers' fears over GM (genetically modified) products and decided to remove all GM ingredients from their products. They have also introduced a policy of only buying organic products and selling them at no extra cost to the customer.

NTL is another company that is destined to be a success story in the early 2000s. They are a fast expanding cable TV company that provides a free internet service for its customers. A new service that is likely to be introduced, when the band-width allows, is video on demand.

2 For a company like BPP, the employees already accept that the customer matters. The company strives to produce a wide range of products and services to suit all customers' needs. Students are invited to comment on products and make suggestions that would lead to improvements. BPP works closely with the examining bodies to produce material that matches the syllabus requirements and they try to make the material user-friendly. Each department/examination area has a manager who is personally responsible for producing a defect-free product within their domain. Typing errors are always a problem in publishing, but the introduction of modern word-processing packages has reduced the incidence of this.

3 This quality standard is aimed at manufacturing companies. It is useful to some companies because it demonstrates they are in control of their

business, and have proved it to a certification body. ISO 9000 registration is a good way of measuring progress and monitoring maintenance of the standard. It reduces the need for customer supplier demonstration of quality assurance procedures by its introduction and ensures that the organisation's product is compatible with EC and USA quality procedures.

There are many different reasons for implementing the standard.

(i) Pressure from large customers
(ii) To maintain contracts with existing customers
(iii) To use the constraints of the standard to prevent scrap
(iv) To reduce auditing of the quality system by customers
(v) To make reference to the standard on company letterhead paper
(vi) To get the kitemark symbol on the company's product
(vii) To enforce discipline on employees

4 The chairman has got the gist. All of them miss the point as to the nature of TQM. The marketing director has a point in that TQM *does* imply a blurring of functional boundaries, but the marketing director *ought* to be pleased that, if TQM is implemented, the marketing concept will be brought into product design. The production director still has not grasped the concept. His idea of quality is 'technical excellence' not fitness for use. The finance director ought to care, as TQM has meaningful cost implications. The row is not pointless: at least the issue is being discussed, which is a beginning.

5 (a) The potential benefits of training for quality include improved quality of output, improved productivity and greater job satisfaction and commitment on the part of employees.

(b) The benefits of quality control come from savings in quality-related costs, from improvements in customer relations and hopefully (because of the quality of the final product) increased sales revenue due to increased sales demand.

6 A wide variety of answers is possible. The article goes on to explain how the bank has monitored the initiative.

(a) It has devised a 100 point scale showing average satisfaction with branch service.

(b) It conducts a 'first impressions' survey of all new customers.

(c) There is also a general survey carried out every six months which seeks the views of a weighted sample of 350 customers per branch.

(d) A survey company telephones each branch anonymously twice a month to test how staff respond to enquiries about products.

(e) A quarter of each branch's staff answer a monthly questionnaire about the bank's products to test their knowledge.

(f) Groups of employees working in teams in branches are allowed to set their own additional standards. This is to encourage participation.

(g) Branches that underperform are more closely watched by 24 managers who monitor the initiative.

Chapter 5:
HEALTH AND SAFETY

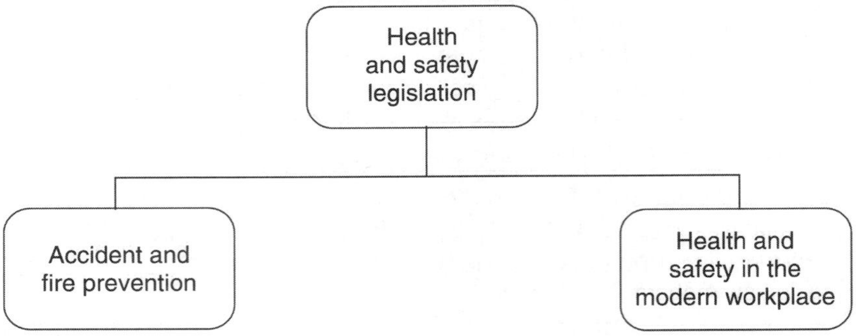

Introduction

Health and safety at work are important for several reasons.

(a) Employees should be protected from pain and suffering. (Obvious – we hope!)

(b) An employer has legal obligations for the health and safety of employees.

(c) Accidents and illness cost the employer money.

(d) The company's image in the market-place (to which it sells goods and services, and from which it recruits labour and buys in other resources) will suffer if its health and safety record is bad.

This chapter looks at the law and best practice relating to health and safety at work.

Your objectives

In this chapter you will learn the following.

(a) Some of the main provisions of health and safety legislation

(b) Accident and fire prevention measures

(c) Some of the existing and emerging threats to health and safety in the modern workplace

1 HEALTH AND SAFETY LEGISLATION

In 1972, a Royal Commission on Safety and Health at Work reported that unnecessarily large numbers of days were being lost each year through industrial accidents, injuries and diseases, because of the 'attitudes, capabilities and performance of people and the efficiency of the organisational systems within which they work'. Since then, major legislation has been brought into effect in the UK, most notably:

(a) Health and Safety at Work Act 1974 ;

(b) the regulations introduced in January 1993 implementing EU directives on Health and Safety.

Some of the most important regulations are as follows.

- Reporting of Injuries, Diseases and Dangerous Occurrences Regulations 1995
- The Health and Safety (First Aid) Regulations 1981
- The Noise at Work Regulations 1989
- The Control of Substances Hazardous to Health Regulations 1994
- The Manual Handling Operations Regulations 1992
- The Workplace (Health, Safety and Welfare) Regulations 1992
- The Provision and Use of Work Equipment Regulations 1992
- The Health and Safety (Display Screen Equipment) Regulations 1992
- The Management of Health and Safety at Work Regulations 1992
- The Personal Protective Equipment at Work Regulations 1992

We will not be able to cover their provisions in detail here. Just be aware that the framework for personnel policy in the area of health and safety is extensive and detailed!

We will begin by looking at the major legal landmarks in the area of health and safety at work. This legislation is refreshingly practical, with lots of measures to be taken and procedures to be put in place. Like other legal provisions we have discussed, the 'law is a floor': remember that these are minimum standards, not a description of best practice.

1.1 The Health and Safety at Work Act 1974

In the UK, the Health and Safety at Work Act 1974 provides for the introduction of a system of approved codes of practice, prepared in consultation with industry. Thus an employee, whatever his/her employment, should find that his/her work is covered by an appropriate code of practice.

Employers also have **specific** duties under the 1974 Act.

(a) All systems (work practices) must be safe.

(b) The work environment must be safe and healthy (well-lit, warm, ventilated and hygienic).

(c) All plant and equipment must be kept up to the necessary standard (with guards on machines and so on).

In addition, information, instruction, training and supervision should be directed towards safe working practices. Employers must consult with **safety representatives** appointed by a recognised trade union, and appoint a **safety committee** to monitor safety policy, if asked to do so. Safety policy and measures should be clearly **communicated in writing** to all staff.

The **employee** also has a duty:

(a) to take reasonable care of himself/herself and others;

(b) to allow the employer to carry out his or her duties (including enforcing safety rules); and

(c) not to interfere intentionally or recklessly with any machinery or equipment.

FOR DISCUSSION

'A baby was put on a social services "at risk" register"', reported The Times in February 1992, 'after his father, a roofer, took him to work up ladders in a sling fixed to his back.' The story continues:

After a two-hour hearing it was decided to place the boy in his godparents' care while his father goes to work. Putting [the child] on a register will allow social workers to ensure the child remains grounded. [The roofer] said that his wife... a bank clerk... was happy with the outcome.

'But I intend to fight this decision in the European Court', he said 'I should be allowed to raise my son as I want to.'

Who do you think is responsible for a person's safety? Should people be allowed to take risks if they 'want to'? Or should measures be taken to protect them 'for their own good'?

1.2 The Management of Health and Safety at Work Regulations 1992

Under the Management of Health and Safety at Work Regulations 1992 employers now have the following additional general duties.

(a) They must carry out risk assessment, generally in writing, of all work hazards. Assessment should be continuous.

(b) They must introduce controls to reduce risks.

(c) They must assess the risks to anyone else affected by their work activities.

(d) They must share hazard and risk information with other employers, including those on adjoining premises, other site occupiers and all subcontractors coming onto the premises.

(e) They should revise safety policies in the light of the above, or initiate safety policies if none were in place previously.

(f) They must identify employees who are especially at risk.

(g) They must provide fresh and appropriate training in safety matters.

(h) They must provide information to employees (including temps) about health and safety.

(i) They must employ competent safety and health advisers.

Employees are also given an additional duty under the 1992 regulations to inform their employer of any situation which may be a danger. This does not reduce the employer's responsibilities in any way, however, because his/her risk assessment programme should have spotted the hazard in any case.

Under the **Health and Safety (Consultation with Employees) Regulations 1996**, employers must consult all of their employees on health and safety matters (such as the planning of health and safety training, any change in equipment or procedures which may substantially affect their health and safety at work or the health and safety consequences of introducing new technology). This involves giving information to employees *and* listening to and taking account of what they say before any health and safety decisions are taken.

1.3 Factories Act 1961

Definition

> A **factory** is defined as a place where manufacturing or processing work is done for the purposes of gain, and where the main purpose of the premises involves manual labour.

The 1961 Act applies only to a factory. This includes buildings ancillary to a place of manufacture and also a slaughterhouse, a laundry, a shipyard, a film set and premises where packing takes place (among other specified categories).

The occupier of a factory has an absolute duty to fence securely all prime movers (machines which provide power), all transmission machinery and every dangerous part of any machinery. Machinery is dangerous if it can be reasonably foreseen that injury to any person can occur in the ordinary course of use.

1.4 The Workplace (Health, Safety and Welfare) Regulations 1992

The workplace regulations deal with matters that have been statutory requirements for many years in the UK under legislation such as the Offices, Shops and Railway Premises Act 1963, although in some cases the requirements have been more clearly defined. The following provisions are made.

(a) **Machinery and equipment.** All equipment should be properly maintained and fenced if dangerous.

(b) **Ventilation**. Air should be fresh or purified.

(c) **Temperature**. The temperature must be 'reasonable' inside buildings during working hours. This means not less than 16°C where people are sitting down, or 13°C if they move about to do their work.

(d) **Lighting** should be suitable and sufficient, and natural if practicable. Windows should be clean and unobstructed.

(e) **Cleaning and decoration**. Floors, walls, ceilings, furniture, furnishings and fittings must be kept clean.

(f) **Room dimensions and space**. Each person should have at least 11 cubic metres of space, ignoring any parts of rooms more than 3.1 metres above the floor or with a headroom of less than 2.0 metres.

(g) **Floors, passages and stairs** must be properly constructed and maintained (without holes, not slippery, properly drained and so on).

(h) **Falls or falling objects.** These should be prevented by erecting effective physical safeguards (fences, safety nets, ground rails and so on).

(i) **Glazing**. Windows should be made of safe materials and if they are openable it should be possible to do this safely.

(j) **Traffic routes.** These should have regard to the safety of pedestrians and vehicles alike.

(k) **Doors and gates.** These should be suitably constructed and fitted with any necessary safety devices (especially sliding doors and powered doors and doors opening in either direction).

(l) **Lifts, escalators and travelators** should function safely and be regularly maintained.

(m) **Sanitary conveniences and washing facilities** must be suitable and sufficient. This means that they should be properly ventilated and lit, properly cleaned and separate for men and women. 'Sufficient' means that undue delay is avoided!

(n) **Drinking water.** An adequate supply should be available with suitable drinking vessels.

(o) **Clothing**. There should be suitable accommodation for outdoor clothing, which should be able to dry out if wet. Facilities for changing clothing should be available where appropriate.

(p) **Rest facilities and eating facilities.** These must be provided unless the employees' workstations are suitable for rest or eating, as is normally the case for offices.

(q) **Fire precautions** should be taken, and appropriate firefighting equipment and clearly marked and unobstructed escape route should be provided. Fire alarms should be installed and tested.

(r) **First aid** equipment should be provided, under the charge of a responsible person who should be trained in first aid, if there are more than 150 employees.

Activity 1 **(1 hour)**

Look at your own college (or workplace) from a health and safety perspective. Compare the provisions (a) to (r) above with what you see within your college/workplace. Make a note of areas where health and safety provisions fall short of requirements.

- **The Health and Safety (First Aid) Regulations 1981** require employers to provide adequate and appropriate equipment, facilities and personnel to enable first aid to be given to employees if they are injured or become ill at work. The minimum contents that should be found in a first aid box, for example, consist of dressings (plasters) and bandages of various sizes.
- **The Health and Safety (Young Persons) Regulations 1997** require employers to take into account the lack of experience, absence of awareness of existing or potential risks and/or the relative immaturity of young employees (aged under 18) when assessing the risks to their health and safety.
- **The Health and Safety (Safety Signs and Signals) Regulations 1996** describe the safety signs and signals that should be provided in the workplace, how they should be used and also require employers to instruct employees on their use and meaning.

In addition to legislation, you need to be aware of helpful guidance on health and safety from other sources. The instruction manual to a piece of equipment or machinery, for example, makes all the difference between a help and a hazard. The Health and Safety Commission issues helpful booklets on matters such as working with VDUs, smoking and alcohol. But there is no substitute for common sense: care in handling chemicals, lifting heavy objects, operating machinery, moving around the workplace (and playing practical jokes) is part of every employee's own 'Safety Policy'. We will now look at some practical measures and requirements for accident and fire prevention in the workplace.

2 ACCIDENT AND FIRE PREVENTION

2.1 Accidents

Apart from obviously dangerous equipment in factories, there are many hazards to be found in the modern working environment. Many accidents could be avoided by the simple application of common sense and consideration by employer and employee, and by safety consciousness encouraged or enforced by a widely acceptable and well publicised **safety policy**.

Activity 2 **(10 minutes)**

What would you expect to be the most common causes of injury in the workplace? List at least five hazards or risky behaviours.

The **cost** of accidents to the employer consists of:

(a) time lost by the injured employee;

(b) time lost by other employees whose work is interrupted by the accident;

(c) time lost by supervision, management and technical staff as a result of the accident;

(d) a proportion of the cost of first aid materials, or even medical staff;

(e) the cost of disruption to operations at work;

(f) the cost of any damage and repairs and modification to the equipment;

(g) the cost of any compensation payments or fines resulting from legal action;

(h) the costs associated with increased insurance premiums;

(i) reduced output from the injured employee on return to work;

(j) the cost of possible reduced morale, increased absenteeism, increased labour turnover among employees;

(k) the cost of recruiting and training a replacement for the injured worker.

An employer may also be liable to an employee in tort if the employee is injured as a result of either:

(a) the employer's failure to take reasonable care in providing safe premises and plant, a safe system of work and competent fellow employees; or

(b) the employer's breach of a statutory duty – say, to fence dangerous machinery.

Although the injured employee's damages may be reduced if the injury was partly a consequence of his/her own contributory negligence, due allowance is made for ordinary human failings, such as inattentiveness, tiredness and so on.

2.2 Accident prevention

The prevention of illness or accidents requires efforts on the part of employers, including workplace design, communication of health and safety policies and procedures, training and so on. Some of the steps which might be taken to reduce the frequency and severity of accidents are as follows.

(a) Developing a safety consciousness among staff and workers and encouraging departmental pride in a good safety record.

(b) Developing effective consultative participation between management, workers and unions so that safety and health rules can be accepted and followed.

(c) Giving adequate instruction in safety rules and measures as part of the training of new and transferred workers, or where working methods or speeds of operation are changed.

(d) Materials handling, a major cause of accidents, should be minimised and designed as far as possible for safe working and operation.

(e) Ensuring a satisfactory standard from the safety angle for both basic plant and auxiliary fittings such as guards and other devices.

(f) Good maintenance – apart from making sound job repairs, temporary expedients to keep production going should not prejudice safety.

(g) In general, the appropriate code of practice for the industry/work environment should be implemented in full.

2.3 Accident reporting

Safety inspections should be carried out to locate and define faults in the system that allow accidents to occur. They may be carried out as a comprehensive audit, working through a checklist; or by using random spot checks, regular checks of particular risk points, or statutory inspections of particular areas, such as lifts, hoists, boilers or pipe-lines. It is essential that checklists used in the inspection process should identify corrective action to be taken, and allocate responsibility for that action. There should be reporting systems and control procedures to ensure that inspections are taking place and that findings are being acted on.

Activity 3 **(10 minutes)**

A scene from everyday office life is shown below. Note down anything that strikes you as being dangerous about this working environment.

An accident report is a management tool, designed to:

(a) identify problems; and
(b) indicate corrective action.

Recurring accidents may suggest the need for special investigation, but only more serious incidents will have to be followed-up in depth. Follow-up should be clearly aimed at preventing recurrence – not placing blame.

The drawing below shows the format of a **typical accident book,** which should by law be kept by any organisation which employs more than 10 people. (The one used by your organisation may be laid out differently, or it might consist of loose-leaf sheets.)

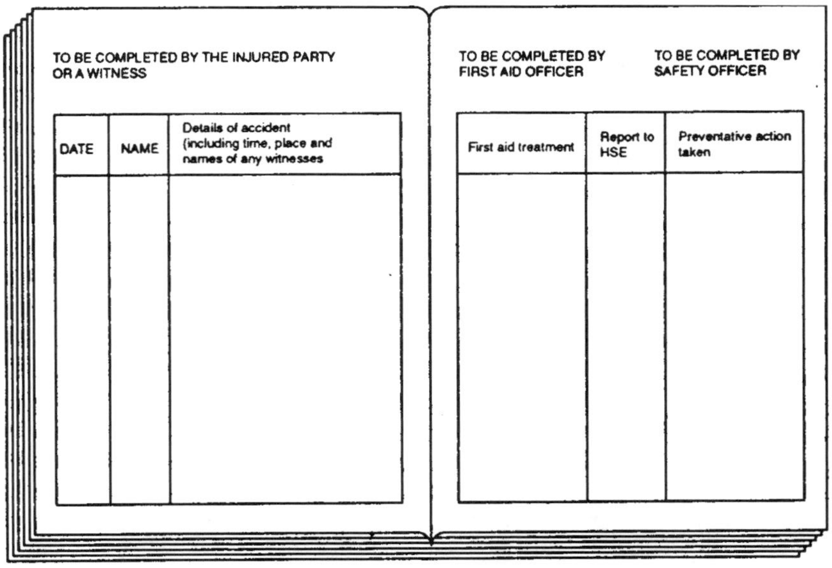

TO BE COMPLETED BY THE INJURED PARTY OR A WITNESS

DATE	NAME	Details of accident (including time, place and names of any witnesses

TO BE COMPLETED BY FIRST AID OFFICER — TO BE COMPLETED BY SAFETY OFFICER

First aid treatment	Report to HSE	Preventative action taken

The **Reporting of Injuries, Diseases and Dangerous Occurrences Regulations 1995** (RIDDOR 95) require employers to do the following.

(a) Notify the environmental health authority or the Health and Safety Executive **immediately** if one of the following occurs.

  (i) There is an accident connected with work and either an employee or self-employed person working on the premises is killed or suffers a major injury (including as a result of physical violence) or a member of the public is killed or taken to hospital.

  (ii) There is a dangerous occurrence.

(b) Send a completed **Accident report form** to do the following.

  (i) Confirm within ten days a telephone report of an accident or dangerous occurrence (as described in (a) above).

  (ii) Notify, within ten days of the accident, any injury which stops someone doing their normal job for more than three days.

  (iii) Report certain work-related diseases.

NOTES

HSE
Health & Safety Executive

Health and Safety at Work etc Act 1974
The Reporting of Injuries, Diseases and Dangerous Occurrences Regulations 1995

Report of an injury or dangerous occurrence

Filling in this form
This form must be filled in by an employer or other responsible person.

Part A

About you

1 What is your full name?

2 What is your job title?

3 What is your telephone number?

About your organisation

4 What is the name of your organisation?

5 What is its address and postcode?

6 What type of work does your organisation do?

Part B

About the incident

1 On what date did the incident happen?

/ /

2 At what time did the incident happen?
(Please use the 24-hour clock eg 0600)

3 Did the incident happen at the above address?

Yes ☐ Go to question 4

No ☐ Where did the incident happen?

☐ elsewhere in your organisation - give the name, address and postcode

☐ at someone else's premises - give the name, address and postcode

☐ in a public place - give the details of where it happened

If you do not know the postcode, what is the name of the local authority?

4 In which department, or where on the premises, did the incident happen?

Part C

About the injured person

If you are reporting a dangerous occurrence, go to Part F.
If more than one person was injured in the same incident, please attach the details asked for in Part C and Part D for each injured person.

1 What is their full name?

2 What is their home address and postcode?

3 What is their home phone number?

4 How old are they?

5 Are they

☐ male?

☐ female?

6 What is their job title?

7 Was the injured person (tick only one box)

☐ one of your employees?

☐ on a training scheme? Give details:

☐ on work experience?

☐ employed by someone else? Give details of the employer:

☐ self-employed and at work?

☐ a member of the public?

Part D

About the injury

1 What was the injury? (eg fracture, laceration)

2 What part of the body was injured?

BPP PUBLISHING

NOTES

3 Was the injury (tick the one box that applies)

- ☐ a fatality?
- ☐ a major injury or condition? (see accompanying notes)
- ☐ an injury to an employee or self-employed person which prevented them doing their normal work for more than 3 days?
- ☐ an injury to a member of the public which meant they had to be taken from the scene of the accident to a hospital for treatment?

4 Did the injured person (tick all the boxes that apply)

- ☐ became unconscious?
- ☐ need resuscitation?
- ☐ remain in hospital for more than 24 hours?
- ☐ none of the above?

Part E

About the kind of accident

Please tick the one box that best describes what happened, then go to part G.

- ☐ Contact with moving machinery or material being machined
- ☐ Hit by a moving, flying or falling object
- ☐ Hit by a moving vehicle
- ☐ Hit by something fixed or stationary

- ☐ Injured while handling, lifting or carrying
- ☐ Slipped, tripped or fell on the same level
- ☐ Fell from a height
  How high was the fall?
  [ ] metres
- ☐ Trapped by something collapsing

- ☐ Drowned or asphyxiated
- ☐ Exposed to, or in contact with, a harmful substance
- ☐ Exposed to fire
- ☐ Exposed to an explosion

- ☐ Contact with electricity or an electrical discharge
- ☐ Injured by an animal
- ☐ Physically assaulted by a person

- ☐ Another kind of accident (describe it in part G)

Part F

Dangerous occurrences

Enter the number of the dangerous occurrence you are reporting. (The numbers are given in the Regulations and in the notes which accompany this form.)

[ ]

Part G

Describing what happened

Give as much detail as you can. For instance

- the name of any substance involved
- the name and type of any machinery involved
- the events that led to the incident
- the part played by any people.

If it was a personal injury, give details of what the person was doing. Describe any action that has since been taken to prevent a similar incident. Use a separate piece of paper if you need to.

[ ]

Part H

Your signature

[ ]

Date

/ /

Where to send the form
Please send it to the Enforcing Authority for the place where it happened. If you do not know the Enforcing Authority, send it to the nearest HSE office.

For official use

Client number	Location number	Event number	
			☐ INV REP ☐ Y ☐ N

NOTES

Definitions

Major injuries include things like fractures other than to fingers, thumbs or toes, amputation, temporary or permanent loss of sight and any other injury which results in the person being admitted to hospital for more than 24 hours.

Dangerous occurrences are 'near misses' that might well have caused major injuries. They include the collapse of a load bearing part of a lift, electrical short circuit or overload causing fire or explosion, the malfunction of breathing apparatus while in use of during testing immediately before use, and many others.

Notifiable diseases include certain poisonings, occupational asthma, asbestosis, hepatitis and many others.

The standard for the notification of injuries and dangerous occurrences is reproduced on the previous page.

NOTES

Activity 4 **(30 minutes)**

Look back at the scene from everyday office life in Activity 3.

Adopt the role of each of the three workers shown and, assuming that you have by now had one of the many accidents possible in this working environment, fill out a report in the Accident Book shown below.

Accident book

	Full name, address and occupation of injured person (1)	Signature of injured person or other person making this entry* (2)	Date when entry made (3)	Date and time of accident (4)	Room/place in which accident happened (5)	Cause and nature of injury † (6)
1						
2						
3						
4						
5						
6						
7						
8						
9						
10						

* If the entry is made by some person acting on behalf of the employee, the address and occupation of that person must also be given

† State clearly the work or process being performed at the time of the accident

2.4 Fire safety and prevention

The main provisions of the **Fire Precautions Act 1971** are that:

(a) there must be adequate means of escape kept free from obstructions;
(b) all doors out of the building must be capable of opening from the inside;
(c) all employees should know the fire alarm system;
(d) there must be an effective and regularly tested fire alarm system;
(e) there must be fire-fighting equipment easily available and in working order.

Specialised buildings are covered by other legislation such as the Fire Safety and Safety of Places of Sport Act 1987. European legislation was implemented in the **Fire Precautions (Workplace) Regulations 1997** which came into force in December 1997. These regulations require employers to:

(a) provide the appropriate number of fire extinguishers and other means for fighting fire;

(b) install fire detectors and fire alarm systems where necessary.

(c) take whatever measures are necessary for fighting fire (eg the drawing up of a suitable emergency plan of action) and nominate a sufficient number of workers to implement these measure and ensure that they are adequately trained and equipped to carry out their responsibilities;

(d) provide adequate emergency routes and exits for everyone to escape quickly and safely;

(e) ensure that equipment and facilities provided to protect workers from the dangers of fire are regularly maintained and any faults found are rectified as quickly as possible.

Apart from **fire precautions** – which are designed to protect employees in the event of a fire – there must be measures for **fire prevention:** that is, to stop it happening! The main causes of fire in industry and commerce tend to be associated with electrical appliances and installations, and smoking is a major source of fires in business premises. The Fire Protection Association (of the UK) suggests the following guidelines for fire prevention and control:

(a) management should accept that fire prevention policies and practices must be established and reviewed regularly;

(b) management should be aware of the possible effects and consequences of fires, in terms of loss of buildings, plant and output, damage to records, effects on customers and workers etc;

(c) fire risks should be identified, particularly as regards sources of ignition, presence of combustible materials, and the means by which fires can spread;

(d) the responsibility for fire prevention should be established;

(e) a fire officer should be appointed;

(f) a fire prevention drill should be established and practised.

The Fire Protection Association provides detailed guidelines for fire prevention, and checklists for use in assessing the adequacy of existing procedures and in designing new procedures.

Activity 5 **(1 hour)**

Do you know what to do if fire breaks out in your college/workplace? Would you recognise the sound of a smoke alarm or fire alarm for what it was? Where is the nearest fire extinguisher? Is it safe to use a water extinguisher for any sort of fire? How do you set off the alarm? Where is the nearest fire exit? Should you leave doors open or shut? Does anybody know you are in the building? If you are not in the building does anybody think that you are?

Find out the answers to these questions!

2.5 Health and safety policy

In order to enhance safety awareness, promote good practice and comply with legal obligations, many employers have a health and safety policy for their staff. Such a policy might have the following features.

(a) Statement of principles.

(b) Detail of safety procedures.

(c) Compliance with the law (eg in siting of fire extinguishers, fire exits) should be enforced.

(d) Detailed instructions should be made available as to how to use equipment.

(e) Training requirements should be identified (eg no person who has not been on a particular training course can use the equipment), as part of the context of human resource planning.

(f) Committees of safety experts, line managers and employees can discuss issues of health and safety. There is no reason for example why safety issues should not be brought up for discussion in a firm's quality circles.

Safety policy must be implemented in detailed practice (such as fire drills and equipment checking) but it is less likely to be consistently observed if senior managers fail to set a good example, to discipline breaches of policy, or to reward health and safety suggestions. The aim is to create a culture in which health and safety are key values.

2.6 A culture of health and safety

Charles Hampden-Turner (in his book **Corporate Culture**) notes that attitudes to safety can be part of a corporate **culture**. He quotes the example of a firm called (for reasons of confidentiality) **Western Oil.**

EXAMPLE: WESTERN OIL

Western Oil had a bad safety record. 'Initially, safety was totally at odds with the main cultural values of productivity (management's interests) and maintenance of a macho image (the worker's culture)... . Western Oil had a culture which put safety in conflict with other corporate values.' In particular, the problem was with its long-distance truck drivers (who in the USA have a culture of solitary independence and self reliance). They sometimes drove recklessly with loads large enough to inundate a small town. The company instituted Operation Integrity to improve safety in a lasting way, changing the policies and drawing on the existing features of the culture but using them in a different way.

The culture had five dilemmas.

(a) **Safety-first versus macho-individualism.** Truckers see themselves as 'fearless pioneers of the unconventional lifestyle... . "Be careful boys!" is hardly a plea likely to go down well with this particular group'. Instead of trying to control the drivers, the firm recommended that they become road safety consultants (or design consultants). Their advice was sought on improving the system. This had the advantage that 'by making drivers critics of the system their roles as outsiders were preserved and promoted'. It tried to tap their heroism as promoters of public safety.

(b) **Safety everywhere versus safety specialists.** Western Oil could have hired more specialist staff. However, instead, the company promoted cross-functional safety teams from existing parts of the business, for example to help in designing depots and thinking of ways to reduce hazards.

(c) **Safety as cost versus productivity as benefit.** 'If the drivers raced from station to station to win their bonus, accidents were bound to occur... . The safety engineers rarely spoke to the line manager in charge of the delivery schedules. The unreconciled dilemma between safety and productivity had been evaded at management level and passed down the hierarchy until drivers were subjected to two incompatible injunctions, work fast and work safely.' To deal with this problem, safety would be built into the reward system.

(d) **Long-term safety versus short-term steering.** The device of recording 'unsafe' acts in operations enabled them to be monitored by cross-functional teams, so that the causes of accidents could be identified and reduced.

(e) **Personal responsibility versus collective protection.** It was felt that if 'safety' was seen as a form of management policing it would never be accepted. The habit of management 'blaming the victim' had to stop. Instead, if one employee reported another to the safety teams, the person who was reported would be free of official sanction. Peer pressure was seen to be a better enforcer of safety than the management hierarchy.

In many companies, considerations of health and safety are not tied up so intimately and obviously with reward systems and other policies. Nor do health and safety issues relate directly to work. However, from this example, we can learn:

(a) the importance of management practice in ensuring safety;
(b) safety (like total quality) is everyone's responsibility;
(c) culture and structures can either enhance or undermine safety policies.

Copies of legislation are readily available from the government and the Health and Safety Executive. Various companies produce newsletters on the issue to keep managers regularly informed. There is no real excuse for management ignorance in this matter.

FOR DISCUSSION

What are the cultural values in your nation, local community and organisation that:

(a) promote health and safety? and
(b) promote risk-taking and ill-health?

The diagram below shows a systematic approach to health and safety.

NOTES

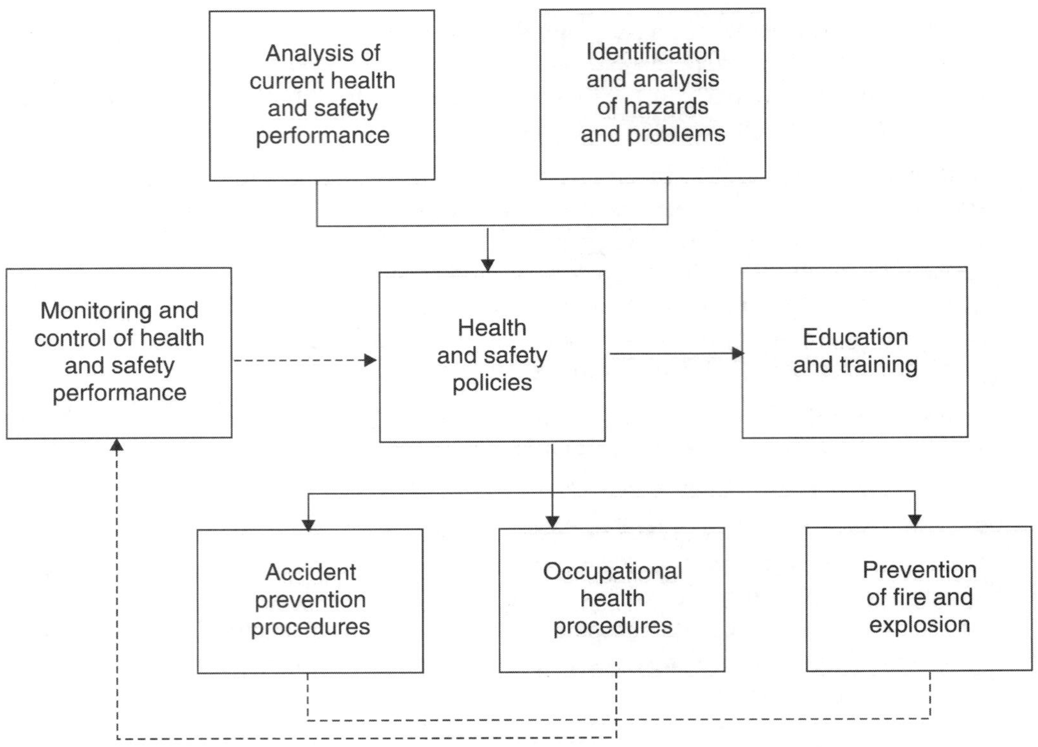

Finally, let us look at some health hazards that have recently started to cause concern.

3 HEALTH AND SAFETY IN THE MODERN WORKPLACE

3.1 Passive smoking

Recent case law has demonstrated that the employer has a duty to protect his/her employees from the effects of passive smoking, which means breathing in tobacco smoke from co-workers even though you don't smoke yourself. Thus, all employers are encouraged to devise smoking policies and procedures at work.

The IPD have produced a code of practice in this area, which recommends that any smoking policy should aim to provide smoke-free air in most areas where smokers and non-smokers meet. The issue should not be about whether people smoke but about where they smoke. Some smokers might wish to cut down or give up smoking, though others will not welcome a smoking policy. A clear written policy should minimise conflict and misunderstanding between employees so that those who wish to smoke are aware of where and when they are free to do so.

3.2 Stress

Organisations should also be aware of the negative effects of stress in the workplace and, in particular, control the work-related causes. These may be summarised as follows.

(a) **Role conflict.** This means the conflict experienced from the various roles played at work; for example the conflicting roles of boss and friend, new supervisor and ex-workmate.

(b) **Role ambiguity.** This means uncertainty about your role in your own mind and the minds of those with whom you come into contact. There is often

NOTES

particular uncertainty about how your work will be evaluated, how much responsibility you have and what others expect of you.

(c) **Role overload/underload**. This means having to do too much work or work which is too hard, or too little work or work which is too easy, boring and repetitive.

(d) **Responsibility for others**. Higher stress is suffered by those who are accountable for success and the performance and welfare of other people.

(e) **Lack of social support**. Isolation and lack of social support increases stress.

(f) **Uncertainty**. Lack of control over decisions which affect you is also a problem.

3.3 Computers

Definition

> **Repetitive strain injury (RSI).** is the term for various complaints associated with sustained computer use, frequently including back ache, eye strain and stiffness or muscular problems of the neck, shoulders, arms or hands.

The *Financial Times* reported in October 1991 that RSI accounted for more than half of all work-related injuries in the USA and that in Australia it had reached almost epidemic proportions. Disorders seem to arise from poor equipment, environment and posture, which lead to muscles being starved of oxygen, the build up of waste products in the body and the compression of nerves.

Although the Health and Safety Executive issued helpful guidelines on working with VDUs some time ago these did not have legal force, and employers remained free to ignore the problem. However, under the Health and Safety (Display Screen Equipment) Regulations 1992, any new workstations put into service have to meet new requirements and existing workstations had to be adapted to comply or be replaced by the end of 1996.

The main provisions of the directive are as follows. (You might like to check them off, if you are a regular VDU user yourself ...)

(a) **VDUs:** these must not flicker, must be free from glare, and must swivel and tilt.

(b) **Keyboards:** must also tilt and be free from glare; the workspace in front of them must be 'sufficient' for the operators to rest their forearms.

(c) **Desks**: these must be free from glare; there must be enough space to allow 'flexible' arrangement of all equipment and documents. Measurements are not specified.

(d) **Chairs:** the seat must be adjustable in height, and the back in height and angle; footrests must be made available if required.

(e) **Lighting:** there must be 'appropriate contrast' between the screen and its background; windows must have some form of blinds.

(f) **Heat and humidity** levels must be 'adequate' on the one hand and not uncomfortable on the other.

BPP PUBLISHING

(g) **Radiation,** for example from computer screens, must be reduced to negligible levels.

(h) **Breaks:** screen work must be 'periodically interrupted by breaks or changes in activity'.

(i) **Eyesight:** the employer must offer free eyesight testing at regular intervals and provide any special glasses that may be needed for screen work.

(j) **Consultation:** employees must be consulted about health and safety measures.

(k) **Training:** training in the proper use of equipment must be provided.

3.4 Working hours

You should be aware that working hours are also a health and safety issue, under the Health and Safety (Young Persons) Regulations 1997. The **Working Time Regulations** have brought into effect the EU working time directive.

Young workers (between 15 and 18) must by and large have:

(a) a 12-hour rest break in every 24 hour period;
(b) a rest period of two days in every seven (consecutive if possible); and
(c) a minimum rest break of 30 minutes, where the working day exceeds $4^{1}/_{2}$ hours.

For adult workers:

(a) The regulations limit working hours to 48 hours a week averaged over a 17-week period (or 26-week period, where continuity of work is necessary, as in health or essential services, 24-hour production or seasonal work). This *can* be extended to a year by collective workplace agreement – to preserve flexible 'annual hours' schemes, for example.

(b) If employees agree individually to work more than 48 hours a week, this should be done in writing, and a record of hours should be retained in case the Health and Safety Executive requires it.

(c) All employees are entitled to a daily rest of 11 consecutive hours in every 24, and a 24-hour rest in every seven days (averaged over 2 weeks) – with adjustments, by collective agreement where necessary.

(d) If the working day exceeds six hours, the employee is entitled to a minimum of 20 minutes' break.

(e) Staff are entitled to a health check before commencing night work, and regularly thereafter. Night work should be limited to an average of 8 in every 24 hours (over 17 weeks). If the work is hazardous, 8 hours is an absolute maximum. Protection is often reduced at night: under the regulations, health and safety protection and prevention services for night workers must be 'equivalent to those available to other workers'.

Activity 6 **(15 minutes)**

Since we have broadened our awareness of what constitutes a potential threat to health ad safety, take some time to think about what other issues personnel policies might cover? Suggest five areas for consideration. (If you are currently employed, check your organisation's manual on health and safety.)

NOTES

Chapter roundup

- The major piece of legislation covering health and safety at work is the Health and Safety at Work Act 1974, which places duties on both employers and employees.
- Regulations under the Act and under EU directives place additional responsibilities regarding health and safety on employers.
- Machine safety, fire prevention, chemicals' handling and so on are obvious areas for attention. However, the average workplace contains many potential hazards, and working conditions (including stress, VDU use and long working hours) can jeopardise health. Detailed safety policies must be formulated and communicated to all staff. It is also important to create a culture in which health and safety are a priority.

Quick quiz

1 Give reasons for the importance of health and safety at work.

2 What are the duties placed on an employee by the HASAW Act 1974?

3 Outline the powers of safety committees.

4 What additional duties have been placed on employers by recent regulations?

5 Explain the term Repetitive Strain Injury.

6 What does the cost of accidents to an employer consist of?

7 What preventive action could be taken to reduce the possibility of illness or accidents at the workplace?

8 What are the main causes of fire in the workplace?

9 What are the main objectives of a smoking policy?

10 What are the major work-related causes of stress?

Answers to quick quiz

1 To protect employees from pain and suffering; legal obligations; the cost of workplace accidents; to improve the company's image. (See Introduction)

2 To take reasonable care of self and others; to allow employers to carry out their duties; not to interfere with machinery/equipment. (See para 1.1)

3 Safety committees can insist that the employer produces a written statement of safety measures and consults with safety representatives. (See para 1.1)

4 Risk assessment; risk control; information on risks and hazards; revise and initiate safety policies; identify 'at risk' employees; training; competence of advisers. (See para 1.2)

5 A syndrome involving back ache, eye strain, stiffness in the neck, shoulders, arms and hands. (See para 3.3)

6 Time lost by employees and management; cost of first aid and staff; cost of disrupted work. (See para 2.1)

7 Safety consciousness; consultation and participation; adequate instruction; minimal materials handling; safety devices on machines; good maintenance; codes of practice. (See para 2.2)

8 Electrical appliances and installations; smoking. (See para 2.4)

9 To provide smoke-free air in most areas where smokers and non-smokers meet; to identify areas where people can smoke; to minimise conflict between smokers and non-smokers. (See para 3.1)

10 Job demands; role conflict; role ambiguity; role overload and underload; responsibility for others; lack of social support; non-participation in decision making. (See para 3.2)

Answers to activities

1 Obviously we do not know the shortcomings of safety measures at your college or work place. Your answer will depend on your following the checklist and identifying what you see in your informal inspection. If you do spot anything which you think might represent a health and safety risk, you should report it to your course tutor or your boss in the first instance.

2 (a) Slippery or poorly maintained floors.
(b) Frayed carpets.
(c) Trailing electric leads.
(d) Obstacles in gangways.
(e) Standing on chairs (particularly swivel chairs!) to reach high shelving.
(f) Staircases used as storage facilities.
(g) Lifting heavy items without bending properly.
(h) Removing the safety guard on a machine to free a blockage.

3 You should have spotted the following hazards

(a) Heavy object on high shelf.
(b) Standing on swivel chair.
(c) Lifting heavy object incorrectly.
(d) Open drawers blocking passageway.
(e) Trailing wires.
(f) Electric bar fire.
(g) Smouldering cigarette unattended.
(h) Overfull waste bin.
(i) Overloaded socket.
(j) Carrying too many cups of hot liquid.
(k) Dangerous invoice 'spike'.

If you can see others, you are probably right.

NOTES

4

Accident book

	Full name, address and occupation of injured person (1)	Signature of injured person or other person making this entry* (2)	Date when entry made (3)	Date and time of accident (4)	Room/place in which accident happened (5)	Cause and nature of injury † (6)
1	TIM SMILEY 22 SPRING ROAD, LONDON OFFICE MANAGER	Tim Smiley	14/9/2000	10/9/2000 17.00	OFFICE FLIT POWDER CO	CAUGHT RIGHT HAND ON INVOICE SPIKE. NEEDED STITCHES
2	FRANCES FINLEY 14 SILVER ST, LONDON DATA ENTRY CLERK	Fran Finley	15 Nov 2000	8 Nov 2000	OFFICE FLIT POWDER CO	TRIPPED ON TRAILING WIRE AND SPRAINED ANKLE
3	FINBAR MCINTOSH 151 QUEEN STREET, LONDON PROGRAMMER	Finbar McIntosh	29 Nov 2000	24 Nov 2000	OFFICE FLIT'S	FELL OFF CHAIR WHILE GETTING EQUIP OFF SHELF - BROKE ARM
4						
5						
6						
7						
8						
9						
10						

* If the entry is made by some person acting on behalf of the employee, the address and occupation of that person must also be given
† State clearly the work or process being performed at the time of the accident

5 This answer is specific to your college/workplace. As an interesting additional piece of learning, though, note how difficult or easy it was to **find out** about fire prevention and safety measures in the organisation.

6 Some areas you might have thought of include:

(a) alcohol on the premesis;

(b) drug taking (including prescription drugs) on the premises;

(c) horse play and practical jokes;

(d) noise (or 'acoustic shock'), particularly from headset use. (In a recent case, 20 BT telephone operators claimed that faulty equipment damaged their hearing: PM 15 May 98);

(e) workplace behaviour: running, throwing things, etc;

(f) tiredness (dangerous objects, dust, slippery objects etc).

BPP PUBLISHING

Chapter 6 :
IMPROVEMENT AND CHANGE

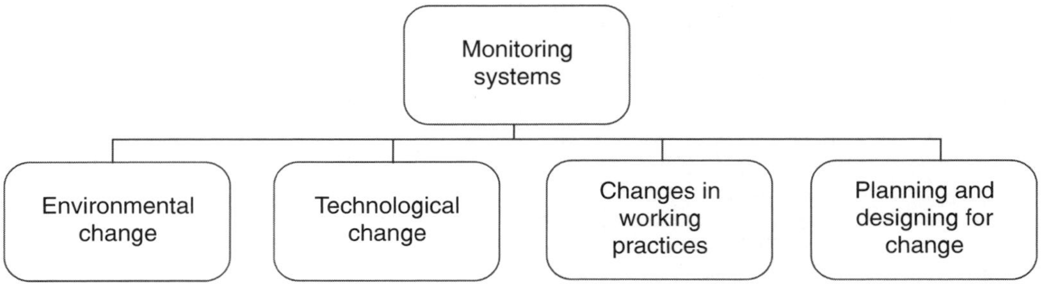

Introduction

Change in organisations is always the result of some external influence. Even seemingly small internal changes can be traced back to an external source. In this chapter we shall consider the environment of the organisation, specifically those influences stemming from political, economic and social forces. We shall then consider the technological influences, focusing on information technology and changes in production technology. Technology has helped to cause various changes in working practices (although technology is not the only stimulus for these). We will look at the examples of down sizing, outsourcing and outworking. All these changes require certain factors to ensure success; arguably, the most important factor is effective communication.

Your objectives

In this chapter you will learn about the following:

(a) Monitoring and control in organisations

(b) The effects of changes in the external environment on communication within organisations

(c) The impact of technological changes and changes in working practices on communications

(d) Changes in organisations relative to changes in communication systems and methods

(e) The effectiveness of communication and potential improvements to it

(f) The aims of organisational development

(g) A programme of organisational development

(h) The methods used to achieve organisational development

Any change that is external to the organisation is said to be a change in the organisational environment. Such external changes may or may not have an impact on the internal fabric of the organisation.

1 MONITORING SYSTEMS

1.1 Monitoring and control

Monitoring in simple terms means watching over something that is happening. Generally the word also carries a sense of warning: detecting things that are going wrong. Active monitoring systems ensure that the organisation is quickly aware of changes in the market place (competitors' actions, changes in customer tastes etc). This is probably best achieved by both formal and informal information collection methods. The organisation will keep abreast (as far as it can) of what its competitors are doing and someone will have an eye on general economic trends, the opinions of political commentators and the progress of scientific research at the *pure* as well as the *applied* stage, in addition to any more specific research work the company may itself be engaged in.

An organisation is a system, and any system must be controlled to keep it steady or enable it to change safely: each system must have a control system. Control is required because unpredictable disturbances arise and enter the system, so that actual results, the outputs of the system, deviate from the expected results or goals. Examples of disturbances in a business system would be the entry of a powerful new competitor into the market, an unexpected rise in labour costs, a decline in quality standards, the failure of a supplier to deliver promised raw materials, or the tendency of employees to stop working in order to chatter or gossip. A control system must ensure that the business is capable of surviving these disturbances by dealing with them in an appropriate manner.

To have a control system, there has to be a plan, standard, budget or any other sort of target or guideline towards which the system as a whole should be aiming. Control is dependent on the receipt and processing of *information*, both to plan in the first place and to compare actual results against the plan, so as to judge what control measures, if any, are needed.

1.2 Process of control

The managerial process of controlling is the measurement and correction of performance to make sure that the enterprise objectives and the plans devised to attain them are accomplished. Control techniques and systems are essentially the same for cash, office procedures, morale or product quality. The basic control process involves three steps:

- establishing standards, ie criteria of performance
- measuring performance against these standards and
- correcting variations from standards and plans

1.3 Feedback

Feedback is information about actual achievements. In a business organisation, it is information about actual results, produced from within the organisation (for example, management accounting control reports) with the purpose of helping with control decisions.

A feature of feedback is that it is information that is gathered by measuring the outputs of the system itself, as distinct from environmental information, which comes from outside the system. For some control systems, notably for control by senior management at a strategic planning level, control information will be gathered from both environmental sources and internal sources. For example, a company might be unable to judge the success or failure of its activities without putting them into the context of the national economy (Is it booming? Is it in recession? How high is the rate of inflation?) and its markets (How well are competitors doing? Is the number of potential customers rising or falling?)

Some form of internally generated feedback is essential if there is to be any effective monitoring within an organisation and the most common types of monitoring systems in businesses, such as budgetary control, stock control and production control systems, are all based on feedback cycles.

A feedback system measures the outputs of a process and then provides information regarding corrective action to the process or the inputs, after the outputs have been produced. In most management problems, because of time lags in implementing the corrective process, this is not good enough. For example, if the manager is informed in August that the administration department has overspent against budget due to a purchase in June, there is nothing that can be done.

Feed forward control will inform management of deviations in time for them to take corrective action. It is used to overcome the time lag problems often encountered by feedback systems. This type of system monitors the inputs into the process to ascertain whether the inputs are as planned; if they are not, the inputs, or perhaps the process, are changed in order to ensure the desired results. In the above example, the administration department would have to submit an estimate for the item they wish to purchase. The organisation would then have to decide whether to refuse the request or change the budget in order to allow the purchase to be made. The diagram below shows feedback/ feedforward control.

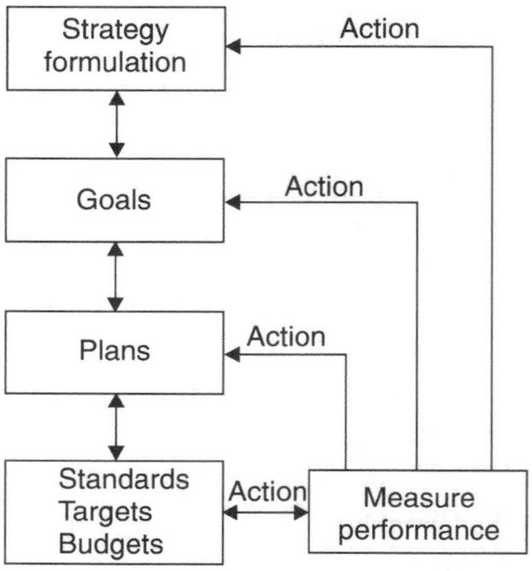

1.4 Critical control points and standards

Actual or expected performance is measured against standards or yardsticks. If the operation is simple, a manager might control through observation of the work being done. However, in most situations this is not possible because of the complexity of the operations and the fact that a manager has better things to do. He or she must choose critical points for special attention and monitor them to be sure that the operation is proceeding as planned. The principle of critical point control states that effective control requires attention to those factors critical to evaluating performance against plans. Managers need to select these points after asking themselves:

- what will best reflect the goals of my department?
- what will best show me when these goals are not being met?
- what will best measure critical deviations?
- what will tell me who is responsible for any failure?
- what standards will cost the least?
- for what standards is information economically available?

1.5 Taking corrective action

Where these are critical deviations from the plan, the action to be taken will vary from organisation to organisation according to the managerial style employed and the structure adopted.

A problem analysis exercise will be carried out, which will cover the following issues.

- Why are current methods and working practices used?
- What problems are restricting the effectiveness of the current system and the reasons for their existence?
- Are alternative methods available to achieve the same or better results?
- What changes can be introduced?
- What performance criteria are required from the system and how they can be measured?

It must be appreciated that some failures to attain standards are symptomatic of more fundamental causes and that tinkering with the system may not lead to any real improvement. Changes in standards and overall objectives should not be ruled out.

2 ENVIRONMENTAL CHANGE

Environmental change can affect the strategy, structure or culture of an organisation. It may affect a combination of them all. Environmental changes are sometimes dramatic, such as a sudden change in public opinion, but it is more frequently the case that changes are insidious and gradual. Organisations which communicate effectively with their environment are well placed to become aware of changes as they occur. Organisations that have become insular may take longer to pick up on such changes.

Pressure for change can come from a variety of sources - political, economic, social and technological. We start by looking at the effects of social pressures.

2.1 Social pressures for change

There are many examples of changes brought about by social pressures for change.

EXAMPLES: CHANGE THROUGH SOCIAL PRESSURE

Green issues

Recent changes in the awareness of the public concerning the potential destruction of various parts of the flora or fauna of our planet have had an impact on many industries. In some of these both the products made and the production processes have had to be changed. For example, paper production may now be from sustainable forests, and canned tuna may be caught by methods that are dolphin friendly.

The National Health Service

The National Health Service has undergone major changes in terms of waiting times and clients' expectations of level of service. Whilst some of this change can be attributed to changes in government policy (political pressures), it is the pressure from the population that has increased the impetus for change.

Communication is important in enabling social pressure for change to grow and to have an effect. Effective communication within the organisations concerned is essential to enable these changes to occur. It is also the case that growth in worldwide communication has increased the social pressures themselves.

Activity 1 **(20 minutes)**

Make a list of four products or industries which have been forced to change in the last ten years as a result of social pressures

In each case, give the reason for the change and indicate in what direction the changes have been made.

Social and political pressures are often interrelated. Here we focus on the effects of political pressures emanating from outside the UK.

2.2 Political pressures for change

European directives have considerable effect on the way UK organisations are run, especially as many UK companies now have links outside this country. The integration process that is occurring between EU member states in respect of working conditions within organisations is forcing many established firms to rethink their staff management policies.

Activity 2 **(1 hour + research)**

In the 1990s the European Union issued a directive concerning works councils. Although the UK has not become party to the Maastricht Treaty from which this directive stems, the directive has had implications for UK firms. For the purpose of this activity, assume that the directive is equally valid in the UK as in other European countries.

The directive instructs that all organisations over a specified size (based on number of employees) must set up works councils through which employees will be kept informed of anything affecting them (directly or indirectly) and at which employees can have their say over working conditions. The works councils will not deal with remuneration matters or other subjects covered by existing collective bargaining agreements.

Write a short essay (500-1000 words) on how you think this directive changed the emphasis of communication within UK organisations.

For organisations to be successful in introducing these changes in a beneficial way, there must be effective communication between all those involved.

EXAMPLE: THE BRITISH CIVIL SERVICE

One of the best examples of radical change within an organisation as a result of political pressure, in recent years, has been the transformation of the British Civil Service. This seemingly self-perpetuating bureaucratic organisation was decimated by the introduction of semi-autonomous government agencies as a result of the Ibbs report. The new structure challenged all that the old system stood for, intending instead to replace it with a flexible, less bureaucratic structure.

Success has been limited by the nature of the communication networks in operation before the changes. Some would argue that, because of the culture of the organisation, the nature of these networks is unlikely to change.

We now look at economic pressures.

2.3 Economic pressures for change

External competition has always been a driving force behind changes in product design and innovation of new products. However, in the economic climate of the recent past, there has been even greater pressure on organisations to find ways to change and to adapt to fierce competition. One of the ways some organisations have achieved this is by the use of strategic alliances. One example is the alliance between Rover and Honda. This alliance was driven by two factors.

(a) The desire by Honda to move into the European market at a time when quotas for non-EU imports were in place.

(b) The declining ability of the UK car manufacturing industry in general, and Rover in particular, to compete in the market, and the necessity of improving competitiveness in order to survive.

The alliance of these two companies allowed them both to achieve their objectives. The continued success of the Rover/Honda alliance depended upon trust built from effective communications. Once these communications broke down, the alliance was doomed to failure.

FOR DISCUSSION

Discuss the following statement in groups.

Increasing competitive pressure will result in greater openness in communications between rivals. The eventual outcome will be such close alliance that each sector of the market will become an effective monopoly.

In order for an organisation to have an innovative culture, the structure needs to be organic. By definition, these structures cannot exist without free and effective communications. Swift action and reaction require the fast flow of information and rapid decision making.

One of the greatest recent changes in the environment of organisations is in the area of technological advances. Technological changes have also had impacts on the strategy, structure and culture of organisations.

3 TECHNOLOGICAL CHANGE

In this section we concentrate on information and production technology. This does not imply that other technological advances do not have an impact on the organisation; these are just intended as two examples of changes in technology that generate pressure on organisations to change.

3.1 Information technology

We have already considered how technological innovation in information dissemination has expanded the means to communicate; here we concentrate on how these advances have (a) pushed organisations to change, and (b) facilitated that change.

Technology has had an impact on the whole strategy of organisations. The globalisation of organisations would have been impossible without present day means and methods of communications. Similarly, the concept of selling to a customer you never see would have remained a small niche market if technological innovation had not allowed television and internet shopping. The growing interest of the UK food retailing industry in the concept of home shopping is testament to the viability of such changes.

Activity 3 **(30 minutes)**

How has improved communications technology facilitated the expansion of the global organisation? Make a list of the factors you consider to be important.

The use of IT-based data collection systems to determine where there are areas of waste has allowed organisations to realise their ambitions to cut costs. This represents a change in the values of the organisation and thus a change in its culture.

Improved communications technology has helped to improve partnership relationships with suppliers to such an extent that raw materials and components can now be delivered exactly when they are needed. This reduces the need for manufacturers to hold large stocks and thus saves money. This is one of the few areas when it is easy to quantify the benefits of highly developed and effective communications systems.

A major impact of information technology has been on working practices, which we shall consider below.

3.2 Production technology

The introduction of automated production and robotics has resulted in a reduction in the size of the shop floor workforce. From the organisation's point of view (although not the workers'), this is a benefit, where costs are cut. This reduction in the numbers of the workforce requires more and better communications between those who remain. When this type of new technology is being introduced, the process of increased communication needs to commence before its introduction. Otherwise, the transformation of the production plant is likely to be hindered by such things as trade union intervention.

NOTES

After the introduction of the new technology, continued communications are necessary to identify training needs and skills shortages.

Activity 4 **(45 minutes)**

Robert and Son is a small factory producing components for the electrical industry. Their system of production has for many years taken the form of a series of production lines, with each line producing a different sub-section of the finished component.

The development of new technology, which partly automates the production of the subsections, now means that it is possible to increase the production capacity. The old system required a large factory floor to house the production lines and a final assembly line where the components were put together and packaged. The new technology reduces the amount of space required, so that all operations can be housed in one building. The production manager has put forward two separate layout plans for the 'new look' plant as shown in Figures 2 and 3. Figure 1 shows the existing layout.

Based on what you know about communications, draw up an advantages and disadvantages list for each of the three layouts. Make a final decision as to which layout to choose. Give reasons for your choice.

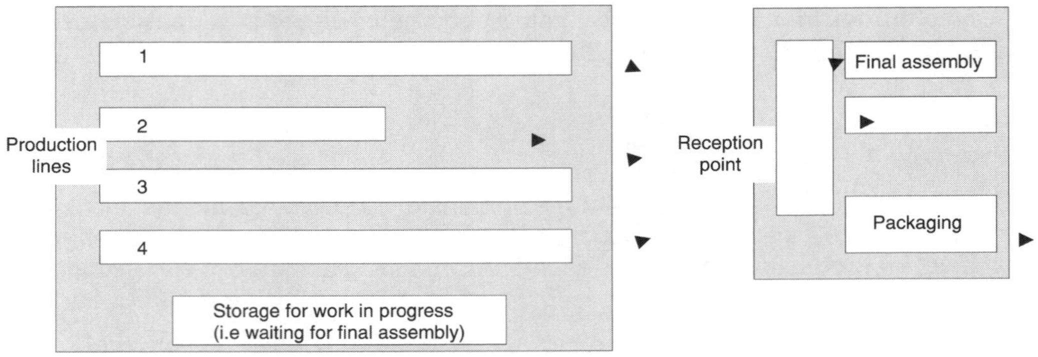

Figure 1 Existing layout

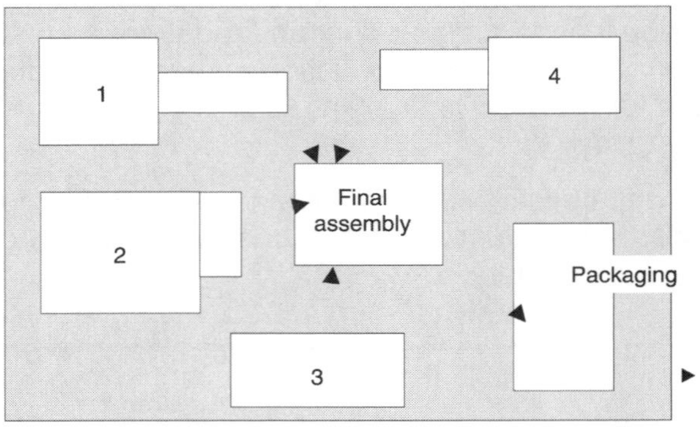

Note: This system is expected to reduce work in progress

Figure 2 Possible new layout (a)

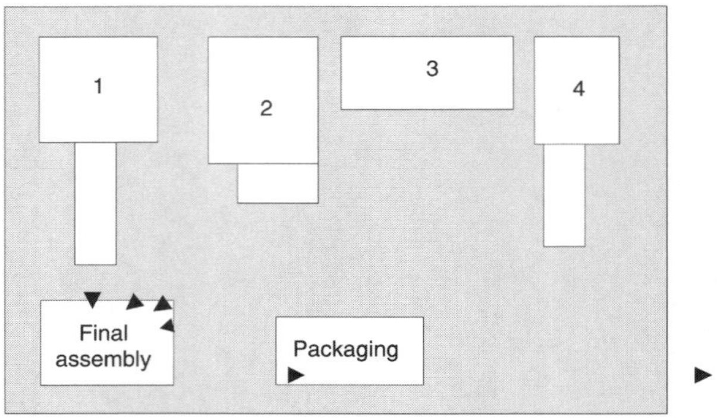

Note: This system is expected to reduce work in progress

Figure 3 Possible new layout (b)

Whatever pressures are exerted by the external environment, the changes that occur within the organisation almost always lead, in some way, to changes in working practices. We shall consider just three of the possibilities.

4 CHANGES IN WORKING PRACTICES

Changes in working practices can be a simple as introducing a new information collection form or as complex as transferring from a paper to computer-based system. However great or small the change, communication plays its part in its introduction and ultimate success.

NOTES

Effective communication will:

(a) allay fear and suspicion about the motivation for the change;
(b) involve the workforce and gain their commitment;
(c) highlight potential problems;
(d) ensure that the change is appropriate;
(e) encourage feedback regarding unexpected side effects of the change;
(f) monitor the results of the change;
(g) facilitate the adaptation of the original plans.

We concentrate here on three contemporary and far reaching changes to working practices. The first of these is 'downsizing'.

4.1 Downsizing

Definitions

> **Downsizing:** the term used to describe the contraction of an organisation so that it concentrates on its core activities.
>
> **De-layering:** the removal of one or more layers of middle management, accompanied by the devolving of responsibility and authority further down the organisation structure.

It is important to note the distinction between downsizing and de-layering. Although they are quite separate concepts, both can have similar effects on the motivation of the workforce, although within differing groups of workers. If communications are poor, the workforce do not understand the strategy that is being followed and the only effect they see is redundancies. This undermines their security and their commitment to the organisation, and, in turn, their performance is likely to suffer. Effective communications can reduce these effects and actively generate a stronger commitment to the change from those workers who remain after the process is complete.

> **Activity 5** **(25 minutes)**
>
> You are the chief executive officer of a large group of companies. You have decided that, in order to consolidate your business with a view to expansion of your core activities in the future, you must sell off some of your smaller enterprises. Make a list of who you think you should communicate with in your environment to ensure that this will be a positive action for your company. Give reasons for communicating with each individual, group or organisation on your list.

4.2 Outsourcing

Definition

Outsourcing: the term used to describe the process of employing outside contractors to perform tasks which, although not core activities of the organisation, were formerly performed in house. Examples can be cleaning, security, legal work and occupational health.

Outsourcing is often the result of downsizing and, as such, can encounter the same problems. Effective communication is especially important to ensure that the outsourced service is to the same standard, or better, and at lower cost than that previously provided in house. Partnership relationships are required with these service providers, and effective communications are the only way to achieve these. (There can be other influencing factors, but without effective communications they will not ensure success.) A great deal of outsourcing has been carried out in public sector organisations, especially as a result of compulsory competitive tendering.

Definition

Compulsory competitive tendering: a process that has been forced onto public-sector organisations by central government. It entails the obligation to ask for tenders to carry out specific activities on behalf of he organisation. This process has to be repeated at regular intervals (yearly or three yearly, typically).

The nature of compulsory competitive tendering inhibits the possibility of developing partnership relationships, and thus the communication is not always as effective as it could be. These problems are just beginning to be highlighted, and may be addressed in the future.

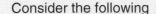

Activity 6 **(25 minutes)**

Consider the following

(a) A local hospital
(b) The council for your locality

Make a list of any activities associated with the above which are outsourced.

Make a second list of activities that you think could be outsourced.

NOTES

4.3 Outworking

Definition

> **Outworking:** the term used to describe a formerly office-based function being carried out primarily from the home of the job holder. This form of working has become popular in the financial services and data processing industries. The effects on the organisation are (a) to reduce overheads on expensive office accommodation and (b) to access the pool of (predominantly) female labour who have child care commitments that prevent them from taking office-based work. Outworking should not be confused with outsourcing.

The advent of the home computer and advances in telecommunications have facilitated the move towards home working. Critics of this working method claim that it will be a passing phase, as the effects of lack of communication on the worker become more evident. However, advances in all technological communication methods mean that the only area that cannot be satisfied is that of face-to-face personal interaction with others. Whilst there is debate as to the importance of interpersonal communication on the performance of the worker, it is clear that it does play a part in job satisfaction and motivation. It remains to be seen whether communications can be so carefully structured and facilitated as to remove this problem.

5 PLANNING AND DESIGNING FOR CHANGE

Organisations have to adapt to external and internal change. As an organisation grows, its structure may not adapt to the changing demands for differentiation and integration. The environment changes but the organisation may not. It may continue with old structures and ways of working long after they have become a liability rather than an asset.

When did your own local tennis or snooker club last shake itself up and make a fresh start? Can you think of any local firms that have restructured themselves? Has their response to the economic changes of the last five years been to try to do more of the same with fewer people?

When organisations become incapable of reaching their potential, they should seek development to improve their effectiveness. This is extremely difficult to do because of the extent of the change in culture and structure that is usually necessary. Any change has to overcome the natural inertia of staff operating in a role in the existing structure. They are busy with their existing jobs. The only way to implement change is to bring in an outsider. Worthwhile change only happens if it is organisation wide.

5.1 Organisation development

Organisation development has become important in the last decade. The pace of change in the environment has quickened. Privatisation, deregulation, recession and global competition have affected public- and private-sector organisations of all types. Social and political changes have been widespread. A policy such as 'Care in the Community' has affected hospitals, general practice, social services, local government, charities and voluntary bodies. The rapid development of the personal computer has transformed work. In 1980 computing power meant a multi-million pound Cray super computer operated by a separate IT department. Twenty years later anyone can have a desk top PC with more calculating power than the Cray at a cost of around £5,000. You can get one capable of most operations for £700. Organisations have been forced to re-examine every aspect of their existence.

Activity 7 **(30 minutes)**

Ask some members of older generations if they can remember how clerical and accounts work were done thirty years ago. Specifically ask them about:

(a) adding up figures in accounts;
(b) how tills operated in shops;
(c) how letters and invoices were prepared.

You may have heard some of this before in the context of how the present generation cannot add up! You should also ask how many people could use a computer, or knew how it worked, in the 1960s.

Compare your findings with how jobs are done today and note how technology has transformed work and methods. It is easy to take today's technology for granted and to forget how recent the change is.

When the top managers of a company realise that it is not operating up to its potential, the way forward is a fundamental reappraisal and redesign of the organisation. Organisation development is the whole process of carrying out a strategy for adapting to change.

Definition

Organisation development is a strategy for improving organisational effectiveness by changing the beliefs, values and structure of organisations through collaboration between an external consultant and the management of the organisation.

There are three features of organisation development (OD).

(a) It is an organisation-wide process.

(b) It is concerned with more than the redesign of the structure and is essentially an education process.

(c) It relies on an external third party consultant - the change agent.

OD programmes have seven distinct stages and we look next at what they involve.

The programme

Each OD programme must be unique because each organisation is different, but they are all likely to follow much the same sequence in introducing and carrying through the required changes. Before the programme can begin, it is essential that senior management recognise the need for development and agree that it should be organisation wide.

Stage 1: preliminary planning

Senior management start by discussing the problem and choosing the change agent. There is then more detailed discussion about the aims and methods of the proposed programme with the agent. This is likely to include:

(a) the aims, methods and potential outcome of the programme;
(b) the role of the consultant and relationship with the management;
(c) the implications for the organisation.

The change agent could have different roles, according to circumstances, as:

(a) educator and facilitator of change;
(b) a catalyst for introducing new ideas and practices;
(c) an expert guiding and leading management in making changes.

Once all these are agreed, the staff of the organisation must be fully informed about the programme. So that their trust is maintained, they must be kept fully informed throughout all its stages. The consultant has to win the trust of all concerned and gain their co-operation.

Stage 2: analysis

The change agent designs a programme for obtaining information. This includes:

(a) documented information such as job descriptions, staff personnel records, budgets and control data;

(b) questionnaires dealing with all aspects;

(c) surveys;

(d) interviews of individuals and/or groups;

(e) collecting statistics;

(f) staff suggestions and proposals.

Activity 8 **(45 minutes)**

Assume that your course is involved in an OD exercise.

Design a short questionnaire to find out how well course members are informed about their results when they complete assignments. You should cover methods of feedback, the time scale and corrective action.

Try your questionnaire on four or five people and from the results say if it shows that there is anything unsatisfactory in the present system and make a suggestion for its improvement.

Stage 3: Diagnosis

All this information is used to buildup a picture of the culture, staff attitudes and operations of the organisation. It is important that staff are involved because they must feel committed to the process. Staff participation may lead them to realise for themselves what is wrong and propose solutions.

The results are discussed with management. An agreed diagnosis of the situation is produced. It is essential that this honestly faces up to the situation. The result is reported back to top management so that the strategy for change can be agreed.

Stage 4: Aims and objectives

When the diagnosis is agreed the change agent and management agree the aims and objectives of the programme of OD. The aims might include improving profitability, increasing market share, entering new markets, changing the culture of the organisation and improving staff motivation. These are then translated into specific objectives, for example:

(a) to achieve a market share of 8% within one year;

(b) to reduce operating costs in marketing and sales by 7% in each of the next three years;

(c) to reduce manufacturing rejects by 15% in six months;

(d) to establish project teams operating in a matrix structure throughout the small appliances division within fifteen months;

(e) to put all staff through specified training programmes within the next three years.

Note that all these objectives are specific, quantifiable and have a timescale for their achievement. Progress can thus be monitored and corrective action taken if required. The outcome of the programme can be checked against the aims.

Stage 5: Action plans

The content and sequence of all the actions required to meet the objectives are set out in a master plan. This could include specific programmes for:

(a) creating an open, problem-solving environment;

(b) increasing knowledge and competence both in specific job-related areas and in general management skills;

(c) building trust and collaboration among groups;

(d) developing reward systems based on personal development as much as on achieving organisational goals;

(e) increasing employee empowerment and the degree of personal autonomy.

Stage 6: Implementation and review

All the plans are put into effect and progress is constantly monitored by the consultant and the management. Progress is reviewed and any necessary changes are made. Parts of a programme may have to be dropped because they have adverse effects. Some parts may lag behind and require more resources of management time to speed them up. Objectives and aims may have to be revised and programmes amended.

Stage 7: Completion and evaluation

As the programme is completed, the results are evaluated against the original aims. At the end of the programme the change agent leaves the organisation.

> **Activity 9** **(10 minutes)**
>
> A new chairman of W H Smith, the news, book, record and DIY chain, announced that the culture of the firm had to change to a more commercial one. He proposed dropping many marginal product lines as part of a complete shake up of the company. Do you consider this is a good preliminary to introducing OD?

The success of any OD programme depends on the change agent; we examine this role next.

5.2 The change agent

An external consultant is preferred for the following reasons.

(a) A consultant will have previous experience of OD, which an internal manager is unlikely to have.

(b) An outsider is not bound by status and can operate across all levels of the hierarchy.

(c) The change agent can be expected to take a more objective view than an insider.

(d) The consultant has more time for the exercise as it is a full-time job, whereas a manager is likely to have other tasks.

(e) The change agent leaves at the end of the programme and does not have to live with the results, unlike a manager who must be wary of making trouble within the organisation.

There are also arguments against using an outsider. These include the following.

(a) An outsider lacks knowledge and understanding of the organisation.

(b) An outsider will take time to become familiar with the organisation.

(c) There is the possibility that a consultant will be resented as a meddler and tool of top management.

5.3 Timespan

Successful OD programmes have sometimes been spread over several years, so that the consultant could become thoroughly familiar with the organisation. The minimum time required for an effective programme is likely to be two years.

5.4 Relationships

The consultant must be capable of building an effective relationship with staff in the organisation and winning over all grades to support the project. The change agent has to build a sound relationship with the management team and establish the trust of all employees. Full information to everyone at all stages is essential.

5.5 Roles

The change agent has many roles, including the following.

(a) Expert and skilled adviser
(b) Analyst
(c) Listener
(d) Catalyst for change
(e) Counsellor
(f) Problem solver

Activity 10 **(5 minutes)**

Why is it that so many change agents brought in by major companies are academics, like Rosabeth Moss Kanter and Tom Peters?

5.6 Establishing the starting point

The consultant has first to establish whether the organisation is ready for OD. This means examining the organisation and asking the following questions.

(a) Are the learning goals of OD appropriate?
(b) Are the key people involved and committed?
(c) Are the culture and values of the organisation such as to make OD feasible?
(d) What are the problems?

Problems in the organisation can be analysed under the following main headings.

(a) Power and authority
(b) Differentiation and integration
(c) Co-operation and conflict
(d) Adaptation to change
(e) Culture and identity

It is not enough for the change agent to concentrate on broad questions of organisation structure and strategy, there must be a process of change at all levels down to individual processes.

5.7 Re-engineering

It is because of the potential problems of bringing in an outsider, and the need to commit members of the organisation to change, that many companies prefer the approach of '**re-engineering the company**'. This involves the same basic process as OD but is started by a leader who is a senior executive who authorises and motivates the overall effort. The process is supervised by a steering committee, composed of senior managers, which develops the overall strategy and monitors progress. Each process is led by a 'process owner' who is a manager with authority for the specific process and the re-engineering effort focused on it. The process owner is supported by a 're-engineering team', a group dedicated to diagnosis, planning the redesign and implementing the programme for that particular process. Each team includes at least one outsider who does not work in the process. There could also be outsiders who are effectively suppliers and customers of the process. Their purpose is to pose awkward questions and initiate new thinking. The objective is to find new and effective ways of doing things.

NOTES

Re-engineering often starts with the appointment of a new chief executive who is effectively a change agent.

EXAMPLE: MAZDA

In 1996 Mazda, the Japanese car manufacturer, appointed Henry Wallace as its new president. Wallace was a British manager in Ford who gained experience in several countries before being appointed Executive Vicepresident of Mazda in 1994. Ford and Mazda have co-operated since the 1960s and Ford took a 25% shareholding in 1979 and raised it to 33.4% in 1996. Mazda made losses in each of the three previous years and lost market share in Japan as well as seeing a drop in exports. Benefits are expected from linking Mazda's research and development with Ford's design capacity. The essential step is to re-engineer Mazda to revitalise it.

FOR DISCUSSION

Many organisations have undergone a transformation when they have moved from the public- to the private-sector, merged or, like building societies, changed from mutual status to Plcs.

How might OD help in these transformations?

We now consider the methods and outcomes of OD.

5.8 Methods and results

Areas of action

There are three main areas of action programmes in OD:

(a) programmes to change behaviour, including team building, improving interpersonal skills, better communication and training in coaching and counselling;

(b) programmes to improve problem solving, including training in goal setting, planning and evaluation;

(c) programmes to make structures effective, including training in systems diagnosis, role analysis and job design.

All these aspects are involved in an OD programme. There is no point in trying to fit new solutions into an inappropriate system. There may have to be radical redesign of the organisation, including delayering of management, outsourcing activities and even selling off parts of the organisation, possibly through a management buy-out.

5.9 Factors leading to success

An OD programme is likely to succeed where:

(a) top management is committed to action;

(b) there is some new element, such .as a new chief executive or a merger which brings a reappraisal of internal problems;

(c) problem areas are honestly and fully analysed and diagnosed;

(d) there is collaboration between line and staff and departments in identifying problems and implementing solutions;

(e) there is a willingness to take risks;

(f) there are new solutions which produce a commitment to action;

(g) there is a reward system that rewards people for the effort of changing;

(h) positive results reinforce the acceptance of new practices.

5.10 Factors preventing success

Effective organisation development is unlikely to occur where:

(a) top management is not totally committed to improvement;

(b) there is impatience for quick results and the timescale necessary (usually at least two years) is not allowed;

(c) top management fails to secure the commitment and support of middle and lower managers;

(d) there is an attempt to fit a major change into an old structure;

(e) ends and means are confused, this includes:

 (i) assuming that training will bring about change in itself without the changes in attitudes, culture .and structure that are necessary;

 (ii) assuming that simply using OD activities, such as management development programmes, constitutes a programme;

 (iii) letting consultants solve problems without management commitment to continuing the changes after the change agent leaves.

6 BUSINESS PROCESS RE-ENGINEERING

Definition

> **Business process re-engineering:** 'the fundamental rethinking and radical redesign of business processes to achieve dramatic improvements in critical contemporary measures of performance, such as cost, quality, service and speed.' (Hammer and Champy)

Investment in technology can be wasted if the fundamental processes of the business remain unaltered. In other words, the apparatus might change and even the techniques, but not the organisation behind it. This might be a reason why, despite all the investments in information technology, the productivity of office workers has not matched the dramatic improvements in manufacturing productivity of recent years.

Business process re-engineering (BPR), is also known as process innovation and core process re-design.

6.1 Development

The concept of BPR was originally formulated in 1990 by Michael Hammer in a seminal article for the *Harvard Business Review.* He contended that: 'In a time of rapidly changing technologies and ever-shorter product life cycles, product development often proceeds at a glacial pace. In an age of the customer, order fulfilment has high error rates and customer enquiries go unanswered for weeks. In a period when asset utilisation is critical, inventory levels exceed many months of demand. The usual methods of boosting performance - process rationalisation and automation - have not yielded the dramatic improvements companies need. In particular, heavy investments in information technology have delivered disappointing results - largely because companies tend to use technology to mechanise old ways of doing business. They leave the existing processes intact and use computers simply to speed them up.'

6.2 How it works

The chief BPR tool is a clean sheet of paper. Re-engineers start from the future and work backwards. They are unconstrained by existing methods, people or departments. In effect, they ask, 'If we were a new company, how would we run the place?' Re-engineers ask two fundamental questions about everything that happens in organisations: 'Why?' and 'What if?'. Only when they receive satisfactory answers to these questions do they then begin to explore better ways of doing things. The critical questions they then ask are:

- What is done?
- How is it done?
- Where is it done?
- When is it done?
- Who does it?
- Why do it?
- Why do it that way?
- Why do it there?
- Why do it then?
- Why that person?

6.3 Processes

By process which Hammer and Champy mean 'a collection of activities that takes one or more kinds of input and creates an output that is of value to the customer.' For example, order fulfilment is a process that takes an order as its input and results in the delivery of the ordered goods. Part of this process is the manufacture of the goods, but under BPR the aim of manufacturing is not merely to **make** the goods. Manufacturing should aim to **deliver** the goods that were **ordered**, and any aspect of the manufacturing process that hinders this aim should be re-engineered. The first question to ask might be 'Do they need to be manufactured at all?'

A **re-engineered process** has certain characteristics.

- Often several jobs are combined into one.
- Workers make decisions.
- The steps in the process are performed in a natural order.
- The same process has different versions depending on the market, or the inputs etc.
- Work is performed where it makes most sense.
- Checks and controls are reduced.
- Reconciliation is minimised.

- A case manager provides a single point of contact.
- The advantages of centralised and decentralised operations are combined.

6.4 Principles of BPR

Hammer presents seven principles for BPR.

(a) Processes should be designed to achieve a **desired outcome** rather than focusing on **existing tasks**.

(b) Personnel who **use the output from a process should perform the process**. For example, a company could set up a database of approved suppliers; this would allow personnel who actually require supplies to order them themselves, perhaps using on-line technology, thereby eliminating the need for a separate purchasing function.

(c) Information processing should be included in the work which produces the information. This **eliminates the differentiation between information gathering and information processing**.

(d) **Geographically dispersed resources should be treated as if they are centralised**. This allows the benefits of centralisation to be obtained, for example, economies of scale through central negotiation of supply contracts, without losing the benefits of decentralisation, such as flexibility and responsiveness.

(e) **Parallel activities should be linked rather than integrated**. This would involve, for example, co-ordination between teams working on different aspects of a single process.

(f) **'Doers' should be allowed to be self-managing**. The traditional distinction between workers and managers can be abolished: decision aids such as expert systems can be provided where they are required.

(g) **Information should be captured once, at source**. Electronic distribution of information makes this possible.

6.5 Characteristics

Because of its strong links to overall strategic planning, BPR cannot be planned meticulously and accomplished in small and cautious steps.

- It tends to be an **all-or-nothing proposition**, often with an uncertain result. It is therefore a **high risk** undertaking and not worth attempting unless there is a pressing need to rethink what the organisation is doing overall or in a major area.
- Many organisations trying BPR do not achieve good results because they **fail to think it through**, do not engage **hearts and minds** sufficiently, act on **bad advice or cannot override established departmental/functional power groups** which have a vested interest in the *status quo*, or in incremental change rather than radical revolution.
- Business process re-engineering has received a great deal of attention in the UK over the last couple of years and there are now concerns that it has been promoted to such an extent that it has become misunderstood. According to a recent independent study of 100 European companies, the Cobra report, BPR has become allied in managers minds with narrow targets such as reductions in staff numbers and cost-cutting measures.

NOTES

- Champy suggests that management itself should be re-engineered. Managers are not, according to Champy, used to thinking in systems terms, so, instead of looking at the whole picture (which might affect their own jobs), they tend to seize on individual aspects of the organisation, such as re-engineering of processes.

CASE EXAMPLES

Barr & Stroud, a Glasgow engineering firm, had to introduce radical changes in response to new business conditions and demands. The changes implemented through BPR included a focus on core competencies, a reduction in management layers from nine to four, and the establishment of multi-disciplinary teams with a brief to strip time and waste out of the organisation.

Many of the more celebrated BPR case histories come from the USA. *Ford* re-engineered its whole accounts payable process, covering the separate functions of purchasing, material control and accounts, with the result that the have introduced a system of invoiceless processing and have reduced their accounts payable staff headcount by 75%. *Union Carbide* eliminated $400 million of fixed costs in just three years; *Mutual Benefit Life* reduced its turnround of customer applications from 5-25 days to 2-5 days and jettisoned 100 field office positions. *IBM Credit* cut their time for preparing quotes from 7 days to one. *Bell Atlantic* reduced its delivery times from 15 days to just one.

---

7 IMPLEMENTING CHANGE

A systematic approach should be established, for planning and implementing changes.

Step

1. Determine need or desire for change in a particular area.
2. Prepare a tentative plan.
   - Brainstorming sessions a good idea, since alternatives for change should be considered (Lippitt 1981)
3. Analyse probable reactions to the change
4. Make a final decision from the choice of alternative options
   - Decision taken either by group problem-solving (participative) or by manager on his own (coercive)
5. Establish a timetable for change
   - 'Coerced' changes can probably be implemented faster, without time for discussions.
   - Speed of implementation that is achievable will depend on the likely reactions of the people affected (all in favour, half in favour, all against etc).
   - Identify those in favour of the change, and perhaps set up a pilot programme involving them. Talk with the others who resist the change.
6. Communicate the plan for change
   - This is really a continuous process, beginning at Step 1 and going through to Step 7.
7. Implement the change. Review the change.
   - Continuous evaluation and modifications

BPP PUBLISHING

7.1 The change process

In the words of John Hunt (*Managing People at Work*): 'Learning also involves re-learning - not merely learning something new but trying to unlearn what is already known.' This is, in a nutshell, the thinking behind Lewin/Schein's three stage approach to changing human behaviour, which may be depicted as follows.

UNFREEZE existing behaviour	⟶	Attitudinal/ behavioural change	⟶	REFREEZE new behaviour

Step 1. **Unfreeze** is the most difficult stage of the process, concerned mainly with 'selling' the change, with giving individuals or groups a **motive** for changing their attitudes, values, behaviour, systems or structures.

(a) If the need for change is immediate, clear and necessary for the survival of the individual or group, the unfreeze stage will be greatly accelerated.

(b) Routine changes may be harder to sell if they are perceived to be unimportant and not survival-based.

(c) Unfreezing processes need four things

- A trigger (eg a crisis).
- Someone to challenge and expose the existing behaviour pattern.
- The involvement of outsiders.
- Alterations to power structure.

Step 2. **Change** is mainly concerned with identifying what the new, desirable behaviour should be, communicating it and encouraging individuals and groups to adopt it. The new ideas must be shown to work.

Step 3. **Refreeze** is the final stage, implying consolidation or reinforcement of the new behaviour. Positive reinforcement (praise, reward) or negative reinforcement (sanctions applied to those who deviate from the new behaviour) may be used.

CASE EXAMPLE

In a Harvard Business Review article (November – December 1997), Pascale, Milleman and Groga described change at *Shell Malaysia*. Its new chairman, who arrived in 1992, found an overstaffed organisation, facing declining revenues and increased competition, and offering poorer standards. The functional departments quarrelled a great deal but the culture did not encourage outright confrontation. Their way of dealing with impasses was 'smooth and avoid'.

'For more than a year, Knight (the new chief executive) tried to achieve authentic alignment among his eight-person executive team. Somehow the goal always eluded his grasp. In exasperation, he scheduled an event to which all 260 of Shell's mid-level and senior mangers were invited. At this unusual gathering:

(a) Knight proposed two new strategic changes.

(b) Managers were asked to deal with the issues in groups and come up with a response.

(c) Most lower level managers agreed with the plans, despite the fact they realised that their operating practices would have to change.

(d) This isolated the 'obstructionist' senior managers, one of whom was fired – 'a firing heard round the world'.

7.2 Strategies for change management

Peter Honey (quoted by Robinson in *Managing after the Superlatives*) suggests that each of the causes of change identified below can be dealt with in a different way.

Cause	How to deal with it
Parochial self-interest	**Negotiation** (eg offer incentives to those resisting on grounds of self-interest).
Misunderstanding	This is best dealt with by **educating and reassuring** people. Trust has to be earned.
Different viewpoints of the situation	Change can be promoted through participation and by **involving potential resisters.**
Low tolerance of change	Force the change through and then **support** the new behaviours it requires. In short, people have to be encouraged (by carrot and stick methods) to adopt the new methods.

7.3 Champion of change model: the role of the change agent

The **champion of change model** recognises the importance of change being led by a **change agent**, who may be an individual or occasionally a group.

Step 1. **Senior management** decide in broad terms what is to be done.

Step 2. They appoint a **change agent** to drive it through. Senior management has three roles.

- Supporting the change agent, if the change provokes conflict between the agent and interest groups in the organisation
- Reviewing and monitoring the progress of the change
- Endorsing and approving the changes, and ensuring that they are publicised

Step 3. The change agent has to **win the support of functional and operational managers,** who have to introduce and enforce the changes in their own departments. The champion of change has to provide advice and information, as well as evidence that the old ways are no longer acceptable.

Step 4. The change agent **galvanises managers into action** and gives them any necessary support. The managers ensure that the changes are implemented operationally, in the field. Where changes involve, say, a new approach to customer care, it is the workers who are responsible for ensuring the effectiveness of the change process.

New information systems developments often need management support and a management sponsor.

Chapter roundup

Changes affecting organisations and communications are inextricably linked for the following reasons.

- By monitoring the system, managers can identify deviations from the plan and introduce alternatives.
- Requirements to change can be identified by communications with the organisational environment.
- The nature of the change needed requires effective communications within the organisation as well as externally.
- The way in which changes are be implemented should be ascertained by internal communication.
- Failure in internal communications can render changes ineffective in reaching the objective
- Poor communications may lead to increased resistance to change.
- Organisation development is a strategy for improving organisational effectiveness by changing the beliefs, values and structure of organisations through collaboration between an external consultant and the management of the organisation.
- OD is an organisation-wide process concerned with more than the redesign of the structure.
- OD relies on an external third party consultant - the change agent.
- The seven stages of an OD programme are: (a) preliminary planning, (b) analysis of the organisation, (c) diagnosis of problems, (d) setting aims and objectives, (e) preparing an action plan, (f) implementing the plan and reviewing progress, (g) completion of the programme and evaluation of the results.
- The change agent leaves after the end of the programme.
- Process re-engineering is similar to OD but depends more on internal teams which look at specific processes.
- OD consists of programmes to change behaviour, improve competencies and restructure the organisation.
- Management commitment to action is essential for the success of OD.

Quick Quiz

1 What external factors can give rise to the need for change?

2 Define 'outworking'.

3 List the differences between outworking and outsourcing.

4 Why can compulsory competitive tendering cause communications to be ineffective?

5 With ineffective communications, what is likely to be the view of the workforce when a process of downsizing is embarked upon?

6 How can effective communications overcome resistance to change?

7 Define 'organisation development'.

NOTES

8 What should be the scope of an OD programme?

9 What is a change agent?

10 Why is an outsider used?

11 What is process re-engineering?

12 What is the essential precondition for the success of an OD programme?

13 List the main areas of OD action programmes.

14 Give three reasons why an OD programme may fail.

Answers to Quick Quiz

1 Any change in the environment of the organisation: political, social, technological or economic. (See para 2)

2 Outworking is when a job is done from home rather than from an office. (See para 4.3)

3 Outworkers are (a) employed directly by the organisation, (b) may perform core activities and are usually individuals. Outsourcing is the practice of contracting out work; such work is usually peripheral or a support activity and is often contracted out to another organisation. (See para 4.2, 4.3)

4 Compulsory competitive tendering can result in communications being ineffective because the constant renewal of contracts inhibits the building of partnership relationships. (See para 4.2)

5 The workforce will only see the effects of downsizing in terms of redundancies, which will create feelings of job insecurity. (See para 4.1)

6 Effective communications can overcome resistance to change by involving the worker in the change process and by increasing understanding between workforce and management. (See para 4)

7 A strategy for improving organisational effectiveness. (See para 5.1)

8 Organisation wide. (See para 5.1)

9 An external consultant brought in to manage the OD programme. (See para 5.2)

10 Because of the combination of previous experience, objectivity, ability to give the job full attention, freedom from status constraints and, because the consultant leaves at the end of the programme, lack of a personal stake in the results. (See para 5.2)

11 A strategy for improving operations by setting up process teams under a process owner to find new effective ways of doing things. (See para 5.7)

12 All levels of management must be committed to it. (See para 5.9)

13 (a) Changing behaviour,
(b) improving problem solving,
(c) restructuring. (See para 5.8)

14 You could have given any of the following.

(a) Lack of management commitment.
(b) Insufficient time.
(c) Confusion of ends and means.
(d) Trying to fit major change into an old, inappropriate structure. (See para 5.10)

Answers to Activities

1 Here are four products/industries that have been forced to change in the fast ten years. You may have thought of other equally valid examples.

(a) The major players in the retail food industry have had to change the focus of their product ranges as a result of pressure from consumers to reduce prices. They have done this by introducing 'own brand' labels.

(b) Building societies have found that they cannot compete against the range of services provided by high street banks, and have thus changed from the traditional mutual society.

(c) Lucozade became less fashionable as concern regarding the sugar contents of food and drink grew. The target market of the drink changed away from the wider consumer towards the young and sporting fraternity.

(d) Fewer fur coats are now sold in the UK as a result of social pressures regarding animal cruelty.

2 Your essay should include the following points.

(a) Works councils could raise the awareness of management regarding the importance of communication with their workforce.

(b) The workforce could begin to feel that their views are important.

(c) Adversarial relationships between workers and management should begin to be broken down.

(d) Greater commitment towards the organisation may result.

(e) No change may occur in attitudes.

(f) Works councils may be 'window dressing' with no substance or commitment from management.

(g) Adversarial relationships could be created between works council and unions.

(h) Union power could be further decreased.

3 Technology has facilitated the expansion of the global organisation by:

(a) speeding up the communication process;
(b) increasing the ability to co-ordinate activities;
(c) facilitating data collection to raise awareness of customers' needs;
(d) allowing standardisation of response;
(e) enabling decision making to be better informed.

4 The relative merits of the two possible new layouts are as follows.

	Advantages	**Disadvantages**
Present layout (Figure 1)	Logical sequence to production	Cost of larger premises
	Production lines do not interfere with each other	Communication difficult between production lines
		Isolation from final assembly stops workers from feeling part of the final product
		Communication difficult along assembly lines

	Advantages	Disadvantages
Layout (a) (Figure 2)	Savings on space Less work-in-progress Central final assembly gives all workers a feeling of completing the product Communication between all workers easier 'Shorter' and 'fatter' production lines make communication and team building easier	All workers will be affected by disruption to one area, even if only mentally
Layout (b) (Figure 3)		Lines 3 and 4 are more isolated from final assembly Communication between lines 3 and 4 and final assembly more difficult

Based on these factors, your choice of layout should be layout (a) (Figure 2.) The reasons are that communications are easier, work-in-progress is reduced, team spirit is facilitated and there is a lower cost from the size of the facilities.

5 You could have included the following in your list.

(a) Trade unions - Effective communications with unions can avoid misinterpretation of your actions and the militant reaction that often accompanies such misunderstandings.

(b) Shareholders, including the money markets in general if a Plc is involved -you may need the agreement of shareholders in order to carry out your strategy. Failure to have your reasons for change understood may result in the strategy being seen as a symptom of financial difficulties. The effects of this on share prices would be detrimental to the proposed sale.

(c) The media - much of the potential misinterpretation can be averted if regular accurate information is communicated to the media.

Note. The activity asked for communication with your environment, so your answer should not include internal communication, such as with the workforce.

6 Your lists could have included the following:

(a) Hospital: security, cleaning services, laundry, sterilisation of instruments, non-emergency transport, portering.

(b) Council: gardening, refuse collection, street lighting, house and footpath maintenance, snow clearance and road gritting, library services, the running of any leisure facility.

7 You will have found that many calculations and operations were still done manually 30 years ago. The first four-function electronic calculator was produced by Sir Clive Sinclair in 1968 and cost about £70, more than a week's wages. Even bank statements were prepared by hand with cheques being posted and cleared manually. Tills printed till rolls but did

NOTES

not calculate change - that required mental arithmetic. The whole array of credit, cash and other plastic cards did not exist. Nor did cash machines and, if they had, the computer systems to manage the accounts did not. Telephones were land line based and the telex was the only way to send documents, with each one being typed in. Letters and documents were produced by typing pools, either from hand-written drafts or from shorthand dictation. Electric typewriters did not have spell checkers. Compare this with today's office.

8 Features you could include in a questionnaire include the following.

(a) Methods of feedback-formal/informal, written/verbal.

(b) Quality of feedback - marks, written report, comments on papers, verbal discussion and their extent and relevance.

(c) Timescale - time from submission to return of assignment and to feedback.

(d) Relevance of feedback to future work.

You might have suggested more written comments for reference or more discussion according to your findings.

9 The new chairman's statement is not a good start as it is likely to cause staff to fear change and redundancies. Also, it is not possible to change a culture by giving orders.

10 Academics such as Kanter and Peters have previous experience, the time available, are usually behavioural scientists trained in the sociological and psychological aspects and are obviously independent.

PART B: UNIT 14

MANAGING PEOPLE

Chapter 7 :
SELECTION AND RECRUITMENT

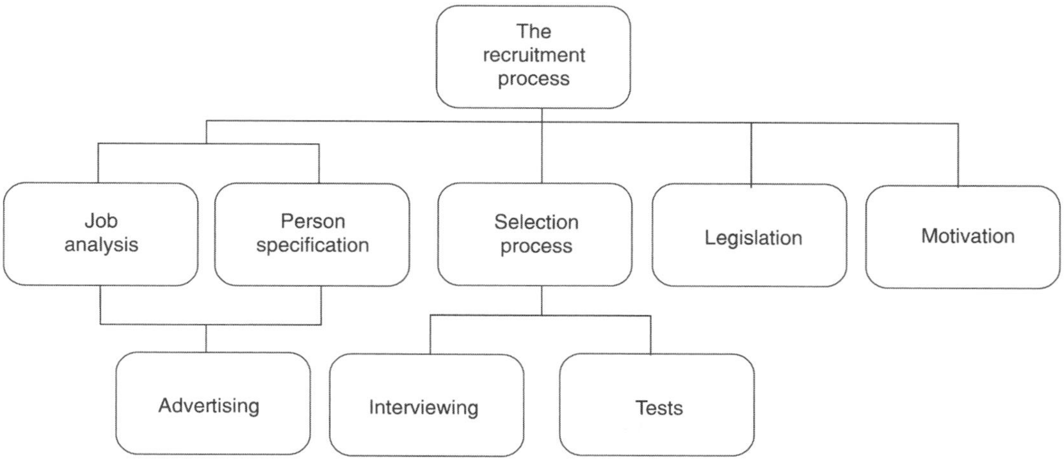

Introduction

The overall aim of the recruitment and selection process in an organisation is to obtain the quantity and quality of employees to fulfil the objectives of the organisation.

The process can be broken down into three main stages.

(i) Defining requirements, including the preparation of job descriptions, job specifications and personnel specifications

(ii) Attracting potential employees, including the evaluation and use of various methods of reaching sources of applicants

(iii) Selecting the appropriate person for the job

The recruitment and selection process is covered by legislation that relates to equal opportunities and discrimination. However, most organisations promote non-discrimination.

Once a person is recruited, it is management's responsibility to ensure that the individual's needs are satisfied and means are found to keep him or her motivated towards achieving the organisation's goals.

Your objectives

In this chapter you will learn about the following.

(a) Analysing and describing the job

(b) Information and documentation needed for clear specifications of personnel required

(c) Assessment and selection methods

(d) Relevant legislation

(e) Individual differences and motivation

1 THE RECRUITMENT PROCESS

1.1 A summary of the process

(a) Detailed **human resource planning** defines what resources the organisation needs to meet its objectives.

(b) The **sources of labour** should be forecast. **Internal** and **external** sources, and media for reaching both, will be considered.

(c) **Job analysis,** so that for any given job there is:

- (i) A **job description**: a statement of the component tasks, duties, objectives and standards
- (ii) A **job specification**: a specification of the skills, knowledge and qualities required to perform the job
- (iii) A **person specification**: a reworking of the job specification in terms of the kind of person needed to perform the job.

(d) An identification of vacancies, from the requirements of the manpower plan or by a **job requisition** from a department, branch or office which has a vacancy.

(e) Preparation and publication of advertising **information,** which will:

- (i) Attract the attention and interest of potentially suitable candidates.
- (ii) Give a favourable (but accurate) impression of the job and the organisation.
- (iii) Equip those interested to make an attractive and relevant application (how and to whom to apply, desired skills, qualifications and so on).

(f) **Processing applications** and assessing candidates.

(g) **Notifying applicants** of the results of the selection process.

NOTES

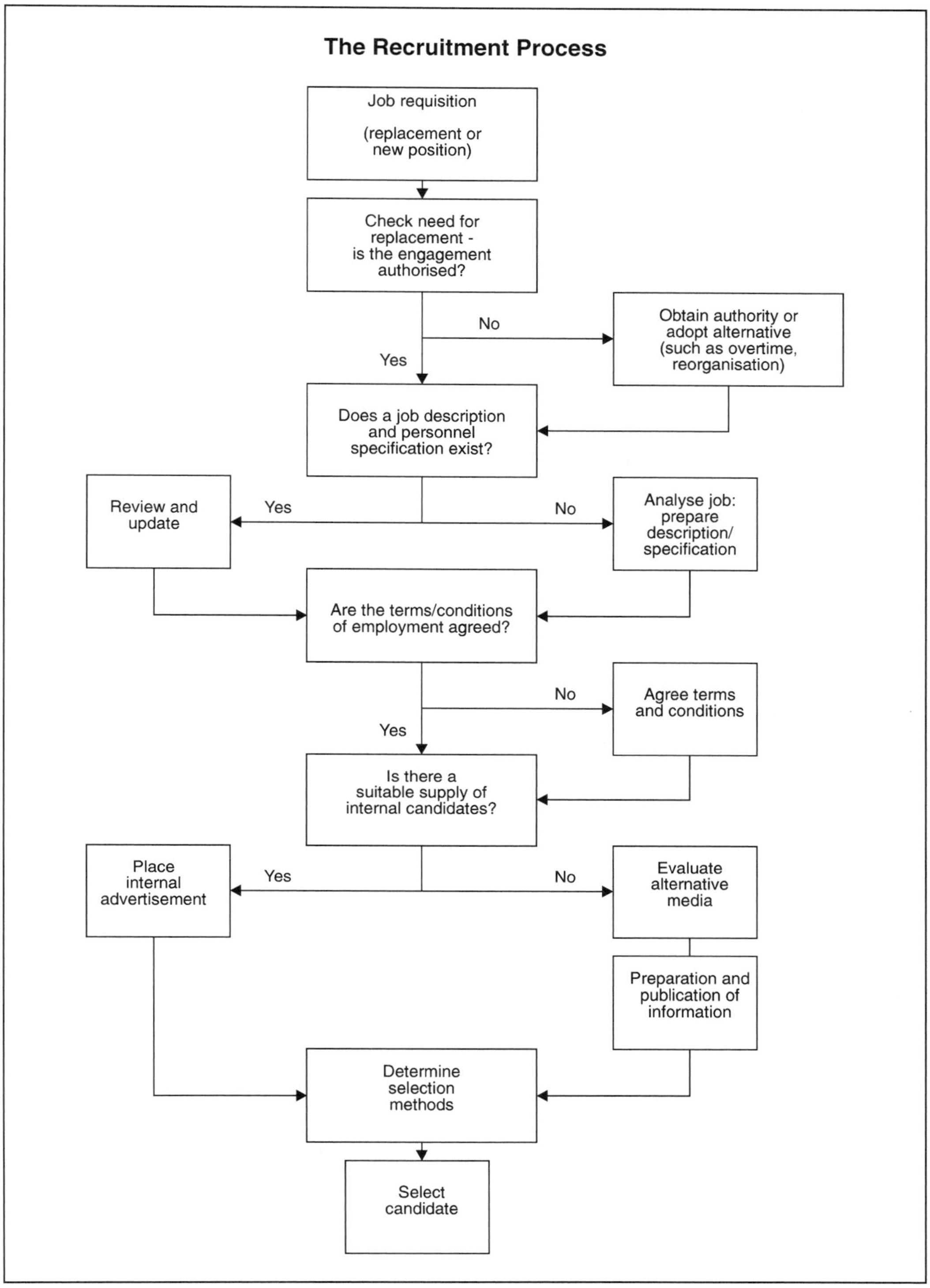

1.2 Recruitment policy

Detailed procedures for recruitment should only be devised and implemented within the context of a coherent **policy**, or code of conduct. A typical recruitment policy might deal with:

- **Internal advertisement** of vacancies
- Efficient and courteous **processing** of applications
- Fair and accurate provision of information to potential recruits
- Selection of candidates on the basis of suitability, without discrimination

NOTES

1.3 The Recruitment Code

The Institute of Personnel and Development has issued a Recruitment Code.

The IPD Recruitment Code

1 Job advertisements should state clearly the form of reply desired, in particular whether this should be a formal application form or by curriculum vitae. Preferences should also be stated if handwritten replies are required.

2 An acknowledgement of reply should be made promptly to each applicant by the employing organisation or its agent. If it is likely to take some time before acknowledgements are made, this should be made clear in the advertisement.

3 Applicants should be informed of the progress of the selection procedures, what there will be (eg group selection, aptitude tests, etc), the steps and time involved and the policy regarding expenses.

4 Detailed personal information (eg religion, medical history, place of birth, family background, etc) should not be called for unless it is relevant to the selection process.

5 Before applying for references, potential employers must secure permission of the applicant.

6 Applications must be treated as confidential.

7 The code also recommends certain courtesies and obligations on the part of the applicants.

Detailed **procedures** should be devised in order to make recruitment activity systematic and consistent throughout the organisation (especially where it is decentralised in the hands of line managers). Apart from the manpower resourcing requirements which need to be effectively and efficiently met, there is a **marketing** aspect to recruitment, as one 'interface' between the organisation and the outside world: applicants who feel they have been unfairly treated, or recruits who leave because they feel they have been misled, do not enhance the organisation's reputation in the labour market or the world at large.

Activity 1 **(30 minutes)**

Find out, if you do not already know, what are the recruitment and selection procedures in your organisation, and who is responsible for each stage. The procedures manual should set this out, or you may need to ask someone in the personnel department.

Get hold of and examine some of the documentation your organisation uses. We show specimens in this chapter, but practice and terminology varies, so your own 'house style' will be invaluable. Compare your organisation's documentation with our example.

2 JOB ANALYSIS

The management of the organisation needs to analyse the sort of work needed to be done.

NOTES

Definition

> **Job analysis** is:
>
> 'the process of collecting, analysing and setting out information about the content of jobs in order to provide the basis for a job description and data for recruitment, training, job evaluation and performance management. Job analysis concentrates on what job holders are expected to do.' (Armstrong)

The definition shows why job analysis is important - the firm has to know what people are doing in order to recruit effectively.

2.1 Information that might be obtained from a job analysis.

Information	Comments
Purpose of the job	This might seem obvious. Someone being recruited to the accounts department will be expected to process or provide financial data. But this has to be set in the context of the organisation as a whole.
Content of the job	The tasks you are expected to do. If the purpose of the job is to ensure, for example, that people get paid on time, the tasks involved include many activities related to payroll.
Accountabilities	These are the results for which you are responsible. In practice they might be phrased in the same way as a description of a task.
Performance criteria	These are the criteria which measure how good you are at the job. For a payroll technician, performance criteria includes task-related matters such as the timeliness and accuracy of your work - which are easily assessed.
Responsibility	This denotes the importance of the job. For example, a person running a department and taking decisions involving large amounts of money is more responsible that someone who only does what he or she is told. Similarly, someone might have a lot of discretion in determining what he or she will do or how he or she spends the day, whereas other people's tasks might be programmed in some detail according to a predictable routine.
Organisational factors	Who does the jobholder report to directly (line manager) or on grounds of functional authority?
Developmental factors	Relating to the job, such as likely promotion paths, if any, career prospects and so forth. Some jobs are 'dead-end' if they lead nowhere.
Environmental factors	Working conditions, security and safety issues, equipment etc.

2.2 Carrying out a job analysis

A job analysis has to be done systematically - that is why it is called an **analysis -** as the purpose is to obtain facts about the job. Therefore the job analysis involves the use of a number of different techniques to gather the data. The stages should be:

Step 1. Obtain documentary information, for main tasks etc

Step 2. Ask managers about more general aspects such as the job's purpose, the main activities, the responsibilities involved and the relationships with others.

Step 3. Ask the job holders similar questions about their jobs - perceptions might differ.

Step 4. Watch people at work - but they may not like it, and they may think you are engaged on a time and motion study.

2.3 Techniques of job analysis

Interviews establish basic facts about the job, from the job holder's point of view. You'll need to get hold of two sorts of information.

(a) **Basic facts** about the job, such as the job title, the jobholder's manager or team leader, people reporting to the jobholder, the main tasks or duties, official targets or performance standards.

(b) More **subjective issues**, which are harder to test which are still important, such as:

- The amount of supervision a person receives
- How much freedom a person has to take decisions
- How hard the job is
- The skills/qualifications you need to carry out the job
- How the job fits in elsewhere with the company
- How work is allocated
- Decision-making authority

This information should always be checked for accuracy.

2.4 Advantages and disadvantages of interviewing

Advantages	Disadvantages
Flexibility	Time consuming
Interactive	Hard to analyse
Easy to organise and carry out	Interviewee might feel on the defensive and might not be entirely frank
New or follow-on questions can be asked in the light of information received	
Reveals other organisational problems	

Interviewing procedures will be covered in greater detail later in this chapter.

Questionnaires are sometimes used in job analysis. Their success depends on the willingness of people to complete them accurately.

- They gather purely factual information
- They can cover large numbers of staff
- They provide a structure to the process of information gathering

NOTES

Checklists and inventories. A checklist would contain a list of activities and the job holder would have to note down how important these are in the job.

Activity description	Time spent on activity	Importance of activity
Processes sales invoices	Less than 10%	Unimportant
	10% to 20%	Not very important
	20-30%	Important
	...and so on	Very important

Observation. People are watched doing the job. This is easy enough for jobs which can be easily observed or which are physical, but is harder for knowledge based work. But observation is quite common in assessing performance - trainee school teachers are observed in the classroom.

Self description. Jobholders are asked to prepare their own job descriptions and to analyse their own jobs. This is quite difficult to do, because people often find it hard to stand back from what they are doing.

Diaries and logs - people keep records of what they do over a period of time, and these can be used by the analyst to develop job descriptions. You may come across something like this in your working life, if, say, you have to keep a timesheet covering work for a particular client, or if it is part of your training record.

Which method should you use? It depends. Any job analysis exercise might involve a variety of methods: Questionnaires or checklists save time. Interviews give a better idea of the detail. Self-description to shows how people *perceive* their jobs, which may be very different from how managers perceive their jobs. Diaries and logs are useful for management jobs, in which a lot is going on.

It is not always easy to carry out a job analysis, especially for managers and supervisors. In part of this text, we identified the growth of the use of **teams** and **flexible working** in which people are expected to exercise initiative. The case example below shows how job analysis techniques can be adapted

CASE EXAMPLE

People Management, 6 March 1997, described **workset**, a job analysis system developed by Belbin. Workset uses colour coding to classify work and working time into seven types.

1 Blue: tasks the job holder carries out in a prescribed manner to an approved standard
2 Yellow: individual responsibility to meet an objective (results, not means)
3 Green: tasks that vary according to the reactions and needs of others
4 Orange: shared rather than individual responsibility for meeting an objective
5 Grey: work incidental to the job, not relevant to the four core categories
6 White: new or creative undertaking outside normal duties
7 Pink: demands the presence of the job holder but leads to no useful results

The manager gives an outline of the proportion of time which the manager expects the jobholder to spend on each 'colour' of work. The job holder then briefs the manager on what has actually been done. This highlights differences: between managers' and jobholders' perceptions of jobs; between the perceptions of different jobholders in the same nominal position, who had widely different ideas as to what they were supposed to do.

Important issues arise when there is a gap in perception. Underperformance in different kinds of work can be identified, and people can be steered to the sort of work which suits them best.

Activity 2 **(10 minutes)**

Analyse your own working time according to the Workset classification above. Do the results surprise you?

2.5 Competences

A more recent approach to job design is the development and outlining of competences.

Definition

A person's **competence** is 'a capacity that leads to behaviour that meets the job demands within the parameters of the organisational environment and that, in turn, brings about desired results', (Boyzatis). Some take this further and suggest that a competence embodies the ability to transfer skills and knowledge to new situations within the occupational area.

2.6 Different sorts of competences.

(a) **Behavioural/personal** competences: underlying personal characteristics people bring to work (eg interpersonal skills); personal characteristics and behaviour for successful performance, for example, 'ability to relate well to others'. Most jobs require people to be good communicators.

(b) **Work-based/occupational competences** refer to 'expectations of workplace performance and the outputs and standards people in specific roles are expected to obtain'. This approach is used in NVQ systems (see below). They cover what people have to do to achieve the results of the job. For example, a competence of a Certified Accountant includes 'produce financial and other statements and report to management'

(c) **Generic competences** can apply to all people in an occupation.

Many lists of competences confuse the following.

- Areas of **work** at which people are competent
- Underlying aspects of behaviour

NOTES

2.7 Examples of competences for managers.

Competence area	Competence
Intellectual	• Strategic perspective • Analytical judgement • Planning and organising
Interpersonal	• Managing staff • Persuasiveness • Assertiveness and decisiveness • Interpersonal sensitivity • Oral communication
Adaptability	
Results	• Initiative • Motivation to achievement • Business sense

These competences can be elaborated by identifying *positive* and *negative* indicators.

3 JOB DESCRIPTION

The job analysis is used to develop the job description.

Definition

> **Job description**. A job description sets out the purpose of a job, where it fits in the organisation structure, the context within which the job holder functions and the principal accountability of job holders and the main tasks they have to carry out.

3.1 Purpose of job description

Purpose	Comment
Organisational	The job description defines the job's place in the organisational structure
Recruitment	The job description provides information for identifying the sort of person needed (person specification)
Legal	The job description provides the basis for a contract of employment
Performance	Performance objectives can be set around the job description

3.2 Contents of a job description

(a) **Job title** (eg Assistant Financial Controller). This indicates the function/department in which the job is performed, and the level of job within that function.

(b) **Reporting to** (eg the Assistant Financial controller reports to the Financial Controller), in other words the person's immediate boss. (No other relationships are suggested here.)

(c) **Subordinates** directly reporting to the job holders.

(d) **Overall purpose** of the job, distinguishing it from other jobs.

(e) **Principal accountabilities or main tasks**

 (i) Group the main activities into a number of broad areas.

 (ii) Define each activity as a statement of accountability: what the job holder is expected to achieve (eg **tests** new system to ensure they meet agreed systems specifications).

(f) The current fashion for multi-skilled teams means that **flexibility** is sometimes expected.

Here are two examples of job descriptions.

JOB DESCRIPTION

1 *Job title:* Baking Furnace Labourer.

2 *Department:* 'B' Baking.

3 *Date:* 20 November 19X0.

4 *Prepared by:* H Crust, baking furnace manager.

5 *Responsible to:* baking furnace chargehand.

6 *Age range:* 20-40.

7 *Supervises work of:* N/A.

8 *Has regular co-operative contract with:* Slinger/Crane driver.

9 *Main duties/responsibilities:* Stacking formed electrodes in furnace, packing for stability. Subsequently unloads baked electrodes and prepares furnace for next load.

10 *Working conditions:* stacking is heavy work and requires some manipulation of 100lb (45kg) electrodes. Unloading is hot (35° - 40°C) and very dusty.

11 *Employment conditions:*

Wages £3.60 ph + group bonus (average earnings £219.46 pw).

Hours: Continuous rotating three-shift working days, 6 days on, 2 days off. NB must remain on shift until relieved.

Trade Union: National Union of Bread Bakers, optional.

NOTES

MIDWEST BANK PLC

1 *Job title:* Clerk (Grade 2).

2 *Branch:* All branches and administrative offices.

3 *Job summary:* To provide clerical support to activities within the bank.

4 *Job content:* Typical duties will include:

(a) Cashier's duties;
(b) Processing of branch clearing;
(c) Processing of standing orders;
(d) Support to branch management.

5 *Reporting structure*

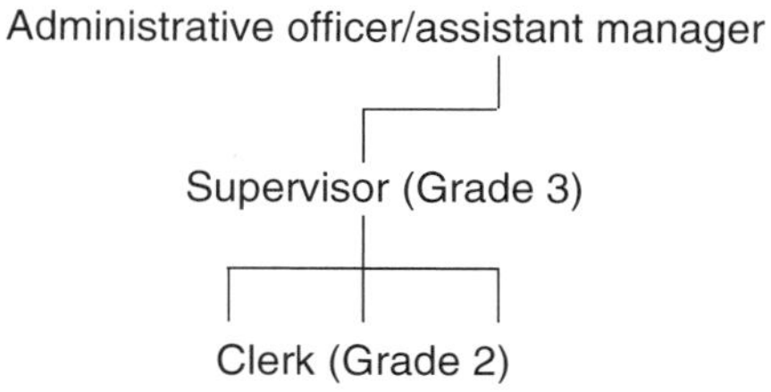

6 *Experience/education:* experience not required, minimum 3 GCSEs or equivalent.

7 *Training to be provided:* initial on-the-job training plus regular formal courses and training.

8 *Hours:* 38 hours per week.

9 *Objectives and appraisal:* Annual appraisal in line with objectives above.

10 *Salary:* refer to separate standard salary structure.

Job description prepared by: Head office personnel department.

Activity 3 **(20 minutes)**

Studying has placed you in a role in which you have to perform a fairly consistent set of duties, in fairly consistent conditions, within a structure that requires you to interact with other people, both superiors and peers (and possibly subordinates). Draw up a job description for yourself.

3.3 Alternatives to job descriptions

Detailed job descriptions are perhaps only suited for jobs where the work is largely repetitive and therefore performed by low-grade employees: once the element of **judgement** comes into a job description it becomes a straitjacket. Many difficulties arise where people adhere strictly to the contents of the job description, rather than responding flexibly to task or organisational requirements.

Perhaps job descriptions should be written in terms of the **outputs and performance levels** expected. Some firms are moving towards **accountability profiles** in which outputs and performance are identified explicitly.

Armstrong suggests a crucial difference between:

(a) A job - a group of tasks.

(b) A role. A part played by people in meeting their objectives by working competently and flexibly within the context of the organisation's objectives, structures and processes.

A **role definition** is wider than a job description. It is less concerned with the details of the job content, but how they interpret the job, and how they perceive them.

CASE EXAMPLE

Guinness

According to *People Management*, 11 September 1997, in May 1996 Guinness Brewing Great Britain introduced a new pay system based on competences.

Restrictive job definitions, lengthy job descriptions and a 24-grade structure were replaced by broad role profiles and three pay bands. Roles are now specified in terms of 'need to do' (primary accountabilities), 'need to know' (experience and knowledge requirements) and 'need to be' (levels of competence).

Competences are defined as 'the skill, knowledge and behaviours that need to be applied for effective performance'. There are seven of them, including commitment to results and interpersonal effectiveness. Roles are profiled against each relevant competence and individuals' actual competences are compared with the requirements through the performance management process.

Activity 4 **(30 minutes)**

Without looking at the real thing, to start with, draw up a job description for your own job and for the job of a personnel officer in your organisation. Now look at the official job descriptions. Are they true, detailed and up-to-date, compared with the actual jobs as you saw them? If not, what does this tell you about (a) job descriptions and (b) perceptions of the personnel function?

4 PERSON SPECIFICATION

Definition

'A **person specification**, also known as a job or personnel specification, sets out the education, qualifications, training, experience personal attributes and competences a job holder requires to perform her or his job satisfactorily.' (Armstrong)

The job description outlines the job: the person specification describes the person needed to do the job. For example, a position of secretary or personal assistant normally requires the holder to have word processing skills.

4.1 Traditional approaches to the person specification

The **Seven Point Plan** put forward by Professor Rodger in 1951 draws the selector's attention to seven points about the candidate.

- **Physical attributes** (such as neat appearance, ability to speak clearly)
- **Attainment** (including educational qualifications)
- **General intelligence**
- **Special aptitudes** (such as neat work, speed and accuracy)
- **Interests** (practical and social)
- **Disposition** (or manner: friendly, helpful and so on)
- Background **circumstances**

4.2 Problems with the Seven Point Plan.

(a) Physical attributes or disposition might include a person's demeanour. **Eye contact** is considered a sign of honesty and frankness in some cultures, but a sign of disrespect in others.

(b) **General intelligence** is not something that can be measured easily. A criticism of IQ tests is that test scores tell you that you are good at doing IQ tests - and not much else.

(c) **Attainment**: educational qualifications - no attention is paid to the circumstances in which these were obtained.

The plan does not identify a person's **potential**, or suggest how it can be aligned precisely to the organisation's requirements.

4.3 Five-Point Pattern

Munro-Fraser's Five Point Pattern is one alternative.

- **Impact on others**: physical attributes, speech, manner
- **Acquired knowledge** and qualifications
- **Innate abilities**: ability to learn, mental agility
- **Motivation**: What sort of goals does the individual set, how much effort goes into achieving them, how successful.
- **Adjustment**: emotional stability, tolerance of slips.

4.4 New approaches: competences

The two methods described above have been in use for many years. More recruiters are using **competences** (see paragraph 2.5) in designing the person specification.

4.5 Preparing the specification

Each feature in the person specification should be classified as:

(a) **Essential.** For instance, honesty in a cashier is essential whilst a special aptitude for conceptual thought is not.

(b) **Desirable.** For instance, a reasonably pleasant manner should ensure satisfactory standards in a person dealing with the public.

(c) **Contra-indicated**. Some features are actively disadvantageous, such as an inability to work in a team when acting as project leader.

PERSON SPECIFICATION: Customer Accounts Manager

	ESSENTIAL	DESIRABLE	CONTRA-INDICATED
Physical attributes	Clear speech Well-groomed Good health	Age 25-40	Age under 25 Chronic ill-health and absence
Attainments	2 'A' levels GCSE Maths and English Thorough knowledge of retail environment	Degree (any discipline) Marketing training 2 years' experience in supervisory post	No experience of supervision or retail environment
Intelligence	High verbal intelligence		
Aptitudes	Facility with numbers Attention to detail and accuracy Social skills for customer relations	Analytical abilities (problem solving) Understanding of systems and IT	No mathematical ability Low tolerance of technology
Interests	Social: team activity		Time-consuming hobbies 'Solo' interests only
Disposition	Team player Persuasive Tolerance of pressure and change	Initiative	Anti-social Low tolerance of responsibility
Circumstances	Able to work late, take work home	Located in area of office	

Activity 5 **(30 minutes)**

Turn your job description for A student into a corresponding Personnel Specification, using the 'essential; desirable; contra-indicated' framework, and either the Seven Point Plan or Five Point Pattern. If you did not do Activity 4, do it now! (You might like to consider into which section of your personnel specification 'laziness' would fall....)

5 ADVERTISING THE POSITION

The object of recruitment advertising is to attract suitable candidates and deter unsuitable candidates.

5.1 Content of the advertisement

It should be:

(a) **Concise**, but comprehensive enough to be an accurate description of the job, its rewards and requirements.

(b) **Attractive** to the maximum number of the right people.

(c) **Positive and honest** about the organisation. Disappointed expectations will be a prime source of dissatisfaction when an applicant actually comes into contact with the organisation.

(d) **Relevant and appropriate to the job and the applicant**. Skills, qualifications and special aptitudes required should be prominently set out, along with special features of the job that might attract - on indeed deter - applicants, such as shiftwork or extensive travel.

The advertisement, based on information set out in the job description, job and person specifications and recruitment procedures, should contain information about:

(a) The **organisation**: its main business and location, at least.

(b) The **job**: title, main duties and responsibilities and special features.

(c) **Conditions**: special factors affecting the job.

(d) **Qualifications and experience** (required, and preferred); other attributes, aptitudes and/or knowledge required.

(e) **Rewards**: salary, benefits, opportunities for training, career development, and so on.

(f) **Application process**: how to apply, to whom, and by what date.

It should encourage a degree of **self-selection**, so that the target population begins to narrow itself down. The information contained in the advertisement should deter unsuitable applicants as well as encourage potentially suitable ones.

5.2 Factors influencing the choice of advertising medium

(a) **The type of organisation**. A factory is likely to advertise a vacancy for an unskilled worker in a different way to a company advertising for a member of the Institute of Personnel and Development for an HRM position.

(b) **The type of job**. Managerial jobs may merit national advertisement, whereas semi--skilled jobs may only warrant local coverage, depending on the supply of suitable candidates in the local area. Specific skills may be most appropriately reached through trade, technical or professional journals, such as those for accountants or computer programmers.

(c) **The cost of advertising**. It is more expensive to advertise in a national newspaper than on local radio, and more expensive to advertise on local radio than in a local newspaper etc.

(d) The **readership and circulation** (type and number of readers/listeners) of the medium, and its suitability for the number and type of people the organisation wants to reach.

(e) The **frequency** with which the organisation wants to advertise the job vacancy, and the duration of the recruitment process.

Activity 6 **(20 minutes)**

Dealing with individuals demands a certain... ...um...

You've heard the old line...
'You don't have to be mad to work here, but it helps'. It's like that at AOK, but in the nicest possible way. We believe that our Personnel Department should operate for the benefit of our staff, and not that staff should conform to statistical profiles. It doesn't make for an easy life, but dealing with people as individuals, rather than numbers, certainly makes it a rewarding one.

We're committed to an enlightened personnel philosophy. We firmly believe that our staff are our most important asset, and we go a long way both to attract the highest quality of people, and to retain them.

AOK is a company with a difference. We're a highly progressive, international organisation, one of the world's leading manufacturers in the medical electronics field.

...Character

As an expanding company, we now need another experienced Personnel Generalist to join us at our UK headquarters in Reigate, Surrey.

Essentially we're looking for an individual, a chameleon character who will assume an influential role in recruitment, employee relations, salary administration, compensation and benefits, or whatever the situation demands. The flexibility to interchange with various functions is vital. Within your designated area, you'll experience a large degree of independence. You'll be strong in personality, probably already experienced in personnel management in a small company. Whatever your background you'll certainly be someone who likes to help people help themselves and who is happy to get involved with people at all levels within the organisation.

Obviously, in a fast growing company with a positive emphasis on effective personnel work, your prospects for promotion are excellent. Salaries are highly attractive and benefits are, of course, comprehensive.

So if you're the kind of personnel individual who enjoys personal contact, problem solving, and will thrive on the high pace of a progressive, international organisation, such as AOK, get in touch with us by writing or telephoning, quoting ref: 451/BPD, to AOK House, Reigate, Surrey.

What do you think of this advertisement? How can you improve it?

5.3 Media for recruitment advertising

(a) **In-house magazine, notice-boards,** e-mail or its 'intra-net'. An organisation might invite applications from employees who would like a transfer or a promotion to the particular vacancy advertised.

(b) **Professional and specialist newspapers or magazines,** such as *Accountancy Age*, *Marketing Week* or *Computing.*

(c) **National newspapers** are used for senior management jobs or vacancies for skilled workers, where potential applicants will not necessarily be found through local advertising.

(d) **Local newspapers** would be suitable for jobs where applicants are sought from the local area.

(e) **Local radio, television and cinema.** These are becoming increasingly popular, especially for large-scale campaigns for large numbers of vacancies.

(f) **Job centres**. Vacancies for unskilled work (rather than skilled work or management jobs) are advertised through local job centres, although in theory any type of job can be advertised here.

(g) **School and university careers offices.** Ideally, the manager responsible for recruitment in an area should try to maintain a close liaison with careers officers. Some large organisations organise special meetings or **careers fairs** in universities and colleges (the so-called 'milk round'), as a kind of showcase for the organisation and the careers it offers.

(h) The **Internet**. Any personal computer user may access the network, independently or via an internet service provider such as CompuServe.

6 THE SELECTION PROCESS IN OUTLINE

Step 1. Deal with responses to job advertisements. This might involve sending **application forms** to candidates. Not all firms bother with these, however, preferring to review CVs.

Step 2. Assess each application or CV against **key criteria** in the job advertisement and specification. Critical factors may include age, qualifications, experience or whatever.

Step 3. **Sort applications** into 'possible', 'unsuitable' and 'marginal'.

'Possibles' will then be more closely scrutinised, and a shortlist for interview drawn up. Ideally, this should be done by both the personnel specialist and the prospective manager of the successful candidate.

Step 4. **Invite candidates for interviews.**

Step 5. Reinforce interviews with **selection testing,** if suitable.

Step 6. Review un-interviewed 'possibles', and 'marginals', and put potential future candidates on hold, or in reserve.

Step 7. Send standard letters to unsuccessful applicants, and inform them simply that they have not been successful. Reserves will be sent a holding letter: 'We will keep your details on file, and should any suitable vacancy arise in future...'.

Step 8. Make a provisional offer to the recruit.

Sometimes Steps 4 and 5 will be reversed, so that **testing** comes before **interviewing.** There are good reasons for this, as we shall see.

7 APPLICATION FORMS

Job advertisements usually ask candidates to fill in a **job application form**, or to send information about themselves and their previous job experience (their CV or **curriculum vitae**), usually with a covering letter briefly explaining why they think they are qualified to do the job.

7.1 Purposes of application forms

Weeding out unsuitable candidates
Identifying possible candidates

Application forms fulfil these jobs in two ways.

Asking specific questions	• The application form will be designed around the personnel specification. So, if a certain number of GCSE's are needed, the applicant will be asked to list educational qualifications. • Certain questions **cannot** be asked by law, on account of equal opportunities legislation.
Finding out more	Give candidates the ability to **write about themselves,** their ambitions, why they want the job. Some application forms ask people to write about key successes and failures. This gives information about the candidate's underlying personality as well as matters such as neatness, literacy and the ability to communicate in writing.

EXAMPLE

Page 1

AOK PLC

APPLICATION FORM

Post applied for ....

PERSONAL DETAILS

Surname Mr/ Mrs/ Miss/Ms
First name
Address

Post code
Telephone (Daytime) (Evenings)
Date of birth
Nationality
Marital status
Dependants

EDUCATION AND TRAINING

- Qualifications

  List academic and/or professional qualifications. (Use initials eg GCSE, 'O' levels, BSc, ACCA, MBA etc).

Education (latest first)

Date		Institution	Exams passed/qualifications
From	To		

TRAINING AND OTHER SKILLS

Please give details of any specialised training courses you have attended.

Please note down other skills such as languages (and degree of fluency), driving licence (with endorsements if any), keyboard skills (familiarity with software package).

EMPLOYMENT

Page 2

Dates		Employer name and address	Title and duties
From	To		

Current salary and benefits ...

INTERESTS

Please describe your leisure/hobby/sporting interests

YOUR COMMENTS

Why do you think you are suitable for the job advertised?

ADDITIONAL INFORMATION

Do you have any permanent health problems? If so, please give details.

When would you be able to start work?

REFERENCES

Please give two references. One should be a former employer.

Name Address	Name Address
Position	Position
Signed	Date

> **Activity 6** **(10 minutes)**
>
> Suggest four possible design faults in job application forms - you may be able to draw on your own personal experience.

7.2 Application forms and CVs

Many firms are either **too small** or cannot be bothered to design a standard application form for all posts. The requirements of a business employing, say, 30 people, are very different from a large employer such as the Civil Service or British Airways. This is why many job advertisements ask for a **curriculum vitae (CV)** and a covering letter.

How a CV is presented will tell you a great deal about the candidate - not only the information on the CV but the candidate's neatness and ability to structure information.

Application forms have the merit of being standardised, so that all candidates are asked the same information. Gaps can thus be identified clearly, and essential information can be asked for. CVs on the other hand are easy to mould and manipulate.

7.3 Sifting application forms and CVs: biodata

For some jobs, hundreds or even thousands of people might apply, and so to reduce all this to manageable proportion, recruiters can use structured ways of sifting the data. Some firms even use computers to identify items on CVs or application forms in order to rank the candidates in order to generate a shortlist.

Biodata is the term given to techniques which aim to score and structure biographical information about a candidate in order to predict work performance.

(a) A **biodata questionnaire**, which might even be appended to the application form, asks specific questions about:

- Demographic details (age, sex, family circumstances)
- Education and professional qualifications
- Previous employment history and work experience
- Positions of responsibility outside work
- Leisure interests
- Career and job motivation

(b) **Each item is given a weight**. For example, education and professional qualifications might account for up to 20 marks; leisure interests might account for up to ten marks. Within each weight the candidate is given a score.

(c) The **scores are added up**, to give the candidate a total. A candidate who scores below a certain level will not be accepted.

Biodata is only really suitable when large numbers of applicants have to be screened. Furthermore, the biodata weights are based on the scores of existing employees, so a large workforce is needed for any meaningful correlation to be made between biodata and work performance.

8 SELECTION METHODS IN OUTLINE

We will briefly list the main selection methods here. The more important are discussed in the following sections.

BPP PUBLISHING

Methods	Examples
Interviewing	• Individual (one-to-one) • Interview panels • Selection boards • Assessment centres
Biodata	
Selection tests	• Intelligence • Aptitudes • Personality • Proficiency
Work sampling	
Group selection methods	

9 INTERVIEWS

Most firms use the selection interview as their main source for decision-making.

9.1 Purpose of the interview

(a) Finding the best person for the job, by giving making the organisation a chance to assess applicants (and particularly their interpersonal communication skills) directly.

(b) Making sure that applicants understand what the job, what the career prospects are and have suitable information about the company.

(c) Giving the best possible impression of the organisation - after all, the candidate may have other offers elsewhere.

(d) Making all applicants feel that they have been given **fair treatment** in the interview, whether they get the job or not.

9.2 Conducting selection interviews: matters to be kept in mind

(a) The **impression** of the organisation given by the interview arrangements.

(b) The **psychological effects** of the location of the interview and seating arrangements.

(c) The **manner and tone** of the interviewers.

(d) Getting the candidates to talk freely (by asking open questions) and honestly (by asking probing questions), in accordance with the organisation's need for **information.**

(e) The **opportunity for the candidate to learn** about the job and organisation.

(f) The control of **bias** or hasty judgement by the interviewer.

9.3 Preparation for the interview

Welcoming the candidate. Candidates should be given:

(a) Clear instructions about the date, time and location - perhaps with a map.
(b) The name of a person to contact.

(c) A place to wait (with cloakroom facilities), perhaps with tea or coffee.

The interview room

(a) The interview is where the organisation 'sells' itself and the candidate aims to give a good impression. The layout of the room should be carefully designed. Being 'interrogated' by two people from the other side of a desk may be completely unsuitable.

(b) Some interviews are **deliberately** tough, to see how a candidate performs under pressure.

The agenda. The agenda and questions will be based on:

(a) The job description and what abilities are required of the jobholder.

(b) The personnel specification. The interviewer must be able to judge whether the applicant matches up to the personal qualities required from the jobholder.

(c) The application form or the applicant's CV: the qualities the applicant claims to possess.

9.4 Conduct of the interview

Questions should be paced and put carefully. The interviewer should not be trying to confuse the candidate, plunging immediately into demanding questions or picking on isolated points; neither, however, should s(he) allow the interviewee to digress or gloss over important points. The interviewer must retain control over the information-gathering process.

Type of question	Comment
Open questions	('Who...? What...? Where...? When...? Why....?) These force candidates to put together their own responses in complete sentences. This encourages them to talk, keeps the interview flowing, and is most revealing ('Why do you want to be a marketing assistant?')
Probing questions	Similar to open questions, these aim to discover the deeper significance of the candidate's answers, especially if they are initially dubious, uninformative, too short, or too vague. ('But what was it about marketing that **particularly** appealed to you?')
Closed questions	Invite only 'yes' or 'no' answers: ('Did you...?, 'Have you...?'). (a) They elicit an answer **only** to the question asked. This may be useful where there are small points to be established ('Did you pass your exam?') (b) Candidates cannot express their personality, or interact with the interviewer on a deeper level. (c) They make it easier for candidates to conceal things ('You never **asked** me...'). (d) They make the interviewer work very hard.

Type of question	Comment
Multiple questions	Two or more questions are asked at once. ('Tell me about your last job? How did your knowledge of accountancy help you there, and do you think you are up-to-date or will you need to spend time studying?'). This encourages the candidate to talk at some length, without straying too far from the point. It might also test the candidate's ability to listen, and to handle large amount of information.
Problem solving questions	Present the candidate with a situation and ask him/her to explain how he/she would deal with it. ('How would you motivate your staff to do a task that they did not want to do?'). Such questions are used to establish whether the candidate will be able to deal with the sort of problems that are likely to arise in the job.
Leading questions	Encourage the candidate to give a certain reply. ('We are looking for somebody who likes detailed figure work. How much do you enjoy dealing with numbers?' or 'Don't you agree that…?' 'Surely…?). The danger with this type of question is that the candidate will give the answer that he thinks the interviewer wants to hear.

Activity 7 **(10 minutes)**

Identify the type of question used in the following examples, and discuss the opportunities and constraints they offer the interviewee who must answer them.

(a) 'So, you're interested in a Business Studies degree, are you, Jo?'

(b) 'Surely you're interested in Business Studies, Jo?'

(c) 'How about a really useful qualification like a Business Studies degree, Jo? Would you consider that?'

(d) 'Why are you interested in a Business Studies degree, Jo?

(e) 'Why particularly Business Studies, Jo?'

9.5 Evaluating the response

(a) The interviewer must **listen carefully** to the responses and evaluate them so as to judge what the **candidate** is:

- Wanting to say
- Trying **not** to say
- Saying, but does not mean, or is lying about
- Having difficulty saying

(b) In addition, the interviewer will have to be aware when he/she is hearing:

- Something he/she needs to know
- Something he/she **doesn't** need to know

- Only what he/she **expects** to hear
- Inadequately - when his or her own attitudes, perhaps prejudices, are getting in the way of an objective response to the candidate

Candidates should be given the opportunity to ask questions. The choice of questions might well have some influence on how the interviewers assess a candidate's interest in and understanding of the job. Moreover, there is information that the candidate will need to know about the organisation, the job, and indeed the interview process.

9.6 Types of interview

Individual or **one-to-one interviews**. These are the **most common** selection method.

(a) **Advantages**

(i) **Direct** face-to-face communication.

(ii) **Rapport** between the candidate and the interviewer: each has to give attention solely to the other, and there is potentially a relaxed atmosphere, if the interviewer is willing to establish an informal style.

(b) The **disadvantage** of a one-to-one interview is the scope it allows for a biased or superficial decision.

(i) The **candidate** may be able to **disguise** lack of knowledge in a specialist area of which the interviewer knows little.

(ii) The **interviewer's** perception may be selective or **distorted**, and this lack of objectivity may go unnoticed and unchecked.

(iii) The greater opportunity for personal rapport with the candidate may cause a **weakening of the interviewer's objective judgement**.

Panel interviews are designed to overcome such disadvantages. A panel may consist of two or three people who together interview a single candidate: most commonly, an HR specialist and the departmental manager who will have responsibility for the successful candidate. This saves the firm time and enables better assessment.

Large formal panels, or **selection boards**, may also be convened where there are a number of individuals or groups with an interest in the selection.

(a) **Advantage**. A number of people see candidates, and share information about them at a single meeting: similarly, they can compare their assessments on the spot, without a subsequent effort at liaison and communication.

(b) **Drawbacks**

(i) Questions tend to be more varied, and more random, since there is **no single guiding force** behind the interview strategy. The candidate may have trouble switching from one topic to another so quickly, especially if questions are not led up to, and not clearly put - as may happen if they are unplanned. Candidate are also seldom allowed to expand their answers and so may not be able to do justice to themselves.

(ii) If there is a **dominating member** of the board, the interview may have greater continuity - but that individual may also influence the judgements of other members.

(iii) Some candidates may not perform well in a formal, artificial situation such as the board interview, and may find such a situation extremely stressful.

(iv) Research shows that **board members rarely agree** with each other in their judgements about candidates.

9.7 The limitations of interviews

Interviews are criticised because **they fail to provide accurate predictions** of how a person will perform in the job, partly because of the nature of interviews, partly because of the errors of judgement by interviewers.

Problem	Comment
Scope	• An interview is **too brief** to 'get to know' candidates in the kind of depth required to make an accurate prediction of work performance. • An interview is an **artificial situation**: candidates may be on their best behaviour or, conversely, so nervous that they do not do themselves justice. Neither situation reflects what the person is really like.
The halo effect	A tendency for people to make an initial **general judgement** about a person based on a **single obvious attribute**, such as being neatly dressed or well-spoken. This single attribute will colour later perceptions, and might make an interviewer mark the person up or down on every other factor in their assessments
Contagious bias	The interviewer changes the behaviour of the applicant by suggestion. The applicant might be led by the wording of questions or non-verbal cues from the interviewer, and change what (s)he is doing or saying in response.
Stereotyping	Stereotyping groups people together who are assumed to share certain characteristics (women, say, or vegetarians), then attributes certain traits to the group as a whole (emotional, socialist etc). It then (illogically) assumes that each individual member of the supposed group will possess that trait.
Incorrect assessment	Qualitative factors such as motivation, honesty or integrity are very difficult assess in an interview.
Logical error	An interviewer might decide that a young candidate who has held two or three jobs in the past for only a short time will be unlikely to last long in any job. (Not necessarily so.)
Inexperienced interviewers	• Inability to evaluate information about a candidate properly • Failure to compare a candidate against the requirements for a job or a personnel specification • Bad planning of the interview • Failure to take control of the direction and length of the interview • A tendency either to act as an inquisitor and make candidates feel uneasy or to let candidates run away with the interview • A reluctance to probe into fact and challenge statements where necessary

While some interviewers may be experts for the human resources function, it is usually thought desirable to include **line managers** in the interview team. They cannot be full-time interviewers, obviously: they have their other work to do. No matter how much training they are given in the interview techniques, they will lack continuous experience, and probably not give interviewing as much thought or interest as they should.

10 TESTS

In some job selection procedures, an interview is supplemented by some form of **selection test**. Tests must be:

(a) **Sensitive** enough to discriminate between different candidates.

(b) **Standardised** on a representative sample of the population, so that a person's results can be interpreted meaningfully.

(c) **Reliable**: in that the test should measure the same thing whenever and to whomever it is applied.

(d) **Valid**: it measures what it is supposed to measure.

10.1 Types of tests

The science of measuring mental capacities and processes is called 'psychometrics'; hence the term **psychometric testing**. Types of test commonly used in practice are:

- Intelligence tests
- Aptitude tests
- Personality tests
- Proficiency tests

Intelligence tests. Tests of **general intellectual ability** typically test memory, ability to think quickly and logically, and problem solving skills.

(a) Most people have experience of IQ tests and the like, and few would dispute their validity as good measure of **general** intellectual capacity.

(b) However, there is no agreed definition of intelligence.

Aptitude tests. Aptitude tests are designed to **measure** and predict an individual's potential for performing a job or learning new skills.

- **Reasoning**: verbal, numerical and abstract
- **Spatio-visual ability**: practical intelligence, non-verbal ability and creative ability
- **Perceptual speed and accuracy**: clerical ability
- '**Manual**' **ability**: mechanical, manual, musical and athletic

Personality tests. Personality tests may measure a variety of characteristics, such as an applicant's skill in dealing with other people, his ambition and motivation or his emotional stability.

CASE EXAMPLE

Probably the best known example is the 16PF, originally developed by Cattell in 1950.

The 16PF comprises 16 scales, each of which measure a factor that influences the way a person behaves.

The factors are functionally different underlying personality characteristics, and each is associated with not just one single piece of behaviour but rather is the source of a relatively broad range of behaviours. For this reason the factors themselves are referred to as source traits and the behaviours associated with them are called surface traits.

The advantage of measuring source traits, as the 16PF does, is that you end up with a much richer understanding of the person because you are not just describing what can be seen but also the characteristics underlying what can be seen.

The 16PF analyses how a person is likely to behave generally including, for example, contribution likely to be made to particular work contexts, aspects of the work environment to which the person is likely to more or less suited, and how best to manage the person.

The validity of such tests has been much debated, but is seems that some have been shown by research to be valid predictors of job performance, so long as they are used **properly.**

Proficiency tests. Proficiency tests are perhaps the most closely related to an assessor's objectives, because they **measure ability to do the work involved**. An applicant for an audio typist's job, for example, might be given a dictation tape and asked to type it.

10.2 Trends in the use of tests

(a) Continuing enthusiasm for personality tests.

(b) The continuing influence of cognitive ability intelligence tests.

(c) A focus on certain popular themes - sales ability or aptitude, customer orientation, motivation, teamworking and organisational culture are mentioned.

(d) The growing diversity of test producers and sources (meaning more choice, but also more poor quality measures).

(e) Expanded packages of tests, including tapes, computer disks, workbooks and so on.

(f) A growing focus on fairness: the most recent edition of the 16PF test, for example, has been scrutinised by expert psychologists to exclude certain types of content that might lead to bias.

10.3 Limitations of testing

(a) There is not always a direct relationship between ability in the test and ability in the job: the job situation is very different from artificial test conditions.

(b) The **interpretation of test results is a skilled task**, for which training and experience is essential. It is also highly subjective (particularly in the case of personality tests), which belies the apparent scientific nature of the approach.

(c) Additional difficulties are experienced with particular kinds of test. For example:

  (i) An aptitude test measuring arithmetical ability would need to be constantly revised or its content might become known to later applicants.

  (ii) Personality tests can often give misleading results because applicants seem able to guess which answers will be looked at most favourably.

NOTES

(iii) It is difficult to design intelligence tests which give a fair chance to people from different cultures and social groups and which test the **kind** of intelligence that the organisation wants from its employees: the ability to **score highly in IQ** tests does not necessarily correlate with desirable traits such as mature **judgement** or **creativity**, merely mental ability.

(iv) Most tests are subject to coaching and practice effects.

(d) **It is difficult to exclude bias from tests.** Many tests (including personality tests) are tackled less successfully by women than by men, or by some candidates born overseas than by indigenous applicants because of the particular aspect chosen for testing.

11 OTHER SELECTION METHODS

11.1 Group selection methods

Group selection methods might be used by an organisation as the final stage of a selection process as a more 'natural' and in-depth appraisal of candidates. Group assessments tend to be used for posts requiring leadership, communication or teamworking skills: advertising agencies often use the method for selecting account executives, for example.

They consist of a series of tests, interviews and group situations over a period of two days, involving a **small number of candidates for a job**. After an introductory session to make the candidates feel at home, they will be given one or two tests, one or two individual interviews, and several group situations in which the candidates are invited to discuss problems together and arrive at solutions as a management team.

11.2 Techniques in such programmes

(a) **Group role-play exercises**, in which they can explore (and hopefully display) interpersonal skills and/or work through simulated managerial tasks.

(b) **Case studies**, where candidates' analytical and problem-solving abilities are tested in working through described situations/problems, as well as their interpersonal skills, in taking part in (or leading) group discussion of the case study.

These group sessions might be thought useful because:

(a) They give the organisation's **selectors a longer opportunity to study the candidates.**

(b) **They reveal more than application forms, interviews and tests alone** about the ability of candidates to persuade others, negotiate with others, and explain ideas to others and also to investigate problems efficiently. These are typically **management skills.**

(c) They reveal more about how the **candidate's personalities and attributes will affect the work team** and his own performance.

11.3 Work sampling

Work sampling involves getting the candidate to spend **some time doing the job**, in actual or simulated conditions. A firm wanting to recruit someone to do typesetting work can simply sit that person down in front of a wordprocessor or PC for a few hours to see how they do the job.

12 LEGISLATION

12.1 Equal opportunities and discrimination

As with other areas of management, recruitment and selection is subject to certain restrictions. The main statutes which affect this subject relate to equal opportunities and discrimination, and include the following:

(i) The Equal Pay Act 1970

(ii) The Sex Discrimination Act 1975

(iii) The Disability Discrimination Act 1995 and The Disability Rights Commission Act 1999

(iv) The Race Relations Act 1976, and

(v) The Rehabilitation of Offenders Act 1974

The Equal Pay Act 1970 makes it clear that where men and women are employed in like work or work of an equivalent nature they will receive the same terms and conditions of employment.

The provisions apply equally to men and women (ie a man can also claim if he has a less favourable term than a woman).

The Sex Discrimination Act 1975 renders it unlawful to make any form of discrimination in employment affairs because of martial status or sex. This applies especially to the selection process as it offers protection to both sexes against unfair treatment on appointment.

There are two kinds of discrimination, direct and indirect.

- Direct discrimination occurs when someone is treated less favourably than someone of the opposite sex – perhaps by being banned from applying for a job because of being a woman. This type of discrimination is not difficult to discover.
- Indirect discrimination. In this case, an employer may relate a condition to an applicant for a job which does not actually seem relevant to it but which suggests that only one sex would be acceptable. An example of this may be advertising so that only men are encouraged to apply.

The Disability Discrimination Act 1995 gives disabled people similar rights to those already enjoyed in relation to sex and race. The **Disability Rights Commission Act 1999** received Royal Assent in July 1999 and has provided for the establishment of a **Disability Rights Commission,** which has the same powers as the Equal Opportunities Commission and the Commission for Racial Equality when determining whether unlawful discrimination has taken place. All accusations of discrimination can be taken to an **employment tribunal** where the penalties are similar to those already in operation for race and sex.

The Race Relations Act 1976 makes it unlawful to discriminate on grounds of:

(i) race
(ii) colour
(iii) nationality, and
(iv) ethnic or national origin.

Rehabilitation of Offenders Act 1974. Although this Act declares that former convictions are not relevant and do not have to be stated at interviews for jobs, many exceptions are given and no remedy is forthcoming where someone is discriminated against during selection.

12.2 Promotion of non discrimination

'Equal opportunities' is a generic term describing the belief that there should be an equal chance for all workers to apply and be selected for jobs, to be trained and promoted in employment and to have that employment terminated fairly. Employers should only discriminate according to ability, experience and potential. All employment decisions should be based solely on a person's ability to do the job in question. No consideration should be taken of a person's sex, age, racial origin, disability or marital status.

A number of employers label themselves as equal opportunity employers, establishing their own particular kind of equal opportunity policy. While some protection is afforded by employment legislation, the majority of everyday cases must rely on good practice to prevail.

Developing and applying good working practice should cover all of the aspects of human resource management including the following:

- (i) recruitment
- (ii) terms and conditions of employment
- (iii) promotion, transfer and training
- (iv) benefits, facilities and services, and
- (v) dismissal

The main areas where good practice can be demonstrated are as follows.

Job analysis – person specifications must not be more favourable to men or women.

Advertisements and documentation must not discriminate on sex or marital status grounds. This means that job titles must be sexless, eg 'salesman' becomes 'sales person'.

Employee interviewing and selection – questions must not be asked at interviews which discriminate by implication, eg asking a women whether or not she intends to have children.

13 MOTIVATION

13.1 Organisational goals and motivation

An organisation has goals, which can only be achieved by the efforts of the people who work in the organisation. Individuals also have their own 'goals' in life and these are likely to be different from those of the organisation. Once recruited, the new employee might be subjected to a variety of techniques to enhance his or her performance at work and help the organisation achieve its goals. This means that the employee must be motivated.

You may be wondering why motivation is important. It could be argued that if a person is employed to do a job, he or she will do that job and no question of motivation arises. If the person does not want to do the work, he or she can resign. The point at issue, however, is the efficiency and effectiveness with which the job is done. If individuals can be motivated, by one means or another, they will work more effectively (ie productivity will rise) or they will produce a better quality of work. There is some debate as to what the actual effects of improved motivation are, efficiency or effectiveness, but it has become widely accepted that motivation is beneficial to the organisation.

It has been argued that some individuals need the 'big stick' treatment to be forced into doing their work well, but that self-disciplined individuals do not need this treatment and will be motivated by a more enlightened approach to superior-subordinate relationships. The best approach to motivating individuals in an organisation will vary with the particular circumstances, or situation, of each organisation.

13.2 Individual differences

In the most basic terms, an individual has needs that he needs to satisfy. The means of satisfying his needs are 'wants'. For example, an individual might feel the need for power, and to fulfil this need he might want money and a position of authority. Depending on the strength of his needs and wants, he may take action to achieve them. If he is successful in achieving them, he will be satisfied. This can be shown in a simple diagram.

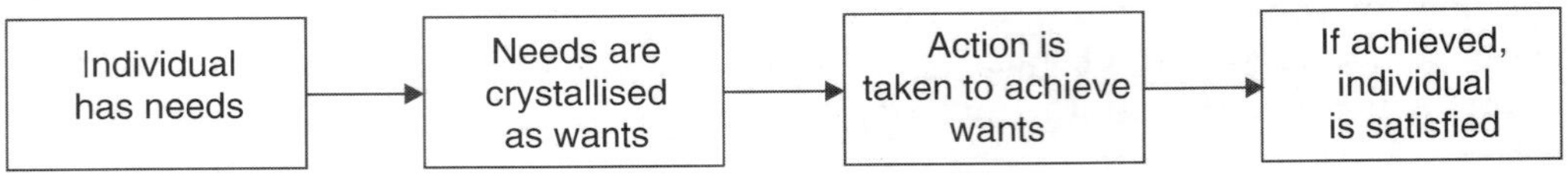

Motivators can be established which act as the 'wants' of an individual. For example, the position of sales director might serve as a 'want' to satisfy an individual's need for power, or access to a senior executives' dining room might serve as a 'want' to satisfy a need for status.

Motivators may exist which are not directly controllable by management. For example, he or she might want to be accepted by workmates to satisfy the need for friendship and affiliation with others and might therefore choose to conform to the norms and adopt the attitudes of the work group – which are not necessarily shared by the organisation as a whole.

Motivation is then the urge or drive to take action to achieve wants. However, an individual might want to be promoted but may not be sufficiently motivated to work harder or more efficiently in order to win the promotion: he or she may not believe that the company really will give promotion in return for working harder. Management has the problem of creating or 'manipulating' motivators which will actually motivate employees to perform in a desired way.

13.3 Motivation theories

The kind of theory we subscribe to, about what motivation is and what can be 'done' with it, will influence our attitudes to management and individuals in organisations. There are various ways of looking at motivation. Handy groups early motivation theories under three headings.

(i) **Satisfaction theories** are based on the assumption that a 'satisfied' worker will work harder (although there is little evidence to support the assumption). Satisfaction may reduce labour turnover and absenteeism, but will not necessarily increase individual productivity. Some theories hold that people work best within a compatible work group, or under a well-liked leader.

(ii) **Incentive theories** are based on the assumption that individuals will work harder to obtain a desired reward, ie positive reinforcement, although most studies are concentrated on money as a motivator. Handy notes that incentive theories can work if:

- the individual perceives the increased reward to be worth the extra effort
- the performance can be measured and clearly attributed to the individual
- the individual wants that particular kind of reward

NOTES

- the increased performance will not become the new minimum standard

(iii) **Intrinsic theories** are based on the belief that higher-order needs are more prevalent in modern man than we give him credit for. People will work hard in response to factors in the work itself – participation, responsibility etc – effective performance is its own reward

Chapter roundup

- Effective recruitment practices ensure that a firm has enough **people with the right skills**.
- Most recruitment practices aim to **fit the person to the job** by identifying the needs of the job and finding a person who satisfies them.
- The recruitment process involves **personnel specialists** and **'line' managers**, sometimes with the help of recruitment **consultants**.
- First the overall **needs of the organisation** have been identified in the recruitment process.
- The account for each individual position a **job analysis** is prepared, which identifies through various investigative techniques, the content of the job.
- A **job description** is developed from the job analysis. The job description outlines the **tasks** of the job and its place within the organisation.
- A **person specification** identifies the characteristics of a person who will be recruited to do the job identified in the job description.
- The person specification can be used to develop the **job advertisement**. The Seven Point Plan and Five Point Pattern are examples.
- In recent years, recruiters have been using the '**competences**' as a means to select candidates. A **competence** is a person's capacity to behave in a particular way for example to fulfil the requirements of a job, or to motivate people. Work-based competences directly relate to the job (eg the ability to prepare a trial balance); behavioural competences relate to underlying issues of personality.
- The process of selection begins when the recruiter receives details of candidates interested in the job, in response, for example, to a job advert, or possibly enquiries made to the recruitment consultant.
- Many firms require candidates to fill out an **application form**. This is standardised and the firm can ask for specific information about **work experience** and **qualifications**, as well as other **personal data**. Some firms do not bother with an application form, being happy to accept CVs with a covering letter.
- Application forms and CVs are then sifted, to weed out unsuitable candidates and to identify others whose applications can be taken further. **Biodata** techniques give weight to the data submitted giving applicants a score.
- Most firms use **interviews**, on a one-to-one basis, using a variety of **open** and **closed questions**. The interviewer should avoid bias in assessing the candidate.
- **Selection tests** can be used before or after interviews. Intelligence tests measures the candidate's general intellectual ability, and personality tests identify the type of person. Other tests are more specific to the job (eg proficiency tests)

NOTES

- Interviews are unreliable as predictors of actual job performance for many posts, but they are traditional and convenient. A combination of interviews with other methods may be used.
- Current legislation that applies to recruitment and selection includes laws on equal pay, sex discrimination, the employment of disabled people, race relations and the rehabilitation of offenders.
- Motivation theories suggest that individuals have needs that must be satisfied. There are a number of different theories. Satisfaction theories are based on the assumption that a 'satisfied' worker will work harder. Incentive theories believe that individuals will work harder to obtain a desired reward, eg more money and intrinsic theories argue that effective performance is its own reward.

Quick quiz

1 What, in brief, are the stages of the recruitment and selection process?

2 Briefly summarise job analysis.

3 What is a currently fashionable approach to drawing up jobs analysis, job descriptions etc?

4 List the components of the Five Point Pattern.

5 What are the characteristics of a good job advertisement?

6 What should application forms achieve?

7 Why are bio-data techniques useful?

8 What factors should be taken into account in an organisation's interview strategy?

9 Why are open questions useful?

10 Why do interviews fail to predict performance accurately?

11 List the desirable features of selection tests

12 Give examples of group selection methods

Answers to quick quiz

1 Identifying/defining requirements; attracting potential employees; selecting candidates. (See para 1.1)

2 **Job analysis**. The process of examining a 'job' to identify the component parts and the circumstances in which it is performed. (See para 2)

3 The use of competences - work based and behavioural. (See para 2.5)

4 Impact on others; acquired knowledge and qualifications; innate abilities; motivation; adjustment. (See para 4.3)

5 Concise; reaches the right people; gives a good impression; relevant to the job, identifying skills required etc. (See para 5.1)

6 They should give enough information to identify suitable candidates and weed out no-hopers, by asking specific questions and by getting the candidate to volunteer information. (See para 7.1)

7 Bio-data techniques enable data in application forms/CVs to be weighted and scored, making it easier to sift candidates' applications. (See para 7.3)

8 In brief, giving the right impression of the organisation and obtaining a rounded, relevant assessment of the candidate. (See para 9.1)

9 They allow the candidate to volunteer more, and open avenues for further questions. (See para 9.4)

10 Brevity and artificiality of interview situation combined with the bias and inexperience of interviewers. (See para 9.7)

11 Sensitive; standardised; reliable; valid. (See para 10)

12 Role play exercises; case studies. (See para 11.1)

Answers to activities

1 Large organisations tend to have standard procedures. In order to ensure a standard process, you might have seen a specialist from the personnel department only. Smaller organisations cannot afford such specialists so you might have been interviewed by your immediate boss - but perhaps someone else might also have interviewed you (your boss's boss) to check you out.

2 (a) Goods points about the advertisement and points for improvement

(i) It is attractively designed in terms of page layout.

(ii) The tone of the headline and much of the body copy is informal, colloquial and even friendly. It starts with a joke, implying that the company has a sense of humour.

(iii) The written style is fluent and attractive.

(iv) It appears to offer quite a lot of information about the culture of the company - how it feels about personnel issues, where it's going etc - as well as about the job vacancy.

Improvements that could be made

Job advertisements carry certain 'responsibilities': they are a form of pre-selection, and as such should be not be just attractive and persuasive, but accurate and complete enough to give a realistic and relevant picture of the post and the organisation.

(i) There is too much copy. Readers may not have the patience to read through so much (rather wordy) prose, particularly since the same phrases are repeated ('progressive international organisation', for example), or look rather familiar in any case ('in the nicest possible ways', 'our staff are our most important asset', 'a company with a difference' etc) and there is very little 'hard' information contained in the ad.

(ii) There are many words and expressions which sound good, and seem to imply good things, but are in fact empty of substance, and commit the organisation to nothing. They are usually the 'stock' expressions like 'committed to an enlightened personnel philosophy': what does that actually mean?

(iii) There are confusing contradictions, eg between the requirements for flexibility, 'interchange with various functions', do 'whatever the situation demands' etc and the more cautious 'within your designated area ...'.

(iv) The copywriters are in places too 'clever' for their own good. The first three lines, for example, could backfire quite badly if a reader failed to catch the next line, or simply didn't appreciate the self-deprecating tone.

(v) The advertisement does not give enough 'hard' information to make effective response likely - and then fails to do its job of facilitating response at all! Despite the invitation to telephone, no number is given. No named corespondent is cited, merely a reference number - despite the claimed emphasis on people as people, not numbers.

(b) **What is learnt about AOK**

The advertisement claims to say quite a lot about AOK, its culture, its people-centredness, its expansion and progressive outlook, flexibility, sense of humour etc. Such claims should always be taken with a pinch of salt. We may, however, infer some things about the company.

(i) It has a strong cultural 'flavour', and believes in 'selling' that culture quite hard. It likes, for example, telling people what it is 'committed to', what it 'firmly believes' etc.

(ii) It tends to stress its good points and opportunities: it certainly sees itself (even allowing for advertising hyperbole) as go-ahead, successful and expanding, flexible, people-oriented.

(iii) It is possibly not as deeply people oriented as it tries to project. The areas of involvement for the Personnel Department enumerated, for example, seem rather limited and administrative: there is no suggestion of a wider strategic role for personnel, such as would indicate that 'people issues' really do affect management outlook.

7 (a) Boxes too small to contain the information asked for.

(b) Forms which are (or look) so lengthy or complicated that a prospective applicant either completes them perfunctorily or gives up (and applies to another employer instead).

(c) Illegal (eg discriminatory) or offensive questions.

(d) Lack of clarity as to what (and how much) information is required.

8 (a) Closed. (The only answer is 'yes' or 'no', unless Jo is prepared to expand on it, at his or her own initiative.)

(b) Leading. (Even if Jo was interested, (s)he should get the message that 'yes' would not be what the interviewer wanted, or expected, to hear.)

(c) Leading closed multiple! ('Really useful' leads Jo to think that the 'correct' answer will be 'yes': There is not much opportunity for any other answer, without expanding on it unasked.)

(d) Open. (Jo has to explain, in his or her own words.)

(e) Probing. (If Jo's answer has been unconvincing, short or vague, this question forces a more specific answer.)

Chapter 8 :
EMPLOYEE DEVELOPMENT

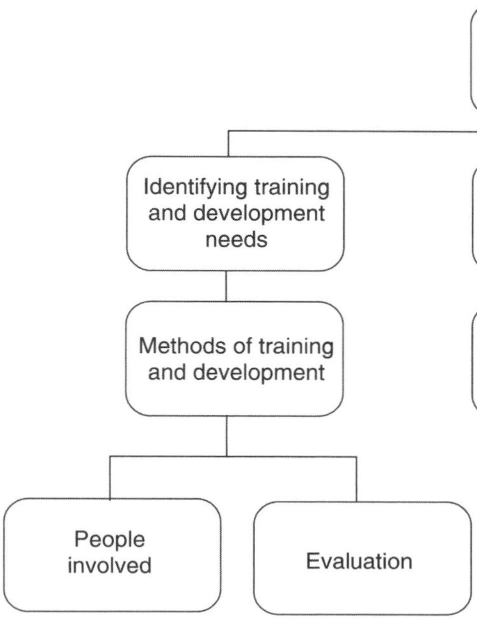

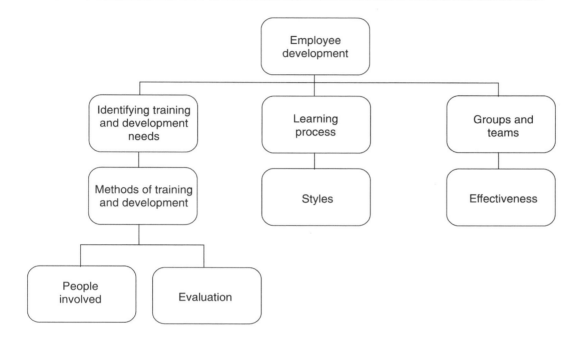

Introduction

Human resource development is the process by which the knowledge, skills and attitudes of employees are enhanced to the benefit of the organisation, the individual and the group. Development is the growth or realisation of a person's ability through conscious or unconscious learning. Training is a planned process to modify attitude, knowledge, skill or behaviour through learning experiences to achieve effective performance in an activity or range of activities.

The different types of learning theory we will be looking at in this chapter include the behaviourist and the cognitive approaches. Learning theory highlights the importance of feedback in sustaining and improving performance.

Your objectives

In this chapter you will learn about the following:

(a) Development and the role of training

(b) Identifying training and development needs

(c) Methods of development and training

(d) The learning process

(e) People involved in training and development

(f) Evaluating training

1 DEVELOPMENT AND THE ROLE OF TRAINING

1.1 Factors affecting job performance

There are many factors affecting a person's performance at work, as shown in the diagram below. Training and development are the ways by which organisations seek to improve the performance of their staff and, it is hoped, of the organisation.

1.2 What is development?

Definitions

> **Development** is 'the growth or realisation of a person's ability and potential through the provision of learning and educational experiences'.
>
> **Training** is 'the planned and systematic modification of behaviour through learning events, programmes and instruction which enable individuals to achieve the level of knowledge, skills and competence to carry out their work effectively'.
>
> (Armstrong, *Handbook of Personnel Management Practice*)

1.3 Overall purpose of employee and management development

- **Ensure** the firm meets current and future performance objectives by...
- **Continuous improvement** of the performance of individuals and teams, and...
- **Maximising people's** potential for growth (and promotion).

1.4 Development activities

- Training, both on and off the job
- Career planning
- Job rotation
- Appraisal (see next chapter)
- Other learning opportunities

> **Activity 1** **(10 minutes)**
>
> Note down key experiences which have developed your capacity and confidence at work, and the skills you are able to bring to your employer (or indeed a new employer!)

Organisations often have a **training and development strategy**, based on the overall strategy for the business. We can list the following steps.

Step 1. Identify the skills and competences are needed by the **business plan**

Step 2. Draw up the **development strategy** to show how training and development activities will assist in meeting the targets of the corporate plan.

Step 3. **Implement** the training and development strategy.

The advantage of such an approach is that the training is:

- Relevant
- Problem-based (ie corrects a real lack of skills)
- Action-oriented
- Performance-related

1.5 Training and the organisation

Benefits for the organisation of training and development programmes

Benefit	Comment
Minimise the learning costs of obtaining the skills the organisation needs	Training supports the business strategy.
Lower costs and **increased productivity**, thereby improving performance	Some people suggest that higher levels of training explain the higher productivity of German as opposed to many British manufacturers
Fewer accidents, and better health and safety	EU health and safety directives require a certain level of training. Employees can take employers to court if accidents occur or if unhealthy work practices persist.
Less need for detailed supervision	If people are trained they can get on with the job, and managers can concentrate on other things. Training is an aspect of **empowerment**.
Flexibility	Training ensures that people have the **variety** of skills needed – multi-skilling is only possible if people are properly trained.

Benefit	Comment
Recruitment and succession planning	Training and development attracts new recruits and ensures that the organisation has a supply of suitable managerial and technical staff to take over when people retire.
Change management	Training helps organisations manage change by letting people know why the change is happening and giving them the skills to cope with it.
Corporate culture	(1) Training programmes can be used to build the corporate culture or to direct it in certain ways, by indicating that certain **values** are espoused. (2) Training programmes can **build relationships** between staff and managers in different areas of the business
Motivation	Training programmes can increase commitment to the organisation's goals

Training cannot do everything. Look at the wheel below paragraph 1.1 again. Training only really covers:

Aspect of performance	Areas covered
Individual	Education; Experience; possibly Personal Circumstances (if successful completion of training is accompanied by a higher salary
Physical and job	Methods of work
Organisational and social	Type of training and supervision

In other words, **training cannot improve performance problems** arising out of:

- Bad management
- Poor job design
- Poor equipment, factory layout and work organisation
- Other characteristics of the employee (eg intelligence)
- Motivation – training gives a person the ability but not necessarily the willingness to improve
- Poor recruitment

Activity 2 **(10 minutes)**

Despite all the benefits to the organisation, many are still reluctant to train. What reasons can you give for this?

NOTES

1.6 Training and the individual

For the individual employee, the benefits of training and development are more clear-cut, and few refuse it if it is offered.

Benefit	Comment
Enhances portfolio of **skills**	Even if not specifically related to the current job, training can be useful in other contexts, and the employee becomes more attractive to employers and more promotable
Psychological benefits	The trainee might feel reassured that he/she is of continuing value to the organisation
Social benefit	People's social needs can be met by training courses – they can also develop networks of contacts
The job	Training can help people do their job better, thereby increasing job satisfaction

2 IDENTIFYING TRAINING AND DEVELOPMENT NEEDS

2.1 The training process in outline

In order to ensure that training meets the real needs of the organisation, large firms adopt a planned approach to training. This has the following steps.

Step 1. Identify and define the **organisation's training needs**. It may be the case that recruitment might be a better solution to a problem than training

Step 2. **Define the learning required** – in other words, specify the knowledge, skills or competences that have to be acquired. For technical training, this is not difficult: for example all finance department staff will have to become conversant with a new accounting system.

Step 3. **Define training objectives** – what must be learnt and what trainees must be able to do after the training exercise

Step 4. **Plan training programmes** – training and development can be planned in a number of ways, employing a number of techniques, as we shall learn about in Section 3. (Also, people have different approaches to learning, which have to be considered.) This covers:

- Who provides the training
- Where the training takes place
- Divisions of responsibilities between trainers, managers and the individual.

Step 5. Implement the training

Step 6. Evaluate the training: has it been successful in achieving the learning objectives?

Step 7. Go back to Step 2 if more training is needed.

NOTES

Activity 3 **(15 minutes)**

Draw up a training plan for introducing a new employee into your department. Repeat this exercise after you have completed this chapter to see if your chosen approach has changed.

2.2 Training needs analysis

Training needs analysis covers three issues.

Current state	Desired state
Organisation's current results	Desired results, standards
Existing knowledge and skill	Knowledge and skill needed
Individual performance	Required standards

The difference between the two columns is the **training gap**. Training programmes are designed to improve individual performance, thereby improving the performance of the organisation.

CASE EXAMPLE

Training for quality

The British Standards for Quality Systems (BS EN ISO 9000: formerly BS 5750) which many UK organisations are working towards (often at the request of customers, who perceive it to be a 'guarantee' that high standards of quality control are being achieved) includes training requirements. As the following extract shows, the Standard identifies training needs for those organisations registering for assessment, and also shows the importance of a systematic approach to ensure adequate control.

The training, both by specific training to perform assigned tasks and general training to heighten quality awareness and t0 mould attitudes of all personnel in an organisation, is central to the achievement of quality.

The comprehensiveness of such training varies with the complexity of the organisation. The following steps should be taken:

1 Identifying the way tasks and operations influence quality in total

2 Identifying individuals; training needs against those required for satisfactory performance of the task

3 Planning and carrying out appropriate specific training

4 Planning and organising general quality awareness programmes

5 Recording training and achievement in an easily retrievable form so that records can be updated and taps in training can be readily identified

BSI, 1990

Training surveys combine information from a variety of sources to discern what the training needs of the organisation actually are. These sources are:

(a) The **business strategy** at corporate level.

(b) **Appraisal and performance reviews** – the purpose of a performance management system is to improve performance, and training maybe recommended as a remedy.

(c) **Attitude surveys** from employees, asking them what training they think they need or would like.

(d) **Evaluation of existing training** programmes.

(e) **Job analysis** (see Chapter 7) can be used. To identify training needs from the job analysis, the job analysis can pay attention to:

   (i) Reported difficulties people have in meeting the skills requirement of the job

   (ii) Existing performance weaknesses, of whatever kind, which could be remedied by training

   (iii) Future changes in the job.

   The job analysis can be used to generate a training specification covering the knowledge needed for the job, the skills required to achieve the result, attitudinal changes required.

2.3 Setting training objectives

The **training manager** will have to make an initial investigation into the problem of the gap between job or competence **requirements** and current performance of **competence**.

If training would improve work performance, training **objectives** can then be defined. They should be clear, specific and related to observable, measurable targets, ideally detailing:

- **Behaviour** - what the trainee should be able to do
- **Standard** - to what level of performance?
- **Environment** - under what conditions (so that the performance level is realistic)?

EXAMPLE

'At the end of the course the trainee should be able to describe ... or identify ... or distinguish x from y ... or calculate ... or assemble ...' and so on. It is insufficient to define the objectives of training as 'to give trainees a grounding in ...' or 'to encourage trainees in a better appreciation of ...': this offers no target achievement which can be measured.

Training objectives link the identification of training needs with the content, methods and technology of training. Some examples of translating training needs into learning objectives are given in *Personnel Management, A New Approach* by D Torrington and L Hall.

Training needs	Learning objectives
To know more about the Data Protection Act	The employee will be able to answer four out of every five queries about the Data Protection Act without having to search for details.
To establish a better rapport with customers	The employee will immediately attend to a customer unless already engaged with another customer.
	The employee will greet each customer using the customer's name where known.
	The employee will apologise to every customer who has had to wait to be attended to.
To assemble clocks more quickly	The employee will be able to assemble each clock correctly within thirty minutes.

Having identified training needs and objectives, the manager will have to decide on the best way to approach training: there are a number of types and techniques of training, which we will discuss below.

3 METHODS OF DEVELOPMENT AND TRAINING

3.1 Incorporating training needs into an individual development programme

This is achieved by a personal development plan

Definition

> A **personal development plan** is a 'clear developmental action plan for an individual which incorporates a wide set of developmental opportunities including formal training.'

The purpose of a personal development plan will cover:

- Improving performance in the existing job
- Developing skills for future career moves within and outside the organisation.

Definition

> **Skills:** what the individual needs to be able to do if results are to be achieved. Skills are built up progressively by repeated training. They may be manual, intellectual or mental, perceptual or social.

3.2 Preparing a personal development plan.

Step 1. **Analyse the current position**. You could do a personal SWOT (strengths, weaknesses, opportunities, threats) analysis. The supervisor can have an input

NOTES

into this by categorising the skills use of the employee on a grid as follows, in a **skills analysis**.

		Performance	
		High	*Low*
Liking of skills	*High*	Like and do well	Like but don't do well
	Low	Dislike but do well	Dislike and don't do well

The aim is to try to incorporate more of the employees' interests into their actual roles.

Step 2. **Set goals to cover performance in the existing job**, future changes in the current role, moving elsewhere in the organisations, developing specialist expertise. Naturally, such goals should have the characteristic, as far as possible of SMART objectives (ie specific, measurable, attainable, realistic and time-bounded).

Step 3. **Draw up an action plan** to achieve the goals, covering the developmental activities listed in paragraph 3.1

Activity 4 **(15 minutes)**

Draw up a personal development plan for yourself over the next month, the next year, and the next five years. You should include your HND/HNC activities.

3.3 Formal training

Formal training

(a) **Courses** may be run by the organisation's training department or may be provided by external suppliers.

(b) **Types of course**

(i) **Day release**: the employee works in the organisation and on one day per week attends a local college or training centre for theoretical learning.

(ii) **Distance learning, evening classes and correspondence courses,** which make demands on the individual's time outside work.

(iii) **Revision courses** for examinations of professional bodies.

(iv) **Block release** courses which may involve four weeks at a college or training centre followed by a period back at work.

(v) **Sandwich courses,** usually involve six months at college then six months at work, in rotation, for two or three years.

(vi) A **sponsored full-time course** at a university for one or two years.

(c) **Computer-based training** involves interactive training via PC. The typing program, Mavis Beacon, is a good example.

(d) **Techniques** used on the course might include lecturers, seminars, role play and simulation.

3.4 Disadvantages of formal training

(a) An individual will not benefit from formal training unless he or she **is motivated to learn**.

(b) If the **subject matter** of the training course does not **relate to an individual's job**, the learning will quickly be forgotten.

3.5 On the job training

Successful on the job training

(a) The assignments should have a **specific purpose** from which the trainee can learn and gain experience.

(b) The organisation must **tolerate any mistakes** which the trainee makes. Mistakes are an inevitable part of on the job learning.

(c) The work should **not be too complex**.

Methods of on the job training

(a) **Demonstration/instruction:** show the trainee how to do the job and let them get on with it. It should combine **telling** a person what to do and **showing** them how, using appropriate media. The trainee imitates the instructor, and asks questions.

(b) **Coaching:** the trainee is put under the guidance of an experienced employee who shows the trainee how to do the job.

   (i) **Establish learning targets**. The areas to be learnt should be identified, and specific, realistic goals (eg completion dates, performance standards) stated by agreement with the trainee.

   (ii) **Plan a systematic learning and development programme.** This will ensure regular progress, appropriate stages for consolidation and practice.

   (iii) **Identify opportunities for broadening the trainee's knowledge and experience:** eg by involvement in new projects, placement on inter-departmental committees, suggesting new contacts, or simply extending the job, adding more tasks, greater responsibility etc.

   (iv) **Take into account the strengths and limitations of the trainee** in learning, and take advantage of learning opportunities that suit the trainee's ability, preferred style and goals.

   (v) **Exchange feedback**. The coach will want to know how the trainee sees his or her progress and future. He or she will also need performance information in order to monitor the trainee's progress, adjust the learning programme if necessary, identify further needs which may emerge and plan future development for the trainee.

(c) **Job rotation:** the trainee is given several jobs in succession, to gain experience of a wide range of activities. (Even experienced managers may rotate their jobs, to gain wider experience; this philosophy of job education is commonly applied in the Civil Service, where an employee may expect to move on to another job after a few years.)

(d) **Temporary promotion:** an individual is promoted into his/her superior's position whilst the superior is absent due to illness. This gives the individual a chance to experience the demands of a more senior position.

(e) **'Assistant to' positions:** a junior manager with good potential may be appointed as assistant to the managing director or another executive director. In this way, the individual gains experience of how the organisation is managed 'at the top'.

(f) **Action learning:** a group of managers are brought together to solve a real problem with the help of an 'advisor' who exposes the management process that actually happens.

(g) **Committees:** trainees might be included in the membership of committees, in order to obtain an understanding of inter-departmental relationships.

(h) **Project work**. work on a project with other people can expose the trainee to other parts of the organisation.

Activity 5 **(15 minutes)**

Suggest a suitable training method for each of the following situations.

(a) A worker is transferred onto a new machine and needs to learn its operation.

(b) An accounts clerk wishes to work towards becoming qualified with the relevant professional body.

(c) An organisation decides that its supervisors would benefit from ideas on participative management and democratic leadership.

(d) A new member of staff is about to join the organisation.

3.6 Induction training

On the first day, a manager or personnel officer should welcome the new recruit. He/she should then introduce the new recruit to the person who will be their **immediate supervisor.**

The immediate supervisor should commence the **on-going process of induction**.

Step 1. Pinpoint the areas that the recruit will have to learn about in order to **start the job**. Some things (such as detailed technical knowledge) may be identified as areas for later study or training.

Step 2. Explain first of all the nature of the job, and the goals of each task, both of the recruit's job and of the department as a whole.

Step 3. Explain about hours of work, and stress the importance of time-keeping. If flexitime is operated, the supervisor should explain how it works.

Step 4. Explain the structure of the department: to whom the recruit will report, to whom he/she can go with complaints or queries and so on.

Step 5. Introduce the recruit to the people in the office. One particular colleague may be assigned to the recruit as a **mentor**, to keep an eye on them, answer routine queries, 'show them the ropes'.

Step 6. Plan and implement an appropriate **training programmes** for whatever technical or practical knowledge is required. Again, the programme should have a clear schedule and set of goals so that the recruit has a sense of purpose, and so that the programme can be efficiently organised to fit in with the activities of the department.

Step 7. Coach and/or train the recruit; and check regularly on their progress, as demonstrated by performance, as reported by the recruit's mentor, and as perceived by the recruit him or herself.

Note that induction is an **on-going process**, embracing mentoring, coaching, training, monitoring and so on. It is not just a first day affair! After three months, six months or one year the performance of a new recruit should be formally appraised and discussed with them. Indeed, when the process of induction has been finished, a recruit should continue to receive periodic appraisals, just like every other employee in the organisation.

Activity 6 **(30 minutes)**

'Joining an organisation with around 8,500 staff, based on two sites over a mile apart and in the throes of major restructuring, can be confusing for any recruit. This is the situation facing the 20 to 30 new employees recruited each month by the Guy's and St Thomas' Hospital Trust, which was formed by the merger of the two hospitals in April.

In a climate of change, new employees joining the NHS can be influenced by the negative attitudes of other staff who may oppose the current changes. So it has become increasingly important for the trust's management executive to get across their view of the future and to understand the feelings of confusion new staff may be experiencing.'

Personnel Management Plus, August 1993

See if you can design a **one day** induction programme for these new recruits, in the light of the above. The programme is to be available to **all** new recruits, from doctors and radiographers to accountants, catering and cleaning staff and secretaries.

4 THE LEARNING PROCESS

There are different schools of learning theory which explain and describe how people learn.

(a) **Behaviourist psychology** concentrated on the relationship between **stimuli** (input through the senses) and **responses** to those stimuli. 'Learning' is the formation of **new** connections between stimulus and response, on the basis of **conditioning**. We modify our responses in future according to whether the results of our behaviour in the past have been good or bad.

(b) The **cognitive approach** argues that the human mind takes sensory information and imposes organisation and meaning on it: we interpret and rationalise. We use feedback information on the results of past behaviour to make **rational decisions** about whether to maintain successful behaviours or modify unsuccessful behaviours in future, according to our goals and our plans for reaching them.

4.1 Effective training programmes

Whichever approach it is based on, learning theory offers certain useful propositions for the design of **effective training programmes**.

Proposition	Comment
The individual should be **motivated** to learn	The advantages of training should be made clear, according to the individual's motives - money, opportunity, valued skills or whatever.
There should be clear **objectives and standards** set, so that each task has some meaning	Each stage of learning should present a challenge, without overloading the trainee or making them lose confidence. Specific objectives and performance standards for each will help the trainee in the planning and control process that leads to learning, and providing targets against which performance will constantly be measured.
There should be timely, relevant **feedback** on performance and progress	This will usually be provided by the trainer, and should be concurrent - or certainly not long delayed. If progress reports or performance appraisals are given only at the year end, for example, there will be no opportunity for behaviour adjustment or learning in the meantime.
Positive and negative **reinforcement** should be judiciously used	Recognition and encouragement enhance an individuals confidence in their competence and progress: punishment for poor performance - especially without explanation and correction - discourages the learner and creates feelings of guilt, failure and hostility
Active **participation** is more telling than passive reception (because of its effect on the motivation to learn, concentration and recollection).	If a high degree of participation is impossible, practice and repetition can be used to reinforce receptivity. However, participation has the effect of encouraging 'ownership' of the process of learning and changing - committing the individual to it as their **own** goal, not just an imposed process.

4.2 Learning styles

The way in which people learn best will differ according to the type of person. That is, there are **learning styles** which suit different individuals. Peter Honey and Alan Mumford have drawn up a popular classification of four learning styles.

(a) **Theorists**

- Seek to understand basic principles and to take an intellectual, 'hands-off' approach based on logical argument. They prefer training to be:
  - Programmed and structured
  - Designed to allow time for analysis
  - Provided by teachers who share his/her preference for concepts and analysis

NOTES

(b) **Reflectors**

- Observe phenomena, think about them and then choose how to act
- Need to work at their own pace
- Find learning difficult if forced into a hurried programme
- Produce carefully thought-out conclusions after research and reflection
- Tend to be fairly slow, non-participative (unless to ask questions) and cautious

(c) **Activists**

- Deal with practical, active problems and do not have patience with theory
- Require training based on hands-on experience
- Excited by participation and pressure, such as new projects
- Flexible and optimistic, but tend to rush at something without due preparation

(d) **Pragmatists**

- Only like to study if they can see its direct link to practical problems
- Good at learning new techniques in on-the-job training
- Aim is to implement action plans and/or do the task better
- May discard good ideas which only require some development

Training programmes should ideally be designed to accommodate the preferences of all four styles. This can often be overlooked especially as the majority of training staff are activitists.

Activity 7 **(10 minutes)**

With reference to the four learning styles drawn up by Honey and Mumford, which of these styles do you think most closely resembles your own? What implications has this got for the way you learn?

4.3 The learning cycle

Another useful model is the **experiential learning cycle** devised by David Kolb. Experiential learning involves **doing**, however, and puts the learners in an active problem-solving role: a form of **self-learning** which encourages the learners to formulate and commit themselves to their own learning objectives.

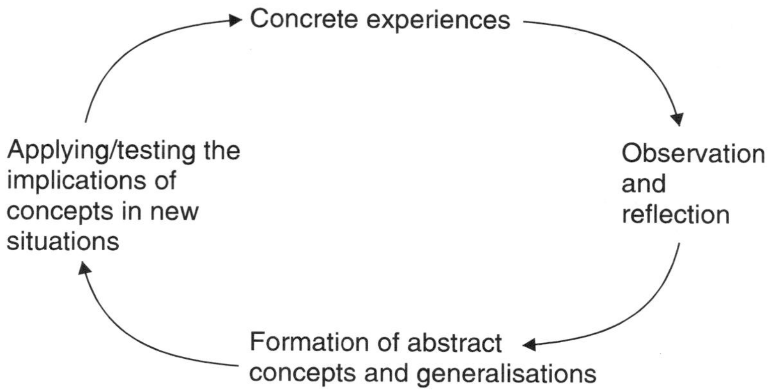

EXAMPLE

An employee interviews a customer for the first time (concrete experience). He observes his own performance and the dynamics of the situation (observation) and afterwards, having failed to convince the customer to buy his product, the employee analyses what he did right and wrong (reflection). He comes to the conclusion that he failed to listen to what the customer really wanted and feared, underneath his general reluctance: he realises that the key to communication is listening (abstraction/ generalisation). In his next interview he applies his strategy to the new set of circumstances (application/testing). This provides him with a new experience with which to start the cycle over again.

Simplified, this 'learning by doing' approach involves:

Act: Analyse action: Understand principles: Apply principles:

> **Activity 8** **(15 minutes)**
>
> With reference to Kolb's learning cycle, think of a situation on your present course where you have been involved in a practical exercise or 'experiential learning'. Illustrate the stages of the learning cycle using your chosen example.

4.4 Barriers to learning

According to Peter Senge, there are seven sources of **learning disability** in organisations which prevent them from attaining their potential - which trap them into 'mediocrity', for example, when they could be achieving 'excellence'.

(a) '**I am my position**'. When asked what they do for a living, most people describe the tasks they perform, not the **purposes** they fulfil; thus they tend to see their responsibilities as limited to the boundaries of their position.

(b) '**The enemy is out there**'. If things go wrong it is all too easy to imagine that somebody else 'out there' was at fault.

(c) **The illusion of taking charge.** The individual decides to be more active in fighting the enemy out there, trying to destroy rather than to build.

(d) **The fixation on events.** Conversations in organisations are dominated by concern about events (last month's sales, who's just been promoted, the new product from our competitor), and this focus inevitably distracts us from seeing the longer-term patterns of change.

(e) **The parable of the boiled frog.** Failure to adapt to gradually building threats is pervasive. (If you place a frog in a pot of boiling water, it will immediately try to scramble out; but if you place the frog in room temperature water, he will stay put. If you heat the water gradually, the frog will do nothing until he boils: this is because 'the frog's internal apparatus for sensing threats to survival is geared to sudden changes in his environment, not to slow, gradual changes'.)

(f) **The delusion of learning from experience.** We learn best from experience, but we never experience the results of our most important and significant decisions. Indeed, we never know what the outcomes would have been had we done something else.

(g) **The myth of the management team.** All too often, the management 'team' is not a team at all, but is a collection of individuals competing for power and resources.

Activity 9 **(20 minutes)**

How far do Senge's seven learning disabilities apply to your own organisation, or to some other significant organisation with which you may be familiar?

For individuals, the barriers may be:

- 'A waste of time': people see no personal benefit from training
- Training programmes employ the wrong techniques for people's learning styles
- Unwillingness to change

4.5 Encouraging learning: what managers can do

Managers can try to **develop the learning organisation**.

- Encourages continuous learning and knowledge generation at all levels
- Has the processes to move knowledge around the organisation
- Can transform knowledge into actual behaviour

Definition

Learning organisation is 'An organisation that facilitates the learning of all its members and continuously transforms itself'.

4.6 The building of the learning organisation

Characteristics	Comments
Systematic problem solving	Problems should be tackled in a scientific way.
Experimentation	Experimentation can generate new insights.
Learn from experience	Knowledge from past failures can help avoid them in future.
Learn from others	Customers and other firms can be a good source of ideas. Learning opportunities should be sought out.
Knowledge transfer	Knowledge should be transferred throughout the organisation.

5 PEOPLE INVOLVED IN TRAINING AND DEVELOPMENT

5.1 The trainee

Many people now believe that the ultimate responsibility for training and development lies, not with the employer, but with the **individual**. People should seek to develop their own skills, to improve their own careers rather than wait for the organisation to impose training upon them. Why? The current conventional wisdom is that:

(a) **Delayering** means there are fewer automatic promotion pathways; promotion was once a source of development but there might not be further promotions available.

(b) Technological change means that new skills are always needed, and people who can find new work will be learning new skills.

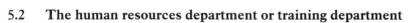

Activity 10 **(10 minutes)**

You are currently studying for the HNC/HND Business qualification. Was this your own decision, or were you encouraged to do so by your employer?

5.2 The human resources department or training department

The human resources department is ideally concerned with developing people. Some organisations have extensive development and career planning programmes. These shape the progression of individuals through the organisation, in accordance with the performance and potential of the individual and the needs of the organisation. Of course, only large organisations can afford or use this sort of approach.

The HR department also performs an **administrative** role by recording what training and development opportunities and individual might be given – in some firms, going on a training programme is an entitlement that the personnel department might have to enforce.

5.3 The supervisor and manager

Line managers and supervisors bear some of the responsibility for training and development within the organisation by identifying:

- The training needs of the department or section
- The current competences of the individuals within the department
- Opportunities for learning and development on the job
- When feedback is necessary.

The **supervisor** may be required to organise training programmes for staff.

5.4 Mentoring

Definition

> **Mentoring** is the use of specially trained individuals to provide guidance and advice which will help develop the careers of those allocate to them. A person's line manager should not be his or her mentor.

Mentors can assist in:

- Drawing up personal development plans
- Advice with administrative problems people face in their new jobs
- Help in tackling projects, by pointing people in the right order

5.5 The training manager

The training manager is a member of staff appointed to arrange and sometimes run training. The training manager generally reports to the **human resources** or **personnel director**, but also needs a good relationship with line managers in the production and other departments where the training takes place.

5.6 Responsibilities of the training manager

Responsibility	Comment
Liaison	With HRM department and operating departments
Scheduling	Arranging training programmes at convenient times
Skills identifying	Discerning existing and future skills shortages
Programme design	Develop tailored training programmes
Feedback	The trainee, the department and the HR department

6 EVALUATING TRAINING

Definitions

> **Validation of training** means observing the results of the course and measuring whether the training objectives have been achieved.
>
> **Evaluation of training** means comparing the actual costs of the scheme against the assessed benefits which are being obtained. If the costs exceed the benefits, the scheme will need to be redesigned or withdrawn.

Ways of validating and evaluating a training scheme

(a) **Trainees' reactions to the experience.** This form of monitoring is rather inexact, and it does not allow the training department to measure the results for comparison against the training objective.

(b) **Trainee learning:** measuring what the trainees have learned on the course by means of a test at the end of it.

(c) **Changes in job behaviour following training.** This is possible where the purpose of the course was to learn a particular skill.

(d) **Organisational change as a result of training:** finding out whether the training has affected the work or behaviour of **other** employees not on the course - seeing whether there has been a general change in attitudes arising from a new course in, say, computer terminal work. This form of monitoring would probably be reserved for senior managers in the training department.

(e) **Impact of training on organisational goals:** seeing whether the training scheme has contributed to the overall objectives of the organisation. This too is a form of monitoring reserved for senior management, and would perhaps be discussed at board level in the organisation. It is likely to be the main component of a cost-benefit analysis.

> **Activity 11** **(10 minutes)**
>
> Outline why it is important to evaluate and validate a training programme and describe possible methods for achieving this.

7 GROUPS AND TEAMS

We all belong to groups. They can be social, casual, formal or informal. Social groups include families, friends, clubs, voluntary organisations, religious societies and some work-related groupings of people, such as a regular lunch-time card school. Some groups are work groups, which may be formally established as part of the organisation or informally created by those working together or sharing an interest. Formal groups include committees.

Definitions

> **Group:** a collection of individuals with a common interest and who share a common identity. A group has a leader, a set of social norms and a reason for its existence. It may be informal or formally established and its existence may be permanent or temporary.
>
> **Team:** a formal group created for a purpose. A team has a leader, an aim and a distinctive culture. It may be formed, for example, to consider the provision of hot drinks in vending machines, to determine corporate strategy, or to win the World Cup.

Groups may come together spontaneously or be formally established. However, they do not become teams until they have gone through the process of team formation.

7.1 Group and team formation

Organisations create formal groups (also referred to as official groups) automatically as departments and specialisms develop. Groups are also created to perform such tasks as exchanging ideas, sharing information, co-ordinating work and performing tasks that require the collective use of skills. The Board of Directors is a formal group; so are the Health and Safety Committee and the night shift operatives in machine shop four.

Informal (or unofficial) groups form at work because of:

(a) people's needs to socialise;
(b) a need for self-help (for example, a baby sitting circle)
(c) a need for protection and collective action (for example, a union).

The aims of an informal group and the organisation may be different. It is important that organisations recognise the existence of informal groups and try to use them constructively, rather than making what are likely to be futile attempts to suppress them.

A group of people can be appointed to be a team, but a group has to go through the process of becoming a team before it can function as one. The composition of the group will affect its ability to become effective. Simply setting up a team does not make a group of people into a team, nor does it make it effective. Teams have to be formed with care.

7.2 Team roles

The most effective groups tend to be no more than a dozen people with members performing each of the following roles..

(a) **Co-ordinator or Chair.** The chair need not be the cleverest, most experienced or best qualified member of the team, but must be someone who works well through other people and is capable of keeping the group focused on its task.

(b) **Shaper**. .A member who is full of passion for achieving the objective. The shaper drives the others and may be impatient and domineering.

(c) **Innovator**. An imaginative member who produces original ideas.

(d) **Monitor/evaluator.** An analytical thinker who sees flaws in arguments and perceives practical problems. The monitor/evaluator is objective and often works alone.

(e) **Resource investigator.** A member who has contacts outside the group and who brings in ideas and resources.

(f) **Company worker.** An administrator who can put ideas into practice.

(g) **Team worker.** A supportive member of the group who encourages the others.

(h) **Finisher**. The member who takes, on the important but unpopular role of pushing the group to meet deadlines. The finisher is also likely to be the one who checks details and ensures nothing is overlooked.

Individuals all have different personalities, traits and preferences. A manager will tend to take on the same preferred role every time. It would be very difficult for someone to act as a finisher if their natural choice was the role of shaper.

R M Belbin, who produced these roles from research reported in 1981, said that the ideal team would consist of one chair or one shaper, one innovator, one monitor/evaluator and one or more of each of the others. A team with two shapers or two innovators would be hampered by conflicts and could be ineffective.

Managers have to select teams from the people they have, and may not be able to create an ideal Belbin team. They should try to analyse individual strengths, especially when replacing members who leave an effective team. The road to disaster is when managers pick people in their own image and end up with an unbalanced group.

7.3 Stages in forming a team

Once a group has formed it has to go through certain stages before it becomes an effective team.

(a) **Forming** - where everyone waits for a lead and finds out about the task, rules and other members.

(b) **Storming** - where someone takes the lead, discussion begins, conflicting ideas and opinions are put forward and there is resistance to doing the task.

(c) **Norming** - when conflict is resolved, co-operation begins, roles are established and group norms of behaviour are established.

(d) **Performing** - when teamwork is achieved, roles are accepted, solutions are discussed and agreed, and activities focus on achieving the goals.

Next we look at group behaviour.

7.4 Group behaviour

Groups establish norms or acceptable standards of behaviour. The things which the group has in common and which characterise it are group norms. All members of the group are expected to conform to these. Groups put pressure on members to conform, and those who wish to belong will do so. Failure to conform can lead to conflict with the rest of the group. In extreme cases an individual can be excluded from all desirable groups and forced to seek another job.

Rituals

Groups develop their own rituals, such as meeting in a certain place for coffee breaks, going to the same pub for lunch or meeting after work on Fridays. Individuals may tend to seek acceptance and pretend to conform to such norms as working late, while regularly making excuses to go on time. Similarly, a member may conceal non-adherence to norms by avoiding some aspects of the social activities of the group - having to catch a particular train or getting a lift can be used to avoid after-work drinking sessions.

Where bonus payments are related to group performance there is much stronger pressure on members to conform. Unauthorised breaks and failure to meet targets that affect the performance of the group as a whole are likely to attract strong pressure to conform.

EXAMPLE: GROUP RITUALS IN THE WORKPLACE

An ice cream factory had several lines for filling different flavours of ice cream into tubs, cartons, choc ices and ice lollies. Each filling line had a team, with a leader who allocated jobs - usually in strict rotation so as to avoid boredom. The elite team worked on choc ices. The lowest level in the pecking order was the team responsible for stacking incoming supplies of cartons and loading delivery trucks.

Each team had its special table in the canteen. The ice lolly team brought in cakes they made and shared them. The stackers and loaders took their breaks elsewhere. The choc ice team took their break at a different time from everyone else. Entry to that group was by invitation and seniority. Managers had learned that it was not a good idea to try to allocate new members to choc ices: there would be an astonishing rise in the number of choc ices incorrectly wrapped or partly coated. Teams organised their own informal breaks on a rota basis. Anyone overstaying would lose the next break as the team leader would not relieve them.

The factory paid bonuses to teams that exceeded monthly targets for filling cartons and tubs. There were strict quality controls which included a variation of not more than $^1/_2$% either side of the declared weight. Quality checks showing unacceptable variations in fill weight led to the conveyor being slowed down and consequent loss of bonuses. Individuals who persistently underfilled in an attempt to earn bonuses were banished to the menial jobs of fetching boxes of empty cartons and removing filled tubs to the cold store. These people would also miss out on rounds of drinks in the Friday pub session.

7.5 Group cohesiveness

Group cohesiveness develops over time as the group moves through the stages to performing. It refers to the ability of a group to stick together. A very cohesive group shows strong loyalty among the members, who stick strongly to the norms of behaviour. A strongly cohesive group can become exclusive, with entry being virtually impossible. Individuals find it much easier to join less cohesive groups and groups in the earlier stages of formation.

Factors which affect the development of group cohesiveness are:

- (a) similarity of work;
- (b) physical proximity in the work place;
- (c) the work flow system and whether or not it gives continuing contact;
- (d) the structure of tasks - whether individualised or group;
- (e) group size - smaller groups are more cohesive;
- (f) threats from outside - where a group sees other groups as the enemy;
- (g) prospects of rewards;
- (h) leadership style of the manager;
- (i) common social factors, such as race, social status and cultural origins.

NOTES

Next we look at the factors that affect the effectiveness of groups, and the features of effective and ineffective groups.

7.6 Group effectiveness

The personalities of group members and the traits they bring to the group play an important part in deciding its effectiveness. As we have seen, two shapers or two innovators would lead to confusion. Personal goals also affect effectiveness. It is easy for groups, especially informal ones, to decide that a low level of productivity is the norm. Groups can be motivated to improve their performance. This requires:

(a) a clearly defined task;
(b) effective leadership;
(c) small group size;
(d) skills and abilities matched to the task;
(e) proximity at work, for example an open plan office;
(f) rewards that are regarded as fair by the group.

Factors for identifying effective work groups

A number of factors are involved in identifying effective and ineffective work groups. Some are quantifiable and others are qualitative.

Effective work group	*Ineffective work group*
Quantifiable factors	
(a) Low rate of labour turnover	(a) High rate of labour turnover
(b) Low accident rate	(b) High accident rate
(c) Low absenteeism	(c) High absenteeism
(d) High output and productivity	(d) Low output and productivity
(e) Good quality of output	(e) Poor quality of output
(f) Individual targets are achieved	(f) Individual targets are not achieved
(g) There are few stoppages and interruptions to work	(g) Time is lost owing to disagreements between supervisor and subordinates
Qualitative factors	
(a) There is a high commitment to the achievement of targets and organisational goals	(a) There is no understanding of organisational goals or the role of the group
(b) There is a clear understanding of the group's work	(b) There is a low commitment to targets
(c) There is a clear understanding of the role of each person within the group	(c) There is confusion and uncertainty about the role of each person within the group
(d) There is a free and open communication between members of the group and trust between members	(d) There is mistrust between group members and suspicion of the group's leader
(e) There is idea sharing	(e) There is little idea sharing
(f) The group is good at generating new ideas	(f) The group does not generate any good new ideas

BPP PUBLISHING

(g) Group members try to help each other out by offering constructive criticisms and suggestions	(g) Group members make negative and hostile criticisms of each other's work
(h) There is group problem solving which gets to the root causes of the work problem	(h) Work problems are dealt with superficially, with attention paid to the symptoms but not the cause
(i) There is an active interest in work decisions	(i) Decisions about work are accepted passively
(j) Group members seek a united consensus of opinion	(j) Group members hold strongly opposed views
(k) The members of the group want to develop their abilities in their work	(k) Group members find work boring and do it reluctantly
(l) The group is sufficiently motivated to be able to carry on working in the absence of its leader	(l) The group needs its leader there to get work done

FOR DISCUSSION

Select a group you are involved in, for example a seminar or tutorial group, and analyse its effectiveness in terms of the features it shows from the above list. How valid are these factors in deciding whether or not a group is effective?

7.7 Relationships with other groups

A group's effectiveness is also affected by its relationships with other groups. Contact with other groups can bring power struggles, personal conflict between leaders, territorial disputes and distrust of motives. Relations in the work place often seem to parallel gang warfare in Los Angeles, where each group will go to any lengths to protect its turf.

Effectiveness can be improved and constructive competition encouraged by:

(a) rewarding groups on the basis of their contribution to the organisation as a whole and their efforts to collaborate, rather than rewarding only individual group performance;

(b) encouraging staff to move across group boundaries so that understanding and co-operation are improved;

(c) avoiding putting groups into situations where one must emerge a winner and another a loser;

(d) encouraging communication between groups through committees, discussion groups, joint planning meetings and so on.

NOTES

Chapter roundup

- In order to achieve its goals, an organisation requires a **skilled workforce**. This is partly achieved by training.
- The main purpose of training and development is to **raise competence and therefore performance standards**. It is also concerned with **personal development**, helping and motivating employees to fulfil their potential.
- A thorough analysis of **training needs** should be carried out as part of a systematic approach to training, to ensure that training programmes meet organisational and individual requirements. Once training needs have been identified, they should be translated into **training objectives**.
- Individuals can incorporate training and development objectives into a personal development plan.
- There are different schools of thought as to how people learn. Different people have different learning styles.
- There are a variety of training methods. These include:
    - Formal education and training
    - On-the-job training
    - Awareness-oriented training
- Managers can design and manage the organisation to encourage learning.

Quick quiz

1. List examples of development opportunities within organisations.
2. List how training can contribute to:
    (a) Organisational effectiveness
    (b) Individual effectiveness and motivation
3. According to ISO 9000, what are the main steps to be adopted in a systematic approach to training?
4. Define the term 'training need'.
5. How should training objectives be expressed?
6. What does learning theory tell us about the design of training programmes?
7. List the four learning styles put forward by Honey and Mumford.
8. List the four stages in Kolb's experiential learning cycle.
9. What are the levels of training validation/evaluation?
10. What is the supervisor's role in training?

Answers to quick quiz

1. Career planning, job rotation, deputising, on-the-job training, counselling, guidance, education and training. (See para 1.4)
2. (a) Increased efficiency and productivity; reduced costs, supervisory problems and accidents; improved quality, motivation and morale.

    (b) Demonstrates individual value, enhances security, enhances skills portfolio, motivates, helps develop networks and contacts. (See para 1.5)

NOTES

3 Identify how operations influence quality; identify individual training needs against performance requirements; plan and conduct training; plan and organise quality awareness programmes; record training and achievement. (See para 2.2)

4 The required level of competence minus the present level of competence. (See para 2.2)

5 Actively - 'after completing this chapter you should understand how to design and evaluate training programmes'. (See para 2.3)

6 The trainee should be motivated to learn, there should be clear objectives and timely feedback. Positive and negative reinforcement should be used carefully, to encourage active participation where possible. (See para 4.1)

7 Theorist, reflector, activist and pragmatist. (See para 4.2)

8 Concrete experience, observation/reflection, abstraction/generalisation, application/testing. (See para 4.3)

9 Reactions, learning, job behaviour, organisational change, ultimate impact. (See para 6)

10 Identifying training needs of the department or section. identifying the skills of the individual employee, and deficiencies in performance. Providing or supervising on-the-job training (eg coaching). Providing feedback on an individuals performance. (See para 5.3)

Answers to activities

1 Few employers throw you in at the deep end – it is far too risky for them! Instead, you might have been given induction training to get acclimatised to the organisation, and you might have been introduced slowly to the job. Ideally, your employer would have planned a programme of tasks of steadily greater complexity and responsibility to allow you to grow into your role(s).

2 Cost: training can be costly. Ideally, it should be seen as an investment in the future or as something the firm has to do to maintain its position. In practice, many firms are reluctant to train because of poaching by other employers – their newly trained staff have skills which can be sold for more elsewhere. This got so bad that staff at one computer services firm were required to pay the firm £4,000 if they left (to go to another employer) within two years of a major training programme.

3 & 4 The answers to these two activities will depend on your own personal situation and that of your employer. There is no 'right or wrong' answer which we can include here.

5 Training methods for the various workers indicated are as follows.

(a) Worker on a new machine: on-the-job training, coaching.

(b) Accounts clerk working for professional qualification: external course - evening class or day-release.

(c) Supervisors wishing to benefit from participative management and democratic leadership: internal or external course. However, it is important that monitoring and evaluation takes place to ensure that the results of the course are subsequently applied in practice.

(d) New staff: induction training.

NOTES

6 Here is the actual programme for new recruits (of all types) at Guy's and St Thomas' Hospital Trust, as published in Personnel Management Plus.

9.00	Welcome	
9.05	Introduction	*Ground rules and objectives for the day*
9.25	Presentation	*The history of Guy's and St Thomas' hospitals*
10.25	Presentation	*Talk on structure of the management team, trust board and executive*
10.45	Group exercise	*With chief executive Tim Matthews on patient care, funding, hospital processes and measuring the care provided*
12.20	Lunch	
1.15	Tour of Guy's	
2.30	Presentation	*Looking at trust with new eyes - suggestions for change*
2.50	Presentation	*Information on staff organisations*
3.10	Presentation	*Security issues, fire drills, health and safety (including handouts)*
3.30	Presentation	*Session on occupational health*
3.40	Presentation	*Local areas and staff benefits*
3.45	Tour of St Thomas'	
4.30	Presentation	*Facilities management and patient care*
4.45	Closing session	*Evaluation and finish*

Particularly important is the focus on patient care and the group exercises. 'Feedback from the participants shows that they enjoy the discussions and learn a lot more about their colleagues and the trust by participating rather than being talked at.'

7 Depending on your answer you will learn most effectively in particular given situations. For example, the theorist will learn best from lectures and books, whereas the activist will get most from practical activities.

8 Which part of Kolb's cycle you have experienced will be individual to you. for example, you may have been involved in a group project where you contributed less than other group members. Here the cycle is as follows:

- Concrete experience (make a poor contribution to group project)
- Observation/reflection (note that you felt unsure about the subject matter of the group project from the outset)
- Abstraction/generalisation (conclude that your style is to keep quiet when unsure in order to avoid showing your ignorance)
- Application/testing (at the next available opportunity speak out if you don't understand something - you will probably not be alone!)

9&10 The answers to these two activities will depend on your own personal situation and that of your employer. There is no 'right or wrong' answer which we can include here.

11 Validation of a new course is important to ensure that objectives have been achieved. Evaluation of it is more difficult, but at least as important because it identifies the value of the training programme to the organisation.

Chapter 9 : MANAGEMENT FUNCTIONS

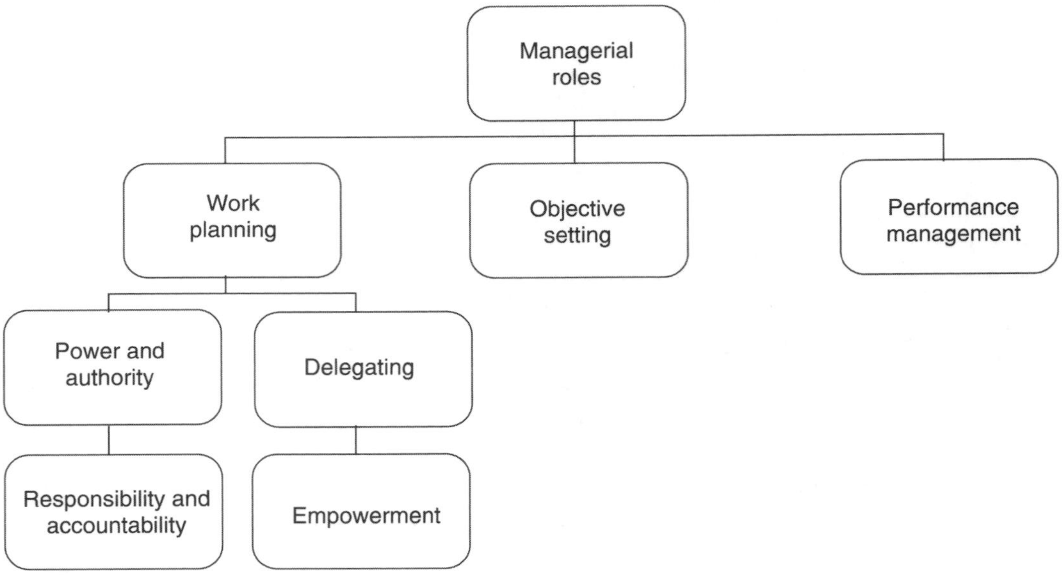

Introduction

The functions of management include *planning* – where managers establish goals, objectives, strategies, and policies and plans to achieve the stated aims of the organisation, and *organising* where managers structure the tasks that need to be performed, and decide which department and which individuals will complete which task and when. Planning helps the organisation to define its purposes and activities. It enables performance standards to be set so that results can be compared with the standard to help managers to see how the organisation is progressing towards its goals.

Because organisations have goals they want to satisfy, they need to direct their activities by:

- Deciding what they want to achieve
- Deciding how and when to do it and who is to do it
- Checking that they do achieve what they want, by monitoring what has been achieved and comparing it with the plan
- Taking action to correct any deviation

Your objectives

In this chapter you will learn about the following:

(a) the role of the manager in the organisation of work

(b) the role of the supervisor in relation to delegation, resource allocation and project planning

(c) the responsibilities of the supervisor

(d) the role of assessing staff

(e) the management tasks involved in organising the work of others

(f) areas of management authority and responsibility

NOTES

1 THE MANAGER

Definition

> **Management** can be defined as: 'getting things done through other people'.

A supervisor is a type of manager.

1.1 Managerial functions

Henri Fayol, who represents the **classical school** of organisation theory, listed the functions of **management**.

Function	Comment
Planning for the future	Selecting objectives and the strategies, policies, programmes and procedures for achieving them.
Organising the work	Establishing a **structure of tasks** to be performed to achieve the goals, **grouping these tasks into jobs** for individuals, creating **groups of jobs** within departments, **delegating authority** to carry out the jobs, providing **systems of information,** and co-ordinating activities.
Commanding	Giving instructions to subordinates to carry out tasks over which the manager has authority for decisions and responsibility for performance.
Co-ordinating	**Harmonising** the activities of individuals and groups within the organisation, reconciling differences of resources.
Controlling	**Measuring** the activities of individuals and groups, to ensure that their performance is in accordance with plans. Deviations from plan are identified and corrected.

Activity 1 **(15 minutes)**

Using Fayol's functions of management, indicate under which of the five headings the activities below fall.

1 Ensuring that the sales department does not exceed its budget.

2 Deciding which products will form the main thrust of advertising during the next financial year.

3 Ensuring that new working practices are communicated to the workforce.

4 Ensuring that the sales department liaises with production on delivery dates.

5 Changing work schedules to reduce idle time.

1.2 Managerial roles: Modern theories

Managerial **functions** are those activities necessary for the **organisation** to be managed. As we saw in the activity above, however, a manager will do a number of **tasks** in each day. Mintzberg suggests that in their daily working lives, managers fulfil three **types** of managerial role.

Role category	Role	Comment
Interpersonal, from formal authority and position	**Figurehead** (or ceremonial)	Representing the company at dinners, conferences etc
	Leader	Hiring, firing and training staff, motivating employees, and reconciling individual needs with the requirements of the organisation
	Liaison	Making contacts with people in other departments
Informational Managers have: • Access to all their staff • Many external contracts	**Monitor**	The manager *monitors* the environment, and receives information from subordinates, superiors and peers in other departments. It might be gossip or speculation.
	Spokesperson	The manager provides information to interested parties either within or outside the organisation
	Disseminator	The manager *disseminates* this information to subordinates
Decisional The manager's formal authority and access to information mean that no one else is in a position to take decisions relating to the work of the department as a whole.	**Entrepreneur**	A manager initiates projects, a number of which may be on the go at any one time.
	Disturbance handler	A manager has to respond to pressures over which the department has no control, taking decisions in unusual or unexpected situations.
	Resource allocator	A manager takes decisions relating to the allocation of scarce resources. The manager determines the department's direction and authorises decisions taken by subordinates.
	Negotiator	Both inside and outside the organisation takes up a great deal of management time.

1.3 Debunking myths about management work

(a) Managers are **not reflective, systematic planners.**

(b) **Managerial work is disjointed** and discontinuous.

(c) Managers **do** have **routine** duties to perform, especially of a ceremonial nature (receiving important guests) or related to authority (signing cheques as a signatory).

(d) Managers prefer verbal (and informal) information to the formal output of management information systems. Verbal information is 'hotter' and probably easier to grasp.

Mintzberg states that general management is, in practice, a matter of **judgement and intuition**, gained from **experience** in **particular situations** rather than from abstract principles. 'Fragmentation and verbal communication' characterise the manager's work.

A manager will play some roles more than others: senior officials, for example, are more likely to be called upon to at as figureheads than team leaders, who will be more concerned with resource allocation and disturbance handling.

Activity 2 **(15 minutes)**

The *Telegraph Magazine* asked a cinema manager: 'What do you actually do? The answer was as follows.

'Everything, apart from being the projectionist and cleaning the lavatories. My office is also the ticket office. If there is a big queue at the confectionery kiosk, I'll help serve and I'll usher people to their seat if we're really busy. Sometimes I go into the cinema before a show and tell the audience about any special events, such as a director coming to give a talk.

'I get in around lunchtime, deal with messages and ensure that the lights and heating are working. I write orders for posters and publicity pictures, popcorn and ice creams and cope with the correspondence for the 2,000 members on our mailing list. I'll brief the projectionist, ushers and kiosk staff and at about 1.45pm the first matinee customers arrive. Our afternoon audience is mainly elderly people and they take some time to settle, so I'll help them to their seats and only start the film when everyone is comfortable. In the evening, more ushers and bar staff arrive and I'll brief them about the programme, seating and timing. While the film is on, I'm selling tickets for the other screen, counting the takings and planning tomorrow. If I get a moment I try to grab something to eat.'

Which of Mintzberg's roles does this manager take on in his 'average' day?

1.4 Managers and leaders

The terms **management** and **leadership** are often used interchangeably, and it will not matter much whether you refer to 'management style' or 'leadership style', for example. However, it is worth noting that it is possible to distinguish between the two ideas.

(a) The functions of management, as discussed above, include planning, organising, co-ordination and controlling. Management is primarily concerned with logic, structure and control. If done well, it produces predictable results, on time.

(b) Leadership, properly considered, involves a different kind of function. It involves essentially people-centred activities, with effects potentially beyond the scope of controlled performance. A leader's special function is to:

 (i) **Create a vision** of something different to the current status quo

 (ii) **Communicate the vision**. This will be particularly powerful if it meets the needs of other people, and if the leader can give it credibility in their eyes

(iii) **Energise, inspire and motivate** others to translate the vision into achievement

(iv) **Create the culture** that will support the achievement, through shared language, rituals, myths and beliefs

In other words, while management have authority by virtue of their position in the organisation to secure the obedience or compliance of their subordinates, leaders direct the efforts of others through vision, inspiration and motivation - forms of **influence**

Definition

> **Influence** is the process by which an individual or group exercises power to determine or modify the behaviour of others.

For routine work, mere **compliance** with directives may be sufficient for the organisation's needs. However, if it wishes to secure **extra input** from its employees – in terms of co-operation, effort and creativity – it may strive for the inspirational quality of leadership, over and above efficient management.

2 THE SUPERVISOR

There are different levels of management in most organisations. A **finance department** in an organisation might be headed by the **finance director** (A) supported by a chief **financial accountant** (B) and chief **management accountant** (C). Lower down in the hierarchy assistant accountants might report to (B) and (C).

The supervisor is the lowest level of management.

Definition

> 'A **supervisor** is a person selected by middle management to take charge of a group of people, or special task, to ensure that work is carried out satisfactorily ... the job is largely reactive dealing with situations as they arise, allocating and reporting back to higher management.' (Savedra and Hawthorn).

2.1 Features of supervision

(a) A supervisor is usually a 'front-line' manager, dealing with the levels of the organisation where the bread-and-butter work is done. The supervisor's **subordinates are non-managerial employees**.

(b) A supervisor does not spend all his or her time on the managerial aspects of his job. Much of the time will be spent doing **technical/operational work** himself.

(c) A supervisor is a '**gatekeeper**' or filter for communication in the organisation.

(d) The supervisor monitors and controls work by means of **day-to-day, frequent and detailed information:** higher levels of management plan and control using longer-term, less frequent and less detailed information, which must be 'edited' or selected and reported by the supervisor.

(e) The **managerial aspects and responsibilities of a supervisor's job are often ill-defined**, and given no precise targets to achievement.

2.2 What do supervisors do?

As a supervisor's job is a junior management job, the tasks of supervision can then be listed under similar headings to the tasks of management.

Planning

- Planning **work** so as to **meet work targets** or schedules set by more senior management
- Planning the **work for each employee;** making estimates of overtime required
- Planning the total **resources** required by the section to meet the total work-load
- Planning work **methods and procedures**
- Attending departmental planning **meetings**
- Preparing **budgets** for the section
- Planning **staff training** and staff development
- Planning the **induction** of new staff
- Planning **improvements** in the work

Organising and overseeing the work of others

- **Ordering** materials and equipment from internal stores or external suppliers
- **Authorising spending** by others on materials, sundry supplies or equipment
- **Interviewing** and selecting staff
- Authorising overtime
- **Allocating work** to staff
- **Allocating equipment** to staff
- Reorganising work (for example when urgent jobs come in)
- Establishing **performance standards** for staff
- Organising transport
- Deciding **job priorities**
- General 'housekeeping' duties
- Maintaining **liaison** with more senior management

NOTES

Activity 3 **(15 minutes)**

Bert Close has decided to delegate the task of identifying the reasons for machine 'down' time (when machines are not working) over the past three months to Brenda Cartwright. This will involve her in talking to operators, foremen and supervisors and also liaising with other departments to establish the effects of this down time. What will Bert need to do to delegate this task effectively? List at least four items he will need to cover with Brenda.

Controlling: making sure the work is done properly

- **Keeping records** of total time worked on the section
- Deciding when sub-standard work must be re-done
- Attending progress control meetings
- Dealing with trade union representatives
- Dealing with personal problems of staff
- Disciplining staff (for late arrival at work and so on)
- Counselling staff
- Ensuring that work procedures are followed
- Ensuring that the quality of work is sustained to the required levels
- Ensuring that safety standards are maintained
- Checking the progress of new staff/staff training, on-the-job training
- Co-ordinating the work of the section with the work of other sections
- Ensuring that work targets are achieved, and explaining the cause to senior management of any failure to achieve these targets

Motivating employees, and dealing with others: appraisal

- Dealing with staff problems
- Dealing with people in other sections
- Reporting to a senior manager
- Dealing with customers
- Motivating staff to improve work performance
- Applying disciplinary measures to subordinates who act unreasonably or work badly
- Helping staff to understand the organisation's goals and targets
- Training staff, and identifying the need for more training

Communicating

- Telling employees about plans, targets and work schedules
- Telling managers about the work that has been done
- Filling in reports (for example absentee reports for the personnel department)
- Writing memos, notes and reports
- Passing information between employees and managers, and between sections
- Collecting information and distributing it to the other persons interested in it.
- Keeping up-to-date with developments

BPP PUBLISHING

'Doing'

- Doing operations work
- Standing in for a senior manager when he or she is on holiday or otherwise absent
- Giving advice to others to help solve problems

Activity 4 **(15 minutes)**

Look at the job of the supervisor (or similar position) in your office (your own job, if you are in such a position).

(a) Identify the (i) managerial and (ii) technical aspects of the job, and list as many as you can. Think of the duties they entail.

(b) Get hold of a copy of the **job description** of a supervisory job (or have a look at one in the organisation manual). Does it bear any relation to the list you compiled yourself? Is it a realistic description of the actual work of the supervisor? Is the 'supervisory' part of the job well-defined (as compared with the technical part)? Are there targets or standards, and training requirements?

(c) Consider your own experience of promotion to a supervisory post (or ask your supervisor). What preparation, training, coaching, and/or advice was given by the manager for this first step into managerial work - was it 'sink or swim'?

3 WORK PLANNING

3.1 The resources at the supervisor's disposal

A supervisor is asked to get a piece of work done, or organise other people to get the work done. A supervisor has resources, as follows.

(a) **Human resources**. A supervisor can deploy his or her staff to do different tasks at different times.

(b) **Material resources,** for example. Some discretion over the use of machinery.

(c) **Financial resources,** within budget guideline.

3.2 Work planning

Work planning is the establishment of work methods and practices to ensure that predetermined objectives are efficiently met at all levels.

(a) **Task sequencing or prioritisation** (ie considering tasks in order of importance for the objective concerned.

(b) **Scheduling or timetabling tasks,** and allocating them to different individuals within appropriate time scales.

(c) **Establishing checks and controls** to ensure that:

(i) Priority deadlines are being met and work is not 'falling behind'.
(ii) Routine tasks are achieving their objectives.

NOTES

(d) **Contingency plans:** arrangements for what should be done if a major upset were to occur, eg if the company's main computer were to break down.

(e) **Co-ordinating the efforts of individuals.**

(f) **Reviewing and controlling performance.**

Some jobs (eg assembly line worker), are entirely routine, and can be performed one step at a time, but for most people, some kind of planning and judgement will be required.

3.3 Assessing where resources are most usefully allocated

A manager or supervisor is responsible for allocating resources between:

(a) **Different ways** to achieve the same objective (eg to increase total profits, sell more, or cut costs etc).

(b) **Competing areas,** where total resources are limited.

ABC analysis (Pareto analysis) suggests that only a small proportion of items will be significant. For example a business might have 99 customers who each spend £10 per month and 1 customer who spends £100,000 per month. Pareto's Law assumes that, for sales, approximately 80% of sales volume is accounted for by 20% of the customers. This means that the manager will:

(a) Concentrate scarce resources on the crucial 20%.
(b) Devise policies and procedures for the remaining 80%, or delegate.

A piece of work will be **high priority** in the following cases.

- **If it has to be completed by a certain time** (ie a deadline)
- **If other tasks depend on it**
- **If other people depend on it**

Routine priorities or regular peak times (eg tax returns etc) can be **planned ahead of time**, and other tasks planned around them.

Non-routine priorities occur when **unexpected demands** are made. Thus planning of work should cover routine scheduled peaks and contingency plans for unscheduled peaks and emergencies.

3.4 Methodical working

Efficiency requires working systematically or methodically.

(a) Ensure that **resources** are available, in sufficient supply and good condition

(b) Organise work in **batches** to save time spent in turning from one job to another

(c) Work to **plans,** schedules, checklists etc

(d) Taking advantage of work **patterns**

(e) Follow up tasks:

- Check on the progress of an operation
- Checking the task is completed when the deadline is reached
- Check payments are made when they fall due
- Retrieve files relevant to future discussions, meetings, correspondence

Activity 5 **(30 minutes)**

Choose a task or event that needs planning.

(a) Make a checklist

(b) Re-arrange items in order of priority and time sequence

(c) Estimate the time for each activity and schedule it, working back from a deadline

(d) Prepare an action sheet

(e) Draw a chart with columns for time units, and rows for activities

(f) Decide what items may have to be 'brought forward' later and how

3.5 Scheduling

Scheduling is where priorities and deadlines are planned and controlled. A schedule establishes a timetable for a logical sequence of tasks, leading up to completion date.

(a) All involved in a task must be given adequate **notice** of work schedules.

(b) The schedules themselves should allow a **realistic time allocation** for each task.

(c) Allowance will have to be made for **unexpected events**.

(d) A **deadline** is the *end* of the longest span of time which may be allotted to a task, ie the last acceptable date for completion. Failure to meet them has a 'knock-on' effect on other parts of the organisation, and on other tasks within an individual's duties. Diary entries may be made on appropriate days (eg: - 'Production completed?' 'Payment received?' 'Bring forward file x' 'One week left for revision').

A number of activities may have to be undertaken in sequence, with some depending on, or taking priority over others.

(a) **Activity scheduling** provides a list of necessary activities in the order in which they must be completed. You might use this to plan each day's work.

(b) **Time scheduling** adds to this the time scale for each activity, and is useful for setting deadlines for tasks. The time for each step is estimated; the total time for the task can then be calculated, allowing for some steps which may be undertaken simultaneously by different people or departments.

3.6 Work programmes and other aids to planning

From activity and time schedules, detailed **work programmes** can be designed for jobs which are carried out over a period of time. Some tasks will have to be started well before the deadline, others may be commenced immediately before, others will be done on the day itself. **Organising a meeting**, for example, may include:

Step 1. Booking accommodation two months before
Step 2. Retrieving relevant files one week before
Step 3. Preparing and circulating an agenda 2-3 days before
Step 4. Checking conference room layout the day before
Step 5. Taking minutes on the day

NOTES

The same applies to stock ordering in advance of production (based on a schedule of known delivery times), preparing correspondence in advance of posting etc.

Once time scales are known and final deadlines set, it is possible to produce **job cards, route cards** and **action sheets**.

Activity	*Days before*	*Date*	*Begun*	*Completed*
1 Request file	6	3.9		
2 Draft report	5	4.9		
3 Type report	3	6.9		
4 Approve report	1	8.9		
5 Signature	1	8.9		
6 Internal messenger	same day	9.9		

Longer-term schedules may be shown conveniently on charts, pegboards or year planners, holiday planners etc. These can be used to show lengths of time and the relationships between various tasks or timetabled events.

3.7 Work allocation

Managers and supervisors divide duties and allocate them to available staff and machinery. Here are all the considerations.

(a) **General tasks.** Some tasks (eg filing, photo-copying) may not have the attention of a dedicated employee. Who will do the work, and will it interfere with their other duties?

(b) **Peak periods** in some tasks may necessitate re-distribution of staff to cope with the work load.

(c) **Status and staff attitudes** must be considered. Flexibility in reassigning people from one job to another or varying the work they do may be hampered by an employee's perception of his or her own status.

(d) Individual **temperaments** and abilities may differ.

(e) Planning should allow for **flexibility** in the event of an employee proving unfit for a task, or more able than his present tasks indicate.

(f) Efforts will have to be **co-ordinated** so that all those involved in a process (eg sales orders) work together as a team or a number of groups.

3.8 Projects

Definition

A **project** is 'an undertaking that has a beginning and an end and is carried out to meet established goals within cost, schedule and quality objectives' (Haynes, *Project Management*).

The difference between project planning and other parts of planning is that a project is not a repetitive activity.

Characteristics of projects

- Specific start and end points

- Well-defined objectives
- The project endeavour is to a degree unique and not repetitious
- The project usually contains costs and time schedules
- A project cuts across many organisational and functional boundaries

3.9 Examples of projects

Project	Comment
Building and construction	Any building project, such as the construction of 'Cyberjaya', a new high-tech city in Malaysia.
Management	Development of an information system.
Supervision	Installing new machinery

The job of **project management** is to foresee as many dangers as possible, and to plan, organise and control activities so that they are avoided.

3.10 The role of the project manager or supervisor

Projects have to be co-ordinated. A project manager's duties are outlined below.

Duty	Comment
Outline project planning	• Developing project targets such as overall costs or timescale (eg project should take 20 weeks). • Dividing the project into activities (eg analysis, programming, testing), and placing these activities into the right sequence, often a complicated task if overlapping. • Developing the procedures and structures, manage the project (eg plan weekly team meetings, performance reviews etc).
Detailed planning	Identifying the tasks, resource requirements, network analysis for scheduling.
Teambuilding	The project manager has to meld the various people into an effective team.
Communication	The project manager must let superiors know what is going on, and ensure that members of the project team are properly briefed.
Co-ordinating project activities	Between the project team and users, and other external parties (eg suppliers of hardware and software).
Monitoring and control	The project manager should estimate the causes for each departure from the standard, and take corrective measures.
Problem-resolution	Unforeseen problems may arise, and it falls upon the project manager to sort them out, or to delegate the responsibility for so doing to a subordinate.
Quality control	There is often a short-sighted trade-off between getting the project out on time and the project's quality.

4 POWER AND AUTHORITY

Organisations feature a large number of different activities to be co-ordinated, and large numbers of people whose **co-operation and support** is necessary for the manager to get anything done. As you have probably noticed if you have worked for any length of time, organisations rarely run as clockwork, and all depend on the directed energy of those within them.

Definition

> **Power** is the **ability** to get things done.

A manager without power, of whatever kind, cannot do his/her job properly, and this applies to supervisors too. Power is not something a person has in isolation: it is exercised over other individuals or groups.

4.1 Types of power

Type of power	Description
Physical, coercive power	This is the power of physical force or punishment. Physical power is absent from most organisations, but organisations can sometimes use hidden forms of coercion to get what they want
Resource power	Access to or control over valued resources is a source of power. For example, managers have a resource of information or other contacts. The amount of resource power a person has depends on the scarcity of the resource, how much the resource is valued by others, and how far the resource is under the manager's control
Legitimate or position power	This is power associated with a particular job or position in the hierarchy. For example, your boss has the power to authorise certain expenses, or organise work. This is equivalent to **authority**
Expert power	A person may have power if his/her experience, qualifications or expertise are recognised. Typically, accountants have a type of expert power because of their knowledge of the tax system.
Personal power	A person may be powerful simply by force of personality, which can influence other people, inspire them etc.
Negative power	This is the power to disrupt operations, such as strike, refusal to communicate information

Definition

> **Authority** is the *right* of a person to ask someone else to do something and expect it to be done. Authority is thus another word for position power.

Managerial authority consists of:

(a) **Making decisions within the scope of authority** given to the position. For example, a supervisor's authority is limited to his/her team and with certain limits. For items of expenditure more than a certain amount, the supervisor may have to go to someone else up the hierarchy.

(b) **Assigning tasks** to subordinates, and expecting satisfactory performance of these tasks.

Activity 6 **(15 minutes)**

What types of authority and power are being exercised in the following case?

Marcus is an accountant supervising a team of eight technicians. He has to submit bank reconciliation statements every week to the chief accountant. However, the company runs four different bank accounts and Marcus gets a team member, Dave, to do it for him.

Marcus asks Isabella to deal with the purchase ledger - the company obtains supplies from all over the world, and Isabella, having worked once for an international bank, is familiar with letters of credit and other documentation involved with overseas trade. Isabella has recently told Marcus that Maphia Ltd, a supplier, should not be paid because of problems with the import documentation, even though Marcus has promised Maphia to pay them.

Marcus is getting increasingly annoyed with Sandra who seems to be leaving Marcus's typing until last, although she says she has piles of other work to do. 'Like reading the newspaper,' thinks Marcus, who is considering pulling rank by giving her an oral warning.

Definition

Line authority is the authority a manager has over a subordinate, arising from their respective positions in the organisation hierarchy. In other words, if you have line authority you an exercise position power over someone immediately below you.

There are other forms of authority which individuals (or departments) may exercise in the organisation.

Definitions

Staff authority is the influence wielded when an expert gives specialist **advice** to another manager or department, even if there is no direct line authority. (An example might be the influence of legal advice from the legal department, or advice on budgetary constraints from the accounts department.)

Functional authority is staff authority which has been built into the structure and policies of the organisation, for example where a specialist department lays down *procedures* and *rules* for other departments to follow within the area of its expertise. (The Personnel department, for example, may impose certain recruitment and selection procedures on other departments.)

5 RESPONSIBILITY AND ACCOUNTABILITY

Definitions

Responsibility is the **obligation** a person has to fulfil a task, which (s)he has been given.

Accountability is a person's liability to be called to account for the fulfilment of tasks they have been given.

You might be a bit confused by the various terms. They are related but they mean different things. But just keep in mind:

	Comment
You are **given authority** to do something	As a supervisor, you have the authority to plan command and control the work of your team, within certain limitations.
You are **responsible for** something	Your boss has left you in charge of the team. He says 'I'd like you to get a balance sheet and P & L prepared by 6pm tonight.' That is your responsibility. You are busy on other things, but you give the balance sheet to one team member and a P & L to the other.
You are **accountable to** someone.	You give the completed balance sheet and P & L to your boss who is annoyed that some of the figures don't agree. You are accountable to the boss: you cannot blame your subordinates; you were given the task, and the authority to make sure it was done. As head of the department you are accountable for what they do.

Activity 7 **(5 minutes)**

Can a person delegate responsibility, authority and accountability to a subordinate?

5.1 Responsibility without authority

In practice, matters are rarely as clear-cut, and in many organisations responsibility and authority are:

	Comments
Not clear	When the organisation is doing something new or in a different way, its existing rules and procedures may be out of date or unable to cope with the new development. Various people may try to 'empire build'. The managers may not have designed the organisation very well.
Shifting	In large organisations there may be real conflict between different departments; or the organisation may, as it adapts to its environment, need to change.

Don't skip this activity as the issues it covers are important. Having completed the activity, you should have some idea of the subject matter of the next two sections.

Activity 8 **(15 minutes)**

You have just joined a small accounts department. The financial controller keeps a very close eye on expenditure and, being prudent, believes that nothing should be spent that is not strictly necessary. She has recently gone on a three week holiday to Venezuela. You have been told that you need to prepare management accounts, and for this you have to obtain information from the payroll department in two weeks time. This is standard procedure. However, there are two problems. One of the other people in your department has gone sick, and a temporary replacement will be needed very shortly. The personnel department say: 'We need a staff requisition from the Financial Controller before we can get in a temp. Sorry, you'll just have to cancel your weekend'. The payroll department is happy to give you the information you need - except directors' salaries, essential for the accounts to be truly accurate.

What is the underlying cause of the problem and what, in future, should you ask the Financial Controller to do to put it right?

6 DELEGATION

Definition

Delegation of authority is when a superior gives to a subordinate part of his or her own authority to make decisions.

Note that delegation can only occur if the superior initially possesses the authority to delegate; a subordinate cannot be given organisational authority to make decisions unless it would otherwise be the superior's right to make those decisions personally.

6.1 Reasons for delegation

Managers and supervisors must delegate some authority because:

(a) There are **physical and mental limitations** to the work load of any individual or group in authority.

(b) Managers and supervisors are free to **concentrate on the aspects of the work** (such as planning), which only they are competent (and paid) to do.

(c) The **increasing size and complexity** of some organisations calls for specialisation, both managerial and technical.

However, by delegating authority to assistants, the supervisor takes on the extra tasks of:

- **Monitoring their performance**
- **Co-ordinating** the efforts of different assistants.

6.2 The process of delegation

Step 1. **Specify the expected performance** levels of the assistant, keeping in mind the assistant's level of expertise.

Step 2. **Formally assign tasks** to the assistant, who should formally agree to do them.

Step 3. **Allocate resources and authority** to the assistant to enable him or her to carry out the delegated tasks at the expected level of performance.

Step 4. **Maintain contact** with the assistant to review the progress made and to make constructive criticism. **Feedback** is essential for control, and also as part of the learning process.

Remember that ultimate **accountability** for the task remains with the supervisor: if it is not well done it is at least partly the fault of poor delegation, and it is still the supervisor's responsibility to get it re-done.

6.3 Problems of delegation

Many managers and supervisors are **reluctant to delegate** and attempt to do many routine matters themselves in addition to their more important duties.

(a) **Low confidence and trust** in the abilities of their staff: the suspicion that 'if you want it done well, you have to do it yourself'.

(b) The burden of **accountability for the mistakes of subordinates**, aggravated by (a) above.

(c) A **desire to 'stay in touch'** with the department or team - both in terms of workload and staff - particularly if the manager does not feel 'at home' in a management role.

(d) **Feeling threatened.** An unwillingness to admit that assistants have developed to the extent that they could perform some of the supervisor's duties. The supervisor may feel threatened by this sense of 'redundancy'.

(e) **Poor control and communication systems** in the organisation, so that the manager feels he has to do everything himself, if he is to retain real control and responsibility for a task, and if he wants to know what is going on.

(f) An **organisational culture** that has failed to reward or recognise effective delegation, so that the manager may not realise that delegation is positively regarded (rather than as shirking responsibility).

(g) **Lack of understanding** of what delegation involves - not giving assistants total control, or making the manager himself redundant.

As an accountant, you might like the idea of a **trust-control dilemma** in a superior-subordinate relationship. The sum of trust and control is a constant amount:

T + C = Y

where T = the trust the superior has in the subordinate, and the trust which the subordinate feels the superior has in him

C = the degree of control exercised by the superior over the subordinate

Y = a constant, unchanging value

If there is any increase in C (if the superior retains more 'control' or authority), the subordinate will immediately recognise that he is being trusted less. If the superior wishes to show more trust in the subordinate, he can only do so by reducing C: by delegating more authority.

6.4 Overcoming the reluctance of managers to delegate

(a) **Train the subordinates** so that they are capable of handling delegated authority in a responsible way. If assistants are of the right 'quality', supervisors will be prepared to trust them more.

(b) Have a system of **open communications**, in which the supervisor and assistants freely interchange ideas and information. If the assistant is given all the information needed to do the job, and if the supervisor is aware of what the assistant is doing:

   (i) The assistant will make better-informed decisions.

   (ii) The supervisor will not panic because he does not know what is going on.

(c) **Ensure that a system of control is established**. If responsibility and accountability are monitored at all levels of the management hierarchy, the dangers of relinquishing authority and control to assistants are significantly lessened.

6.5 When to delegate

(a) Is the **acceptance** of staff affected required (for morale, relationships, ease of implementation of the decision etc)?

(b) Is the **quality** of the decision most important? Many technical financial decisions may be of this type, and should be retained by the supervisor if he or she alone has the knowledge and experience to make them.

(c) Is the **expertise or experience** of assistants relevant or **necessary** to the task, and will it enhance the quality of the decision?

(d) Can **trust** be placed in the competence and reliability of the assistants?

(e) Does the **decision** require tact and confidentiality, or, on the other hand, maximum exposure and assimilation by employees?

In instances where **reference upwards** to the manager's own superior may be necessary, the manager should consider:

(a) Whether the decision is **relevant** to the superior: will it have any impact on the boss's area of responsibility, such as strategy, staffing, or the departmental budget?

(b) Whether the superior has **authority** or **information** relevant to the decision that the manager does not possess: for example, authority over issues which affect other departments or interdepartmental relations, or information only available at senior levels.

(c) The **political climate** of the organisation: will the superior expect to be consulted, and resent any attempt to make the decision without his authority?

Activity 9 **(15 minutes)**

You are the manager of an accounts section of your organisation and have stopped to talk to one of the clerks in the office to see what progress he is making. He complains bitterly that he is not learning anything. He gets only routine work to do and it is the same routine. He has not even been given the chance to swap jobs with someone else. You have picked up the same message from others in the office. You discuss the situation with Jean Howe the recently appointed supervisor. She appears to be very busy and harassed. When confronted with your observations she says that she is fed up with the job. She is worked off her feet, comes early, goes late, takes work home and gets criticised behind her back by incompetent clerks.

What has gone wrong?

7 EMPOWERMENT

Empowerment and delegation are related.

Definition

Empowerment is the current term for making workers (and particularly work teams) responsible for achieving, and even setting, work targets, with the freedom to make decisions about how they are to be achieved.

Empowerment goes in hand in hand with:

(a) **Delayering** or a cut in the number of levels (and managers) in the chain of command, since responsibility previously held by middle managers is, in effect, being given to operational workers.

(b) **Flexibility**, since giving responsibility to the people closest to the products and customer encourages responsiveness - and cutting out layers of communication, decision-making and reporting speeds up the process.

(c) **New technology**, since there are more 'knowledge workers'. Such people need less supervision, being better able to identify and control the means to clearly understood ends. Better information systems also remove the mystique and power of managers as possessors of knowledge and information in the organisation.

7.1 Reasons for empowerment

'The people lower down the organisation possess the knowledge of what is going wrong with a process but lack the authority to make changes. Those further up the structure have the authority to make changes, but lack the profound knowledge required to identify the right solutions. The only solution is to change the culture of the

NOTES

organisation so that everyone can become involved in the process of improvement and work together to make the changes.' (Max Hand)

The change in organisation structure and culture as a result of empowerment can be shown in the diagram below.

Traditional hierarchical structure: fulfilling management requirements

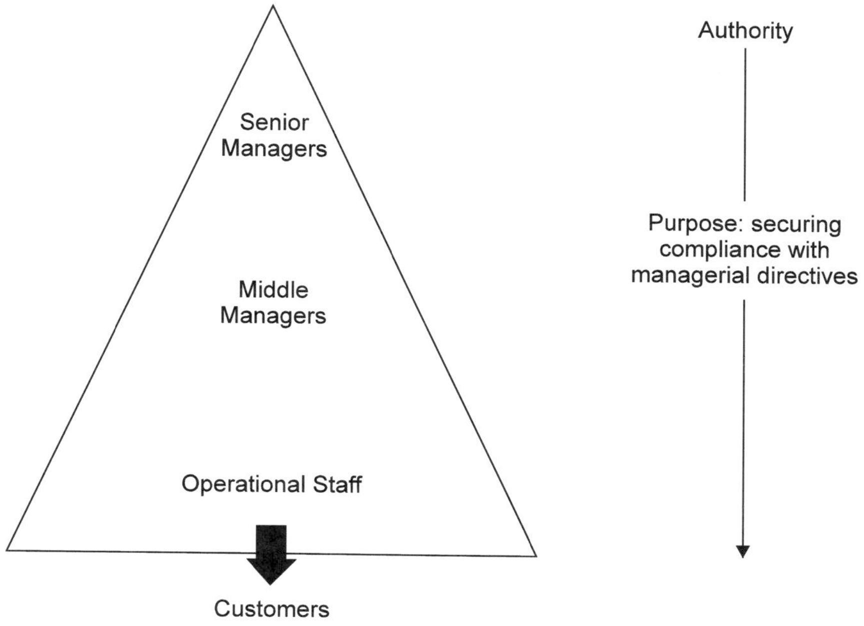

Empowerment structure: supporting workers in serving the customer

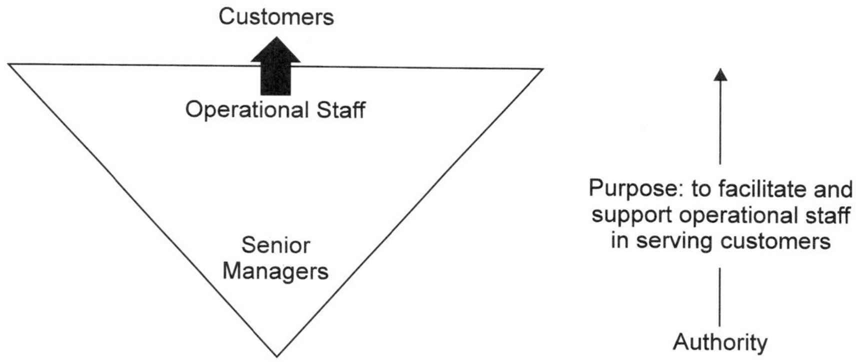

The argument, in a nutshell, is that by empowering workers (or 'decentralising' control of business units, or devolving/delegating responsibility, or removing levels in hierarchies that restrict freedom), not only will the job be done more effectively but the people who do the job will get more out of it.

CASE EXAMPLE

The validity of this view and its relevance to modern trends appears to be borne out by the approach to empowerment adopted by *Harvester Restaurants*, as described in *Personnel Management*. The management structure comprises a branch manager and a 'coach', while everyone else is a team member. Everyone within a team has one or more 'accountabilities' (these include recruitment, drawing up rotas, keeping track of sales targets and so on) which are shared out by the team members at their weekly team meetings. All the team members at different times act as 'co-ordinator' to the person responsible for taking the snap decisions that are frequently necessary in a busy restaurant. Apparently all of the staff involved agree that empowerment has made their jobs more interesting and has hugely increased their motivation and sense of involvement.

---

8 OBJECTIVE SETTING

For learning and motivation to be effective, it is essential that people know exactly what their objectives are. This enables them to do the following.

- Plan and direct their effort towards the objectives
- Monitor their performance against objectives and adjust (or learn) if required
- Experience the reward of achievement once the objectives have been reached

8.1 Types of objectives for individuals and teams

Individual objectives must be directed towards, or 'dovetailed' with organisational goals. Each managerial job must be focused on the success of the business as a whole, not just one part of it, so that the results can be measured in terms of his or her contribution. People must know what their targets of performance are.

Work objectives – at team level, they relate to the purpose of the team and the contribution it is expected to make to the goals of the department and the organisation. At individual level, they are related specifically to the job. They clarify what the individual is expected to do and they enable the performance of the individual to be measured.

Standing aims and objectives include qualitative aims – issues such as promptness and courtesy when dealing with customer requests – and quantified targets, eg for a sales team would be to ensure that all phone calls are picked up within three rings.

Output or improvement targets have most of the features of SMART objectives. A sales person may be given a target of increasing the number of sales made in a particular district in a certain time. Many organisations have targets that involve the number of defects in goods produced, or seek to find ways of working more efficiently.

Development goals deal with how an individual can improve his or her own performance and skills. These goals are set at the appraisal interview and are part of the performance measurement system.

8.2 Management by objectives (MBO)

Integrating the organisation's and the individual's objectives is not always easy. The hierarchy of objectives illustrated below shows a cascade of objectives from the organisation to the individual.

NOTES

STRATEGIC PLANS - (Longer term)

↓

TACTICAL PLANS - (Shorter term, for product market development, resource development, operations and organisation)

↓

UNIT OR DEPARTMENTAL PLANS

↓

INDIVIDUAL MANAGERS' OBJECTIVES

Basically the MBO approach involves the systematic setting of targets and checking of progress for each management position.

The first stage sets the unit objectives required for all departments (steps 1-4 below).

Step 1. They must be set first of all in terms of primary targets, eg relating to achievement of production schedules and delivery dates, the quality of output or efficiency in the use of resources (labour, productivity, material usage or services).

Step 2. For each of these primary targets, secondary targets (or sub targets) will be set.

Step 3. Is the identification of the individual managers within the unit who are in a position to influence the achievement of each of them.

Step 4. Top management will then make a unit improvement plan for each unit of the business, setting out specifically the objectives for improvement, the performance standards and the time scale.

The second stage is to agree and define the key result areas (known as KRAs). These are those areas where an individual's failure to perform would damage an important company objective. The key results of an information systems manager might be as given below.

ITEM	**KEY RESULT**
Service to users	To ensure that users get regular software upgrades, with appropriate help lines and training
Use of resources and efficiency level	The time when users cannot access the network must not exceed 5%
Costs	The cost per operating hour must not exceed £60
Quality	Queries from users must be responded to within ten minutes

The next step is to define one or two improvement objectives for each key result area, eg to improve the defective product rate to one per ten thousand manufactured, within four months.

Review periods will be planned where manager and subordinates can discuss progress at regular intervals. At the final review period, results will be compared to objectives and a factual, constructive discussion will attempt to find the reasons for shortfalls.

9 PERFORMANCE MANAGEMENT: AN INTRODUCTION

Definition

Performance management is: 'a means of getting better results...by understanding and managing performance within an agreed framework of planned goals, standards and competence requirements. It is a process to establish a shared understanding about what is to be achieved, and an approach to managing and developing people..[so that it]...will be achieved' (Armstrong, Handbook of Personnel Management Practice).

9.1 Features of performance management

Armstrong 'unpacks' this definition, and describes some other features of performance management.

Aspect	Comment
Agreed framework of goals, standards and competence requirements	As in MBO, the manager and the employee agree about a standard of performance, goals and the skills needed.
Performance management is a process	Managing people's performance is an everyday issue to generate real results. It is not just a system of form filling.
Shared understanding	People need to understand the nature of high levels of performance so they can work towards them.
Approach to managing and developing people	(1) How managers work with their teams (2) How team members work with managers and each other. (3) Developing individuals to improve their performance.
Achievement	The aim is to enable people to realise their potential and maximise their contribution to the organisation's well being.
Line management	A performance management system is primarily the concern, not of experts in the personnel/HRM department, but of the managers responsible for driving the business.
All staff	Everybody is involved in the success of the organisation, so managers must be included in the system.

Aspect	Comment
Specific	As each organisation has unique issues to face, performance management systems cannot really be bought off the peg.
Future-based	Performance management is forward-looking, based on the organisation's future needs and what the individual must do to satisfy them

9.2 The process of performance management

Step 1. From the **business plan**, identify the requirements and competences required to carry it out.

Step 2. Draw up a **performance agreement**, defining the expectations of the individual or team, covering standards of performance, performance indicators and the skills and competences people need.

Step 3. Draw up a **performance and development plan** with the individual. These record the actions needed to improve performance, normally covering development in the current job. They are discussed with job holders and will cover, typically:

- The areas of performance the individual feels in need of development
- What the individual and manager agree is needed to enhance performance
- Development and training initiatives

Step 4. **Manage performance continually throughout the year,** not just at appraisal interviews done to satisfy the personnel department. Managers can review actual performance, with more informal interim reviews at various times of the year.

(a) High performance is reinforced by praise, recognition, increasing responsibility. Low performance results in coaching or counselling

(b) Work plans are updated as necessary.

(c) Deal with performance problems, by identifying what they are, establish the reasons for the shortfall, take control action (with adequate resources) and provide feedback

Step 5. Performance review. At a defined period each year, success against the plan is reviewed, but the whole point is to assess what is going to happen in future.

Organisations are introducing such systems for much the same reason as they pursued management by objectives, in other words, to:

- Tie in individual performance with the performance of the organisation
- Indicate where training and development may be necessary

NOTES

Chapter roundup

- Organisations typically employ managers to direct them. The classic functions of managers were: **planning**, **organising**, **commanding**, **co-ordinating** and **controlling** (Fayol). In businesses, we can add the need to achieve **economic results.**
- A manager's job is not clear-cut and systematic in practice. More recent descriptions of the manager's role (Mintzberg) describe **interpersonal** roles (figurehead, leader, liaison), **informational** roles (monitor, disseminator, spokesperson) and **decisional** roles (entrepreneur, disturbance-handler, resource allocator, negotiator).
- The **supervisor** is at the first level of management, being closest to operational work. A supervisor is a person normally selected to take charge of a group of people or special task to ensure that work is carried out satisfactorily, as well as fulfilling his or her own tasks.
- Supervisors often have to plan the use of **resources** in their section and **schedule** activities to ensure that work is done on time, to standard and to budget. Supervisors might act as project managers: a **project** is a defined task with a beginning and an end point.
- **Power** is the ability to get things done.
- There are many types of power in organisations: position or **legitimate power**, expert power, personal power, resource power and negative power are examples.
- **Authority** is related to position power. It is the right to take certain decisions within certain boundaries.
- A person with **responsibility** is given a task to get done. Such a person must have the necessary authority to command resources and staff to get the job. Responsibility without authority is stressful for the individual.
- Responsibility can be **delegated**, but the person delegating responsibility still remains accountable to his or her boss that the job has been done to the right standard. Accountability is not delegated.
- **Delegation** is necessary to get work distributed throughout the organisation. Successful delegation requires the resolution of the Trust-Control dilemma. Some managers and supervisors are reluctant to delegate.
- Successful delegation requires that people have the right skills and the authority to do the job, and are given feedback.
- **Empowerment** takes the process of delegation further. Its advantages are not simply that it releases managers to do more important things, but that front line staff are closest to customers are best able to take decisions concerning them.
- Management by objectives is a way of integrating the organisation's and the individual's objectives. The process is one where managers agree specific, measurable goals with each employee on a regular basis. The employee is then responsible for attaining these goals within a certain time. After this time has elapsed the employee and superior need to discuss results or establish new objectives.
- Performance management suggests that people must agree performance standards, that the responsibility for performance management is principally that of line management, and that it is a conscious commitment to developing and managing people in organisations. It is a continuous process.

Quick quiz

1. List the traditional management functions.
2. List three categories of managerial roles.
3. 'A supervisor's job is like any other manager's.' Do you agree?
4. List some aids to planning work.
5. What is unusual about project management?
6. What is legitimate power?
7. Give an example of negative power
8. Why might functional authority be a good thing for the organisation?
9. Why can't accountability be delegated?
10. Why are there problems in determining authority and responsibility?
11. List the stages in the process of delegation.
12. List some problems in delegation.

Answers to quick quiz

1. The functions of management are: planning, organising, co-ordinating, controlling and commanding. (See para 1.1)
2. Interpersonal, informational, decisional. (See para 1.2)
3. No - a supervisor is in charge of non-managerial employees, whereas a manager might be in charge of other managers in the levels below; a supervisor's job often contains a technical aspect. (See para 2.1)
4. Scheduling, deadlines, contingency plans, job cards. (See para 3.2)
5. A project has specific start and end points, whereas other activities might be continuous. (See para 3.8)
6. Legitimate power is power arising from formal position in the organisation hierarchy; authority, in other words. (See para 4.1)
7. Going on strike; refusal to communicate; withhold information; delaying etc. (See para 4.1)
8. Because it is exercised impersonally, impartially and automatically. (See para 4.1)
9. Because the delegator has been given the task by his/her own boss. (See Para 5)
10. Because the boundaries are often unclear and shifting. (See para 5.1)
11. Specify performance levels; formally assign task; allocate resources and authority; give feedback. (See para 6.2)
12. Low trust, low competence, fear, worry about accountability. (See para 6.6)

Answers to activities

1. Fayol's functions would define the activities: 1 = controlling; 2 = planning; 3 = commanding; 4 = co-ordinating; 5 = organising.

2 Your answer may well be that the cinema manager takes on all of Mintzberg's roles, although **figurehead** and **negotiator** play a very minor part in his day.

3 Your answer should include some of the following.

To delegate, Bert must identify the objectives of the task; explain the limits within which Brenda will work, such as liaising with the sales department but not contacting customers; establish deadlines; indicate in what format the results should be made (oral report, written report, memo); and agree how progress will be monitored (brief weekly meetings, weekly memo or informal chats).

4 & 5. Your answer will depend on your own specific circumstances and the situation/example you have chosen.

6 Marcus exercises position power because he has the right, given to him by the chief accountant, to get his staff, such as Dave, to do bank reconciliations. Dave does not do bank recs because of Marcus's personality or expertise, but because of the simple fact that Marcus is his boss. Marcus also exercises position power by getting Isabella to do the purchase ledger. However, Isabella exercises expert power because she knows more about import/export documentation than Marcus. She does not have the authority to stop the payment to Maphia, and Marcus can ignore what she says, but that would be a bad decision. Sandra is exercising negative power as far as Marcus is concerned, although she is claiming, perhaps, to exercise resource power - her time is a scarce resource. No-one appears to be exercising physical power as such, although Marcus's use of the disciplinary procedures would be a type of coercive power.

7 Responsibility for a task can be delegated, simply by using your authority to give the job to someone else. But accountability cannot be delegated: you are still accountable for the work you have delegated to a junior. It is your job to ensure the job is done: you are accountable to your boss.

8 The immediate problem is that the Financial Controller should have considered these issues before she went to Venezuela. The underlying cause, as far as you are concerned, is that you have responsibility to do a task but without the authority - to obtain all the information you need and to hire a temp - to do the job. In future the Financial Controller should, when delegating the task, delegate the authority to do it.

9 The problem appears to be that the new supervisor is taking too much of the department's work on to herself. While she is overworked, her subordinates are apparently not being stretched and as a result motivation and morale amongst them are poor. The supervisor herself is unhappy with the position and there is a danger that declining job satisfaction will lead to inefficiencies and eventually staff resignations.

There could be a number of causes contributing to the problem.

(a) Jean Howe may have been badly selected, ie she may not have the ability required for a supervisory job.

(b) Alternatively she may just be unaware of what is involved in a supervisor's role. She may not have realised that much of the task consists of managing subordinates; she is not required to shoulder all the detailed technical work herself.

(c) There may be personality problems involved. Jean Howe regards her clerks as incompetent and this attitude may arise simply form an inability to get on with them socially. (Another possibility is that her staff actually are incompetent.)

(d) The supervisor does much of the department's work herself. This may be because she does not understand the kind of tasks which can be delegated and the way in which delegation of authority can improve the motivation and job satisfaction of subordinates.

As manager you have already gone some way towards identifying the actual causes of the problem You have spoken to some of the subordinates concerned and also to the supervisor. You could supplement this by a review of personnel records relating to Jean Howe to discover how her career has progressed so far and what training she had received (if any) in the duties of a supervisor. You may then be in a position to determine which of the possible causes of the problems are operating in this case.

Chapter 10 :
MOTIVATION AND EVALUATION OF PERFORMANCE

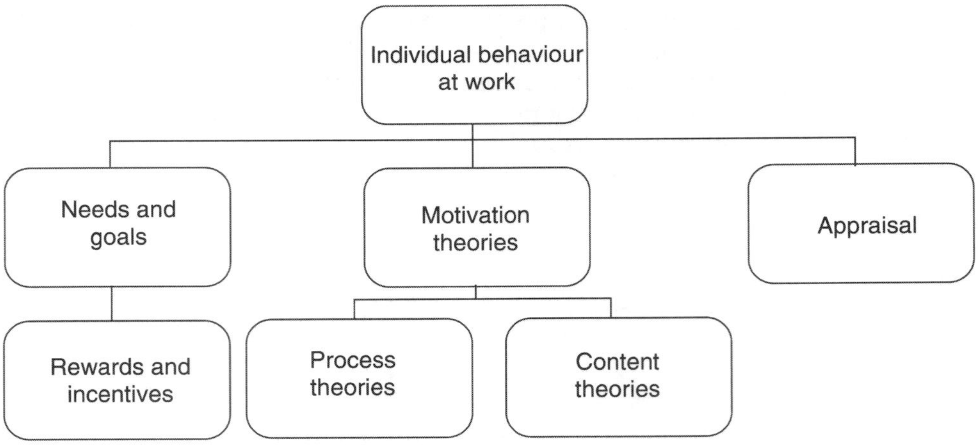

Introduction

Much research has been undertaken in an attempt to understand what motivates individual employees at work and how managers can improve it.

The motivational strategy that is decided on will depend on the beliefs held and the culture that prevails in the organisation. Maslow's theory holds that human needs form a hierarchy ranging from the lowest-order needs (physiological needs) to the highest order need – self actualisation. According to Herzberg's two factor theory, there are two sets of motivating factors. Vroom's expectancy theory suggests that people are motivated to reach a goal if they think the goal is worthwhile and can see that the activities will help them achieve the goal.

Your objectives

In this chapter you will learn about the following.

(a) Individual behaviour at work

(b) Needs and goals

(c) Theories of motivation

(d) Rewards and incentives

(e) Pay as a motivator

1 INDIVIDUAL BEHAVIOUR AT WORK

1.1 Personality

In order to identify, describe and explain the differences between people, psychologists use the concept of personality.

Definition

> **Personality** is the total pattern of characteristic ways of thinking, feeling and behaving that constitute the individual's distinctive method of relating to the environment.

1.2 Self and self-image

Personality develops from dynamic process whereby the individual interacts with his or her environment and other people, through experience.

(a) **Self-image.** If people regularly praise your hard work for example, you may have an image of yourself as a successful worker. People tend to behave, and expect to be treated, in accordance with their self-image.

(b) **Personality development.** People tend, as they mature, to become more actively independent, to take on more equal or superior relationships (moving from child-adult, to adult-adult and adult-child relationships) and to develop self control and self awareness.

1.3 Personality and work behaviour

An individual should be 'compatible' with ' work' in three ways.

Compatibility	Comments
With the task	Different personality types suit different types of work. A person who appears unsociable and inhibited will find sales work, involving a lot of social interactions, intensely stressful - and will probably not be very good at it.
With the systems and management culture of the organisation	Some people hate to be controlled, for example, but others (or an 'authoritarian' personality type) want to be controlled and dependent in a work situation, because they find responsibility threatening.
With other personalities in the team	Personality clashes are a prime source of conflict at work. An achievement-oriented personality, for example, tends to be a perfectionist, is impatient and unable to relax, and will be unsociable if people seem to be getting in the way of performance: such a person will clearly be frustrated and annoyed by laid-back sociable types working (or not working) around him.

1.4 Incompatibility

Where incompatibilities occur the manager or supervisor will have to:

(a) **Restore compatibility**: this may be achieved by reassigning an individual to tasks more suited to his personality type, for example, or changing management style to suit the personalities of the team.

(b) **Achieve a compromise**: individuals should be encouraged to:

(i) **Understand the nature** of their differences. Others have the right to be themselves (within the demands of the team); personal differences should not be 'taken personally', as if they were adopted deliberately to annoy.

(ii) **Modify their behaviour** if necessary.

(c) **Remove the incompatible personality**. In the last resort, obstinately difficult or disruptive people may simply have to be weeded out of the team.

Activity 1 **(10 minutes)**

Look at the following list and number the qualities in priority order. 1 is very important, 2 is quite important, 3 is unimportant.

(a) Good appearance	(f) A pleasant personality
(b) Ability to do the job	(g) The ability to reason
(c) Ability to answer questions clearly	(h) Being interested in further training
(d) A pleasant speaking voice	(i) Being used to working in a team
(e) Being objective	(j) Being a good listener

1.5 Perception

Different people 'see' things differently and human beings behave in (and in response to) the world, not 'as it really is', but as they see it.

Definition

Perception is the psychological process by which stimuli or in-coming sensory data are selected and organised into patterns which are meaningful to the individual.

Perception may be determined by any or all of the following.

(a) **The context**. People 'see what they want to see': whatever is necessary or relevant in the situation in which they find themselves. You might notice articles on management in the newspapers while studying this module which normally you would not notice.

(b) **The nature of the stimuli**. Our attention tends to be drawn to large, bright, loud, unfamiliar, moving and repeated (not repetitive) stimuli. Advertisers know it.

(c) **Internal factors**. Our attention is drawn to stimuli that match our personality, needs, interests, expectations and so on If you are hungry, for example, you will pick the smell of food out of a mix of aromas.

(d) **Fear or trauma.** People are able to avoid seeing things that they don't want to see: things that are threatening to their security of self-image, or things that are too painful for them.

A complementary process of **perceptual organisation** deals with the **interpretation** of the data which has been gathered and filtered.

1.6 Perception and work behaviour

People do not respond to the world 'as it really is', but as they **perceive it to be**. If people act in ways that seem illogical or contrary to you, it is probably not because of stupidity or defiance, but because they simply do not see things in the same way you do.

(a) Consider whether **you** might be misinterpreting the situation.

(b) Consider whether **others** might be misinterpreting the situation or interpreting it differently from you.

(c) When tackling a task or a problem get the people involved to **define the situation** as they see it.

(d) Be aware of the most common clashes of perception at work.

  (i) **Managers and staff.** The experience of work can be very different for managerial and non-managerial personnel. Efforts to bridge the gap may be viewed with suspicion.

  (ii) **Work cultures**. Different functions in organisations may have very different time-scales and cultures of work, and will therefore perceive the work, and each other, in different ways.

  (iii) **Race and gender.** A joke, comment or gesture that one person may see as a 'bit of a laugh' may be offensive - and construed as harassment under the law - to another.

NOTES

Activity 2 **(15 minutes)**

Identify the perceptual problem(s) in the following cases.

(a) An autocratic manager tries to adopt a more participative style of management, in order to improve the morale of his staff. He tells them they will be given more responsibility, and will be 'judged and rewarded accordingly'. For some reason, morale seems to worsen, and several people ask to transfer to other departments.

(b) A woman has just been promoted to the management team. At the first management meeting, the chairman introduces her to her new colleagues - all male - and says: 'At least we'll get some decent tea in these meetings from now on, eh?' Almost everyone laughs. For some reason, the woman does not contribute much in the meeting, and the chairman later tells one of his colleagues: 'I hope we haven't made a mistake. She doesn't seem to be a team player at all.'

(c) A new employee wanders into the office canteen, and is offered a cup of coffee by a youngster in jeans and an T-shirt, who has been chatting to the canteen supervisor. The youngster joins the man at his table (to his surprise) and asks how he likes working there so far. After a while, glancing uneasily at the man behind the serving counter, the new employee asks: 'Is it OK for you to be sitting here talking to me? I mean, won't the boss mind?' The youngster replies: 'I am the boss. Actually, I'm the boss of the whole company. Biscuit?'

1.7 Attitudes

Attitudes are our general standpoint on things: the positions we have adopted in regard to particular issues, things and people, as we perceive them.

Definition

An **attitude** is 'a mental state ... exerting a directive or dynamic influence upon the individual's response to all objects and situations with which it is related.'

Attitudes are thought to contain three basic components.

- Knowledge, beliefs or disbeliefs, perceptions
- Feelings and desires (positive or negative)
- Volition, will or the intention to perform an action

1.8 Attitudes and work

Behaviour in a work context will be influenced by:

(a) **Attitudes to work:** the individual's standpoint on working, work conditions, colleagues, the task, the organisation and management.

(b) **Attitudes at work:** all sorts of attitudes which individuals may have about other people, politics, education, religion among other things, and which they bring with them into the work place - to act on, agree, disagree or discuss.

Positive, negative or neutral attitudes to other workers, or groups of workers, to the various systems and operations of the organisation, to learning - or particular training initiatives - to communication or to the task itself will obviously influence performance at work. In particular, they may result in varying degrees of:

- Co-operation or conflict between individuals and groups, or between departments
- Co-operation with or resistance to management
- Success in communication - interpersonal and organisation wide
- Commitment and contribution to the work

Activity 3 **(15 minutes)**

Suggest four elements which would make up a positive attitude to work. (An example might be the belief that you get a fair day's pay for a fair day's work.)

1.9 Non-work factors that might influence attitudes to work, or affecting work:

(a) **Class and class consciousness:** attitudes about the superiority or inferiority of others, according to birth, wealth and education; attitudes to money and work (necessity or career?).

(b) **Age**. Attitudes to sexual equality, family and morality can vary widely from one generation to the next.

(c) **Race, culture or religion**. These will affect the way people regard each other and their willingness to co-operate in work situations. Culture and religion are also strong influences on attitudes to work.

(d) **Lifestyle and interests.** Attitudes to these areas affect interpersonal relations and self-image, as well as the relative importance of work and leisure to the individual.

(e) **Sex**. Attitudes to the equality of the sexes and their various roles at work and in society may be influential in:

  (i) **Interpersonal relations at work**: sexist attitudes and language

  (ii) **The self concept of the individual:** women at work may be made to feel inferior, incompetent or simply unwelcome, while men working for female managers might feel threatened

  (iii) **Attitudes to work.** Stereotypical role profiles ('a women's place is in the home', 'the man has to support the family') may be held by both sexes and may create feelings of guilt, resentment or resignation about wanting or having to work.

1.10 Intelligence

Intelligence is a wide and complex concept. Intelligence/ability takes many forms.

(a) **Analytic intelligence**: measured by IQ test.

(b) **Spatial intelligence**: the ability to see patterns and connections, most obvious in the creative artist or scientist.

(c) **Musical intelligence**: 'the good ear' that musicians, mimics and linguists have.

(d) **Physical intelligence**: obvious in athletes and dancers.

(e) **Practical intelligence**: some people can make and fix things without theoretical knowledge.

(f) **Intra-personal intelligence**: the ability to know, be sensitive to and express oneself, observable in poets, artists and mystics.

(g) **Inter-personal intelligence**. The ability to relate to the work through others; essential in leaders.

2 NEEDS AND GOALS

2.1 Needs

Individual behaviour is partly influenced by human biology, which requires certain basics for life. When the body is deprived of these essentials, biological forces called **needs** or **drives** are activated (eg hunger), and dictate the behaviour required to end the deprivation: each, drink, flee and so on. However, we retain freedom of choice about **how** we satisfy our drives: they do not dictate specific or highly predictable behaviour. (Say you are hungry: how many specific ways of satisfying your hunger can you think of?)

2.2 Goals

Each individual has a different set of goals. The relative importance of those goals to the individual may vary with time, circumstances and other factors including the following.

Influence	Comment
Childhood environment and education	Aspiration levels, family and career models and so on are formed at early stages of development
Experience	This teaches us what to expect from life: we will either strive to repeat positive experiences, or to avoid or make up for negative ones.
Age and position	There is usually a gradual process of 'goal shift' with age. Relationships and exploration may preoccupy young employees. Career and family goals tend to conflict in the 20-40 age group: career launch and 'take-off' may have to yield to the priorities associated with forming permanent relationships and having children.
Culture	Some studies suggest that Japanese goals show a greater concern than in Europe for relationships at work and a lesser preoccupation with power and autonomy.
Self-concept	All the above factors are bound up with the individual's own self-image. The individual's assessments of his own abilities and place in society will affect the relative strength and nature of his needs and goals.

You should now be able to identify some of the needs and goals that people might have, where they might come from and why the might change. So why are they relevant to a manager?

2.3 The significance of personal goals

(a) People behave in such a way as to **satisfy their needs and fulfil their goals.**

(b) An **organisation is in a position to offer some of the satisfactions** people might seek: relationships and belonging, challenge and achievement, progress on the way to self-actualisation, security and structure and so on.

(c) The **organisation can therefore influence people** to behave in ways it desires (to secure work performance) by **offering them the means to satisfy their needs** and fulfil their goals in **return for** that behaviour. This process of influence is called **motivation**.

(d) If people's needs are being met, and goals being fulfilled, at work, they are more likely to have a positive attitude to their work and to the organisation.

3 THEORIES OF MOTIVATION

Managers might have certain **basic assumptions** about subordinates. Such assumptions were usefully summarised by Douglas MacGregor.

3.1 McGregor's Theory X and Theory Y

(a) **Theory X**. This is the theory that most people **dislike work and responsibility and will avoid both if possible**. Because of this, most people must be coerced, controlled, directed and/or threatened with punishment to get them to make an adequate effort. Managers who believe in this theory brandish the stick.

(b) **Theory Y**. **Physical and mental effort in work is as natural as play or rest**. The ordinary person does not inherently dislike work: according to the conditions it may be a source of satisfaction or punishment. At present the potentialities of the average person are not being fully used. A manager with this sort of attitude to his staff is likely to be a democratic, consultative type.

Both are rather crude simplifications, resting on assumptions as to how people are motivated.

Activity 4 **(10 minutes)**

What factors in yourself or your organisation motivate you to:

(a) Turn up to work at all?
(b) Do an average day's work?
(c) 'Bust a gut' on a task or for a boss?

Go on - be honest!

BPP PUBLISHING

NOTES

Definitions

Motivation is 'a decision-making process through which the individual chooses the desired outcomes and sets in motion the behaviour appropriate to acquiring them'. (Buchanan and Huczynski).

Motives: 'learned influences on human behaviour that lead us to pursue particular goals because they are socially valued'. (Buchanan and Huczynski).

3.2 Meaning of motivation

In practice the words **motives** and **motivation** are commonly used in different contexts to mean the following.

(a) **Goals or outcomes** that have become desirable for a particular individual. We say that money, power or friendship are motives for doing something.

(b) The **mental process of choosing desired outcomes**, deciding how to go about them (and whether the likelihood of success warrants the amount of effort that will be necessary) and **setting in motion** the required behaviours.

(c) The **social process** by which **other people motivate us** to behave in the ways they wish. Motivation in this sense usually applies to the attempts of organisations to get workers to put in more effort.

Many theories try to explain motivation and why and how people can be motivated. One classification is between content and process theories.

3.3 Content theories

(a) **Content theories** ask the question: '**what** are the things that motivate people?'

They assume that human beings have a *set* of needs or desired outcomes. Maslow's hierarchy theory and Herzberg's two-factor theory, both discussed shortly, are two of the most important approaches of this type.

(b) **Process theories** ask the question: '**how** can people be motivated?'

They explore the process through which outcomes **become** desirable and are pursued by individuals. This approach assumes that people are able to select their goals and choose the paths towards them, by a conscious or unconscious process of calculation. Expectancy theory and Handy's 'motivation calculus', discussed soon, are theories of this type.

3.4 Maslow's hierarchy of needs

Maslow outlined seven needs, as in the diagram below, and put forward certain propositions about the motivating power of each need.

NOTES

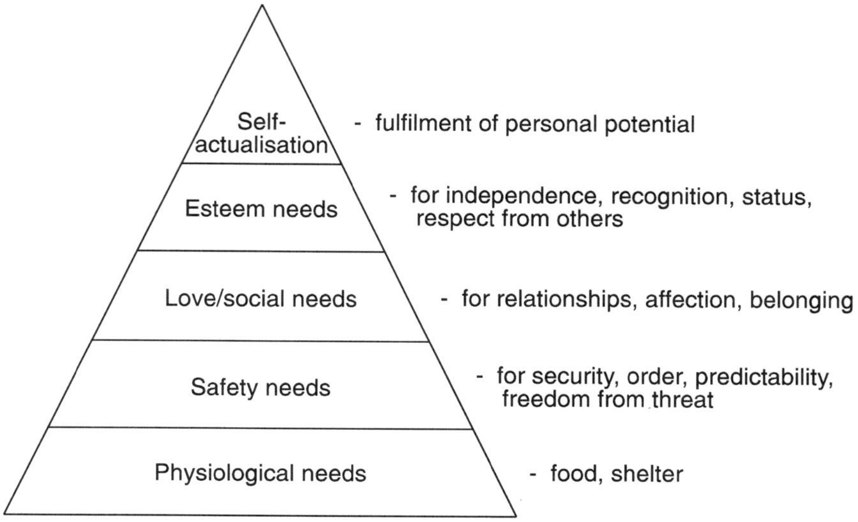

(a) Any individual's needs can be arranged in a '**hierarchy** of relative pre-potency'.

(b) Each level of need is **dominant until satisfied**; only then does the next level of need become a motivating factor.

(c) A need which has been satisfied no longer motivates an individual's behaviour. The need for self-actualisation can rarely be satisfied.

(d) In addition, Maslow described:

   (i) Freedom of enquiry and expression needs (for social conditions permitting free speech, and encouraging justice, fairness and honesty)

   (ii) Knowledge and understanding needs (to gain knowledge of the environment, to explore, learn).

Activity 5 **(10 minutes)**

Decide which of Maslow's categories the following fit into.

(a) Receiving praise from your manager
(b) A family party
(c) An artist forgetting to eat
(d) A man washed up on a desert island
(e) A pay increase
(f) Joining a local drama group
(g) Being awarded the OBE
(h) Buying a house

3.5 Problems with Maslow's hierarchy

(a) An individual's behaviour may be in response to **several needs**. Work, after all, can either satisfy or thwart the satisfaction of a number of needs.

(b) The **same need may cause different behaviour** in different individuals.

(c) It ignores the concept of **deferred gratification** by which people are prepared to ignore current suffering for the promise of future benefits.

(d) **Empirical verification is hard to come by**. In particular tests revealed it had a bias towards US and UK cultures.

3.6 Herzberg's two-factor theory

Herzberg's two-factor theory identified **hygiene factors** and **motivator factors**.

(a) **Hygiene factors** are based on a **need to avoid unpleasantness.**

If inadequate, they cause **dissatisfaction** with work. They work analogously to sanitation, which minimises threats to health rather than actively promoting 'good health'. Unpleasantness demotivates: pleasantness is a steady state. Hygiene factors (the conditions of work) include:

- Company policy and administration
- Salary
- The quality of supervision
- Interpersonal relations
- Working conditions
- Job security

(b) **Motivator factors** are based on a **need for personal growth.**

They actively create job satisfaction and are effective in motivating an individual to superior performance and effort. These factors are:

- Status (this may be a hygiene factor too)
- Advancement
- Gaining recognition
- Responsibility
- Challenging work
- Achievement
- Growth in the job

A lack of motivators at work will encourage employees to concentrate on bad hygiene factors such as to demand more pay. Stemming from his fundamental division of motivator and hygiene factors, Herzberg encouraged managers to **change the job** itself (the type of work done, the nature of tasks, levels of responsibility) rather than conditions of work. (We discuss this in Section 6 below.)

3.7 Process theories

Expectancy theory

Expectancy theory (Victor Vroom) states that people will decide how much they are going to put into their work, according to two factors.

(a) **Valence:** the value that they place on this outcome (whether the positive value of a reward, or the negative value of a punishment)

(b) **Expectancy:** the strength of their expectation that behaving in a certain way will in fact bring out the desired outcome.

Expectancy x *Valence* = *Force of motivation.*

CASE EXAMPLE

Expectancy theory in action

This example illustrates the complexity of expectancy theory when applied to, say, the case of an insurance company sales representative who is male and in his 50s. For a given level of effort (E), he may perceive the possible outcomes as follows.

(a) A 75% chance of selling 17 policies in a week
(b) a 15% chance of selling 13 policies in a week
(c) A 10% chance of selling 30 policies in a week

There is 100% probability that this given level of effort (E) will produce the following effects.

(a) Exhaustion
(b) Sarcastic comments from his colleagues
(c) Aggravation to his sciatica

If he succeeds in selling 17 policies a week, the perceived outcomes will be as follows.

(a) Praise from his manager
(b) Accusations from colleagues about setting impossibly high standards
(c) Sufficient earnings (from commission) to buy a present for his wife

If he only sells 13 policies in the week, the perceived outcomes will be as follows.

(a) Criticism from his manager

(b) Tacit approval from colleagues

(c) A poor level of commission on earnings and income, leading to disapproval from his wife.

Selling 20 policies in a week will generate these perceived outcomes:

(a) Loud praise from his manager
(b) Extreme hostility from his colleagues
(c) Family expectations that income on this level will be sustained

The sales representative must assign a probability to each of these outcomes, eg a 75% probability that selling 17 policies will produce accusations from colleagues, and a 60% probability that selling 17 policies will produce praise from his manager.

Finally, the sales representative must attach a **valence** to each of the expected outcomes. Earning enough money to buy a present for his wife may have **high valence** for him; attracting the disapproval of colleagues may have **low valance.**

It can be seen from this (much simplified) example that trying to predict which choice will be made, in any given situation, becomes impossibly arduous.

3.8 Handy's motivation calculus

Charles Handy suggests that for any individual decision, there is a conscious or unconscious **motivation calculus** which is an assessment of three factors.

(a) The individual's own set of needs.

(b) The desired results - what the individual is expected to do in his job.

(c) 'E' factors (effort, energy, excitement in achieving desired results, enthusiasm, emotion, and expenditure).

NOTES

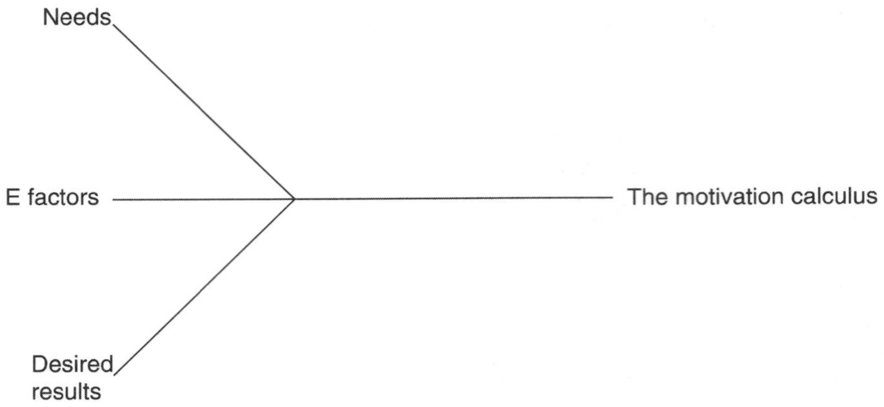

The **motivation decision** will depend on:

- The **strength of the individual's needs**
- The **expectancy** that expending 'E' will lead to a desired result
- How far the result will be **instrumental** in satisfying the individual's needs

Consequences for management

(a) **Intended results should be made clear,** so that the individual can complete the calculation by knowing **what is expected**, the **reward**, and **how much 'E'** it will take.

(b) Individuals are more committed to **specific goals** which they **have helped to set themselves**.

(c) **Feedback.** Without knowledge of **actual results,** there is no check that the 'E' expenditure was justified (and will be justified in future).

(d) If an individual is **rewarded** according to performance tied to standards (management by objectives), however, he or she may well set lower standards: the instrumentality part of the calculus (likelihood of success and reward) is greater if the standard is lower, so less expense of 'E' is indicated.

3.10 Motivation and performance

Motivation, from the manager's view, is the controlling of the work environment and the offering of rewards in such a way as to encourage extra performance from employees.

You may be wondering whether motivation is really so important. It could be argued that if a person is employed to do a job, he will do that job and no question of motivation arises. If the person doesn't want to do the work, he can resign. So why try to motivate people?

(a) Motivation is about getting *extra* levels of commitment and performance from employees, over and above mere compliance with rules and procedures. If individuals can be motivated, by one means or another, they might work more efficiently (and productivity will rise) or they will produce a better quality of work.

(b) The case for **job satisfaction** as a factor in improved performance is not proven.

(c) The key is to work 'smarter'.

Motivation can be a negative process (appealing to an individual's need to **avoid** unpleasantness, pain, fear etc) as well as a positive one (appealing to the individual's need to attain certain goals).

(a) **Negative motivation** is wielding the big stick: threatening dismissal or demotion, reprimand etc - it is negative reinforcement.

(b) **Positive motivation** is dangling the carrot, and may be achieved by:

  (i) The offer of extrinsic rewards, such as pay incentives, promotion, better working conditions etc

  (ii) Internal or psychological satisfaction for the individual ('virtue is its own reward'), a sense of achievement, a sense of responsibility and value etc.

3.11 Morale

Definition

> '**Morale**' is a term drawn primarily from a military context, to denote the state of mind or spirit of a group, particularly regarding discipline and confidence. It can be related to 'satisfaction', since 'low morale' implies a state of dissatisfaction.
>
> Morale relates to how a group feels.

The 'signs' by which morale is often gauged are by no means clear cut.

(a) Low productivity is not invariably a sign of low morale. In fact there may be little correlation between morale and output.

(b) High labour turnover is not a reliable indicator of low morale: the age structure of the workforce and other factors in natural wastage will need to be taken into account. Low turnover, likewise, is no evidence of high morale: people may be staying because of lack of other opportunities in the local job market, for example.

(c) There is some evidence that satisfaction correlates with mental health - so that symptoms of stress or psychological failure may be a signal to management that all is not well, although again, a range of non-work factors may be contributing.

(d) Attitude surveys may indicate workers' perception of their job satisfaction, by way of interview or questionnaire.

4 REWARDS AND INCENTIVES

Definitions

> A **reward** is a token (monetary or otherwise) given to an individual or team in recognition of some contribution or success.
>
> An **incentive** is the offer or promise of a reward for contribution or success, designed to motivate the individual or team to behave in such a way as to earn it. (In other words, the 'carrot' dangled in front of the donkey!)

Not all the incentives that an organisation can offer its employees are directly related to **monetary** rewards. The satisfaction of **any** of the employee's wants or needs maybe seen as a reward for past of incentive for future performance.

Different individuals have different goals, and get different things out of their working life: in other words they have different **orientations** to work. There are any number of reasons why a person works, or is motivated to work well.

(a) The 'human relations' school of management theorists regarded **work relationships** as the main source of satisfaction and reward offered to the worker.

(b) Later writers suggested a range of 'higher' motivations, notably:

- **Job satisfaction,** interest and challenge in the job itself - rewarding work
- **Participation** in decision-making - responsibility and involvement

(c) **Pay** has always occupied a rather ambiguous position, but since people need money to live, it well certainly be part of the reward 'package' an individual gets from his work.

4.1 Intrinsic and extrinsic factors

The **rewards offered to the individual** at work may be these.

(a) **Extrinsic rewards**

These are external to the individual, and are given to him by others, such as wage or salary, bonuses and prizes, working conditions, a car, training opportunities.

(b) **Intrinsic rewards**

There are within individual himself: feelings of companionship, comfort, sense of achievement, enjoyment of status and recognition, interest in the job, responsibility, pride in the organisation's success etc.

The system of rewards used in an organisation or in the department will largely depend on:

- The **assumptions the managers make** about their subordinates' working life
- The **employees' goals**

Child has outlined six management **criteria for a reward system**. It should:

(a) Encourage people to **fill job vacancies** and to stay in their job (ie not leave).

(b) Increase the **predictability of employees' behaviour,** so that employees can be depended on to carry out their duties consistently and to a reasonable standard.

(c) Increase **willingness to accept change** and flexibility. (Changes in work practices are often 'bought' from trade unions with higher pay.)

(d) Foster and **encourage innovative behaviour**.

(e) **Reflect the nature of jobs** in the organisation and the skills or experience required. The reward system should therefore be consistent with seniority of position in the organisation structure, and should be thought fair by all employees.

(f) **Motivate** (increase commitment and effort).

4.2 The job as a motivator

The job itself can be used as a motivator, or it can be a cause of dissatisfaction.

Definition

> **Job design** is the incorporation of the tasks the organisation needs to be done into a job for one person.

One of the consequences of mass production was what might be called a micro-division of labour, or **job simplification.**

(a) **Little training**. A job is divided up into the smallest number of sequential tasks possible. Each task is so simple and straightforward that it can be learned with very little training.

(b) **Replacement**. If labour turnover is high, this does not matter because unskilled replacements can be found and trained to do the work in a very short time.

(c) **Flexibility**. Since the skill required is low, workers can be shifted from one task to another very easily. The production flow will therefore be unaffected by absenteeism.

(d) **Control**. If tasks are closely defined and standard times set for their completion, production is easier to predict and control.

(e) **Quality**. Standardisation of work into simple tasks means that quality is easier to predict. There is less scope for doing a task badly, in theory.

4.3 Disadvantages

(a) The work is **monotonous** and makes employees tired, bored and dissatisfied. The consequences will be high labour turnover, absenteeism, spoilage, unrest.

(b) **People work better** when their work is **variable,** unlike machines.

(c) An individual doing a simple task feels like a small cog in a large machine, and has no **sense of contributing to the organisation's end product** or service.

(d) Excessive specialisation **isolates** the individual in his or her work and inhibits not only social contacts with 'work mates', but knowledge generation.

(e) In practice, excessive job simplification leads to **lower quality, through inattention**.

Herzberg suggest three ways of improving job design, to make jobs more interesting to the employee, and hopefully to improve performance: job enrichment, job enlargement and job rotation.

4.4 Job enrichment

Definition

> **Job enrichment** is planned, deliberate action to build greater responsibility, breadth and challenge of work into a job. Job enrichment is similar to **empowerment** although the emphasis of job enrichment is on the individual rather than on the team.

A job may be enriched by:

(a) Giving the job holder **decision-making capabilities of a 'higher' order.** What is, mundane detail at a high level can represent significant job interest at a lower level.

(b) Giving the **employee greater freedom** to decide how the job should be done.

(c) Encouraging employees **to participate** in the planning decisions of their superiors.

(d) Giving the employee regular **feedback.**

Job enrichment alone will not **automatically** make employees more productive. 'Even those who want their jobs enriched will expect to be rewarded with more than job satisfaction. Job enrichment is not a cheaper way to greater productivity. Its pay-off will come in the less visible costs of morale, climate and working relationships'. (Handy).

4.5 Job enlargement

Definition

> **Job enlargement** is the attempt to widen jobs by increasing the number of operations in which a job holder is involved.

By reducing the number of repetitions of the same work, the dullness of the job should also be reduced. Job enlargement is therefore a **'horizontal' extension** of an individual's work, whereas job enrichment is a 'vertical' extension.

(a) Just by giving an employee tasks which span a larger part of the total production work should **reduce boredom.**

(b) Enlarged jobs can provide a **challenge and incentive.** For example, a trusted employee might be given added responsibilities, for example:

- **Checking the quality of output**
- **On the job training** of new recruits

(c) Enlarged jobs might also be regarded as 'status' jobs within the department, and as stepping stones towards promotion.

4.6 Job rotation

Job rotation might take two forms.

(a) An employee might be **transferred to another job** after a period of, say, two to four years in an existing job, in order to give him or her a new interest and challenge, and to bring a fresh person to the job being vacated.

(b) **Job rotation might be regarded as a form of training.** Trainees might be expected to learn a bit about a number of different jobs, by spending six months or one year in each job before being moved on. The employee is regarded as a 'trainee' rather than as an experienced person holding down a demanding job.

4.7 Job optimisation

A **well designed job** should therefore provide the individual with:

- **Scope** for setting his own work standards and targets
- **Control** over the pace and methods of working
- **Variety** by allowing for inter-locking tasks to be done by the same person
- **Voice**: A chance to add his comments about the design of the product, or his job
- **Feedback** of information to the individual about his performance

4.8 Participation as a motivator

People want more interesting work and to have a say in decision-making. These expectations are a basic part of the movement towards greater **participation** at work.

The methods of achieving increased involvement have largely crystallised into two main streams.

(a) **Immediate participation** is used to refer to the involvement of employees in the **day-to-day** decisions of their work group.

(b) **Distant participation** refers to the process of including company employees at the top levels of the organisation which deal with long-term policy issues including investment and employment. Typical examples of this type of participation would be found in any major German company with the **two-tier** board structure. although firms in the EU are to have **works councils**.

Participation can involve employees and make them feel committed to their task, given the following conditions (5 Cs).

- **Certainty**. Participation should be genuine.
- **Consistency.** Efforts to establish participation should be made consistently over a long period.
- **Clarity.** The purpose of participation is made quite clear.
- **Capacity.** The individual has the ability and information to participate effectively.
- **Commitment.** The manager believes in participation.

Motivation through **employee satisfaction** is not a useful concept because employee satisfaction is such a **vague idea**. Drucker suggested that employee satisfaction comes about through encouraging - if need be, by pushing - employees to accept responsibility. There are four ingredients to this.

(a) **Careful placement of people in jobs** so that an individual is suited to the role.

(b) **High standards of performance in the job**, so that the employee should know what to aim for.

(c) **Providing the worker with feedback control information.** The employee should receive routine information about how well or badly he or she is doing without having to be told by his boss.

(d) **Opportunities for participation** in decisions that will give the employee managerial vision.

5 PAY AS A MOTIVATOR

Extrinsic rewards include:

- Basic pay and overtime legal minimum
- Bonuses
- Performance-related pay
- Share-ownership schemes
- Benefit car or allowance
- Holiday entitlement
- Sick pay and maternity pay over the
- Contributions to a pension scheme
- Private health care
- Sickness and disability insurance
- Crèches
- Season ticket loans

You may be able to think of some more.

Pay is important because:

- It is an important cost
- People feel strongly about it
- It is a legal issue (minimum wage, equal opportunities legislation)

5.1 How is pay determined?

As pay is such a **complex** issue, there are a number of ways by which organisations determine pay.

(a) '**Job evaluation**'. This is a systematic process for establishing the relative worth of jobs within an organisation. Its purpose is to:

(i) Provide a rational basis for the design and maintenance of an equitable and defensible pay structure

(ii) Help manage differences existing between jobs within the organisation

(iii) Enable consistent decisions to be made on grading and rates of pay

(iv) Establish the extent to which there is comparable worth between jobs so that equal pay can be provided for work of equal value.'

The salary structure is based on **job content**, and **not on the personal merit** of the job-holder. (The individual job-holder can be paid extra personal bonuses in reward for performance.)

(b) **Fairness.** Pay must be **perceived** and felt to match the level of work, and the capacity of the individual to do it.

(c) **Negotiated pay scales**. Pay scales, differentials and minimum rates may have been negotiated at plant, local or national level, according factors such as legislation, government policy, the economy, trade unions, the labour market.

(d) **Market rates.** Market rates of pay will have most influence on pay structures where there is a standard pattern of supply and demand in the open labour market. If an organisation's rates fall below the benchmark rates in the local or national labour market from which it recruits, it will have trouble attracting and holding employees.

(e) **Individual performance in the job**.

5.2 What do people want from pay?

Pay has a central - but ambiguous - role in motivation theory. It is not mentioned explicitly in any need list, but it **offers the satisfaction of many of the various needs**

(a) Physiological - pay for food, shelter

(b) Security

(c) Esteem needs - pay might be a mark of status, but also a level of pay may be a sign of fairness

(d) Self-actualisation - pay gives people resources to pursue self-actualisation outside the working environment

Individuals may also have needs unrelated to money, however, which money cannot satisfy, or which the pay system of the organisation actively denies. So to what extent is pay an inducement to better performance: a motivator or incentive?

Although the size of their income will affect their standard of living, most people tend not to be concerned to **maximise** their earnings. They may like to earn more but are probably more concerned to:

(a) Earn **enough**

(b) Know that their pay is **fair** in comparison with the pay of others both inside and outside the organisation

Pay is more of a 'hygiene' factor than a motivator factor. It gets taken for granted, and so is more usually a source of dissatisfaction than satisfaction. However, pay is the **most important of the hygiene factors**, according to Herzberg. It is valuable not only in its power to be converted into a wide range of other satisfactions but also as a consistent measure of worth or value, allowing employees to compare themselves and be compared with other individuals or occupational groups inside and outside the organisation. But this clearly **conflicts with performance-related pay**.

CASE EXAMPLE

The Affluent Worker research of Goldthorpe, Lockwood et al (1968) illustrated an **instrumental** orientation to work (the attitude that work is not an end in itself but a means to other ends). The highly-paid Luton car assembly workers experienced their work as routine and dead-end. The researchers concluded that they had made a rational decision to enter employment offering high monetary reward **rather** than intrinsic interest: they were getting out of their jobs what they most wanted from them.

The Luton researchers did not claim that all workers have an instrumental orientation to work, however, but suggested that a person will seek a suitable balance of:

- The rewards which are important to him
- The deprivations he feels able to put up with

Even those with an instrumental orientation to work have limits to their purely financial aspirations, and will cease to be motivated by money if the deprivations - in terms of long working hours poor conditions, social isolation or whatever- become too great. In other words, if the 'price' of pay is too high.

High taxation rates may also weigh the deprivation side of the calculation; workers may perceive that a great deal of extra effort will in fact earn them little extra reward

---

Unlike other 'hygiene' or 'motivator' factors at work, pay is the only factor which is impossible to 'leave behind' at the office.

(a) Furthermore, if pay is a dominant motivator, then you would expect **difficulties in recruiting** for certain lower paid jobs. Academic research is not particularly well paid, but the job has other satisfactions, such as interest, status or esteem.

(b) Pay is thus only one of several **intrinsic or extrinsic rewards** offered by work. If pay is used to motivate, it can only do so in a **wider context of the job** and the other rewards. **Thanks, praise and recognition** are also relevant.

5.3 Performance related pay (PRP)

Definition

> **Performance related pay (PRP)** is related to output (in terms of the number of items produced or time taken to produce a unit or work), or results achieved (performance to defined standards in key tasks, according to plan).

The most common individual PRP scheme for wage earners is straight **piecework:** payment of a fixed amount per unit produced, or operation completed.

For managerial and other salaried jobs, however, a form of **management by objectives** will probably be applied. PRP is often awarded at the discretion of the line manager, subject to the budget overall. Guidelines may suggest, for example, that those rated exceptional get a rise of 10% whereas those who have performed less well only get, say, 3%.

(a) Key results can be identified and specified, for which merit awards will be paid.

(b) There will be a clear model for evaluating performance and knowing when, or if, targets have been reached and payments earned.

(c) The exact conditions and amounts of awards can be made clear to the employee, to avoid uncertainty and later resentment.

For service and other departments, a PRP scheme may involve **bonuses** for achievement of key results, or **points schemes**, where points are awarded for performance of various criteria (efficiency, cost savings, quality of service and so on). Certain points totals (or the highest points total in the unit, if a competitive system is used) then win cash or other awards.

Here are the supposed benefits and problems of performance related pay.

(a) **Benefits of PRP cited**

- Improves **commitment** and capability
- **Complements other HR initiatives**
- Improves focus on the business's performance objectives
- Better **two-way communications**
- Greater **supervisory responsibility**
- It **recognises achievement** when other means are not available

(b) **Potential problems cited**

- Subjectivity
- Supervisors' commitment and ability
- Translating appraisals into pay
- Divisive/against team working
- Union acceptance/employee attitudes

CASE EXAMPLE

People Management (September 1996) reported several local authorities who had withdrawn from their PRP schemes. PRP was adopted by around 70 councils between 1988 and 1991: the figure is now in decline. The London Borough of Brent dropped PRP because of the difficulty in measuring performance and a general unease about its position in local government. Cambridgeshire Country Council axed its PRP scheme as part of an overhaul of salary policy, while the London Borough Lewisham abandoned PRP in favour of other programmes such as Investors in People, and ISO 9000, claiming that it demotivated more people than it inspired.

Activity 6 **(10 minutes)**

Why might PRP fail to motivate?

5.4 Rewarding the team

Group bonus schemes

Group incentive schemes typically offer a bonus for a which achieves or exceeds specified targets. Offering bonuses to a **whole team** may be appropriate for tasks where individual contributions cannot be isolated, workers have little control over their individual output because tasks depend on each other, or where team-building is particularly required. It may enhance team-spirit and co-operation as well as provide performance incentives, but it may also create pressures within the group if some individuals are seen to be 'not pulling their weight'.

Profit-sharing schemes

Profit-sharing schemes offer employees (or selected groups of them) bonuses, directly on profits or 'value added'. Profit sharing is based on the belief that all employees can contribute to profitability, and that that contribution should be recognised. The effects may include profit-consciousness and motivation in employees, commitment to the future prosperity of the organisation etc.

The actual incentive value and effect on productivity may be wasted, however, if the scheme is badly designed.

(a) The sum should be **significant**.

(b) There should be a **clear and timely link** between effort/performance and reward. Profit shares should be distributed as frequently as possible with the need for reliable information on profit forecasts, targets etc and the need to amass significant amounts for distribution.

(c) The scheme should only be introduced if profit forecasts indicate a **reasonable chance of achieving** the above: profit sharing is welcome when profits are high, but the potential for disappointment is great.

(d) The greatest effect on productivity arising from the scheme may in fact arise from its use as a focal point for discussion with employees, about the relationship between their performance and results, areas and targets for improvement etc. Management must be seen to be **committed** to the principle.

5.5 Share schemes

Some firms choose to reward employees and managers by way of shares, again allowing them to participate in the success of the company as measured by the share price. In effect, the employee is allowed to purchase, at a future date, shares in the firm at the current price or perhaps at a discount. If the share price has risen the employee can sell the shares and make a profit.

(a) This is used often in the remuneration of chief executives; there has been some criticism especially with regard to rewarding executives of privatised utilities.

(b) Many firms have introduced such schemes for all their staff. There have been some tax incentives also.

6 THE PURPOSE OF APPRAISAL

Definition

> **Performance appraisal** is the process whereby an individual's performance is reviewed against previously agreed goals, and where new goals are agreed which will develop the individual and improve performance over the forthcoming review period.

6.1 Uses of appraisal

Jeannie Brownlow has decided to leave Gold and Silver where she has worked for five years as a supervisor. When the personnel manager asked for her reasons she said, 'I'm fed up. You don't know where you are here. No one tells you if you're doing the job well, but they jump on you like a ton of bricks if anything goes wrong. Talk about "no news is good news" – that's the way it is here'.

Monitoring and evaluating the performance of individuals and groups is an essential part of people-management. It has several uses.

(a) Identifying the current level of performance to provide a basis for informing, training and developing team members to a higher level.

(b) Identifying areas where improvement is needed in order to meet acceptable standards of performance.

(c) Identifying people whose performance suggests that they might be suitable for promotion in future.

(d) Measuring the individual's or team's level of performance against specific standards, to provide a basis for reward above the basic pay rate (in other words, individual or group bonuses).

(e) Measuring the performance of new team members against the organisation's (and team's) expectations, as a means of assessing whether selection procedures have been successful.

(f) Improving communication about work tasks between managers and team members, as a result of discussing the assessment.

(g) In the process of defining what performance should be, establishing what key results and standards must be reached for the unit to reach its objectives.

It may be argued that a particular, deliberate stock-taking exercise is unnecessary, since managers are constantly monitoring and making judgements about their subordinates and (theoretically) giving their subordinates feedback information from day to day.

6.2 Why have a system?

It must be recognised that, if no system of formal appraisal is in place:

(a) managers may obtain random impressions of subordinates' performance (perhaps from their more noticeable successes and failures), but not a coherent, complete and objective picture;

(b) managers may have a fair idea of their subordinates' shortcomings – but may not have devoted time and attention to the matter of improvement and development;

(c) judgements are easy to make, but less easy to justify in detail, in writing, or to the subject's face;

(d) different managers may be applying a different set of criteria, and varying standards of objectivity and judgement, which undermines the value of appraisal for comparison, as well as its credibility in the eyes of employees;

(e) managers rarely give their subordinates adequate feedback on their performance. Most people dislike giving criticism as much as receiving it.

> **Activity 7** **(15 minutes)**
>
> List four disadvantages to the individual of not having an appraisal system.

A typical system would therefore involve:

(a) identification of **criteria** for assessment;

(b) the preparation of an **appraisal report**;

(c) an **appraisal interview**, for an exchange of views about the results of the assessment, targets for improvement, solutions to problems and so on;

(d) the preparation and implementation of **action plans** to achieve improvements and changes agreed; and

(e) **follow-up**: monitoring the progress of the action plan.

Definition

> A **criterion** (plural: **criteria**) is a factor or standard by which something can be judged or decided. For example, 'meeting output targets' is one criterion for judging work performance.

We will now look at each stage in turn. First of all, what is the basis of appraisal going to be?

6.3 What should be monitored and assessed?

Managers must broadly monitor and assess the same things, so that comparisons can be made between individuals. On the other hand, they need to take account of the fact that jobs are different, and make different demands on the jobholder. If every individual were rated on 'communication skills' and 'teamworking', for example, you might have a good basis for deciding who needed promoting or training – but what about a data inputter or research scientist who does not have to work in a team or communicate widely in your organisation?

> **Activity 8** **(20 minutes)**
>
> Think of some other criteria which you would want to use in assessment of some jobs – but which would not be applicable in others.

There is also the important question of whether you assess **personality** or **performance**: in other words, do you assess what the individual is, or what (s)he does? Personal qualities like reliability or outgoingness have often been used as criteria for judging people. However, they are not necessarily relevant to job performance: you can be naturally outgoing, but still not good at communicating with customers, if your product knowledge or attitude is poor. Also, personality judgements are notoriously vague and unreliable: words like 'loyalty' and 'ambition' are full of ambiguity and moral connotations.

In practical terms, this has encouraged the use of competence or results-based appraisals, where performance is measured against specific, job-related performance criteria.

So how does a manager choose what criteria to base the assessment on? Most large organisations have a system in place, with pre-printed assessment forms setting out all the relevant criteria and the range of possible judgements. (We reproduce such a form later in this chapter). Even so, a team manager should critically evaluate such schemes to ensure that the criteria for assessment are relevant to his or her team and task – and that they remain so over time, as the team and task change.

Relevant criteria for assessment might be based on the following.

(a) **Job analysis:** the process of examining a job, to identify its component tasks and skill requirements, and the circumstances in which it is performed.

Analysis may be carried out by observation, if the job is routine and repetitive it will be easy to see what it involves. Irregular jobs, with lots of 'invisible' work (planning, thinking, relationship-building and so on) will require interviews and discussions with superiors and with the job holders themselves, to find out what the job involves.

The product of job analysis is usually a **job specification** which sets out the activities (mental and physical) involved in the job, and other factors in its social and physical environment. Many of the aspects covered – aptitudes and abilities required, duties and responsibilities, ability to work under particular conditions (pressure, noise, hazards), tolerance of teamwork or isolation and so on – will suggest criteria for assessment.

(b) **Job descriptions:** more general descriptions of a job or position at a given time, including its purpose and scope, duties and responsibilities, relationship with other jobs, and perhaps specific objectives and expected results. A job description offers a guide to what competences, responsibilities and results might be monitored and assessed.

(c) **Departmental or team plans, performance standards and targets**. These are the most clear-cut of all. If the plan specifies completion of a certain number of tasks, or production of a certain number of units, to a particular quality standard, assessment can be focused on whether (or how far) those targets have been achieved. (Personality and environmental factors may be relevant when investigating why performance has fallen short – but do not cloud the assessment of performance itself.)

Let us now look at some of the performance monitoring and reporting methods used in organisations.

7 APPRAISAL PROCEDURES

7.1 Monitoring and reporting

Overall assessment

This is much like a school report. The manager simply writes narrative judgements about the appraisee. The method is simple – but not always effective, since there is no guaranteed consistency of the criteria and areas of assessment from manager to manager (or appraisal to appraisal). In addition, managers may not be able to convey clear, precise or effective judgements in writing.

Guided assessment

Assessors are required to comment on a number of specified characteristics and performance elements, with guidelines as to how terms such as 'application', 'integrity' and 'adaptability' are to be interpreted in the work context. This is a more precise, but still rather vague method.

Grading

Grading adds a comparative frame of reference to the general guidelines. Managers are asked to select one of a number of levels or degrees (Grades 1–5 say) which describe the extent to which an individual displays a given characteristic. These are also known as rating scales, and have been much used in standard appraisal forms (for example, see the diagram of an appraisal form on the following page). Their effectiveness depends to a large extent on two things.

(a) **The relevance of the factors chosen for assessment.** These may be nebulous personality traits, for example, or clearly-defined work-related factors such as job knowledge, performance against targets, or decision-making.

(b) **The definition of the agreed standards or grades.** Grades A-D might simply be labelled 'Outstanding – Satisfactory – Fair – Poor', in which case assessments will be rather subjective and inconsistent. They may, on the other hand, be more closely related to work priorities and standards, using definitions such as 'Performance is good overall, and superior to that expected in some important areas', or 'Performance is broadly acceptable, but the employee needs training in several major areas and motivation is lacking'.

Numerical values may be added to gradings to give rating scores. Alternatively a less precise graphic scale may be used to indicate general position on a plus/minus scale, as shown here.

Factor: job knowledge

High |——✓——| Average |————|Low

NOTES

Personnel Appraisal: Employees in Salary Grades 5-8

Date of Review	Time on Position Yrs Mths	S.G.	Age Yrs	Name
Period of Review	Position Title			Area

Important: Read guide notes carefully before proceeding with the following sections

Section One	Performance Factors						Section Two	Personal Characteristics				
	N/A	U	M	SP	E	O		1	2	3	4	5
Administrative Skills							Initiative					
Communications – Written							Persistence					
Communications – Oral							Ability to work with others					
Problem Analysis							Adaptability					
Decision Making							Persuasiveness					
Delegation							Self-Confidence					
Quantity of Work							Judgement					
Development of Personnel							Leadership					
Development of Quality Improvements							Creativity					

Section Three Highlight Performance Factors and particular strengths/weaknesses of employee which significantly affect Job Performance

Overall Performance Rating (taking into account ratings given)

Prepared by: Signature .... Date .... Position Title ....

Section Four Comments by Reviewing Authority

I R Review Initial

Signature .... Date .... Position Title .... Date

Section Five Supervisor's Notes on Counselling Interview

Signature .... Date .... Position Title ....

Section Six Employees Reactions and Comment

Signature .... Date ....

Performance Classification

Outstanding performance is characterised by high ability which leaves little or nothing to be desired.

Personnel rated as such are those who regularly make significant contributions to the organisation which are above the requirements of their position. Unusual and challenging assignments are consistently well handled.

Excellent performance is marked by above-average ability, with little supervision required.

These employees may display some of the attributes present in '**outstanding**' performance, but not on a sufficiently consistent basis to warrant that rating. Unusual and challenging assignments are normally well handled.

Satisfactory Plus performance indicates fully adequate ability, without the need for excessive supervision.

Personnel with this rating are able to give proper consideration to normal assignments, which are generally well handled. They will meet the requirements of the position. '**Satisfactory plus**' performers may include those who lack the experience at their current level to demonstrate above-average ability.

Marginal performance is in instances where the ability demonstrated does not fully meet the requirements of the position, with excessive supervision and direction normally required.

Employees rated as such will show specific deficiencies in their performance which prevent them from performing at an acceptable level.

Unsatisfactory performance indicates an ability which falls clearly below the minimum requirements of the position.

'**Unsatisfactory**' performers will demonstrate marked deficiencies in most of the major aspects of their responsibilities, and considerable improvement is required to permit retention of the employee in his current position.

Personal Characteristics Ratings

1 – Needs considerable improvement – substantial improvement required to meet acceptable standards.
2 – Needs improvement – some improvement required to meet acceptable standards.
3 – Normal – meets acceptable standards.
4 – Above normal – exceeds normally acceptable standards in most instances.
5 – Exceptional – displays rare and unusual personal characteristics.

BPP PUBLISHING

Results-orientated schemes

All the above techniques may be used with more or less results-orientated criteria. A wholly results-orientated approach sets out to review performance against specific targets and standards of performance, which are agreed – or even set – in advance by a manager and subordinate together. This is known as performance management and was mentioned in the previous chapter.

Activity 9 **(15 minutes)**

Give three advantages of a performance management approach to appraisal.

In introducing 'performance management', we have raised the possibility that an employee might be involved in monitoring and evaluating his or her own performance. If targets are clear, and the employee is able to be honest and objective, self-assessment may be both effective and satisfying.

7.2 Who does the appraising?

Organisations have begun to recognise that the employee's immediate boss is not the only (or necessarily the best) person to assess his or her performance. Other 'stakeholders' in the individual's performance might be better, including the people (s)he deals with on a day to day basis:

(a) the current (and perhaps previous) boss (including temporary supervisors);
(b) peers and co-workers (peer appraisal);
(c) subordinates; (upward appraisal)
(d) external customers; or
(e) the employee him or herself (self appraisal).

7.3 360 degree feedback

360-degree feedback is an approach which collects comments and feedback on an individual's performance from all these sources (usually anonymously using questionnaires) and adds the individual's own self-assessment.

The advantages of 360-degree feedback are said to be as follows.

(a) It highlights every aspect of the individual's performance, and allows comparison of the individual's self-assessment with the views of others. (Rather revealing, in most cases.)

(b) Feedback tends to be balanced, covering strengths in some areas with weaknesses in others, so it is less discouraging.

(c) The assessment is based on real work – not artificial (eg interview) situations. The feedback is thus felt to be fairer and more relevant, making it easier for employees to accept the assessment and the need for change and development.

Activity 10 **(20 minutes)**

Peter Ward, who introduced 360-degree feedback at Tesco in 1987, gives an example of the kinds of questionnaire that might be used as the instrument of 360-degree feedback. 'A skill area like "communicating", for example, might be defined as "the ability to express oneself clearly and to listen effectively to others". Typical comments would include "Presents ideas or information in a well-organised manner" (followed by rating scale); or: "Allows you to finish what you have to say".'

Rate yourself on the two comments mentioned here, on a scale of 1–10. Get a group of friends, fellow-students, even a tutor or parent, to write down, anonymously, on a piece of paper their rating for you on the same two comments. Keep them in an envelope, unseen, until you have a few.

Compare them with your self-rating. If you dare... What drawbacks did you (and your respondents) find to such an approach?

7.4 Upward appraisal

A notable modern trend, adopted in the UK by companies such as BP, British Airways and some television companies, is upward appraisal, whereby employees are rated not by their superiors but by their subordinates. The followers appraise the leader.

The advantages of this method might be as follows.

(a) Subordinates tend to know their (one) superior better than superiors know their (many) subordinates.

(b) Instead of the possible bias of an individual manager's ratings, the various ratings of several employees may reflect a rounded view.

(c) Subordinates' ratings have more impact, because it is less usual to receive feedback from below: a manager's view of good management may be rather different from a team's view of being managed!

(d) Upward appraisal encourages subordinates to give feedback and raise problems they may have with their boss, which otherwise would be too difficult or risky for them.

Activity 11 **(15 minutes)**

Imagine you had to do an upward appraisal on your boss, parent or teacher. Suggest the two major problems that might be experienced with upward appraisal.

Having reported on an individual's performance – whether in a written narrative comment, or on a prepared appraisal form – a manager must discuss the content of the report with the individual concerned.

7.5 The appraisal interview

There are basically three ways of approaching appraisal interviews.

(a) The **tell and sell** method. The manager tells the subordinate how (s)he has been assessed, and then tries to 'sell' (gain acceptance of) the evaluation and any improvement plans.

(b) The **tell and listen** method. The manager tells the subordinate how (s)he has been assessed, and then invites comments. The manager therefore no longer dominates the interview throughout, and there is greater opportunity for counselling as opposed to pure direction. The employee is encouraged to participate in the assessment and the working out of improvement targets and methods; change in the employee may not be the sole key to improvement, and the manager may receive helpful feedback about job design, methods, environment or supervision.

(c) The **problem-solving** approach. The manager abandons the role of critic altogether, and becomes a counsellor and helper. The discussion is centred not on assessment of past performance, but on future solutions of the employee's work problems. The employee is encouraged to recognise the problems, think solutions through, and commit himself to improvement. This approach is more involving and satisfying to the employee and may also stimulate creative problem-solving.

EXAMPLE

A survey of appraisal interviews given to 252 officers in a UK government department found that:

(a) interviewers have difficulty with negative performance feedback (criticism), and tend to avoid it if possible;

(b) negative performance feedback (criticism) is, however, more likely to bring forth positive post-appraisal action, and is favourably received by appraisees, who feel it is the most useful function of the whole process, if handled frankly and constructively;

(c) the most common fault of interviewers is talking too much.

The survey recorded the preference of appraisees for a 'problem-solving' style of participative interview, over a one-sided 'tell and sell' style.

Many organisations waste the opportunity represented by appraisal for **upward communication**. If an organisation is working towards empowerment, it should harness the aspirations and abilities of its employees by asking positive and thought-provoking questions.

(a) Do you fully understand your job? Are there any aspects you wish to be made clearer?

(b) What parts of your job do you do best?

(c) Could any changes be made in your job which might result in improved performance?

(d) Have you any skills, knowledge, or aptitudes which could be made better use of in the organisation?

(e) What are your career plans? How do you propose achieving your ambitions in terms of further training and broader experience?

7.6 Follow-up

After the appraisal interview, the manager may complete his or her report with an overall assessment and/or the jointly-reached conclusion of the interview, with recommendations for follow-up action. This may take the following forms.

(a) Informing appraisees of the results of the appraisal, if this has not been central to the review interview. (Some people argue that there is no point making appraisals if they are not openly discussed, but unless managers are competent and committed to reveal results in a constructive, frank and objective manner, the negative reactions on all sides may outweigh the advantages.)

(b) Carrying out agreed actions on training, promotion and so on.

(c) Monitoring the appraisee's progress and checking that (s)he has carried out agreed actions or improvements.

(d) Taking necessary steps to help the appraisee to attain improvement objectives, by guidance, providing feedback, upgrading equipment, altering work methods or whatever.

If follow-up action is not taken, employees will feel that appraisal is all talk and just a waste of time, and that improvement action on their side will not be appreciated or worthwhile.

7.7 Assessing potential

Definition

> **Potential review** is the use of appraisal to forecast where and how fast an individual is progressing.

Potential review can be used as feedback to the individual to indicate the opportunities open to him or her in the organisation in the future. It will also be vital to the organisation in determining its management promotion and succession plans.

Information for potential assessment will include:

(a) strengths and weaknesses in the employee's existing skills and qualities;

(b) possibilities and strategies for improvement, correction and development;

(c) the employee's goals, aspirations and attitudes, with regard to career advancement, staying with the organisation and handling responsibility;

(d) the opportunities available in the organisation, including likely management vacancies, job rotation/enrichment plans and promotion policies for the future.

No single review exercise will mark an employee down for life as 'promotable' or otherwise. The process tends to be on-going, with performance at each stage or level in the employee's career indicating whether (s)he might be able to progress to the next step. However, an approach based on performance in the current job is highly fallible.

L J Peter pointed out that managers tend to be promoted from positions in which they have proved themselves competent, until one day they reach a level at which they are no longer competent – promoted 'to the level of their own incompetence'!

Moreover, the management succession plan of an organisation needs to be formulated in the long term. It takes a long time to equip a manager with the skills and experience needed at senior levels, and the organisation must develop people continuously if it is to fill the shoes of departing managers without crisis.

Some idea of **potential** must therefore be built into appraisal. It is impossible to predict with any certainty how successful an individual will be in what will, after all, be different circumstances from anything (s)he has experienced so far. However, some attempt can be made to:

(a) determine key **indicators of potential:** in other words, elements believed to be essential to management success; these include past track record, and also administrative, interpersonal and analytical skills; leadership; orientation towards work, and a taste for making money; or a suitable mix of any of these;

(b) simulate the conditions of the position to which the individual would be promoted, to assess his or her performance. This may be achieved using case studies, role plays, presentations or team discussions and so on. An alternative approach might be to offer some **real** experience (under controlled conditions) by appointing the individual to assistant or deputy positions or to committees or project teams, and assessing his or her performance. This is still no real predictor of his or her ability to handle the **whole** job, on a continuous basis and over time, however, and it may be risky, if the appraisee fails to cope with the situation.

In theory, systematic appraisal schemes may seem fair to the individual and worthwhile for the organisation, but in practice the system often goes wrong. Let's see how, and what can be done.

8 PROBLEMS WITH APPRAISAL SCHEMES

8.1 Criticisms of appraisal schemes

Even the best objective and systematic appraisal scheme is subject to personal and interpersonal problems!

(a) Appraisal is often **defensive on the part of the subordinate,** who believes that criticism may mean a low bonus or pay rise, or lost promotion opportunity.

(b) Appraisal is often **defensive on the part of the superior**, who cannot reconcile the role of judge and critic with the human relations aspect of interviewing and management. (S)he may in any case feel uncomfortable about 'playing God' with the employee's future.

(c) The superior might show **conscious or unconscious** bias in the appraisal or may be influenced by rapport (or lack of it) with the interviewee. Systems without clearly-defined standard criteria will be particularly prone to the subjectivity of the assessor's judgements.

(d) The manager and subordinate may both be **reluctant to devote time and attention to appraisal**. Their experience in the organisation may indicate that the exercise is a waste of time (especially if there is a lot of form-filling) with no relevance to the job, and no reliable follow-up action.

(e) The organisational culture may **simply not take appraisal seriously:** interviewers are not trained or given time to prepare, appraisees are not encouraged to contribute, or the exercise is perceived as a 'nod' to Human Resources with no practical results.

Activity 12 **(15 minutes)**

What would you anticipate the effects of appraisal on employee motivation to be?

8.2 Improving the system

The appraisal scheme should itself be assessed (and regularly re-assessed). Here's a handy checklist.

(a) **Relevance**

(i) Does the system have a useful purpose, relevant to the needs of the organisation and the individual?

(ii) Is the purpose clearly expressed and widely understood by all concerned, both appraisers and appraisees?

(iii) Are the appraisal criteria relevant to the purposes of the system?

(b) **Fairness**

Is there reasonable standardisation of criteria and objectivity throughout the organisation?

(c) **Serious intent**

(i) Are managers committed to the system – or is it just something the personnel department thrusts upon them?

(ii) Who does the interviewing, and are they properly trained in interviewing and assessment techniques?

(iii) Is reasonable time and attention given to the interviews – or is it a question of 'getting them over with'?

(d) **Co-operation**

(i) Is the appraisal a participative, problem-solving activity – or a tool of management control?

(ii) Is the appraisee given time and encouragement to prepare for the appraisal, so that he can make a constructive contribution?

(iii) Does a jointly-agreed, concrete conclusion emerge from the process?

9 INTERPERSONAL SKILLS AND FEEDBACK

9.1 Interpersonal behaviour

Interpersonal behaviour describes interaction between people – a two way process such as communicating, delegating, negotiating, resolving conflict, persuading, selling, using and responding to authority. It is also a way of defining an individual's behaviour in relationship to other people.

The way you behave in response to other people includes:

(a) How you perceive other people
(b) Listening to and understanding other people
(c) Behaving in a way that builds on this understanding
(d) Giving and receiving feedback

We use feedback information on the results of past behaviour to make rational decisions about whether to maintain successful behaviours or modify unsuccessful behaviours in the future, according to our goals and our plans for reaching them.

Development options that improve employees' effectiveness in their current jobs are called 'position related' while those that develop opportunities for career advancement are called 'career related'.

We are going to explain three activities that could be considered appropriate for employee development – coaching, mentoring and counselling.

9.2 Coaching

Managers help employees achieve objectives on a daily basis. Coaching is a behavioural control technique used by the manager to give on-going guidance and instruction, to follow day-to-day progress, and to give feedback.

Coaching is the ability to improve the job performance of employees. It is active, instead of passive, and is involved with guiding performance. Managers, who emphasise formal training and day-to-day coaching, reap the benefits of competence, high performance, commitment and co-operative behaviour.

The coaching process includes the following steps.

(a) *Establish learning targets* – the areas to be learned about should be identified and specific, realistic goals, eg completion dates or performance standards stated by agreement with the trainee

(b) *Plan a systematic learning and development programme* – this will ensure regular progress and appropriate stages for consolidation and practice

(c) *Identify opportunities for broadening the trainee's knowledge and experience* – eg by involvement in new products, placement on inter-departmental committees, suggesting new contacts or simply extending the job by adding more tasks, greater responsibility etc

(d) *Take into account the strengths and limitations of the trainee* in learning, and take advantage of learning opportunities that suit the trainee's ability, preferred style and goals.

(e) *Exchange feedback* – the coach will want to know how the trainee sees his or her progress and future and will also need performance information to monitor the trainee's progress, adjust the learning programme if necessary, identify further needs which may emerge and plan future development for the trainee

9.3 Mentoring

Mentoring is a process where one person offers help, guidance, advice and support to facilitate the learning or development of another.

Mentors can assist in:

(a) Drawing up personal development plans
(b) Advice with administrative problems people face in their new jobs
(c) Help in tackling projects, by pointing people in the right direction

Mentoring should not be seen as an additional or supplementary management task. It is an approach to management that puts the learning and development of the person at the heart of the process, offering advice and guidance to facilitate development. It is a good way of breaking down internal barriers between departments or groups and promoting equal opportunities. Mentoring offers a constructive alternative to the more traditional development methods by:

(a) giving structure and continuity to development in the workplace
(b) providing learners with a sounding board and facility for trust and confidentiality
(c) focusing learning on the learner, not the tutor
(d) transferring knowledge and skills
(e) enabling quicker and more effective induction on new employees
(f) providing structure for improved succession planning
(g) enabling learners to focus on their own experience
(h) allowing failure to be tolerated and used as a learning tool
(i) helping the learner to solve real problems and make real decisions
(j) providing continuous personal support and motivation

9.4 Counselling

Unlike mentoring, which focuses on learning and supporting the learner through the learning process, and coaching which focuses on the task and ensuring that the learner gains competence, counselling focuses on the person and enabling an individual to explore situations and responses.

Counselling can be defined as 'a purposeful relationship in which one persons helps another to help himself. It is a way of relating and responding to another person so that that person is helped to explore his thoughts, feelings and behaviour with the aim of reaching a clearer understanding. The clearer understanding may be of himself or of a problem, or of one in relation to the other' (Rees).

The need for workplace counselling can arise in many situations, eg:

(a) during appraisal
(b) in grievance or disciplinary situations
(c) following change, such as promotion or relocation
(d) on redundancy or dismissal
(e) as a result of personal or domestic difficulties
(f) in cases of sexual harassment or violence at work

Effective counselling is not merely a matter of pastoral care for individuals but is very much in the organisation's interests. The benefits include the following.

(a) Prevents underperformance, reduces labour turnover and absenteeism and increases commitment from employees

(b) Demonstrates an organisation's commitment to and concern for its employees

(c) Gives employees the confidence and encouragement necessary to take responsibility for self and career development

(d) Recognises that the organisation may be contributing to the employee's problems and therefore provides an opportunity to reassess organisational policy and practice

Chapter roundup

- Personality is the total pattern of an individual's thoughts, feelings and behaviours. It is shaped by a variety of factors, both inherited and environmental.
- **Perception** is the process by which the brain selects and organises information in order to make sense of it. People behave according to what they perceive - not according to what 'really is'.
- People develop attitudes about things, based on what they think, what they feel and what they want to do about it. Attitudes are formed by perception, experience and personality which in turn are shaped by wider social influences.
- Ability is the capacity to do something. It is often equated with intelligence. It is now recognised that there are many types of ability/intelligence, not all of which are based on mental dexterity or verbal fluency.
- People have certain innate needs. Maslow has categorised needs as physiological, security, love/social, esteem and self-actualisation. People also have goals, through which they expect their needs to be satisfied.
- Content theories of motivation suggest that each person has a package of needs: the best way to motivate an employee is to find out what his/her needs are and offer him/her rewards that will satisfy those needs.
  - Abraham Maslow identified a hierarchy of needs which an individual will be motivated to satisfy, progressing towards higher order satisfactions, such as self-actualisation.
  - Frederick Herzberg identified two basic need systems: the need to avoid unpleasantness and the need for personal growth. He suggested factors which could be offered by organisations to satisfy both types of need: 'hygiene' and 'motivator' factors respectively.
- Process theories of motivation do not tell managers what to offer employees in order to motivate them but help managers to understand the dynamics of employees' decisions about what rewards are worth going for. They are generally variations on the expectancy model: $F = V \times E$
- Various means have been suggested or improving job satisfaction but there is little evidence that a satisfied worker actually works harder.
- Pay is the most important of the hygiene factors, but it is ambiguous in its effect on motivation.

- Ways in which managers can improve employees' motivation range from encouraging employees to accept responsibility to careful design of jobs (including job enrichment, job enlargement and job rotation) to increasingly sophisticated and performance-related pay and incentive schemes.
- The main points of an appraisal system can be conveyed diagrammatically as follows.
  - *Performance appraisal*

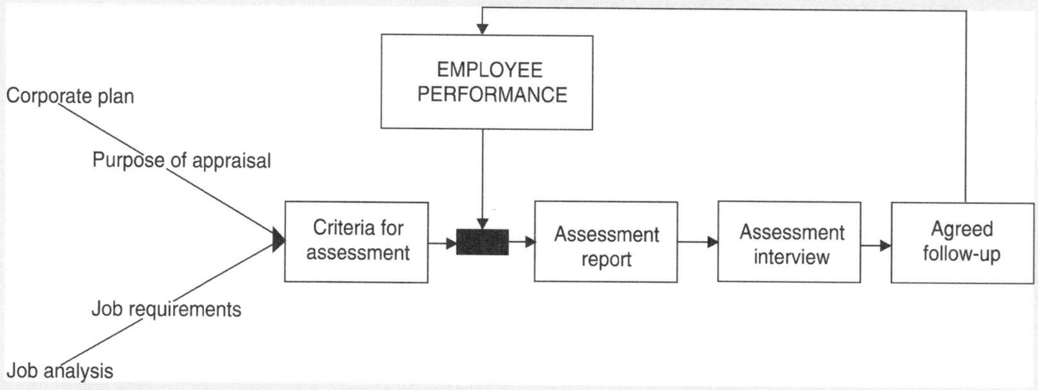

  - Potential appraisal indicates:
    - the individual's promotability (present and likely future);
    - the individual's training and development needs;
    - the direction and rate of progress of the individual's development;
    - the future (forecast) management resource of the organisation;
    - the management recruitment, training and development needs of the organisation.

Quick quiz

1. List three factors for a manager to consider in managing 'personality' at work.
2. Give three examples of areas where people's perceptions commonly conflict.
3. What are the three components of an 'attitude'?
4. Give three examples of non-work factors that might influence attitudes to work.
5. List the five categories in Maslow's Hierarchy of Needs.
6. List three ways in which an organisation can offer motivational satisfaction.
7. What is the difference between a reward and an incentive?
8. List five motivator and five hygiene factors.
9. Explain the formula 'F = V × E'.
10. What are the purposes of appraisal?
11. What bases or criteria of assessment might an appraisal system use?

12 Outline a results-oriented approach to appraisal, and its advantages.

13 What is upward appraisal?

14 What follow-up should there be after an appraisal?

15 How can appraisal be made more positive and empowering to employees?

16 What kinds of criticism might be levelled at appraisal schemes by a manager who thought they were a waste of time?

17 What techniques might be used to measure an employee's potential to become a successful senior manager?

Answers to quick quiz

1 The compatibility of an individual's personality with the task, with the systems and culture of the organisation and with other members of the team. (See para 1.3)

2 Managers and staff, work culture, race and gender. (See para 1.6)

3 Knowledge, feelings and desires, volition. (See para 1.7)

4 Class, age, race, culture or religion, interests and sex. (See para 1.9)

5 Physiological, safety, love/social, esteem, self-actualisation. (See para 3.4)

6 Relationships, belonging, challenge, achievement, progress, security, money. (See para 3.8)

7 A reward is given for some contribution or success. An incentive is a promise or offer of reward. (See para 4)

8 Motivator - status, advancement, recognition, responsibility, challenging work, achievement, growth. Hygiene - company policy and administration, salary, quality of supervision, relationships, job security, working conditions. (See para 3.6)

9 Force of motivation - Valence $\times$ Expectation. (See para 3.7)

10 Identifying performance levels, improvements needed and promotion prospects; deciding on rewards; assessing team work and encouraging, communication between manager and employee. (See para 6.1)

11 Job analysis, job description, plans, targets and standards. (see para 6.3)

12 Performance against specific, mutually agreed targets and standards. (See para 7.1)

13 Subordinates appraise superiors. (See para 7.4)

14 Appraisees should be informed of the results, agreed activities should be taken, progress should be monitored and whatever resources or changes are needed should be provided or implemented. (See para 7.6)

15 Ensure the scheme is relevant, fair, taken seriously and co-operative. (See para 8.2)

16 The manager may say that he or she has better things to do with his or her time, that appraisals have no relevance to the job and there is no reliable follow-up action, and that they involve too much paperwork. (See para 8.1)

17 Key indicators of performance should be determined and the employee should be assessed against them. The employee could be placed in positions simulating the responsibilities of senior management. (See para 7.7)

Answers to activities

1 You probably felt as we did that none of the qualities listed were unimportant. You probably had similar priorities to ours, as follows.

1 = b, c, e, g, j. 2 = a, d, f, h,i.

2 The perceptual problems in the situations given are as follows.

(a) The manager perceives himself as 'enlightened', and his style as an opportunity and gift to his staff. He clearly thinks that assessment and reward on the basis of more responsibility is a positive thing, probably offering greater rewards to staff. He does not perceive his use of the work 'judged' as potentially threatening: he uses it as another word for 'assessed'. His staff obviously see things differently. 'More responsibility' means their competence - maybe their jobs - are on the line. Feeling this way, and with the expectations they have of their boss (based on past experience of his autocratic style), they are bound to perceive the work 'judged' as threatening.

(b) The chairman thinks he is being funny. Maybe he is only joking about the woman making the tea - but he may really perceive her role that way. He lacks the perception that his new colleague may find his remark offensive. From the woman's point of view, she is bound to be sensitive and insecure in her first meeting and with all male colleagues: small wonder that, joke or not, she perceives the chairman's comment as a slap in the face. The chairman later fails to perceive the effect his joke has had on her, assuming that her silence is a sign of poor co-operation or inability to communicate.

(c) This is a case of closure leading to misinterpretation. The new employee sees the informal dress, the position behind the counter, and the offer of coffee: his brain fills in the gaps, and offers the perception that the youngster must be the tea-boy. Perceptual selectivity also plays a part filtering out awkward information that does not fit his expectations (like the fact that the 'tea-boy' comes to chat with him).

3 Elements of a positive attitude to work may include a willingness to:

(a) Commit oneself to the objectives of the organisation, or adopt personal objectives that are compatible with those of the organisation.

(b) Accept the right of the organisation to set standards of acceptable behaviour for its members.

(c) Contribute to the development and improvement of work practices and performance.

(d) Take advantages of opportunities for personal development at work.

4 As this activity is concerned with your own personal circumstances, there is no model answer.

5 Maslow's categories for the listed circumstances are as follows.

(a) Esteem needs

(b) Social needs

(c) Self-actualisation needs

(d) He will have physiological needs

(e) Safety needs initially; esteem needs above in a certain income level

(f) Social needs or self-actualisation needs

(g) Esteem needs

(h) Safety needs or esteem needs

6 (a) The rewards from PRP are often too small to motivate effectively. Anyhow, some employees may not expect to receive the rewards and hence will not put in the extra effort.

(b) It is often unfair, especially in jobs where success is determined by uncontrollable factors.

(c) As people are rewarded individually, they are less willing to work as a team. Consequently 'teamwork' might be included as a factor to be rewarded - but this is hard to measure.

(d) People concentrate on performance indicators rather than on longer-term issues such as innovation or quality. In other words, people put all their energy into hitting the target rather than doing their job better.

(e) PRP schemes have to be well designed to ensure performance is measured properly, people consider them to be fair and there is consent to the scheme.

(f) Performance is often hard to measure.

(g) If too many factors have to be taken into account, the whole process becomes subjective and unfair.

7 Disadvantages to the individual of not having an appraisal system include the following. The individual is not aware of progress or shortcomings, is unable to judge whether s/he would be considered for promotion, is unable to identify or correct weaknesses by training and there is a lack of communication with the manager.

8 You will have come up with your own examples of criteria to assess some jobs but not others. You might have identified such things as:

(a) numerical ability (applicable to accounts staff, say, more than to customer contact staff or other non-numerical functions);

(b) ability to drive safely (essential for transport workers – not for desk-bound ones);

(c) report-writing (not applicable to manual labour, say);

(d) creativity and initiative (desirable in areas involving design and problem-solving not routine or repetitive jobs in mass production or bureaucratic organisations).

9 Advantages of performance management include the following.

(a) The subordinate is more involved in appraisal of his or her own performance, because he or she is able to evaluate his or her success or progress in achieving specific, jointly-agreed targets. The sense of responsibility and independence may encourage job satisfaction and commitment.

(b) The manager is therefore relieved of his or her role as judge, to an extent, and becomes a counsellor. A primarily problem-solving approach may be adopted (what does the employee require in order to do a better job?)

(c) Learning and motivation theories suggest, as we have seen, that clear and known targets are important in determining behaviour.

10 Drawbacks to 360-degree appraisal include:

(a) respondents' reluctance to give negative feedback to a boss – or friend;

(b) the suspicion that management is passing the buck for negative feedback, getting people to 'rat' on their friends;

(c) the feeling that the appraisee is being picked on, if positive feedback is not carefully balanced with the negative.

11 Problems with upward appraisal include fear of reprisals or vindictiveness (or extra form-processing). Some bosses in strong positions might feel able to refuse to act on results, even if a consensus of staff suggested that they should change their ways.

12 The effects of appraisal on motivation are a tricky issue.

(a) Feedback on performance is regarded as vital in motivation, because it enables an employee to make calculations about the amount of effort required in future to achieve objectives and rewards. Even negative feedback can have this effect – and is more likely to spur the employee on to post-appraisal action.

(b) Agreement of challenging but attainable targets for performance or improvement also motivates employees by clarifying goals and the value (and 'cost' in terms of effort) of incentives offered.

(c) A positive approach to appraisal allows employees to solve their work problems and apply creative thinking to their jobs.

However, people rarely react well to criticism – especially at work, where they may feel that their reward or even job security is on the line. In addition, much depends on the self-esteem of the appraisee. If s(he) has a high self-image, (s)he may be impervious to criticism. If s(he) has a low self-image, (s)he may be depressed rather than motivated by criticism.

Chapter 11 :

DISCIPLINARY AND GRIEVANCE PROCEDURES

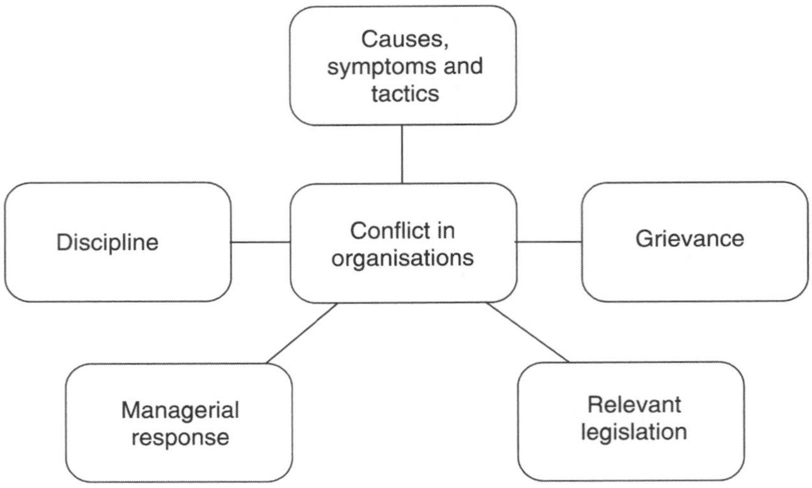

Introduction

There are various theorise of the organisation as a co-operative or a conflict-ridden structure. Conflict can exist at an individual or group level. The main aim of grievance and disciplinary procedures is to provide the standard means for resolving conflict. The last resort, for either employer or employee, will be to terminate the contract, but steps will usually be taken to sort out problems before this stage.

The employer, in resolving conflict, employs disciplinary procedures and the employee adopts grievance procedures – but both should be clearly defined. Both procedures, when seen together, are ways of policing unacceptable behaviour.

Hopefully, industrial action and its harmful effects on corporate performance may be mitigated. At the very least, standard procedures will minimise the problem of adopting different treatments for similar incidents. Additionally, employers will have a stronger legal case – should this be necessary – if they have adopted standard procedures, such as the ACAS code.

Your objectives

In this chapter you will learn about the following:

(a) The main causes of conflict within an organisation

(b) Procedures for managing conflict

(c) Suitable frameworks (both internal and external to the organisation) for dealing with grievance and disciplinary matters

(d) The need for effective organisational procedures

(e) The role of management in respect of disciplinary matters

(f) Ways in which the outcome of the disciplinary process should be communicated to the individual concerned

(g) The relevant legislation

NOTES

1 CONFLICT IN ORGANISATIONS

The existence of **conflict** in organisations might be considered inevitable or unnatural, depending on your viewpoint.

1.1 The 'happy family' view: conflict is unnatural

The happy family view presents organisations as:

(a) **Co-operative structures**, designed to achieve agreed common objectives, with no systematic conflict of interest.

(b) **Harmonious environments**, where conflicts are **exceptional** and arise from:

- Misunderstandings
- Personality factors
- The expectations of inflexible employees
- Factors outside the organisation and its control

Conflict is thus **blamed** on bad management, lack of leadership, poor communication, or 'bloody-mindedness' on the part of individuals or interest groups that impinge on the organisation. The theory is that a strong culture, good two-way communication, co-operation and motivational leadership will 'eliminate' conflict.

Activity 1 **(15 minutes)**

How accurate is the 'happy family' perspective when applied to your own organisation, or to any organisation with which you are sufficiently familiar?

To what extent would you subscribe to the claim that the 'happy family' view is publicised by managers within their own organisations, not so much as an accurate description of reality, but rather because adoption of the 'happy family' perspective itself helps to reduce the level of articulated conflict?

1.2 The conflict view

In contrast, some see organisations as **arenas** for conflict on individual and group levels.

(a) Members battle for limited resources, status, rewards and professional values.

(b) **Organisational politics** involve constant struggles for control, and choices of structure, technology and organisational goals are part of this process. Individual and organisational interests will not always coincide.

1.3 The 'evolutionary' view

This view regards conflict as a means of **maintaining the status quo**, as a useful basis for **evolutionary change**.

- **Conflict** keeps the organisation **sensitive to the need to change**, while reinforcing its essential framework of control.
- The **legitimate pursuit of competing interests** can balance and preserve social and organisational arrangements.

This '**constructive conflict**' view may perhaps be the most useful for managers and administrators of organisations, as it neither:

(a) Attempts to dodge the issues of conflict, which is an observable fact of life in most organisations; nor

(b) Seeks to pull down existing organisational structures altogether.

Conflict can be highly desirable. Conflict is constructive, when its effect is to:

- Introduce different **solutions** to problems
- **Define power relationships** more clearly
- Encourage **creativity**, the testing of ideas
- **Focus attention** on individual contributions
- **Bring emotions** out into the open
- **Release hostile feelings** that have been, or may be, repressed otherwise

Conflict can also be destructive. It may:

- **Distract attention** from the task
- **Polarise** views and 'dislocate' the group
- Subvert **objectives** in favour of secondary goals
- Encourage **defensive** or 'spoiling' behaviour
- Force the group to **disintegrate**
- Stimulate emotional, **win-lose conflicts**, ie hostility

CASE EXAMPLE

Tjosvold and Deerner researched conflict in different contexts. They allocated to 66 student volunteers the roles of foremen and workers at an assembly plant, with a scenario of conflict over job rotation schemes. Foremen were against, workers for.

One group was told that the organisational norm was to 'avoid controversy'; another was told that the norm was 'co-operative controversy', *trying* to agree; a third was told that groups were out to win any arguments that arose, 'competitive controversy'. The students were offered rewards for complying with their given norms. Their decisions, and attitudes to the discussions, were then monitored.

(a) Where controversy was avoided, the foremen's views dominated.

(b) Competitive controversy brought no agreement - but brought out feelings of hostility and suspicion.

(c) Co-operative controversy brought out differences in an atmosphere of curiosity, trust and openness: the decisions reached seemed to integrate the views of both parties.

But can real managers and workers be motivated to comply with useful organisational 'norms' in this way?

1.4 Conflict between groups

Conflicts of interest may exist throughout the organisation - or even for a single individual. There may be conflicts of interest between local management of a branch or subsidiary and the organisation as a whole.

- Sales and production departments in a manufacturing firm (over scheduling, product variation)
- Trade unions and management.

Interest groups such as trade unions tend to wield greater power in conflict situations than their members as individuals. Trade Unions are organisations whose purpose it is to promote their members' interests. (Strike action has to be preceded by a ballot.)

> **Activity 2** **(10 minutes)**
>
> What other examples of 'conflicts of interest' can you identify within an organisation? Having selected some instances, can you detect any common patterns in such conflicts?

CASE EXAMPLE

Conflict can also operate **within** groups.

In an experiment reported by Deutsch (1949), psychology students were given puzzles and human relation problems to work at in discussion groups. Some groups ('co-operative' ones) were told that the grade each individual got at the end of the course would depend on the performance of his group. Other groups ('competitive' ones) were told that each student would receive a grade according to his own contributions.

No significant differences were found between the two kinds of group in the amount of interest and involvement in the tasks, or in the amount of learning. But the co-operative groups, compared with the competitive ones, had greater productivity per unit time, better quality of product and discussion, greater co-ordination of effort and sub-division of activity, more diversity in amount of contribution per member, more attentiveness to fellow members and more friendliness during discussion.

1.5 Conflict and competition

Sherif and Sherif conducted a number of experiments into groups and competing groups.

(a) People tend to identify with a group.

(b) New members of a group quickly learn the norms and attitudes of the others, no matter whether these are 'positive' or 'negative', friendly or hostile.

(c) When a group competes, this is what happens to it **within the group**.

  (i) Members close ranks, and submerge their differences; loyalty and conformity are demanded.

  (ii) The 'climate' changes from informal and sociable to work and task-oriented; individual needs are subordinated to achievement.

  (iii) Leadership moves from democratic to autocratic, with the group's acceptance.

  (iv) The group tends to become more structured and organised.

  (v) The opposing group begins to be perceived as 'the enemy'.

  (vi) Perception is distorted, presenting an idealised picture of 'us' and a negative stereotype of 'them'.

  (vii) Communication between groups decreases.

NOTES

In a 'win-lose' situation, where competition is not perceived to result in benefits for both sides.

(a) The **winning** group will:

- Retain its cohesion
- Relax into a complacent, playful state
- Return to group maintenance and concern for members' needs
- Be confirmed in its group 'self-concept' with little re-evaluation

(b) The **losing** group might behave as follows.

(i) Deny defeat if possible, or place the blame on the arbitrator, or the system

(ii) Lose its cohesion and splinter into conflict, as 'blame' is apportioned.

(iii) Be keyed-up, fighting mad.

(iv) Turn towards work-orientation to regroup, rather than members' needs or group maintenance.

(v) Tend to learn by re-evaluating its perceptions of itself and the other group. It is more likely to become a cohesive and effective unit once the 'defeat' has been accepted.

Members of a group will act in unison if the group's existence or patterns of behaviour are threatened from outside. Cohesion is naturally assumed to be the result of positive factors such as communication, agreement and mutual trust - but in the face of a 'common enemy' (competition, crisis or emergency) cohesion and productivity benefit.

Activity 3 **(20 minutes)**

How applicable are Sherif's 1965 research findings to the cause, symptoms and treatment of conflict in a modern organisation? In what ways, if at all, could Sherif's findings be used as a means of improving employee performance within an organisation?

2 CAUSES, SYMPTOMS AND TACTICS OF CONFLICT

2.1 Causes of conflict

(a) **Differences in the objectives** of different groups or individuals.

(b) **Scarcity of resources**.

(c) **Interdependence of two departments** on a task. They have to work together but may do so ineffectively.

(d) **Disputes about the boundaries of authority.**

(i) The technostructure may attempt to encroach on the roles or 'territory' of line managers and usurp some of their authority.

(ii) One department might start '**empire building**' and try to take over the work previously done by another department.

(e) **Personal differences**, as regards goals, attitudes and feelings, are also bound to crop up. This is especially true in **differentiated organisations**, where people employed in the different sub-units are very different.

2.2 Symptoms of conflict

- Poor communications, in all 'directions'
- Interpersonal friction
- Inter-group rivalry and jealousy
- Low morale and frustration
- Widespread use of arbitration, appeals to higher authority, and inflexible attitudes

2.3 The tactics of conflict

(a) **Withholding information** from one another

(b) **Distorting information.** This will enable the group or manager presenting the information to get their own way more easily.

(c) **Empire building**. A group (especially a specialist group such as research) which considers its influence to be neglected might seek to **impose rules, procedures**, restrictions or official requirements on other groups, in order to bolster up their own importance.

(d) **Informal organisation**. A manager might seek to by-pass formal channels of communication and decision-making by establishing informal contacts and friendships with people in a position of importance.

(e) **Fault-finding** in the work of other departments: department X might duplicate the work of department Y - hoping to prove department Y 'wrong' - and then report the fact to senior management.

3 MANAGERIAL RESPONSE TO CONFLICT

3.1 Management responses to the handling of conflict

Not all of these are effective.

Response	Comment
Denial/withdrawal	'Sweeping it under the carpet'. If the conflict is very trivial, it may indeed blow over without an issue being made of it, but if the causes are not identified, the conflict may grow to unmanageable proportions.
Suppression	'Smoothing over', to preserve working relationships despite minor conflicts. As Hunt remarks, however: 'Some cracks cannot be papered over'.
Dominance	The application of power or influence to settle the conflict. The disadvantage of this is that it creates all the lingering resentment and hostility of 'win-lose' situations.

Response	Comment
Compromise	Bargaining, negotiating, conciliating. To some extent, this will be inevitable in any organisation made up of different individuals. However, individuals tend to exaggerate their positions to allow for compromise, and compromise itself is seen to weaken the value of the decision, perhaps reducing commitment. **Negotiation** is: 'a process of interaction by which two or more parties who consider they need to be jointly involved in an outcome, but who initially have different objectives seek by the use of argument and persuasion to resolve their differences in order to achieve a mutually acceptable solution'.
Integration/ collaboration	Emphasis must be put on the task, individuals must accept the need to modify their views for its sake, and group effort must be seen to be superior to individual effort.
Encourage co-operative behaviour	Joint problem-solving team, goals set for all teams/departments to follow.

Activity 4 **(25 minutes)**

In the light of the above consider how conflict could arise, what form it would take and how it might be resolved in the following situations.

(a) Two managers who share a secretary have documents to be typed.

(b) One worker finds out that another worker who does the same job as he does is paid a higher wage.

(c) A company's electricians find out that a group of engineers have been receiving training in electrical work.

(d) Department A stops for lunch at 12.30 while Department B stops at 1 o'clock. Occasionally the canteen runs out of puddings for Department B workers.

(e) The Northern Region and Southern Region sales teams are continually trying to better each others results, and the capacity of production to cope with the increase in sales is becoming overstretched.

3.2 The win-win model

One useful model of conflict resolution is the **win-win model**. This states that there are three basic ways in which a conflict or disagreement can be worked out.

Method	Frequency	Explanation
Win-lose	This is quite common.	**One party gets what (s)he wants at the expense of the other party**: for example, Department A gets the new photocopier, while Department B keeps the old one (since there were insufficient resources to buy two new ones). However well-justified such a solution is (Department A needed the facilities on the new photocopier more than Department B), there is often lingering resentment on the part of the 'losing' party, which may begin to damage work relations.
Lose-lose	This sounds like a senseless outcome, but actually **compromise** comes into this category. It is thus very common.	**Neither party gets what (s)he really wanted**: for example, since Department A and B cannot both have a new photocopier, it is decided that neither department should have one. However 'logical' such a solution is, there is often resentment and dissatisfaction on *both* sides. (Personal arguments where neither party gives ground and both end up storming off or not talking are also lose-lose: the parties may not have lost the argument, but they lose the relationship ...) Even positive compromises only result in half-satisfied needs.
Win-win	This may not be common, but working towards it often brings out the best solution.	**Both parties get as close as possible to what they really want**. How can this be achieved?

It is critical to the **win-win approach** to discover **what both parties really want** - as opposed to:

- What they think they want (because they have not considered any other options)
- What they think they can get away with
- What they think they need in order to avoid an outcome they fear

For example, Department B may want the new photocopier because they have never found out how to use all the features (which do the same things) on the old photocopier; because they just want to have the same equipment as Department A; or because they fear that if they do not have the new photocopier, their work will be slower and less professionally presented, and they may be reprimanded (or worse) by management.

The important questions in working towards win-win are:

- What do you want this for?
- What do you think will happen if you don't get it?

These questions get to the heart of what people really need and want.

In our photocopier example, Department A says it needs the new photocopier to make colour copies (which the old copier does not do), while Department B says it needs the new copier to make clearer copies (because the copies on the old machine are a bit blurred). Now there are **options to explore**. It may be that the old copier just needs fixing, in order for Department B to get what it really wants. Department A will still end up getting the new copier - but Department B has in the process been consulted and had its needs met.

EXAMPLE: THE WIN-WIN APPROACH

Two men are fighting over an orange. There is only one orange, and both men want it.

(a) If one man gets the orange and the other does not, this is a **win-lose** solution.

(b) If they cut the orange in half and share it (or agree that neither will have the orange), this is a **lose-lose** solution - despite the compromise.

(c) If they talk about what they each need the orange for, and one says 'I want to make orange juice' and the other says 'I want the skin of the orange to make candied peel', there are further options to explore (like peeling the orange) and the potential for both men to get exactly what they wanted. This is a **win-win** approach.

Win-win is not always possible: It is **working towards it** that counts. The result can be mutual respect and co-operation, enhanced communication, more creative problem-solving and - at best - **satisfied needs all round**.

Activity 5 **(20 minutes)**

Suggest a (i) win-lose, (ii) compromise and (iii) win-win solution in the following scenarios.

(a) Two of your team members are arguing over who gets the desk by the window: they both want it.

(b) You and a colleague both need access to the same file at the same time. You both need it to compile reports for your managers, for the following morning. It is now 3.00pm, and each of you will need it for two hours to do the work.

(c) Manager A is insisting on buying new computers for her department before the budgetary period ends. Manager B cannot understand why - since the old computers are quite adequate - and will moreover be severely inconvenienced by such a move, since her own systems will have to be upgraded as well, in order to remain compatible with department A. (The two departments constantly share data files.) Manager B protests, and conflict erupts.

4 DISCIPLINE

Definition

> **Discipline** can be considered as: 'a condition in an enterprise in which there is orderliness in which the members of the enterprise behave sensibly and conduct themselves according to the standards of acceptable behaviour as related to the goals of the organisation'.

Another definition of 'positive' and 'negative' discipline makes the distinction between methods of maintaining sensible conduct and orderliness which are technically co-operative, and those based on warnings, threats and punishments.

(a) Positive (or constructive) discipline relates to procedures, systems and equipment in the work place which have been designed specifically so that the employee has **no option** but to act in the desired manner to complete a task safely and successfully. A machine may, for example, shut off automatically if its safety guard is not in place.

(b) **Negative discipline** is then the promise of **sanctions** designed to make people choose to behave in a desirable way. Disciplinary action may be punitive (punishing an offence), deterrent (warning people not to behave in that way) or reformative (calling attention to the nature of the offence, so that it will not happen again).

The best discipline is **self discipline**. Even before they start to work, most mature people accept the idea that following instructions and fair rules of conduct are normal responsibilities that are part of any job. Most team members can therefore be counted on to exercise self discipline.

4.1 Types of disciplinary situations

There are many types of disciplinary situations which require attention by the manager. Internally, the most frequently occurring are these.

- Excessive absenteeism
- Poor timekeeping
- Defective and/or inadequate work performance
- Poor attitudes which influence the work of others or reflect on the image of the firm
- Breaking rules regarding rest periods and other time schedules
- Improper personal appearance
- Breaking safety rules
- Other violations of rules, regulations and procedures
- Open insubordination such as the refusal to carry out a work assignment.

Managers might be confronted with disciplinary problems stemming from employee behaviour *off* the job. These may be an excessive drinking problem, the use of drugs or some form of narcotics, or involvement in some form of law breaking activity. In such circumstances, whenever an employee's off-the-job conduct has an impact upon performance on the job, the manager must be prepared to deal with such a problem within the scope of the disciplinary process.

4.2 Disciplinary action

The purpose of discipline is not punishment or retribution. Disciplinary action must have as its goal the improvement of the future behaviour of the employee and other members of the organisation. The purpose obviously is the avoidance of similar occurrences in the future.

The suggested steps of progressive disciplinary action follow ACAS guidelines.

Step 1. **The informal talk**

If the infraction is of a relatively minor nature and if the employee's record has no previous marks of disciplinary action, an informal, friendly talk will clear up the situation in many cases. Here the manager discusses with the employee his or her behaviour in relation to standards which prevail within the enterprise.

Step 2. **Oral warning or reprimand**

In this type of interview between employee and manager, the latter emphasises the undesirability of the subordinate's repeated violation, and that ultimately it could lead to serious disciplinary action.

Step 3. **Written or official warning**

These are part of the ACAS code of practice. A written warning is of a formal nature insofar as it becomes a permanent part of the employee's record. Written warnings, not surprisingly, are particularly necessary in unionised situations, so that the document can serve as evidence in case of grievance procedures.

Step 4. **Disciplinary layoffs, or suspension**

This course of action would be next in order if the employee has committed repeated offences and previous steps were of no avail. Disciplinary lay-offs usually extend over several days or weeks. Some employees may not be very impressed with oral or written warnings, but they will find a disciplinary layoff without pay a rude awakening.

Step 5. **Demotion**

This course of action is likely to bring about dissatisfaction and discouragement, since losing pay and status over an extended period of time is a form of constant punishment. This dissatisfaction of the demoted employee may easily spread to co-workers, so most enterprises avoid downgrading as a disciplinary measure.

Step 6. **Discharge**

Discharge is a drastic form of disciplinary action, and should be reserved for the most serious offences. For the organisation, it involves waste of a labour resource, the expense of training a new employee, and disruption caused by changing the make-up of the work team. There also may be damage to the morale of the group.

NOTES

Activity 6 **(15 minutes)**

How (a) accessible and (b) clear are the rules and policies of your organisation/office: do people really know what they are and are not supposed to do? Have a look at the rule book or procedures manual in your office. How easy is it to see - or did you get referred elsewhere? is the rule book well-indexed and cross-referenced, and in language that all employees will understand?

How (a) accessible and (b) clear are the disciplinary procedures in your office? Are the employees' rights of investigation and appeal clearly set out, with ACAS guidelines? Who is responsible for discipline?

4.3 Relationship management in disciplinary situations

Even if the manager uses sensitivity and judgement, imposing disciplinary action tends to generate resentment because it is an unpleasant experience. The challenge is to apply the necessary disciplinary action so that it will be least resented.

(a) **Immediacy**

Immediacy means that after noticing the offence, the manager proceeds to take disciplinary action as *speedily* as possible, subject to investigations while at the same time avoiding haste and on-the-spot emotions which might lead to unwarranted actions.

(b) **Advance warning**

Employees should know in advance (eg in a Staff Handbook) what is expected of them and what the rules and regulations are.

(c) **Consistency**

Consistency of discipline means that each time an infraction occurs appropriate disciplinary action is taken. Inconsistency in application of discipline lowers the morale of employees and diminishes their respect for the manager.

(d) **Impersonality**

Penalties should be connected with the act and not based upon the personality involved, and once disciplinary action has been taken, no grudges should be borne.

(e) **Privacy**

As a general rule (unless the manager's authority is challenged directly and in public) disciplinary action should be taken in private, to avoid the spread of conflict and the humiliation or martyrdom of the employee concerned.

4.4 Disciplinary interviews

Preparation for the disciplinary interview

(a) **Gathering the facts** about the alleged infringement

(b) **Determination of the organisation's position:** how valuable is the employee, potentially? How serious are his offences/lack of progress? How far is the organisation prepared to go to help him improve or discipline him further?

(c) **Identification of the aims of the interview**: punishment? deterrent to others? improvement? Specific standards of future behaviour/performance required need to be determined.

(d) **Ensure that the organisation's disciplinary procedures have been followed**

   (i) Informal oral warnings (at least) have been given.

   (ii) The employee has been given adequate notice of the interview for his own preparation.

   (iii) The employee has been informed of the complaint against his right to be accompanied by a colleague or representative and so on.

4.5 The content of the disciplinary interview

Step 1. The manager will explain the purpose of the interview.

Step 2. The charges against the employee will be delivered, clearly, unambiguously and without personal emotion.

Step 3. The manager will explain the organisation's position with regard to the issues involved: disappointment, concern, need for improvement, impact on others. This can be done frankly - but tactfully, with as positive an emphasis as possible on the employee's capacity and responsibility to improve.

Step 4. The organisation's expectations with regard to future behaviour/performance should be made clear.

Step 5. The employee should be given the opportunity to comment, explain, justify or deny. If he is to approach the following stage of the interview in a positive way, he must not be made to feel 'hounded' or hard done by.

Step 6. The organisation's expectations should be reiterated, or new standards of behaviour set for the employee.

   (i) They should be specific and quantifiable, performance related and realistic.

   (ii) They should be related to a practical but reasonably short time period. A date should be set to review his progress.

   (iii) The manager agrees on measures to help the employee should that be necessary. It would demonstrate a positive approach if, for example, a mentor were appointed from his work group to help him check his work. If his poor performance is genuinely the result of some difficulty or distress outside work, other help (temporary leave, counselling or financial aid) may be appropriate.

Step 7. The manager should explain the reasons behind any penalties imposed on the employee, including the entry in his personnel record of the formal warning. He should also explain how the warning can be removed from the record, and what standards must be achieved within a specified timescale. There should be a clear warning of the consequences of failure to meet improvement targets.

Step 8. The manager should explain the organisation's appeals procedures: if the employee feels he has been unfairly treated, there should be a right of appeal to a higher manager.

Step 9. Once it has been established that the employee understands all the above, the manager should summarise the proceedings briefly.

Records of the interview will be kept for the employee's personnel file, and for the formal follow-up review and any further action necessary.

Activity 7 **(20 minutes)**

Outline the steps involved in a formal disciplinary procedure (for an organisation with unionised employees) and show how the procedure would operate in a case of:

(a) Persistent absenteeism
(b) Theft of envelopes from the organisation's offices

4.6 The ACAS Code of Practice

This highlights the features of a good disciplinary system.

ACAS Code of Practice

Disciplinary and grievance procedures should:

- be in written form*
- specify to whom they apply (all, or only some of the employees?)
- be capable of dealing speedily with disciplinary matters
- indicate the forms of disciplinary action which may be taken (such as dismissal, suspension or warning)
- specify the appropriate levels of authority for the exercise of disciplinary actions
- provide for individuals to be informed of the nature of their alleged misconduct
- allow individuals to state their case, and to be accompanied by a fellow employee (or union representative)
- ensure that every case is properly investigated before any disciplinary action is taken
- ensure that employees are informed of the reasons for any penalty they receive
- state that no employee will be dismissed for a first offence, except in cases of gross misconduct
- provide for a right of appeal against any disciplinary action, and specify the appeals procedure

** The ACAS code of practice does not extend to informal 'first warnings', but these are an important part of the organisation's policy: don't forget them!*

5 GRIEVANCE

Definition

> A **grievance** occurs when an individual thinks that he is being wrongly treated by his colleagues or supervisor; perhaps he or she is being picked on, unfairly appraised in his annual report, unfairly blocked for promotion or discriminated against on grounds of race or sex.

When an individual has a grievance he should be able to pursue it and ask to have the problem resolved. Some grievances should be capable of solution informally by the individual's manager. However, if an informal solution is not possible, there should be a formal grievance procedure.

5.1 Grievance procedures

Formal grievance procedures, like disciplinary procedures, should be set out in **writing** and made available to all staff. These procedures should do the following things.

(a) State what **grades of employee** are entitled to pursue a particular type of grievance.

(b) State the **rights of the employee** for each type of grievance. For example, an employee who is not invited to attend a promotion/selection panel might claim that he has been unfairly passed over. The grievance procedure must state what the individual would be entitled to claim. In our example, the employee who is overlooked for promotion might be entitled to a review of his annual appraisal report, or to attend a special appeals promotion/selection board if he has been in his current grade for at least a certain number of years.

(c) State what the **procedures for pursuing a grievance** should be.

Step 1. The individual should discuss the grievance with a staff/union representative (or a colleague). If his case seems a good one, he should take the grievance to his immediate boss.

Step 2. The first interview will be between the immediate boss (unless he is the subject of the complaint, in which case it will be the next level up) and the employee, who has the right to be accompanied by a colleague or representative.

Step 3. If the immediate boss cannot resolve the matter, or the employee is otherwise dissatisfied with the first interview, the case should be referred to his own superior (and if necessary in some cases, to an even higher authority).

Step 4. Cases referred to a higher manager should also be reported to the personnel department. Line management might decide at some stage to ask for the assistance/advice of a personnel manager in resolving the problem.

(d) **Distinguish between individual grievances and collective grievances.** Collective grievances might occur when a work group as a whole considers that it is being badly treated.

(e) Allow for the **involvement of an individual's or group's trade union** or staff association representative. Indeed, many individuals and groups might prefer to initiate some grievance procedures through their union or association rather than through official grievance procedures. Involvement of a union representative from the beginning should mean that management and union will have a common view of what procedures should be taken to resolve the matter.

(f) **State time limits** for initiating certain grievance procedures and subsequent stages of them. For example, a person who is passed over for promotion should be required to make his appeal within a certain time period of his review, and his appeal to higher authority (if any) within a given period after the first grievance interview. There should also be timescales for management to determine and communicate the outcome of the complaint to the employee.

(g) **Require written records** of all meetings concerned with the case to be made and distributed to all the participants.

5.2 Grievance interviews

The dynamics of a grievance interview are broadly similar to a disciplinary interview, except that it is the subordinate who primarily wants a positive result from it. Prior to the interview, the manager should have some idea of the complaint and its possible source. The meeting itself can then proceed through three phases.

Step 1. **Exploration**. What is the problem: the background, the facts, the causes (manifest and hidden)? At this stage, the manager should simply try to gather as much information as possible, without attempting to suggest solutions or interpretations: the situation must be seen to be open.

Step 2. **Consideration**. The manager should:

(i) Check the facts

(ii) Analyse the causes - the problem of which the complaint may be only a symptom

(iii) Evaluate options for responding to the complaint, and the implication of any response made

It may be that information can be given to clear up a misunderstanding, or the employee will - having 'got it off his chest' - withdraw his complaint. However, the meeting may have to be adjourned (say, for 48 hours) while the manager gets extra information and considers extra options.

Step 3. **Reply**. The manager, having reached and reviewed his conclusions, reconvenes the meeting to convey (and justify, if required) his decision, hear counter-arguments and appeals. The outcome (agreed or disagreed) should be recorded in writing.

Grievance procedures should be seen as an employee's right. To this end, managers should be given formal training in the grievance procedures of their organisation, and the reasons for having them. Management should be persuaded that the grievance procedures are beneficial for the organisation and are not a threat to themselves (since many grievances arise out of disputes between subordinates and their boss).

Activity 8 **(20 minutes)**

Find your organisation's grievance procedures in the office manual, or ask your union or staff association representative. Study the procedures carefully. Think of a complaint or grievance you have (or have had) at work. Have you taken it to grievance procedures? If so, what happened: were you satisfied with the process and outcome? If not, why not?

6 RELEVANT LEGISLATION

As with other areas of employment, there are statutes that cover the disciplinary and grievance procedures in an organisation. These include dismissal and the termination of employment.

6.1 Termination of employment

The Employment Rights Act 1996 lays down minimum periods of notice for both employer and employee. A contract of employment may not permit either side to give less than the minimum period of notice. However, either party may waive his right to notice or take a payment in lieu, and the Act does not affect the right to terminate a contract without notice in the event of gross misconduct.

The contract of employment may be terminated by either party for any reason or for no reason upon giving notice of a reasonable length, unless the contract is one for a fixed term or unless it specifically restricts the reason for which it may be terminated.

At common law either party may lawfully terminate the contract summarily, eg sacking without giving any notice, if the other party has committed a serious breach of the contract. The general principle justifying summary dismissal is that the employee's conduct prevents further satisfactory continuance of the employer-employee relationship, eg misconduct including disobedience, insolence and rudeness, committing a criminal act such as stealing, or causing injury through practical jokes.

6.2 Dismissal

Dismissal is the ultimate sanction in any disciplinary procedure. However, dismissals occur most frequently in the form of redundancy. Statistics published by the Department of Employment list the major reasons for dismissal as redundancy, sickness, unsuitability and misconduct in that order. Legislation in Britain during the 1970s, notably the Industrial Relations Act 1971, the Trades Unions and Labour Relations Act 1974 and the Employment Protection Act 1975, the Employment Protection (Consolidation) Act 1978 and now the Employment Rights Act 1996, makes it a difficult and costly business to dismiss employees because of the provisions for employees to challenge the employer's decision. However, in recent statistics published by the Department of Employment it was revealed that only a proportion of cases of unfair dismissal actually reach industrial tribunals; the majority are dealt with by some form of conciliation and arbitration.

Dismissal may be fair or unfair:

Fair dismissal – there is a statutory obligation for an employer to show that a dismissal is fair. In this case a dismissal is fair if it is related to:

(a) **A lack of capability or qualifications** – where the employee lacks the qualifications, skill, aptitude or health to do the job properly. However, in all cases the employee must be given the opportunity to improve the position or in the case of health be considered for alternative employment.

(b) **Misconduct** includes the refusal to obey lawful and reasonable instructions, absenteeism, insubordination over a period of time and some criminal actions. In the last case, the criminal action should relate directly to the job; it can only be grounds for dismissal if the result of the criminal action will affect the work in some way.

(c) **A statutory bar** occurs when employees cannot pursue their normal duties without breaking the law, eg drivers who have been banned.

Unfair dismissal – in all cases there are two stages of proof. Firstly, the circumstances that represent fair grounds for dismissal must be established, and secondly, the tribunal must decide whether dismissal is fair in the circumstances of the case in question.

For dismissal to be automatically unfair, it must be for one of the following reasons.

(a) Trade union membership or non-membership
(b) Pregnancy
(c) Sex or race discrimination
(d) Revelation of a non-relevant spent conviction

6.3 Provisions for unfair dismissal

Where employees feel that they have been unfairly dismissed they have the right to take their case to the industrial tribunal. The tribunal will normally refer the case to ACAS (Advisory Conciliation and Arbitration Service) in the hope of gaining an amicable settlement. The possible solutions or remedies for unfair dismissal include:

(a) **Withdrawal of notice** by the employer. This is the preferred remedy as stated in the Employment Rights Act.

(b) **Reinstatement (order of industrial tribunal)** – this treats the employee as though he or she had never been dismissed. The employee is taken back to his old job with no loss of earnings and privileges.

(c) **Re-engagement (order of industrial tribunal)** – the employee is offered a different job in the organisation and loses continuity of service. Both reinstatement and re-engagement were provisions introduced by the Employment Protection Act 1975.

(d) **Compensation (order of industrial tribunal)** – if an employer refuses to re-employ then the employee receives compensation made up of a penalty award of 13-26 weeks' pay (more in the case of discrimination), a payment equivalent to the redundancy entitlement and an award to compensate for loss of earnings, pension rights and so on. Some form of compensation may also be appropriate in cases of reinstatement and re-engagement.

NOTES

Chapter roundup

- **Conflict** can be viewed as:
  - Inevitable owing to the class system
  - A continuation of organisation politics by other means
  - Something to be welcomed as it avoids complacency
  - Something resulting from poor management
  - Something which should be avoided at all costs
- Conflict is possible owing to the different degrees of **power**, **influence** and **authority** that different groups have. Negative power, for example, is the power to disrupt.
- Conflict can be **constructive**, if it introduced new information into a problem, if it denies a problem or if it encourages creativity. It can be destructive if it distracts attention from the task or inhibits communication.
- One constructive response to conflict is the '**win-win**' **model**.
- **Discipline** has the same end as **motivation** - ie to secure a range of desired behaviour from members of the organisation.
  - Motivation may even be called a kind of **self discipline** - because motivated individuals exercise choice to behave in the way that the organisation wishes.
  - Discipline however, is more often related to **negative motivation**, an appeal to the individual's need to avoid punishment, sanctions or unpleasantness.
- Progressive **discipline** includes the following **stages**.
  - Informal talk
  - Oral warning
  - Written/official warning
  - Lay-off or suspension
  - Dismissal
- **Grievance procedures** embody the employee's right to appeal against unfair or otherwise prejudicial conduct or conditions that affect him and his work.
- **Grievance interviews** follow: exploration, consideration, reply.
- **Legislation** that applies to discipline and grievance relates to dismissal and termination of employment as set out in the Employment Rights Act 1996.

Quick quiz

1. What are the features of the 'happy family view' of the organisation?
2. Give an alternative to the happy family view.
3. When can conflict be constructive?
4. What happens when two groups are put in competition with each other?
5. What are the possible outcomes of conflict, according to the 'win-win' model?
6. What causes conflict?
7. What is discipline?

8 What is progressive discipline?

9 What factors should a manager bear in mind in trying to control the disciplinary situation?

10 Outline typical grievance procedures, or the grievance procedures of your own firm.

Answers to quick quiz

1 Organisations are co-operative and harmonious. Conflict arises when something goes wrong. (See para 1.1)

2 Conflict is inevitable, being in the very nature of the organisation. Conflict can be constructive. (See para 1.2)

3 It can introduce solutions, define power relations, bring emotions, hostile or otherwise, out into the open. (See para 1.3)

4 They become more cohesive internally and more achievement-orientated. (See para 1.5)

5 Win-lose, lose-lose, win-win. (See para 3.2)

6 Different objectives, scarcity of responses, personal differences, interdependence of departments. (See para 2.1)

7 People behave according to the standard the organisation has set. (See para 4)

8 A system whereby the disciplinary action gets more severe with repeated 'offence'. (See para 4.2)

9 Immediacy, advance warning, consistency, impersonality, privacy. (See para 4.3)

10 Grievance procedures should state employees' rights, the procedures distinguish between individual and collective grievances state time limits. The interview should explore the facts, consider the issues and provide a resolution. (See para 5.1)

Answers to activities

1 The 'happy family' perspective rarely fits most organisations, even those pursuing a common ideological goal, like a political party. Such organisations regularly face conflict (eg the Conservatives' divisions over Europe), if only about how to attain their goals. Cynics argue that managers promote the 'happy family' view to suppress conflict. Asda at one time referred to all its staff as 'colleagues'.

2 Conflicts occur anywhere in an organisation. Individuals, groups, departments or subsidiaries compete for scarce (financial/human/physical) resources.

3 Sherif's work applies to conflict in organisations. To improve employee performance, win-lose conflict can be turned towards competitors, who become 'the enemy'.

4 (a) Both might need work done at the same time. Compromise and co-ordinated planning can help them manage their secretary's time.

(b) Differential pay might result in conflict with management - even an accusation of discrimination. There may be good reasons for the difference (eg length of service). To prevent conflict such information should be kept confidential. Where it is public, it should be seen to be not arbitrary.

(c) The electricians are worried about their jobs, and may take industrial action. Yet if the engineers' training is unrelated to the electricians' work, management can allay fears by giving information. The electricians cannot be given a veto over management decisions: a 'win-lose' situation is inevitable, but both sides can negotiate.

(d) The kitchen should plan its meals better - or people from both departments can be asked in advance whether they want puddings.

(e) Competition between sales regions is healthy as it increases sales. the conflict lies between sales regions and the production department. In the long-term, an increase in production capacity is the only solution. Where this is to possible, proper co-ordination methods should be instituted.

5 (a) (i) Win-lose: one team member gets the window desk, and the other does not. (Result: broken relationships within the team.)

(ii) Compromise: the team members get the window desk on alternate days or weeks. (Result: half satisfied needs.)

(iii) Win-win: what do they want the window desk for? One may want the view, the other better lighting conditions. This offers options to be explored: how else could the lighting be improved, so that both team members get what they really want? (Result: at least, the positive intention to respect everyone's wishes equally, with benefits for team communication and creative problem-solving.)

(b) (i) Win-lose: one of you gets the file and the other doesn't.

(ii) Compromise: one of you gets the file now, and the other gets it later (although this has an element of win-lose, since the other has to work late or take it home).

(iii) Win-win: you photocopy the file and both take it, or one of your consults his or her boss and gets an extension of the deadline (since getting the job done in time is the real aim - not just getting the file). These kind of solutions are more likely to emerge if the parties believe they can both get what they want.

(c) (i) Win-lose: Manager A gets the computers, and Manager B has to upgrade her systems.

(ii) Compromise: Manager A will get some new computers, but keep the same old ones for continued data-sharing with Department B. Department B will also need to get some new computers, as a back-up measure.

(iii) Win-win: what does Manager A want the computers for, or to avoid? Quite possibly, she needs to use up her budget allocation for buying equipment before the end of the budgetary period: if not, she fears she will lose that budget allocation. Now, that may not be the case, or there may be other equipment that could be more usefully purchased - in which case, there is no losing party.

NOTES

7 Apart from the outline of the steps involved - which can be drawn from the chapter, this question raises an interesting point about the nature of different offences, and the flexibility required in the handling of complex disciplinary matters.

- There is clearly a difference in kind and scale between
  - unsatisfactory conduct (eg absenteeism)
  - misconduct (eg insulting behaviour, persistent absenteeism, insubordination) and
  - 'gross misconduct' (eg theft or assault).
- The attitude of the organisation towards the purpose of disciplinary action will to a large extent dictate the severity of the punishment.
  - If it is punitive it will 'fit the crime'.
  - If it is reformative, it may be a warning only, and less severe than the offence warrants.
  - If it is deterrent, it may be more severe than is warranted (ie to 'make an example').

The absenteeism question assumes that counselling etc. has failed, and that some sanction has to be applied, to preserve credibility. The theft technically deserves summary dismissal (as gross misconduct), but it depends on the scale and value of the theft, the attitude of the organisation to use of stationery for personal purposes (ie is it theft?) etc. Communicating the situations given might best be done as follows.

(a) Telephone, confirmed in writing (order form, letter)

(b) Noticeboard or general meeting

(c) Fact-to-face conversation. it would be a good idea to confirm the outcome of the meeting in writing so that records can be maintained.

(d) Either telephone or face-to-face.

BPP PUBLISHING

PART C: UNIT 15

MANAGING INFORMATION

Chapter 12 :
INFORMATION GATHERING

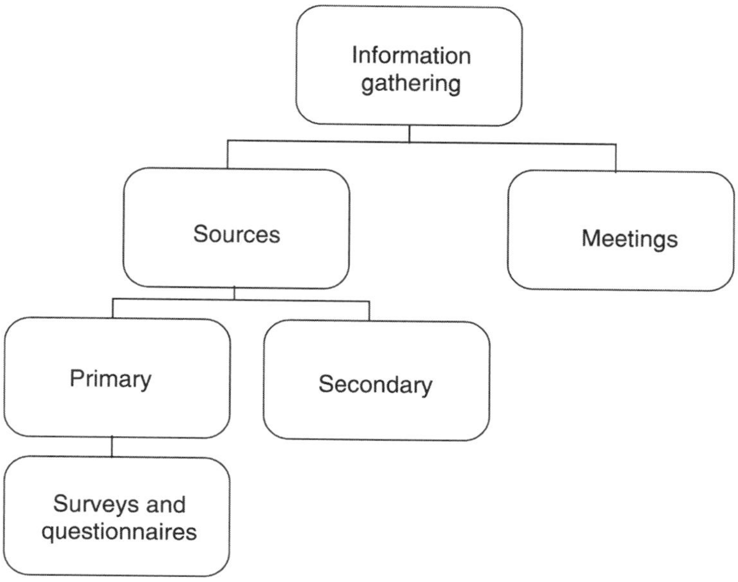

Introduction

The first two headings in the Edexcel Guidelines for Unit 15, *Managing Information*, are concerned with types and sources of information. Much of this ground should already be familiar to you from the HNC/HND Core Unit 7 Course Book, *Management Information Systems*. You should try the first activity in this chapter, and refer back to that Course Book should you encounter any difficulties.

Your objectives

In this chapter you will learn about the following:

(a) Different types of information

(b) Primary and secondary sources of information

(c) The main methods of gathering information

BPP PUBLISHING

NOTES

1 TYPES OF INFORMATION

First of all try these activities to revise the main types of information.

Activity 1 **(10 minutes)**

What may information be used for by an organisation?

Activity 2 **(10 minutes)**

What are the main types of information?

Activity 3 **(10 minutes)**

What do you regard as the qualities of good information?

Activity 4 **(10 minutes)**

How can poor information be improved?

1.1 Quantitative and qualitative information

Quantitative information is information which can be measured, for example, that included in financial statements. You should refer back to Chapter 6 of the HNC/HND Core Unit 2 Course Book, *Managing Financial Resources,* to refresh your memory with regard to this.

Qualitative information is not capable of being measured numerically, but reflects some characteristic, for example the colour of a product.

1.2 Marketing information

The importance of marketing information is covered in the HNC/HND Course Book for Core Unit 1, *Marketing*.

1.3 Financial information

This was covered in detail in the HNC/HND Core Unit 2, Course Book, *Managing Financial Resources.*

2 PERSONNEL ADMINISTRATION AND MANAGEMENT SYTEMS

2.1 Employee records

Definition

> **Employee records** are those kept by an organisation about each of its employees. They are built up and added to as the employee's career with the organisation progresses.

The information kept in an employee's record will be:

(a) his or her original application form, interview record and letters of reference;

(b) his or her contract of employment, giving details such as period of notice, conditions and terms of work;

(c) **standing** details about the employee, such as:

(i) age;
(ii) home address;
(iii) current position/grade in the organisation;
(iv) details of pay;
(v) details of holiday entitlement;
(vi) date of birth;
(vii) date of commencement of employment;

(d) **accumulated** details, gathered over the employee's work history.

> **Activity 5** **(15 minutes)**
>
> From your knowledge of the role of the personnel function, suggest some of the information that it might gather about an employee throughout his/her career with the organisation.

These data will have to be kept continuously flowing in from the department where the employee works.

The diagram on the following page is an example of an employee record card in a paper-based system.

There will also be collective employee records, such as:

- age and length of service distributions;
- total wage/salary bill; wage rates and salary levels;
- overtime statistics;
- absenteeism, labour turnover statistics;
- accident rates and costs;
- grievances, disciplinary action, disputes;
- training records.

NOTES

EXAMPLE

Employee record card

Name:

Employee record card

Date of Birth	Nationality	Sex ☐ M ☐ F
National insurance no.	No. of dependants	
☐ Single ☐ Engaged ☐ Married	☐ Separated ☐ Divorced	☐ Widowed
Job related physical disabilities	Registration No.	
Education		
Higher education		
Qualifications		
Company training		
Other skills (e.g. languages)	Driving licence	
Pension scheme	Date eligible	Date joined

Address	
Tel.	Postcode
First change	
Address	
Tel.	Postcode
Second change	
Address	
Tel.	Postcode

Employment history

Dates From	To	Position	Pay (£)	Reason for change or termination

Training history

Dates From	To	Courses attended

In emergency inform

Next of kin (1)	Next of kin (2)
Name	Name
Address	Address
Tel. (work)	Tel. (work)
Tel. (home)	Tel. (home)
General practitioner	
Name	
Address	
Tel.	

Major medical conditions

Heart condition ☐
Epilepsy ☐
Diabetes ☐
Asthma ☐

Medication
Name
Dose
Location

Records required by statute include the following.

- Hours of work: hours, breaks and overtime of young employees (16–18) on outside duties; hours of work of women and young persons employed in factories; hours of work of drivers.
- Disabled employees: names of registered disabled persons.
- Statutory Sick Pay: the Official Deductions Working Sheet.
- Safety: notifiable accidents, dangerous occurrences and illnesses (under RIDDOR 95); records and dates of first aiders' qualifications and training; records of first aid treatment given.
- PAYE records, under the jurisdiction of the Inland Revenue: details of gross pay, taxable pay, tax due, tax deducted, National Insurance contributions, statutory sick pay and maternity pay (Form P11).

ACAS (1981) recommended that records should also show the following.

- The numbers and occupations of employees required for efficient production, including future production plans.
- How well the age balance of the work force is being maintained.
- The rate of labour turnover and retention of key workers.
- How many and which employees have the potential for promotion within the organisation.

2.2 Personnel returns

Personnel returns may be required in the UK by:

(a) the Health and Safety Executive – health and safety statistics;

(b) Department of Employment or employers' associations – manpower and earnings statistics;

(c) industrial training boards – training statistics;

(d) the Department of Social Security and Inland Revenue – manpower, earnings, pension and other benefit statistics.

2.3 Management information

Decision-making in a range of personnel activities will require statistical information, or data about individuals, for various reasons.

(a) **Human resource planning**. Forecasting the future demand for labour will require ratio-trend analysis, environmental information about the market and competitor action and so on. Forecasting the future supply of labour will require information about the labour market, as well as, for each category of labour within the organisation, turnover, age distribution, promotions etc.

(b) **Planning recruitment and selection**. Job and person specifications will be the basis of both activities. Study of past recruitment campaigns, the cost/success rate of advertising media and offered incentives will help in the design of new recruitment campaigns. Data on the success of interview and testing techniques in selection (did the high-scorers also do well in performance assessment on the job?) may likewise lead to improvements.

NOTES

(c) **Planning training programmes.** Analyses of future manpower and job requirements and training specifications will determine needs for the subjects to be covered, types of course, numbers to be trained and so on.

(d) **Planning and reviewing remuneration systems.** Statistics of earnings fluctuations, average (as opposed to target) salaries, cost per unit of output, rates of pay in competitor organisations and the market in general, etc., will help in reviewing pay systems, structure and levels of pay.

(e) **Improving employee satisfaction and relations.** Work methods, supervision or disciplinary procedures may be improved by analysing disciplinary cases, causes of disputes, statistics on labour turnover, absenteeism or grievances.

(f) **Improving health, safety and fire precautions**, by analysing statistics on sickness, accidents and incidents in the organisation, and reports and returns on industrial disease, health hazards, inspection and audit methods and so on.

2.4 Information resources

Remember that there are sources of information outside the organisation, as well as within the organisation's files.

The 'expert system' of the personnel function may include:

- books and journals on personnel issues, demography and other statistics. In the UK, for example, there is the Abstract of Statistics, People Management, Pay Magazine (payroll issues), European Update (published by the IPD) and many others;
- consultants, personnel managers in other organisations, conferences and seminars;
- the Internet (if you are interested, check out the IPD's website: www.ipd.co.uk).

FOR DISCUSSION

'It's all very well to say "work smarter, not harder". But we've got plenty of information. We don't need more information. What we need is the 'smarts' to use it more wisely and more effectively. Where can we buy that?'

Do you sympathise with this view? Or is 'more information, better information'?

3 SOURCES OF INFORMATION

Some of the topics identified here you have covered already, while some will be new.

3.1 Internal and external information

These two sources of information were covered in the HNC/HND Course Book for Core Unit 7, *Management Information Systems*. You should refer back to that Course Book to refresh your memory.

NOTES

3.2 Primary and secondary information

	Secondary information	Primary information
What it is	Data neither collected directly by the user nor specifically for the user, often under conditions unknown to the user – in other words, data collected not by YOU but by someone else for their own purposes or for general use	Data that is collected specifically by or for the user, at source, in other words by YOU.
Quantitative, 'factual' or 'objective' example	**Government reports** – in the UK a good example is Social Trends, which contains government statistics about British society, employment in different industries, attitudes and so on. A company's **published financial statements** summarise and interpret company transactions data for the benefit of **shareholders**, not necessarily for your precise needs.	A survey you conduct with a questionnaire you have designed, with regard to a sample. You aim to get a statistically significant result. An experiment
Qualitative example	An article in a student publication or in a book about theories of motivation.	A focus group you have conducted to talk about a specific topic.

4 FINDING AND USING SECONDARY INFORMATION

4.1 Internal sources of secondary information

Accounts department

- Procedures manual
- Management accounts - balance sheets
- Financial data
- Accounting policies
- Tax details
- Working capital

Sales and marketing department

- Sales reports by region
- Sales by customer
- Sales by product
- Competitor intelligence
- Market prospects and reports
- Customer complaints
- Marketing research reports
- Brand strategy and values
- Distribution chains

Production and operations

- Operations data
- Efficiency and capacity detail
- Process flow charts
- Detailed product costings
- Input prices
- Supply chain

Human resources

- Number of employees
- Recruitment procedures
- Training programmes
- Staff turnover details
- Details of pay

4.2 External secondary data

- Books
- Journals and articles

EXAMPLE

The UK has a large and developed printing and publishing industry. The trade body, PIRA, aims to promote best practice and has an extensive publication programme. Two examples - of many industry publications - are:

- The Bookseller - for the retail book trade
- Paper focus - for paper buyers

The **Internet** is an excellent source of secondary data if used with care.

(a) For example, you can use a **search engine** which will bring up websites of interest. Some websites will allow you to download articles. Some of these websites - the **Economist Intelligence Unit** is one - offer articles for download. Another is www.ft.com. Many of these will be in PDF (portable document file) format. You will need to download **Adobe Acrobat Reader** for this - fortunately Acrobat Reader is **free** and it is possible that the site will have a link to Adobe to enable you to download the software yourself.

(b) Your internet service provider may also refer you to magazines and on-line newspapers.

Government ministries and agencies

Government agencies are good sources of economic and other statistical information. Most countries have an agency that provides national statistics. This varies significantly from country to country in terms of what is produced and the format, but you should be able to find:

(a) Economic data (eg UK Annual Abstract of Statistics)
(b) Social data (eg on population size and structure)
(c) Market data (eg export promotion

Regulatory bodies and industry associations

There are many quasi-government and other public sector bodies which can provide data on particular industry sectors.

Other sources

There are some sources of data which you may not be able to access in a personal capacity, but which your employer might have access to, by virtue of being in a particular industry or dealing with clients from a particular industry. These include:

- A business directory (eg Kompass)
- Market research data (eg Nielson consumer surveys)

4.3 Using secondary information

Secondary information is used in many business situations, not just in academic research. Secondary information:

- Can provide a backdrop to primary information
- Can act as a substitute for field research
- Can be used as a technique in itself

Backdrop to primary research

Secondary information may also be used to set the **parameters** for primary research. In an **unfamiliar field,** it is natural that the researcher will carry out some **basic research** in the area, using journals, existing reports, the press and any contacts with relevant knowledge. Such investigations will provide guidance on a number of areas.

- Possible data sources
- Data collection
- Methods of collection (relevant populations, sampling methods and so on)

Substitute for primary information

The (often substantial) **cost** of primary research **might be avoided** should existing secondary data be sufficient. Given the low response rate available for questionnaires, secondary research might do the job just as well. There are some situations however, in which secondary data is bound to be **insufficient**.

4.4 A technique in itself

Some types of information can **only be acquired through secondary information,** in particular **trends** over time. The **historical data** published on, say, trends in the behaviour of an industry over time, cannot realistically be replaced by a one-off study.

4.5 How reliable is secondary information?

The quality of the secondary information

(a) Preparers may have an axe to grind; trade associations may not include data which runs counter to the interest of its members.

(b) Why was **the data** being collected in the first place? Random samples with a poor response rate are particularly questionable). Government statistics and information based on them are often relatively dated, though information technology has speeded up the process).

(c) **How were parameters defined**?

Advantages arising from the use of secondary information.

(a) Secondary information may solve the problem **without** the need for any primary research: **time and money is thereby saved**.

(b) Secondary information sources are a great deal **cheaper** than those for primary information.

(c) Secondary information, while not necessarily fulfilling your information needs, can be of great use by:

  (i) **Setting the parameters**, defining a hypothesis, highlighting variables, in other words, helping to focus on the central problem

  (ii) **Providing guidance**, by showing past methods of research and so on, for primary data collection

  (iii) **Helping to assimilate the primary research** with past research, highlighting trends and the like

4.6 Issues to bear in mind in using secondary information

Topic	Comment
Relevance	The data may not be relevant to your objectives in terms of the data content itself, classifications used or units of measurement.
Cost	Although secondary data is usually cheaper than primary data, some specialist reports can cost large amounts of money.
Availability	Secondary data may not exist in the specific product or market area.
Bias	The secondary data may be biased, depending on who originally carried it out and for what purpose. Attempts should be made to obtain the most original source of the data, to assess it for such bias.
Statistical accuracy	Was the sample representative? Was the questionnaire or other measurement instrument(s) properly constructed? Were possible biases in response or in non-response dealt with and accounted for? Was the data properly analysed using appropriate statistical techniques? Was a sufficiently large sample used? Does the report include the raw data? In addition, was any raw data omitted from the final report, and why?
Sufficiency	Even after fulfilling all the above criteria, the secondary data may be insufficient and primary research would therefore be necessary.

The golden rule when using secondary data is **use only meaningful information**.

(a) **Begin with internal sources** and a firm with a good management information system should be able to provide a great deal of data.

(b) External information should be consulted in order of ease and speed of access: directories, catalogues and indexes before books, abstracts and periodicals

(c) **Do not accept it at face value.** The **Internet, for example, is a mine of misinformation.**

5 SURVEYS AND QUESTIONNAIRES

The data used in a statistical survey, whether variables or attributes, can be either **primary information** or **secondary information**.

Primary and secondary information both have their advantages and limitations.

Primary information	Secondary information
Advantage	**Advantage**
The investigator knows where the data came from and is aware of any inadequacies or limitations in the data.	Cheaply available.
Disadvantage	**Disadvantages**
It is expensive to collect primary data.	The investigator did not collect the data and is therefore unaware of any inadequacies or limitations in the data.

5.1 Survey methods of collecting information

There are two basic methods of collecting primary information from individuals.

(a) They can be asked questions.
(b) Their behaviour can be observed.

This involves the collection of information using **surveys**, for example structured interviews, postal questionnaires or, possibly, e-mailed questionnaires.

5.2 Errors in survey methods of collecting data

There are three main types of error that can appear in survey methods of collecting data.

(a) **Sampling error**. It is quite usual for a sample of the population to be surveyed, rather than the entire population. If the sample surveyed is **not representative** of the population from which it is drawn, a sampling error will arise.

(b) **Response error** arises because respondents are either **unable** or **unwilling** to **respond**.

5.3 Interviews

There are basically two types of interview that can be used to collect quantitative data, the **personal (face to face) interview** and the **telephone interview**.

Advantages of personal interviews

(a) The interviewer is able to **reduce respondent anxiety** and **allay potential embarrassment**, thereby increasing the response rate and decreasing the potential for error.

(b) The routing ('if yes go to question 7, if no go to question 10') of questions is made easier due to the experience of the interviewer.

(c) Interviewers can ask, within narrow limits, for a respondent's answer to be clarified.

NOTES

(d) The questions can be given in a **fixed order** with a **fixed wording** and the answers can be recorded in a **standard manner**. If there is more than one interviewer involved in the survey this will reduce variability.

(e) **Standardised questions** and ways of recording the responses mean that less skilled interviewers may be used, thereby reducing the cost of the survey.

(f) **Pictures, signs** and **objects** can be used.

Disadvantages of personal interviews

(a) They can be **time consuming**.

(b) They can be **costly** to complete.

(c) Questionnaires can be **difficult to design**.

(d) Questions must often be kept relatively simple, thus restricting the depth of data collected.

(e) Questions must normally be **closed** because of the difficulties of recording answers to open questions.

(f) Interviewers cannot probe vague or ambiguous replies.

5.4 Arranging interviews and meetings

(a) If the matter is at all sensitive, you may need to get authorisation from a senior member of the organisation.

(b) If you are interviewing people you do not know, give them advance warning.

(c) **Do not just turn up**. Always book a time in advance. If the interviewee works in an open plan office, you may want to **book a place**. (You can book meetings via e-mail or use Microsoft Outlook.)

5.5 Telephone surveys

Advantages

(a) The response is **rapid**.

(b) There is a **standard sampling frame** - the **telephone directory**, which can be systematically or randomly sampled.

(c) A **wide geographical area** can be covered fairly cheaply.

(d) It may be **easier to ask sensitive or embarrassing questions**.

Disadvantages

(a) A **biased sample** may result from the fact that a large proportion (about 10%) of people do not have telephones (representing certain portions of the population such as old people or students) and many of those who do are ex-directory.

(b) It is **not possible to use 'showcards'** or pictures.

(c) The **refusal rate is much higher** than with face-to-face interviews, and the interview often cut short.

(d) It is **not possible to see the interviewee's expressions** or to develop the rapport that is possible with personal interviews.

(e) The interview **must be short**.

NOTES

5.6 Postal surveys

We are using the term 'postal' survey to cover all methods in which the questionnaire is given to the respondent and returned to the investigator without personal contact. Such questionnaires could be posted but might also be left in pigeonholes or on desks.

Postal questionnaires have the following **advantages** over personal interviews.

(a) The **cost per person** is likely **to be less**, so more people can be sampled, and central control is facilitated.

(b) It is usually possible to **ask more questions** because the people completing the forms (the respondents) can do so in their own time.

(c) **All respondents are presented with questions in the same way**. There is no opportunity for an interviewer to influence responses (interviewer bias) or to misrecord them.

(d) It may be **easier to ask personal or embarrassing questions** in a postal questionnaire than in a personal interview.

(e) Respondents **may need to look up information for the questionnaire**. This will be easier if the questionnaire is sent to their homes or places of work.

5.7 E-mail survey

Surveys can be done via e-mail, even though 'spamming' people with unwanted email is not likely to win you any friends.

(a) If you are conducting an e-mail survey at work, you can **attach** a document or spreadsheet to the email, asking the respondent to open the document or spreadsheet, complete it, save it and return.

(b) You may be able to ask your questions in the e-mail itself, asking the respondent to reply and return the e-mail.

5.8 Quantitative research questionnaire design

Designing the questionnaire

The sampling process can be an important contributor to the quality and value of the survey process. Where survey findings are technically suspect, this is most commonly because there are **flaws in the design of the questionnaire.**

Core principles of questionnaire design

- **Decide precisely what information** you wish to obtain from each individual question
- **Ensure that the question gives you this information** as precisely as possible
- Ensure that there is **no possibility of misunderstanding or ambiguity** about the question or its answer

Common pitfalls

(a) **Ambiguity and uncertainty about language or terminology**. Don't assume people will understand what you mean.

(b) **Lack of clarity about the information required**. You should always stop and ask yourself some fundamental questions. Why am I asking this question? What is it intended to find out? What exactly do I want to know? **Will this question give me the information I need?** These questions are often not explicitly addressed, with the result that the wrong question (or only part of the right question) is asked. In an employee survey, for example, the questionnaire could ask:

> Which of the following do you feel are barriers to your undertaking further training or development in your own time?
>
> - Lack of spare time
> - Lack of motivation
> - Personal/domestic commitments
> - Cost

The respondents could tick most **if not all** of these options. The survey designer really wanted to ask not **whether** these factors were seen as barriers, but **which** were the most significant barriers and **how** significant they were.

(c) **Conflation of multiple questions into one**. In a survey, for example, respondents could be asked, 'How often does your workgroup meet to discuss performance, quality and safety issues?' The assumption behind this question - is that managers called workgroups together to discuss all three of these issues. Some workgroups may not meet at all, some may meet infrequently and some could meet relatively often but may only discuss performance issues.

(d) **Making unjustified assumptions**. For example, 'In reviewing your performance, which of the following methods does your manager use?' The assumption here, of course, is that the manager reviews the respondent's performance at all.

5.9 Leading questions

The question may still provide misleading data if it appears to be **leading the respondent towards a particular answer**. People may still feel **uncertain** about its outcomes and they may still feel **suspicious of your motives** for conducting it. In such cases, some may feel very keen to give the 'right' answer - the answer that they believe you or the organisation would like to hear.

5.10 Agree/disagree' and other formats

This problem occurs most commonly when respondents are asked to **indicate their level of agreement or disagreement** with a particular statement. It is prudent, therefore, to include a **mixture of positive and negative statements**, which do not suggest any intrinsic preference.

In some cases, the choice of statement can **significantly undermine the value of the information obtained**. 'The quality of work in my department is generally excellent'. If the respondent agrees with this statement the meaning was clear - that he or she thought the quality of work in the department was generally excellent. However, if the respondent **disagreed** with the statement, the meaning was less clear. Did they think the quality was moderate or even poor?

In general, the questions in a written questionnaire should be of the **multiple choice** type, so providing the basis for quantitative analysis.

Survey questions can be divided into two broad categories; those **exploring attitudes** or opinions and those **seeking some form of factual information.**

(a) In the former category would generally fall, for example, the 'agree/disagree' format, such as 'Safety is always a paramount concern for the organisation. Do you:

- Agree strongly?
- Agree slightly?
- Disagree slightly?
- Disagree strongly'?

(b) In the latter category might fall questions about, say, the frequency of workgroup meetings or about recent experience of training.

Respondents **are commonly reluctant to give extreme responses** and prefer to hover around the middle ground. If you have an odd number of items in your scale, you may find that respondents disproportionately opt for the neutral option. There are benefits in forcing respondents off the fence by **offering only an even number of options,** so that the respondent has to choose between, say, 'agree slightly' and 'disagree slightly'. In this way, you gain a clearer perspective on the **true direction of opinion.**

Where you are asking to identify preferences from among a number of options, you may ask respondents to **rank the options against a given criterion**, such as 'Which of the following do you think are the most important contributors to high workgroup performance? (Please rank in order of importance.)'

(a) If you use this format, you should remember to indicate **how the ranking should be applied**. Is number 1 the **most** or the **least** important factor? Ranking questions can seem **confusing** to respondents and are best used sparingly. In any cases, it is rarely worth asking respondents to rank more than the first three or four items. Beyond that, rankings usually become fairly arbitrary.

(b) A more straightforward approach is to ask respondents simply to **select one item** - 'Which of the following do you think is the single most important contributor to high workgroup performance? (Please tick one only.)' Although slightly less detailed, this question is easier both to complete and to analyse.

In collecting **factual** information, you may again wish to **use scales** where the required information lies on a continuum. For example, 'How many days have you spent training in the past 12 months? Fewer than 3 days/4 - 6 days/6 - 10 days/more than 10 days.'

Where you are exploring more discrete items of information, you may simply ask respondents to **select the most relevant items**. For example, you might ask, 'Which of the following types of training have you undertaken in the last year? (Please tick any that apply.)' In this case, you are not asking respondents to evaluate the options against one another, but simply to make a choice between those that are and those that are not significant. This format can also be applied in cases of **opinions and attitudes**.

5.11 Building the questionnaire

The overall structure of the questionnaire can take a number of forms, depending on the purpose and nature of the survey. As a general rule, when you are exploring a given topic, you should aim to be as systematic as possible in **progressing from the general to the specific**.

(a) **Context**. Typically, your initial aim should be to gain an understanding of the **broad context** within which opinions are held.

(b) You can then progress to gaining an understanding of the **nature and strength of opinion** in a given area.

(c) **Detail**. Finally, you can move, step by step, towards identifying the **detail that underpins these**.

5.12 Questionnaire length and layout

There is generally a trade-off between questionnaire length and the level of response. The **longer and more detailed** the questionnaire, the **more likely** you are to encounter **resistance** from potential respondents.

Despite these caveats, the following crude guidelines for different forms of questionnaire administration may be helpful.

(a) **Cold surveys**. Where the questionnaire is being sent out with no preparation and where respondents have no particular incentive to respond, you should aim for an absolute maximum of 4 sides of paper and no more than 15 to 20 questions (including sub-questions), but in many cases, it will be preferable to aim for just 1 or 2 sides of paper and even fewer questions. The key issue here is likely to be one of presentation. You will want to suggest that the survey is easy to complete and will involve comparatively little of the respondent's time. Therefore, simple, 'user-friendly' layout is likely to be an even more significant issue than the overall length.

(b) **Postal questionnaires**. Where respondents have been briefed and prepared, but are nevertheless expected to complete the questionnaire entirely in their own time, you should generally aim for a questionnaire of some 6 to 8 sides of paper, ideally with no more than 30 to 40 questions. If potential respondents put the questionnaire to one side, the chances are that a substantial proportion will not get around to completing it at all.

(c) **Questionnaires completed in work time**. Where the **organisation** allocates some work time to completing the questionnaire, you can generally risk a rather longer questionnaire - probably up to 10 to 12 pages and 50 to 60 questions.

Some other general points about questionnaire design are also worth stressing. First, make sure that you provide **clear instructions** throughout, indicating precisely how the questionnaire should be completed. These should be simply phrased and as concise as possible. It is also a good idea to **provide some examples** of specific question types and how they should be completed. As always, one good example is worth several dozen words of explanation.

Laying out the questionnaire

(a) If respondents have to complete the questionnaire themselves, it must be approachable and as short as possible. Consider the use of **lines, boxes, different type faces and print sizes and small pictures**. Use plenty of space.

(b) Consider the use of **tick boxes**. Is it clear where ticks go or how to respond in each case? For analysis, will it be easy to transfer responses from the forms to a summary sheet or a computer? Consider pre-coding the answers.

(c) Explain the **purpose of the survey** at the beginning of the questionnaire and where possible guarantee confidentiality. Emphasise the date by which it must be returned.

(d) At the end of the questionnaire, **thank the respondent** and make it clear what they should do with the completed questionnaire.

Pilot tests

It is vital to **pilot test questionnaires** since mistakes, ambiguities and embarrassments in a questionnaire can be expensive once the main data collection phase has been entered. Do not send any questionnaire out 'cold' without getting someone else to work through it in detail.

The Likert scale

This approach can be summarised in three steps - (a), (b) and (c).

(a) A list of statements is prepared about the topic being researched, and a test group of respondents is asked to rate each statement on a scale from strong agreement to strong disagreement.

(b) A numerical value is given to each response:

5 Strongly agree
4 Agree
3 Don't know
2 Disagree
1 Strongly disagree

(c) Each respondent's scores for all the statements are added up to give a total score for the topic, which may reflect overall positive or negative attitudes: responses to individual statements can also be analysed to get more meaningful information about the pattern of responses.

Likert scales are simple to prepare and administer. You may have been asked to complete such an inventory test over the telephone, or seen one in a magazine. However, again you should be aware that scale values have no absolute meaning, and are limited in their statistical uses, on an 'interval' scale.

An example of a questionnaire using a variety of techniques can be found on the next page.

6 QUALITATIVE RESEARCH

Qualitative research is another process which aims to collect primary data. Its main methods are the open-ended interview, whether this be a depth interview (one-to-one) or a group discussion (focus group), and projective techniques. The form of the data collected is narrative rather than isolated statements reduceable to numbers. **Its main purpose is to understand people's behaviour and perceptions rather than to measure them.**

The key to qualitative research is to allow the respondents to say what they feel and think in response to flexible, 'prompting' questioning, rather than to give their responses to set questions and often set answers in a questionnaire.

NOTES

Name	*Description*	*Example*
	CLOSED-END QUESTIONS	
Dichotomous	A question with two possible answers.	'In arranging this trip, did you personally phone British Airways?' Yes ☐ No ☐
Multiple choice	A question with three or more answers.	'With whom are you travelling on this flight?' No one ☐ Spouse ☐ Spouse and children ☐ Children only ☐ Business associates/ friends/relatives ☐ An organised tour group ☐
Likert scale	A statement with which the respondent shows the amount of agreement/	'Small airlines generally give better service Strongly disagree 1 ☐ Disagree 2 ☐ Neither agree nor disagree 3 ☐ Agree 4 ☐ Strongly agree 5 ☐
Semantic differential	A scale connecting two bipolar words, where the respondent selects the point	*British Airways* Large - Small Experienced - - - - - - - - - - - - - - - Inexperienced
Importance scale	A scale that rates the importance of some attribute.	Extremely important 1 ☐ Very important 2 ☐ Somewhat important 3 ☐ Not very important 4 ☐ Not at all important 5 ☐
Rating scale	A scale that rates some attribute from 'poor' to 'excellent'.	Excellent Very good Good Fair Poor
Intention-to-buy scale	A scale that describes the respondent's intention to buy.	'If an inflight telephone was available on a long flight, I would' Definitely buy 1 ☐ Probably buy 2 ☐ Not sure 3 ☐ Probably not buy 4 ☐ Definitely not buy 5 ☐
	OPEN-END QUESTIONS	
Completely unstructured	A question that respondents can answer in an almost unlimited number of ways.	'What is your opinion of British Airways?'
Word association	Words are presented, one at a time, and respondents mention the first word that comes to mind.	'What is the first word that comes to mind when you hear the following' Airline__________ British__________ Travel__________
Sentence completion	An incomplete sentence is presented and respondents complete the sentence.	'When I choose an airline, the most important consideration in my decision is __________ ,
Story completion	An incomplete story is presented, and respondents are asked to complete it.	'I flew B.A. a few days ago. I noticed that the exterior and interior of the plane had bright colours. This aroused in me the following thoughts and
Picture completion	A picture of two characters is presented, with one making a statement. Respondents are asked to identify with the other and fill in the empty balloon.	
Thematic Apperception Test (TAT)	A picture is presented and respondents are asked to make up a story about what they think is happening or may happen in the picture.	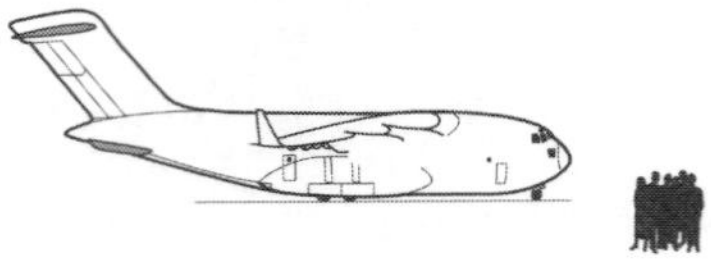

BPP PUBLISHING

6.1 Unstructured interviews

Neither interviewer or respondent is bound by the structure of a questionnaire in an **unstructured interview**. Interviewers may have a checklist of topics to cover in questioning, but they are free to word such questions as they wish. The order in which questions are covered may also be varied. This will allow the respondent to control the data flow and for the interviewer to explore more thoroughly particular views of the respondent and why they are held. Unstructured interviews are a very useful way of capturing data which is qualitative in nature. Such interviews may also provide the researcher with relevant questions which could be put to a wider audience of respondents using structured or semi-structured interview techniques, especially if quantitative data is required.

6.2 Depth interviews

Motivational research often uses the psychoanalytic method of **depth interviews**. The pattern of questioning should assist the respondent to explore deeper levels of thought. Motives and explanations of behaviour often lie well **below the surface**. It is a **time-consuming** and **expensive** process. Taped interviews and analysis of transcripts are often used. A single individual or a small team may conduct depth interviewing. Depth interviews may have fewer than ten respondents.

Strengths of depth interviews

(a) **Longitudinal information** (such as information on decision-making processes) can be gathered from one respondent at a time, thereby aiding clarity of interpretation and analysis.

(b) Intimate and **personal material** can be more easily accessed and discussed.

(c) Respondents are **less likely to confine themselves** simply to reiterating socially acceptable attitudes.

Disadvantages

(a) They are **time consuming** to conduct and to analyse. **Each depth interview needs to be written up shortly afterwards and reflected on.** If each interview lasts between one and two hours, a maximum of two per day is often all that is possible.

(b) They are more **costly** than group discussions.

(c) There is a temptation to begin treating depth interviews as if they were simply another form of questionnaire survey, thinking in terms of quantitative questions like 'how many' rather than qualitative issues like 'how', 'why' or 'what'.

(d) A certain amount of expertise is needed in depth interviews.

In a depth interview the key line of communication is between the interviewer and the respondent. They have an **open-ended conversation**, not constrained by a formal questionnaire, and the qualitative data are captured as narrative by means of an audio or video tape.

6.3 Focus groups

Focus groups are useful in providing the researcher with **qualitative data**. Qualitative data can often provide greater insight than quantitative data and does not lend itself to the simple application of standard statistical methods.

Focus groups usually consist of 8 to 10 respondents and an interviewer taking the role of group moderator. The group moderator introduces topics for discussion and intervenes as necessary to encourage respondents or to direct discussions if they threaten to wander too far off the point. The moderator will also need to control any powerful personalities and prevent them from dominating the group.

Group discussions may be **audio or video tape recorded** for later analysis and interpretation. The researcher must be careful not to generalise too much from such small scale qualitative research. **Group discussion is very dependent on the skill of the group moderator**. It is inexpensive to conduct, it can be done quickly and it can provide useful, timely, qualitative data.

Focus groups are often used at the early stage of research to get a feel for the subject matter under discussion and to create possibilities for more structured research. Four to eight groups may be assembled and each group interviewed for one, two or three hours.

Advantages of focus groups

(a) The group environment with 'everybody in the same boat' can be **less intimidating** than other techniques of research which rely on one-to-one contact (such as depth interviews).

(b) What respondents say in a group often **sparks off experiences** or ideas on the part of others.

(c) **Differences between consumers** are highlighted, making it possible to understand a range of attitudes in a short space of time.

(d) It is **easier to observe groups** and there is more to observe simply because of the intricate behaviour patterns within a collection of people.

(e) **Social and cultural influences** are highlighted.

(f) Groups provide a **social context** that is a 'hot-house' reflection of the real world.

(g) Groups are **cheaper and faster** than depth interviews.

Disadvantages of focus groups

(a) Group processes may **inhibit some people from making a full contribution** and may encourage others to become exhibitionistic.

(b) Group processes **may stall** to the point where they cannot be retrieved by the moderator.

(c) Some groups may **take a life of their own**, so that what is said has validity only in the short-lived context of the group.

(d) It is not usually possible to identify **which group members said what**, unless the proceedings have been video recorded.

(e) It is **not easy to find a common time** when all can participate.

7 MEETINGS

7.1 The role of meetings

Meetings play an important part in the life of any organisation, whether they are:

(a) **Formal meetings** required by government legislation or the Articles of a company, and governed by strict rules and conventions laid down in the organisation's formal constitution.

(b) **Discussions** held informally for information exchange, problem-solving and decision-making.

A well-organised, well-aimed and well-led meeting can be extremely effective in many different contexts.

(a) **Executive decision-making**; for example, by a group of directors, managers, or government officials.

(b) The **relaying of decisions** and instructions (downward 'briefings').

(c) The **provision of advice** and information for management planning and decision-making (upward 'briefings' or reporting).

(d) **Participative problem-solving**, by consultation with people in different departments or fields, such as through a task force, working party, committee or quality circle.

(e) **Brainstorming**: free exchanges with a view to generating new approaches and ideas.

Anthony Jay has argued that 'even the most apparently futile of meetings serves some wider **corporate purpose**, as well as preserving the mental health of those who attend'. In other words, not all meetings are about '**getting things done**', and 'getting things done' is only one of the purposes of having meetings at all.

7.2 Other purposes

The wider corporate purposes of meetings may include the following.

(a) **Ritual**. A manager's '**ceremonial' role** is acted out in meetings. Often, meetings form the ritual ending of months of negotiation: the final 'handshake'.

(b) **Communication and personal contact**. A meeting helps people to get to know one another. Establishing good personal relationships is important in organisational life.

(c) '**Letting off steam**'. There is sometimes a good purpose in having an argumentative session in which grievances get aired. Disagreement might be seen as a useful way of **generating new ideas**.

(d) **Motivation and satisfaction**. The fact, or at least the illusion, of participation in decisions may improve individual motivation.

(e) **Representation**. Meetings enable the various different interests in a decision to be represented as 'equals'.

(f) **Delay**. Meetings can be used to delay decisions, which may be of benefit to the organisation or to managers.

(g) '**Nailing colours to the mast**'. Meetings can also be used to put individuals on the spot in public (and in the written minutes of the meeting). They can enforce commitment, or at least indicate where battle lines are drawn.

(h) **Inspiration**. Some meetings can be inspirational, if they are used to persuade, cajole or encourage a sense of values.

(i) **Unification**. Finally, bringing people together underlines the fact that they belong to the same organisation, and in theory should be working to the same purpose.

7.3 The structure of meetings

To achieve their purpose, those who attend a meeting must generally conform or respond to a measure of **organisation** and **procedure**.

(a) There is usually a **chairperson**, or at least an organiser, who guides the proceedings of the meeting and aims to maintain order. A meeting can hardly function efficiently if it is (or is allowed to become) a sort of Tower of Babel in which everybody talks at once and nobody listens.

(b) There is often a **sequence of business**, or at least of speeches, to express points of view or reach decisions on the common purpose of the meeting. It is not essential to formalise this point with an agenda, but meetings usually do have one.

(c) The purpose of the meeting is achieved by reaching some **decision or expression of opinion** at the end of the discussion. In some circumstances this may lead to taking a vote to determine what is the majority view.

An **informal meeting**, such as might be called from time to time by a department head or working party, may take the form of a **group discussion** 'chaired' by a leader, and **informally documented**: notes handed round or taken during the meeting, a summary of arguments and decisions reached provided afterwards.

Formal meetings, however, are governed by strict rules and conventions (and generate formal documentation) for the announcement, planning, conduct and recording of the proceedings.

Principal among the documents are the:

(a) **Notice***:* the announcement of and 'invitation' to the meeting.
(b) **Agenda***:* the list of items of business to be discussed at the meeting.
(c) **Minutes***:* the written record of a meeting, approved by those present.

Chapter roundup

- Employee records are kept by an organisation about each of its employees. These records generally go back to the application form and letters of reference and build up the accumulated details gathered over the employee's work history.
- Primary data is information collected specifically for the study under consideration. Secondary data is 'data neither collected directly by the user nor specifically for the user, often under conditions that are not well known to the user' (American Marketing Association).
- Surveys include structured interviews, postal questionnaires or e-mailed questionnaires. The method used for the survey will depend on the relative importance and cost of the information. The trade-off may be between primary data, which is expensive to collect, and secondary data, that is cheaply available but may be inadequate or prone to error.
- Questionnaires should be designed with care. You should decide exactly what information you need to obtain from each question and ensure that there is no possibility of misunderstanding or ambiguity. It is very easy to assume that people will understand what you mean. In collecting factual information you might want to use scales where the required information lies on a continuum, eg an age range.
- Qualitative research methods include unstructured and depth interviews, focus groups and projective techniques. There are advantages and disadvantages with each of these methods, although the depth interview is the most expensive and time-consuming method of collecting primary data.
- Meetings may be formal or informal. Some formal meetings are required by law, such as the annual general meeting of a plc, and those who attend must generally conform or respond to a measure of organisation and procedure. An informal meeting may take the form of a group discussion chaired by a leader and informally documented.

Quick quiz

1. In the personnel administration and management system, what would be included in the standing details about an employee?
2. You have just found out the prices of a competitor's product for your supervisor. The information was on their web site and was also given over the phone when you rang them. How would you class this information?
3. Give two examples – one qualitative and one quantitative – of secondary information.
4. If you download a document in a PDF (portable document file) format, what brand of reader do you need?
5. What are the basic methods of collecting primary information from individuals?
6. Why might a survey method of collecting data have a sampling error?
7. When you are designing survey questions, why should you offer an even number of items in your scale for respondents to choose from?
8. Which is the most costly method of qualitative research?
9. What is the role of the chairperson in a meeting?

10 Describe the three main documents associated with formal meetings.

Answers to quick quiz

1 The standing details would include address, date of birth, position, pay, holiday entitlement and date of commencement of employment. (See para 2.1)

2 Data that is collected specifically by you at source is considered primary information. The prices of a product would also be considered as factual and therefore quantitative in nature. (3.2)

3 A qualitative example of secondary information is a customer complaint and a quantitative example is a detailed product costing. (4.1)

4 To read a PDF file you need to use Adobe Acrobat Reader.

5 There are two basic methods of collecting primary information from individuals. They can be asked questions and their behaviour can be observed. (5.1)

6 If the sample surveyed is not representative of the population from which it is drawn, a sampling error will occur. (5.2)

7 Respondents are generally reluctant to give extreme responses and prefer to tick around the middle ground. Having an odd number might leave you with many respondents opting for the neutral option. With an even number you get a clearer idea of the true direction of opinion. (5.10)

8 The depth interview is the most time-consuming and expensive method. (6.2)

9 The chairperson usually guides the proceedings of the meeting and aims to keep order. (7.3)

10 The **meeting notice** is the announcement of and invitation to the meeting

Agenda lists the items of business to be discussed at the meeting

Minutes are the written record of the meeting, approved by those present. (7.3)

Answers to activities

1 All organisations require information for a range of purposes. These can be categorised as follows.

- Information for planning
- Information for controlling
- Information for recording transactions
- Information for performance measurement
- Information for decision making

Planning

Planning requires a knowledge of the available resources, possible time-scales and the likely outcome under alternative scenarios. Information is required that helps decision making, and how to implement decisions taken.

Controlling

Once a plan is implemented, its actual performance must be controlled. Information is required to assess whether it is proceeding as planned or whether there is some unexpected deviation from plan. It may consequently be necessary to take some form of corrective action.

Recording transactions

Information about each transaction or event is required. Reasons include:

(a) Documentation of transactions can be used as evidence in a case of dispute.

(b) There may be a legal requirement to record transactions, for example for accounting and audit purposes.

(c) Operational information can be built up, allowing control action to be taken.

Performance measurement

Just as individual operations need to be controlled, so overall performance must be measured. Comparisons against budget or plan are able to be made. This may involve the collection of information on, for example, costs, revenues, volumes, time-scale and profitability.

Decision making

Just as decision making can be analysed into three levels, so information necessary to make decisions within an organisation can be analysed in the same way.

2 Strategic information

Strategic information is used to plan the objectives of the organisation, and to assess whether the objectives are being met in practice. Such information includes overall profitability, the profitability of different segments of the business, future market prospects, the availability and cost of raising new funds, total cash needs, total manning levels and capital equipment needs.

Strategic information is:

- Derived from both internal and external sources
- Summarised at a high level
- Relevant to the long term
- Concerned with the whole organisation
- Often prepared on an 'ad hoc' basis
- Both quantitative and qualitative
- Uncertain, as the future cannot be predicted

Tactical information

Tactical information is used to decide how the resources of the business should be employed, and to monitor how they are being and have been employed. Such information includes productivity measurements (output per man hour or per machine hour) budgetary control or variance analysis reports, and cash flow forecasts, manning levels and profit results within a particular department of the organisation, labour turnover statistics within a department and short-term purchasing requirements.

Tactical information is:

- Primarily generated internally (but may have a limited external component)
- Summarised at a lower level

- Relevant to the short and medium term
- Concerned with activities or departments
- Prepared routinely and regularly
- Based on quantitative measures

Operational information

Operational information is used to ensure that specific tasks are planned and carried out properly within a factory or office.

In the payroll office, for example, operational information relating to day-rate labour will include the hours worked each week by each employee, his rate of pay per hour, details of his deductions, and for the purpose of wages analysis, details of the time each man spent on individual jobs during the week. In this example, the information is required weekly, but more urgent operational information, such as the amount of raw materials being input to a production process, may be required daily, hourly, or in the case of automated production, second by second.

Operational information is:

- Derived from internal sources
- Detailed, being the processing of raw data
- Relevant to the immediate term
- Task-specific
- Prepared very frequently
- Largely quantitative

3 'Good' information is information that adds to the understanding of a situation. The qualities of good information are outlined in the following table.

NOTES

Quality		Example
A	ccurate	Figures should add up, the degree of rounding should be appropriate, there should be no typos, items should be allocated to the correct category, assumptions should be stated for uncertain information.
C	omplete	Information should includes everything that it needs to include, for example external data if relevant, or comparative information.
C	ost-beneficial	It should not cost more to obtain the information than the benefit derived from having it. Providers or information should be given efficient means of collecting and analysing it. Presentation should be such that users do not waste time working out what it means.
U	ser-targeted	The needs of the user should be borne in mind, for instance senior managers need summaries, junior ones need detail.
R	elevant	Information that is not needed for a decision should be omitted, no matter how 'interesting' it may be.
A	uthoritative	The source of the information should be a reliable one (not, for instance, 'Joe Bloggs Predictions Page' on the Internet unless Joe Bloggs is known to be a reliable source for that type of information).
T	imely	The information should be available when it is needed.
E	asy to use	Information should be clearly presented, not excessively long, and sent using the right medium and communication channel (e-mail, telephone, hard-copy report etc).

4

Feature	Example of possible improvements
Accurate	Use computerised systems with automatic input checks rather than manual systems. Allow sufficient time for collation and analysis of data if pinpoint accuracy is crucial. Incorporate elements of probability within projections so that the required response to different future scenarios can be assessed.
Complete	Include past data as a reference point for future projections. Include any planned developments, such as new products. Information about future demand would be more useful than information about past demand. Include external data.
Cost-beneficial	Always bear in mind whether the benefit of having the information is greater than the cost of obtaining it.

BPP PUBLISHING

Feature	Example of possible improvements
User-targeted	Information should be summarised and presented together with relevant ratios or percentages.
Relevant	The purpose of the report should be defined. It may be trying to fulfil too many purposes at once. Perhaps several shorter reports would be more effective. Information should include exception reporting, where only those items that are worthy of note - and the control actions taken by more junior managers to deal with them - are reported.
Authoritative	Use reliable sources and experienced personnel. If some figures are derived from other figures the method of derivation should be explained.
Timely	Information collection and analysis by production managers needs to be speeded up considerably, probably by the introduction of better information systems.
Easy-to-use	Graphical presentation, allowing trends to be quickly assimilated and relevant action decided upon. Alternative methods of presentation should be considered, such as graphs or charts, to make it easier to review the information at a glance. Numerical information is sometimes best summarised in narrative form or vice versa. A 'house style' for reports should be devised and adhered to by all. This would cover such matters as number of decimal places to use, table headings and labels, paragraph numbering and so on.

5 Accumulated employment information includes:

(i) training;

(ii) professional qualifications acquired;

(iii) holidays taken;

(iv) positions held previously in the organisation: transfers and promotions;

(v) history of accidents, sick leave and absence;

(vi) appraisal forms;

(vii) results of proficiency tests;

(viii) disciplinary measures taken against him/her.

Chapter 13 :
ANALYSIS OF INFORMATION

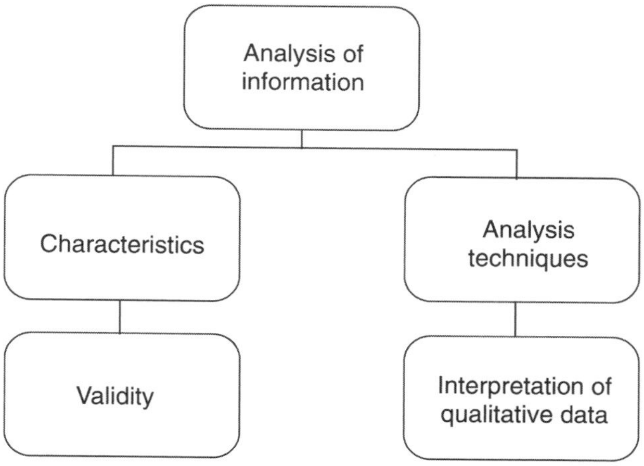

Introduction

Data must be processed or analysed in some way to form information that is useful in the decision-making process of the organisation. As well as being an important ingredient in its day-to-day activities of helping with decision-making, information can also be seen as a valuable strategic resource that can help an organisation gain competitive advantage. For example, credit card companies can analyse expenditure and use the results to specifically target mailshots at likely customers.

There are many different techniques that can be applied to gathered data. Most of them will ensure the relevant levels of accuracy, consistency, relevance, sufficiency and reliability in outcomes.

Your objectives

In this chapter you will learn about the following:

(a) The characteristics of information

(b) Analysing information to inform decision-making

(c) Analysis techniques

(d) Sampling theory

(e) Analysing and interpreting qualitative data

1 THE CHARACTERISTICS OF INFORMATION

1.1 Information and data

Information is different from data, and although the two terms are often used interchangeably in everyday language, it is important to make a clear distinction between them, as follows.

The word '**data**' means facts. Data consists of numbers, letters, symbols, raw facts, events and transactions, which have been recorded but not yet processed or analysed into a form which is suitable for making decisions. Data on its own is not generally useful, whereas information is very useful.

Information is data which has been processed or analysed in such a way that it has a meaning to the person who receives it, who may then use it to improve the quality of decision-making.

For example, in cost accounting the accounting system records a large number of facts (data) about materials, times, expenses and other transactions. These facts are then classified and summarised to produce accounts that are organised into reports, which are designed to help management to plan and control the firm's activities. Note that as data is converted into information some of the detail is eliminated and replaced by summaries, which are easier to interpret.

1.2 Value of information

Information should have some value, otherwise it would not be worth the cost of collecting it and filing it. The benefits obtainable from the information must also exceed the cost of acquiring it, and whenever management is trying to decide whether or not to produce information for a particular purpose (for example, whether to computerise an operation or to build a financial planning model) a cost/benefit study ought to be made.

For information to have value, it must lead to a decision to take action which results in reducing costs, eliminating losses, increasing sales, better utilisation of resources, prevention of fraud (audit requirements) or providing management with information about the consequences of alternative courses of action.

Information which is provided but not used has no actual value. A decision taken on the basis of information received also has no actual value. It is only the action taken as a result of the decision that realises actual value for the organisation. The cost of collecting the data bears no relation to its value. An item of information that leads to an actual increase of profit of £900 is not worth having if it cost £999 to collect.

1.3 Types of management information required

Most managers need information on the resources available to them. For example:

What resources are available?	• Finance, stocks of raw materials, spare machine capacity, labour availability, the balance of expenditure remaining for a certain budget or the target date for completion of a job.
At what rate are the resources being consumed?	• How fast is the labour force working, how quickly are the raw materials being used up, how quickly are other expenses being incurred and how quickly is finance being consumed?
How well are the resources being used?	

A manager uses resources in the light of information received. The board of a company decides how much of available funds should be allocated to any particular activity, and the same problem faces the manager of a factory or department, or even a foreman, for example which machines should be used and which workers should be put on certain jobs. Having used information to decide what should be done, a manager then needs feedback (or else control information from the environment) to decide how well it is being done.

1.3 Levels of information

Information within an organisation (as distinct from information provided by an organisation to external users, such as shareholders, the general public, pressure groups, competitors, suppliers, customers etc) can be analysed into three levels.

(a) **Strategic information** is used by senior management for decision-making described as strategic planning, that is planning the objectives of their organisation and assessing whether the objectives are being met in practice. Such information includes overall profitability, the profitability of different segments of the business, future market prospects, the availability and cost of raising new funds, total cash needs, total manning levels and capital equipment needs. Much of this information must come from environmental sources, although internally generated information is also used.

(b) **Tactical information** is used by middle management. This information includes productivity measurements, budgetary control or variance analysis reports, cash flow forecast, short term purchasing requirements, manning levels and profit results within a department. A large proportion of this information will be generated from within the organisation and is likely to have an accounting emphasis. Tactical information is usually prepared regularly, perhaps weekly or monthly (whereas strategic information is communicated irregularly) and is used for the decision-making known as 'management control'.

(c) **Operational information** is used by front-line managers such as supervisors and foremen, to ensure that specific tasks are planned and carried out properly within the office or factory. For example, in the payroll office operational information relating to day-rate labour will include the hours worked each week by employees, the rate of pay per hour, details of deductions, and for the purpose of wage analysis, details of the time each person spent on individual jobs during the week.

The amount of detail provided in information is likely to vary with the purpose for which it is needed and operational information is likely to go into much more detail than tactical information, which in turn will be more detailed than strategic information. What is information to one level of management may be the raw data, which needs to be further analysed, for another.

1.4 Qualities of information

Just as raw materials can be turned into a good product or a sub-standard one, so raw data can be processed or analysed into good or bad information. Good information is information that has value to the user. It is useful to the recipient, can be relied upon and helps in the decision making process. The basic qualities of good information are that it should be:

(a) **Complete (sufficient)**. The reliability of information increases with its completeness. However, the appropriate level of completeness varies enormously, according to the type of information. For example, it is a fundamental principle of financial accounting that all the transactions should be included in the books. The law would be broken if transactions were deliberately left out. In the same way personnel records should contain details of all employees.

However, suppose a buyer has to make a decision about purchasing commonly available raw materials. In order to obtain the best price he obtains quotes from suppliers. Does he have to ask for quotes from **all** the suppliers? Clearly not, because to do so might delay the purchase and incur unnecessary costs. He would therefore obtain quotes from a representative sample. This is an example of the cost of information influencing its completeness. Thus, rather than arguing that all information must be absolutely complete, we are left with the concept that information should be sufficient for its purpose.

(b) **Relevant**. Information must be relevant to the problem under consideration. It is often the case that reports contain irrelevant sections, which cloud the understanding and can irritate the user searching to find what is required. In the same way, financial analyses can sometimes confuse the reader by presenting a mixture of relevant and irrelevant information, or information with unnecessary detail. The concept of relevance is closely linked to those of understandability and significance, which are dealt with below.

(c) **Timely**. Some information might be communicated at once whereas other items of information are not needed for some time and so must be filed away. Information can only be of use if it is received in time to influence the decision making process. Occasionally this means a compromise in terms of completeness. Routine information should be produced at time intervals that are relevant to the process involved. For example, information on the temperature of a chemical process may be reported every hour, while routine production statistics and management accounts are produced monthly.

Financial accounting reports to shareholders are produced quarterly or less frequently. It is pointless producing information more frequently than it is used. On the other hand, once information is available, there should be the minimum possible delay in reporting it. For example, the annual report to the shareholders of a certain private company is produced nine months after the year-end reporting a modest profit. In the intervening nine months the company has suffered from increased competition at the same time as a general down-turn in the market, resulting in significant losses. Clearly the annual report is of little use to the decision problems of the shareholders in those circumstances.

(d) **Accurate**. Information should be sufficiently accurate for its intended purpose and the decision maker should be able to rely on the information. However, there is often some trade-off in terms of cost and it is possible to supply information in a much more accurate form than is required. The key question is whether increased accuracy will improve the quality of the user's decision making. For example, in deciding whether to make a component in-house or buy the equivalent part from an outside supplier we need an estimate of the internal production cost of making the component, which we may estimate by examining the costs of producing test samples. The required accuracy of these estimates depends on how close the internal production cost appears to be to the external buying cost. If the two costs are very similar, a higher level of accuracy in the measurement of the internal production cost is warranted, but if the internal cost is clearly much cheaper, the accuracy of the estimate is less important.

In addition to the accuracy with which information is measured, there is the further question of the accuracy with which it is reported. For example, data in the accounting system is collected with accuracy to the nearest penny. For some purposes this is necessary, for example paying suppliers and employees and receiving cash from debtors. However in reports given to cost centre mangers, the figures are usually rounded to an acceptable level of accuracy (say to the nearest £100 or £1,000) which makes the information easier to assimilate. In the same way, top management, who are examining summary financial reports of the whole organisation, may be satisfied with results reported correct to the nearest £100,000 or million pounds.

When calculating figures for financial reports, care should be taken to avoid **spurious** accuracy. Information can only be as accurate as the raw data. For example, if in a process costing calculation the cost of producing 9,600 litres is £12,400 and these figures are measured correct to the nearest hundred, it would be spurious accuracy to report the cost per litre as £1.27835. The appropriate level of accuracy is £1.28 or even £1.30 because the volume is only measured corrected to two significant figures.

(e) **Understandable**. Information that is easy to understand is more likely to produce action. Because managers are busy they will resent having to spend unnecessary time interpreting badly presented reports. Managers can, however, often assist their own cause by specifying the format, layout and style of presentation of the information they need. Modern computer packages contain tables, graphics and charts, all of which can assist in speeding up and improving the understanding process.

Information must be understandable by the person receiving it. It is pointless presenting it in a way that assumes knowledge and abilities that the recipient could not be expected to have.

(f) **Significance**. Part of the art of keeping information simple and understandable is to highlight the significant factors, screening out any facts that are not important enough to affect the decision-making process. Information has no value if the user already knows it: we say that information must have a 'surprise' value. This significant information is both new and important for the decision making process. For example, when reporting production or financial figures to managers it is often useful to operate a system of exception reporting. Facts that simply tell the manager that things are going according to plan need not be reported at all. The system concentrates on significant deviations from plan, in other words variances. This principle is even more important when a computer report summarises the work it is processing. The information that two invoices have been rejected is of more importance than the fact that 1,000 invoices have been processed without problem.

(g) **Confidence in the information received**. Good information commands the confidence of the user. Information should be accurate and the person to whom it is communicated should also be confident that it is accurate. The quality of communications is determined by the confidence that key people throughout the organisation have in each other's ability. Communication between managers, or between managers and employees, can help to increase confidence and thereby improve performance. Confidence, in turn, can improve the quality of communications. A subordinate who is confident that his superior is capable and knows what he is doing will be likely to provide him with reliable information of a standard that he expects his superior to find acceptable.

There is therefore a cycle of genuine confidence breeding success and vice versa. Information received in which a manager has confidence will be acted on by him or her more readily, and a manager who is confident that the correct decision has been made communicates that conviction to subordinates, thus improving the likelihood of success in the consequent action.

Activity 1 **(10 minutes)**

Explain why the accuracy of information required at the different levels of management might reduce as you go from operational, through tactical to strategic management.

2 VALIDITY OF INFORMATION

The following table could be used in an assessment of the validity of information.

Guideline	Comment
Common sense	Clearly data which is 'dated', which emanates from dubious sources or which is based on unrepresentative samples should be treated with caution.
Statistical approaches	There are a variety of sampling methods for survey data as already described, which are appropriate to different situations. All of them involve some degree of risk (some probability of error). The degree of risk of statistical error can, however, be computed.
Expert judgement	The same data can be interpreted differently by different people The following array - 98.7, 98.6, 98.6, 98.4, 98.1, 98.1- might be regarded by a statistician as a declining trend but to a business manager the figures may represent a very steady state.
The intuitive approach	Some people have a better feel for figures than others and seem able to judge the value and validity of data intuitively. However, this requires specific knowledge and experience.
The questioning approach	Always question the origin and the basis of the data. Recognise that human errors occur when manipulating data, that bias can occur in questionnaire design: ask to see the questionnaire, check the figures. Furthermore, for information released to the public domain, bear in mind that: (a) Governments and political parties tend to be very selective in the data they choose to use (b) Many newspapers follow a 'political' line and are likely to be selective or even biased (c) Most journalists are not trained statisticians and may interpret data incorrectly

NOTES

3 ANALYSIS OF QUANTITIVE DATA

Analysing raw data - the words and sentences, or the metric or non-metric measurements taken in the collection phase - requires three processes:

(a) **data reduction:** summarising data in order to identify the key features;

(b) **data presentation:** illustrating the data's key features in a way that will be understood by the target audience; and

(c) **drawing conclusions.**

Definitions

Quantitative data are data that can be measured. For example, the temperature on each day of August (which can be measured in degrees (fahrenheit or celsius) or the time it takes you to travel to work each day (which can be measured in hours and minutes) are quantitative data.

Contrast this with **qualitative data**, which cannot easily be measured but reflects some quality of what is being observed. Whether somebody is male or female is qualitative data: there is no measure of *how* male or *how* female somebody is.

Data analysis involves analysing masses of data so as to summarise its essential features and relationships in order that, by generalising, patterns of behaviour, particular outcomes or future results can be determined.

A useful way of think about data analysis is to separate it into problems where:

(a) we have more than one value for only one set of variables or unit of analysis **(univariate analysis)**;

(b) we have more than one value for two sets of variables/units of analysis **(bivariate analysis);** and

(c) we have more than one value for more than two sets of variables/units of analysis **(multivariate analysis)**.

This is not nearly as scary as it sounds.

In **univariate** analysis we concentrate on reducing the raw data to meaningful figures and looking at what is typical. In **bivariate** analysis we concentrate on how the values of two variables are related, and in **multivariate** analysis we attempt to see how three or more variables interact together: seeing how things typically respond to one another.

If a group of people are aged 24, 19, 27 and 19 what age is representative of the group or, in other words, what is their average age? In fact we will examine 3 different ways of selecting a representative or average.

4 AVERAGES

4.1 The arithmetic mean

This is the best known type of average. It is calculated by the formula

$$\text{Arithmetic mean} = \frac{\text{Sum of values of items}}{\text{Number of items}}$$

BPP PUBLISHING

NOTES

For example, if three bakers sell bread, the mean price of a loaf of bread is the 3 individual prices added together and divided by three.

EXAMPLE: THE ARITHMETIC MEAN

The demand for a product on each of 20 days was as follows (in units).

3 12 7 17 3 14 9 6 11 10 1 4 19 7 15 6 9 12 12 8

The arithmetic mean of daily demand is

$$\frac{\text{Sum of demand}}{\text{Number of days}} = \frac{185}{20} = 9.25 \text{ units}$$

4.2 The advantages and disadvantages of the arithmetic mean

The advantages of the arithmetic mean are as follows.

(a) It is widely understood.

(b) The value of every item is included in the computation of the mean.

(c) It is supported by mathematical theory and is suited to further statistical analysis.

The disadvantages of the arithmetic mean are as follows.

(a) Its value may not correspond to any actual value. For example, the 'average' family might have 2.3 children, but no family has exactly 2.3 children.

(b) An arithmetic mean might be distorted by extremely high or low values. For example, the mean of 3, 4, 4 and 6 is 4.25, but the mean of 3, 4, 4, 6 and 15 is 6.4. The high value, 15, distorts the average and in some circumstances the mean would be a misleading and inappropriate figure.

Activity 2 **(5 minutes)**

What is the arithmetic mean of the following figures?

12 46 1 77 25

4.3 The mode

The mode is an average which means 'the most frequently occurring value'.

EXAMPLE: THE MODE

The daily demand for a product in a 10 day period is as follows.

Demand	*Number of days*
	Units
6	3
7	6
8	1
	10

The mode is 7 units, because it is the value which occurs most frequently.

BPP PUBLISHING

4.4 The advantages and disadvantages of the mode

The mode will be a more appropriate average to use than the mean in situations where it is useful to know the most common value. For example, when we want to know what sort of product is most in demand with customers the mode is easy to find, it is uninfluenced by a few extreme values and it can be used for data which are not even numerical (unlike the mean and median). The main disadvantage of the mode is that it ignores dispersion around the modal value, and unlike the mean, does not take every value into account. There can also be two or more modes within a set of data and it is unsuitable for further statistical analysis.

4.5 The median

The third type of average is the median. The median is the middle value of a set of values when the values have been placed in numerical order.

EXAMPLE 1: THE MEDIAN

What is the median of the following nine values?

8	6	9	12	15	6	3	20	11

We must firstly put the values in order:

3	6	6	8	9	11	12	15	20

Now we select the middle value, which in this case is the fifth value, so the median is 9.

EXAMPLE 2: THE MEDIAN

What is the median of the following 10 values?

8	6	7	2	1	11	3	2	6	2

We must firstly put the values in order:

1	2	2	2	3	6	6	7	8	11

Now we select the middle value but in this case we have an even number of values so there is no value in the set which is on its own in the middle. We need to select halfway between the fifth and sixth values, so half way between 3 and 6. In this case the answer is $4\frac{1}{2}$ which we could have calculated as $(3 + 6)/2 = 9/2 = 4\frac{1}{2}$.

4.6 The advantages and disadvantages of the median

The median is only of interest where there is a range of values and the middle item is of some significance. Perhaps the most suitable application of the median is in comparing changes in a 'middle of the road' value over time where most values inevitably fall close to the middle value. An example might be the age at which women marry: the median would show a gradual rise during the twentieth century. The median (like the mode) is unaffected by extremely high or low values. On the other hand, it fails to reflect the full range of values, and is unsuitable for further statistical analysis.

Activity 3 **(15 minutes)**

A group of hourly paid workers are paid at the following hourly rates:

£2.50 £2.75 £2.75 £2.75 £3.00 £3.40 £3.75 £3.90 £5.75 £9.50

The workers claim their average wage is £2.75 but the management claim it is actually just over £4. Which type of averages are they talking about and which type of average do you think is the best or fairest representative of the workers' hourly rates?

FOR DISCUSSION

In the previous activity you may have realised that there are often different ways to process or interpret data to produce statistics. Another example is when an advertiser states 'In tests to compare product X with product Y, 8 out of 10 people who expressed a preference said that they preferred product X'. This seems at first glance to mean 80% preferred product X but how many people were asked? If 100 people were asked then only 8% preferred product X, 2% preferred product Y and 90% did not care which product they had and expressed no preference.

You are probably starting to understand why many people mistrust statistics and market research results. In the vast majority of cases, the statistics that are presented are accurate and true but sometimes the way they are presented emphasises certain aspects and omits to show other aspects. Try to think of ways that unscrupulous people could use this to their own advantage.

Averages are not the only way of analysing data to find out what is most typical. You will often hear an analysis such as 70% said Yes, 25% said No and 5% were Don't Knows. Data is expressed in this way when a large number of people have been asked.

5 FREQUENCY ANALYSIS

5.1 Frequency analysis

If a large number of measurements of a particular variable is taken (for example the number of items purchased per customer per week) some values may occur more than once. A frequency distribution (or frequency table) is obtained by recording the number of times each value occurs.

Definition

A **variable** is something that can have different values. For example the number of customers that come into your shop per hour is a variable: the number of customers changes, while the things it is measured against (your shop, per hour) do not.

EXAMPLE: A FREQUENCY DISTRIBUTION

The quantity of items purchased by 20 customers during one week was as follows.

65	69	70	71	70	68	69	67	70	68
72	71	69	74	70	73	71	67	69	70

If the number of occurrences is placed against each purchase quantity, a frequency 'distribution' is produced.

Items purchased	*Number of customers (frequency)*
65	1
66	0
67	2
68	2
69	4
70	5
71	3
72	1
73	0
74	1
	20

The number of customers corresponding to a particular volume of purchases is called a frequency. When the data are arranged in this way it is immediately obvious that 69 and 70 units are the most common volumes of purchases per customer per week.

Make sure you have noted the term distribution as illustrated above. It is important over the next few pages.

5.2 Percentages

Percentages are used to indicate the **relative** size or proportion of items, rather than their absolute size. For example, if one car salesman sells ten Fords, six Vauxhalls and four Renaults, the **absolute** values of car sales and the **percentage** of the total sales of each type would be as follows.

	Fords	*Vauxhalls*	*Renaults*	*Total*
Absolute numbers	10	6	4	20
Percentages	50%	30%	20%	100%

The idea of percentages is that the whole of something can be thought of as 100%. The whole of a cake, for example, is 100%. If you share it out equally with a friend, you will get half each, or 100%/2 = 50% each.

To turn a percentage into a fraction or decimal you divide by 100. To turn a fraction or decimal back into a percentage you multiply by 100%. Consider the following.

(a) $0.16 = 0.16 \times 100\% = 16\%$
(b) $4/5 = (4/5) \times 100\% = (400/5)\% = 80\%$
(c) $40\% = 40/100 = 2/5 = 0.4$

There are three main types of situations involving percentages.

(a) You may want to calculate a percentage of a figure, having been given the percentage.

Question: What is 40% of £64?
Answer: 40% of £64 = 0.4 × £64 = £25.60.

(b) You may want to state what percentage one figure is of another, so that you have to work out the percentage yourself.

Question: What is £16 as a percentage of £64?
Answer: £16 as a percentage of £64 = (16/64) × 100% = 25%

In other words, put the £16 as a fraction of the £64, and then multiply by 100%.

(c) You may have to fill in the missing number.

Question: If the price with a 20% discount is £5, what is the full price?
Answer: £5 must be 80%, so the full price is (£5 ÷ 80) × 100 = £6.25.

Proportions

A proportion means writing a percentage as a proportion of 1 (that is, as a decimal).

100% can be thought of as the whole, or 1. 50% is half of that, or 0.5. Consider the following.

Question: There are 14 women in an audience of 70. What proportion of the audience are men?

Answer: Number of men = 70 – 14 = 56
Proportion of men = 56/70 = 0.8

(a) 56/70 is the **fraction** of the audience made up by men.
(b) 0.8 is the **proportion** of the audience made up by men.
(c) 80% is the **percentage** of the audience made up by men.

Note that 56/70 is not very meaningful to most people. It can be simplified to four-fifths. A scientific calculator or a spreadsheet will do this for you.

One of the problems with averages that we identified above was that they do not give a very clear idea of the variation or spread of values they represent. This is called 'dispersion' and there are several ways of taking account of it.

6 MEASURES OF DISPERSION

6.1 The range

The range of a set of values is the difference between the highest and the lowest values in the set. If a group of people are aged 28, 25, 32, 21 and 29 then the range of their ages is (32 – 21) = 11. The main properties of the range as a measure of the spread of a set of values are as follows.

(a) It is easy to find and to understand.
(b) It is easily affected by one or two extreme values.
(c) It gives no indication of spread between the extremes.
(d) It is not suitable for further statistical analysis.

6.2 Quartiles (and similar measures)

Quartiles are one means of identifying the range within which proportions of the values being analysed occur. The lower quartile is the value below which 25% of the values fall and the upper quartile is the value above which 25% of the values fall. It follows that 50% of the total number of values fall between the lower and the upper quartiles. The quartiles and the median also divide the values into four groups of equal size, hence the term quartiles.

In a similar way, the values could be divided into ten equal groups, and the value of each dividing point is referred to, not as a quartile, but as a **decile**. When a series of values is divided into 100 parts, the value of each dividing point is referred to as a percentile. For example, in a series of 200 values, the **percentiles** would be the second, fourth, sixth, eighth and so on, up to the 198th item, in rising order of values.

Quartiles, deciles and percentiles, and any other similar dividing points for analysis are referred to collectively as **quantiles**. The purpose of quantiles is to analyse the dispersion of data values: how widely the values are dispersed about the mean.

For example, a marketing researcher might find that the mean number of bottles of cola consumed per household per month was three. This could mean that every household consumes between two and four bottles, but equally it could mean that a sizeable number consume no bottles and a sizeable number consume ten or more bottles. Not every household, therefore, is an equally good target for marketing activities.

The most important measure of spread in statistics is the standard deviation. It is denoted by s or σ. The symbol s is used for the standard deviation of a sample of values (cola-consuming households in Swindon, say), and σ is used for the standard deviation of a population of values (all cola-consuming households).

6.3 The standard deviation

The standard deviation is used in conjunction with the arithmetic mean (the simple average that we described right at the beginning of this chapter). The standard deviation provides a measure of how widely spread the values used to calculate the mean are around that central point.

The standard deviation's main properties are as follows.

(a) It is based on *all* the values measured and so is more comprehensive than dispersion measures based on quantiles, such as the quartile deviation.

(b) It is suitable for further statistical analysis.

(c) It is more difficult to understand and calculate than some other measures of dispersion.

The importance of the standard deviation lies in its suitability for further statistical analysis, as we shall see in the following sections.

7 SAMPLING THEORY

7.1 Collecting and analysing samples

Definitions

> In statistical terms, the **population** is used to refer to the set of all the items we are interested in. Sometimes it is very difficult or impossible to gain data about every item in the population so we get data from just some of the items, in other words we use a **sample** of the population.
>
> **Descriptive statistics** are used to summarise the actual data that we have collected. If we measure the height of everyone in a group and calculate the mean and standard deviation of these heights then we are using descriptive statistics. If we have statistics from a sample of the population we cannot say with certainty those statistics are true for the whole population. However, some sophisticated statistical techniques have been developed for making inferences or estimates about the population based on data from a sample of the population. These techniques are known as **inferential statistics** and usually include a **confidence level** which gives an indication of how certain we are about the accuracy of the results.

In the first part of this chapter we looked at distributions occurring as a result of considering a 'population' of items. We can also construct probability distributions, known as sampling distributions, for samples rather than whole populations and, when we start taking fairly large random **samples** (over 30) from a population and measuring the **mean** of those samples, we find an uncanny relationship with the normal distribution.

A distribution of the means of these samples has the following important properties.

(a) It is very close to being normally distributed. The larger the samples the more closely will the sampling distribution approximate to a normal distribution.

(b) The mean of the sampling distribution is the same as the population mean, μ.

(c) The sampling distribution has a standard deviation which is called the **standard error of the mean.**

7.2 Confidence levels, limits and intervals

From our knowledge of the properties of a normal distribution, together with the rule that sample means are normally distributed around the true population mean, with a standard deviation equal to the standard error, we can predict the following.

(a) 68% of all sample means will be within one standard error of the population mean.

(b) 95% of all sample means will be within 1.96 standard errors of the population mean.

(c) 99% of all sample means will be within 2.58 standard errors of the population mean.

Let us look at it another way.

NOTES

(a) With 68% probability, the population mean lies within the range: sample mean ± one standard error.

(b) With 95% probability, the population mean lies within the range: sample mean ± 1.96 standard errors.

(c) With 99% probability, the population mean lies within the range: sample mean ± 2.58 standard errors.

These degrees of certainty (such as 95%) are known as **confidence levels**, and the ends of the ranges (such as sample mean + 2.58 standard errors) around the sample mean are called **confidence limits**. The ranges (such as sample mean ± one standard error) are called **confidence intervals.**

7.3 What does it all mean?

What it means is that, if you take a reasonably large sample of representative items and find out something about them, you can be confident up to a certain level that something is true of the whole population of items.

Suppose, for example, you measured the height of 100 mature labradors and found that the average was, say, 30cm with a standard deviation of 2cm. You could then be 99% certain that the average height of all mature labradors was in the range of 30 ±(2.58 × 2) = 24.84cm to 35.16cm. (This gives you a basis for designing a range of labrador leisure-wear, or whatever!)

In practice you will probably be able to leave the figurework to marketing research specialists or company statisticians. The important thing is that you understand enough of the jargon to appreciate the scientific basis of such an analysis rather than be blinded by it.

FOR DISCUSSION

The media are very keen to publicise opinion poll statistics. Try to find some examples and discuss how the data may have been collected and how the statistics quoted could have been arrived at.

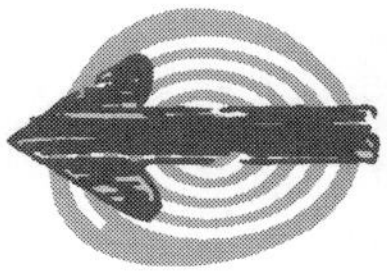

The practical implication in terms of managing information is that a vast amount of time, effort and money can be saved if you only have to consider a sample rather than every single item in a population.

7.4 Sample sizes from an administrative viewpoint

Although it is possible to calculate an ideal sample size from a statistical point of view, administrative and practical factors have to be taken into account. These factors are summarised below.

(a) The amount of money and time available.

(b) The aims of the survey.

(c) The degree of precision required.

(d) The number of sub-samples required.

BPP PUBLISHING

NOTES

(e) The larger the sample size, the more precise will be the information given about the population, but above a certain size, little extra information is given by increasing the size. A sample therefore only need be large enough to be reasonably representative of the population.

7.5 Estimation and small samples

Be aware that although we can calculate the standard error using the standard deviation of the sample, this is only true for very large samples. Smaller samples may not be as closely representative of the population as a whole.

8 ANALYSIS AND INTERPRETATION OF QUALITATIVE DATA

8.1 Using qualitative data

Collecting qualitative data means the recording of words, phrases, sentences and narrative which explains or describes people's thoughts, feelings and intentions. The key task in analysis is to summarise what people said. It is then possible to classify responses into categories, analyse them to some extent using statistics, and then analyse the content.

Summarising the wealth of data gathered may take some time. It involves scanning over the questionnaires or discussion transcripts and picking out:

(a) Key ideas, on the grounds of novelty, excitement or conviction;

(b) Key words and phrases, which seem to sum up the attitudes of the respondents.

It will then be possible to reduce the data to a logical sequence of key points.

Alternatively, it may be possible to identify categories into which responses fall, and classify all responses into these categories. While this is a more systematic method, it may not give due weight to those results which were perceived to be important at the time of the research.

If it is possible to categorise responses then the frequencies of each can be calculated and some degree of statistical method is possible. Thus, a response with which 'nearly all' the respondents agreed has a much higher frequency than one with which very few concurred. This method is particularly useful where differences in the 'demographics' of the groups are highlighted, such as language and humour variations between old and young.

Key words or phrases used in the research should be quoted in a report, but they must be regarded as illustrative rather than representative.

While qualitative data can generate hypotheses, researchers cannot test them easily. The conclusions which can be drawn are those to do with observing relationships, sequences and patterns, but how far these are causal would have to be tested by quantitative techniques.

NOTES

Chapter roundup

- Information is data that has been processed or analysed so that it can be used to improve decision-making. This information is analysed differently for the three management levels – operational, tactical and strategic.
- For information to be useful it must possess certain qualities, eg it must be complete, relevant, timely, accurate, understandable and significant. It must also command the confidence of the user.
- To assess the validity of information, you should apply some or all of the following: common sense, a statistical approach, expert judgement, the intuitive approach or the questioning approach.
- Analysing data requires three processes – data reduction to identify the key features, data presentation so that it is understood by the user and drawing conclusions.
- Analysis techniques include averages, frequency analysis and measure of dispersion.
- Because we know about normal distributions and standard errors when we take a reasonably large sample of representative items and find out something about them, we can be confident up to a certain level that something is true of the whole population of items.
- Analysing and interpreting qualitative information is not very scientific. It can mean picking out key ideas on the grounds of novelty, excitement or conviction. It can involve selecting key words and phrases that seem to sum up the attitudes of the respondents to questions.

Quick quiz

1 How does data differ from information?

2 Information within the organisation is used at the three levels of management. What are these levels?

3 What do we mean when we say that information should have a 'surprise' value?

4 Why should you question the origin and the basis of data?

5 Distinguish between univariate, bivariate and multivariate analysis.

6 What are the main disadvantages associated with the arithmetic mean?

7 What is the difference between a percentage and a proportion?

8 Describe the term 'sample population'.

9 From an administrative point of view, what factors need to be taken into account when deciding on sample sizes?

10 What conclusions can be drawn from qualitative data?

Answers to quick quiz

1 Information is data that has been analysed or processed to give it meaning and improve the quality of decision-making for the user. (See para 1.1)

2 From the top management down to the front-line management, the information can be described as strategic, tactical and operational. (1.4)

3 It means that the significant information is both new and important for the decision-making process. It is often referred to as exception reporting. (1.5)

4 The questioning approach ensures that you recognise that human errors occur when manipulating data and that bias can occur in questionnaire design. Information released to the public domain is not necessarily correct. Political parties can be selective in the data they choose to portray, newspapers may be biased and journalists are not trained statisticians and may interpret data incorrectly. Even on the internet, information is not correct just because the computer 'says so'. (2)

5 With univariate analysis the raw data is reduced to meaningful figures so that we can see what is typical. Bivariate analysis concentrates on how the values of two variables are related and multivariate analysis shows how three or more variables interact together, ie how things typically respond to each other.

6 The calculated value may not correspond to a real value, eg the average class size in UK schools may work out at 31.6 but no class has that number of children. The mean may also be distorted by extremely high or low values, eg a mature student aged 60 in a group of 10 students with ages ranging between 18 and 21 will distort the average. (4.2)

7 A percentage is where you think of the whole of something as 100%, so that if you divide it by 5, you get 20%. A proportion means writing a percentage as a proportion of 1 as a decimal. 100% can be thought of as 1 and dividing it by 5 gives you a proportion of 0.2. (5.2)

8 When we are talking about statistics, the population refers to the set of all the items we are interested in, for example the number of students sitting this examination in a certain year. Because it would be very difficult to find out from all of them which study guide they were using, we just get data from some of them. In other words, we use a sample of the population. (7.1)

9 The factors that affect the size of a sample include the amount of time and money available, the aims of the survey, the degree of precision and the number of sub-samples required.

10 The conclusion that can be drawn from qualitative data are those relating to observing relationships, sequences and patterns.

Answers to activities

1 Operating managers and supervisors might need information that is accurate to the nearest penny, second or kilogram. For example, a cashier will do a bank reconciliation to the exact penny and purchase ledger staff will pay creditors exactly what they are owed. Managers of departments might be satisfied with revenues and costs rounded to the nearest £100 and £1,000, since greater detail would serve no purpose. For example, in budgeting, revenue and cost figures are usually rounded up to the nearest £100 or £1,000 because trying to be more exact would usually only give a spurious accuracy. Senior managers in a medium-sized to large organisation might be satisfied with figures to the nearest £10,000, £100,000 or even a million pounds. Estimates to the nearest £ at this level of decision making would be so inappropriate that they would seem ridiculous and so, oddly enough, perhaps undermine the user's confidence in the accuracy of estimates, ie have a counter-productive effect.

NOTES

2 The arithmetic mean is 12 + 46 + 1 + 77 + 25 = 161 ÷ 5 = 32.2

3 The workers are basing their average on the mode, which is the most frequently occurring value, ie £2.75, whilst the management are basing their average on the mean which means adding the ten values and then dividing the sum by ten, ie £4. A fairer representative of the workers' hourly rates might be to take the median. To do this we would select the middle value – midway between the fifth and sixth values. The rate would then show as £3.20 ((£3.00 + £3.40) ÷ 2).

Chapter 14 :
RECORDING AND STORING INFORMATION

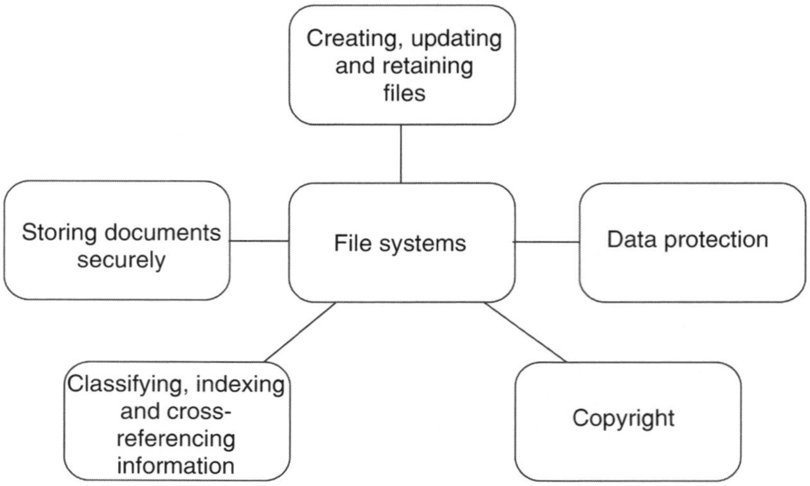

Introduction

For most people working in an office environment, recording and storing information takes up the majority of their working day. Whether it is done manually or on a computer, the lifeblood of the organisation is the flow of information throughout the systems. Unfortunately for some systems, they can become congested when users are not sure what to record, what to store and what to discard.

Your objectives

In this chapter you will learn about the following:

(a) Filing systems

(b) Classifying, indexing and cross-referencing information

(c) Storing documents securely

(d) Creating, updating, and retaining files

(e) Recording item movements

(f) Computerised systems

1 FILING SYSTEMS

The information source that you will use most frequently in practice is the paperwork generated by the activities of your own organisation. This is held in **files** and so we are now going to look at the characteristics of a **filing system**, and at how files are organised and stored.

This chapter should help you to deal with files in practice - getting hold of them, finding documents within them, putting new documents into them, opening new files, keeping track of files, and knowing when to thin them out or throw them away. We discuss **manual filing systems** first, but many of the principles of data storage and retrieval apply to computer documents as well as physical documents.

1.1 Information flow

Filing is an integral part of the process of **creating information** that will lead to an activity or decision of some kind. Creating and using information is not just a matter of processing input data to create output information. Other things happen in the information-creating process.

(a) **Copies of information** are made: documents are duplicated so that everyone who needs a copy gets one.

(b) Information has to be **sent to the people who need it**, and it has to be properly received by them.

(c) Not all information is needed straight away. Or if it is, it might be needed again later, for reference. This means that information has to be **filed away** somewhere, for a time that might range from a very brief period to years. The same item of information might be stored in several different files, once by each person or group who will want to use it again some time.

(d) Information on file will be needed again, sooner or later.

Definition

Information retrieval is the term used to describe getting information out of file for use in further data processing.

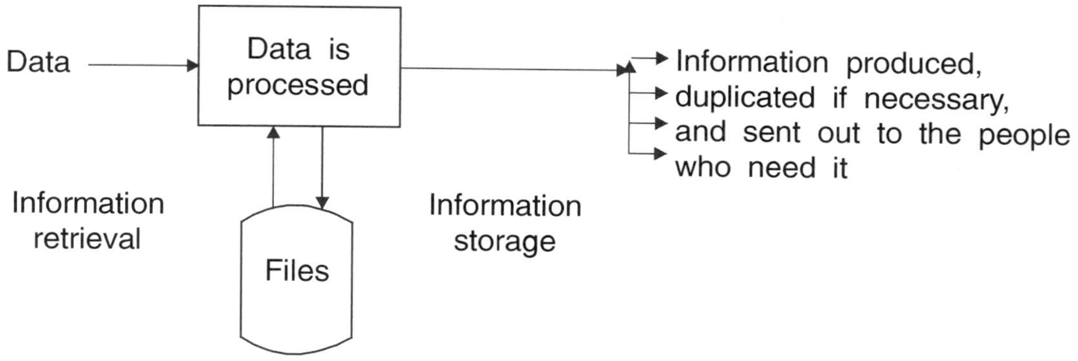

1.2 The features of a filing system

Information for business users takes many forms. Whatever form documents and recorded information take, if they are to be of any use, they must be maintained in such a way that:

(a) **Authorised people** (and only authorised people) can get to the information they require quickly and easily

(b) Information can be **added, updated and outdated** as necessary

(c) Information is **safe from fire, loss or handling damage** for as long as it is required (but not necessarily for ever)

(d) Accessibility, flexibility and security are achieved as **cheaply** as possible

1.3 Files

Definition

> A **file** is a collection of data records with similar characteristics.

Examples of files

- A sales or purchase ledger.
- A cash book.
- A price list.
- A collection of letters, memos and other papers all relating to the same matter, usually kept within a single folder.
- A collection of data records or documents in an electronic 'file' on computer disk or in a computer database.

> **Activity 1** **(10 minutes)**
>
> Apart from these basic records - grouped items of information - what other items of information might pass through organisations needing to be kept track of? Give at least five examples.

1.4 What makes a good filing system?

A **filing system** should:

- Contain all the information that users might want
- Be classified and indexed in such as way as to make it easy to find information quickly
- Be suited to the people who will use it
- Be reliable and secure
- Be flexible enough to allow for expansion

NOTES

- Be cost-effective to install and maintain - there is no point spending more to hold information on file than the information is actually worth
- Allow users to retrieve information within an acceptable period of time

Activity 2 **(10 minutes)**

Your organisation has just received the following letter. List the details that are likely to be used when deciding where it should be filed. What other department would you send a copy of the letter to?

SANDIMANS LTD

72 High Street, Epsom
Surrey EP12 4AB

Your reference: Z/0335/MJD
Our reference: BRC/1249/871

Mr G Latchmore
Purchasing Department
Lightfoot & Co
7 West Broughton St
LONDON W12 9LM

Dear Mr Latchmore

Stationery supplies

I refer to your letter of 11 April 2001.

I am afraid that we are still unable to trace receipt of your payment of £473.20 in settlement of our invoice number 147829. I should be grateful if you would look into this and issue a fresh cheque if necessary.

Your sincerely

Mandy Sands

Mandy Sands

So, with all of this information floating around, how are we going to locate a particular item of information? We need to make sure that our information is held in an organised fashion, and that we have procedures in place which enable us to find what we are looking for quickly and easily. The next section of this chapter considers the ways in which we can track down the information that we are looking for.

2 CLASSIFYING, INDEXING AND CROSS-REFERENCING INFORMATION

2.1 Classifying information

When information is filed, it has to be filed in such a way that its **users know where it is and how to retrieve it** later when it is needed. This means having different files for different types of information, and then **holding each file in a particular order.** Information in an individual file might be divided into categories and then held in a particular order within each category.

Definition

> **Classification** is the process of grouping related items of information together into categories that reflect the relationship between them.

2.2 Ways in which information can be grouped together, or classified

(a) By **name** (for example correspondence relating to a particular person or company).

(b) By **geography** (for example all documents relating to a particular country, area or city).

(c) By **subject matter** (for example all documents relating to a particular contract, transaction or type of problem).

(d) By **date** (for example all invoices for a certain month or year).

(e) By **department** (for example profits or costs for each department or employees of each department).

Once broad classifications are established, the material can be **put into a sequence** which will make individual items easier to retrieve. Again there are various systems for arranging files.

(a) **Alphabetical order** - for example customers listed in name order.

(b) **Numerical order** - for example invoices listed in numerical order of invoice numbers.

(c) **Alpha-numerical** (A1, A2, A3, B1, B2 and so on).

(d) **Chronological order** - for example letters within a subject file listed by the date they were written.

These ways of subdividing and arranging data in a logical way within suitable categories make it possible to store, find and also **index** or **cross-reference** information efficiently (as we will discuss later in this section).

We shall now have a look at some of these systems for arranging information.

2.3 Alphabetical classification

The most common means of classification is **alphabetical**. In an alphabetical name system, items are filed according to the first and then each following letter of a person's or company's name (for example in the phone book). This sounds simple enough, and indeed it is most of the time, but there are some rules which must be followed .

The system works by **surname**. The hyphen is ignored in double-barrelled names. When surnames are the same, initials or first names are taken into account. All of this is illustrated below.

Dawson
Ullyott
Vivian
Watkins
Williams
Williams
Williamson
Winters, Douglas
Winters, George

Initials. Names made up of initials may come before whole-word names.

PBAB Parties Ltd
Party Time Ltd

Prefixes are included as part of the surname.

De Beauvoir
Le Bon
McVitee
Von Richthofen

Mc, Mac etc are all treated as if they were Mac, so:

McGraw
MacLaverty

and St is usually treated as Saint, so:

St Angela's Convent
Saint George's Chapel.

Titles and common words. Words such as 'Mr', 'Mrs', 'Sir', 'The', 'A' are ignored for filing purposes (or most names would be under M or T!) while departments, ministries, offices, local authorities and so on are filed under the key part of their name:

Stanwick, B (Mrs)
Stock Exchange (The)
Trend, N U (Prof)
Finance, Ministry of

Bromley, London Borough of
Fair Trading, Department of
Foreign Office

Businesses with names like 'Phillip Smith Ltd', 'Frank Tilsley & Son' etc are sometimes listed under the first letter of the surname (as usual) but perhaps more often under the first letter of the whole name (P and F in the examples given).

Numbers which appear as names may also count as if they were spelled out as words:

84 Charing Cross Road (under 'E' for Eighty)
2001: A Space Odyssey (under 'T' for Two)
3i plc (under 'T' for Three).

You will find things arranged differently in some cases. Rules do vary from system to system. **Get to know the ones you have to work with in your organisation.**

The **alphabetical name system** is used, for example, in files of clients or customers, students, employees or members and also for index cards and cross-referencing (which we will come to a bit later). It is a simple to use and easily expandable system: there is a 'right' place for files, so they can simply be taken out or slotted in as necessary.

NOTES

2.4 Numerical classification

Numerical sequence is natural where standard documents are concerned. Invoices, for example, are numbered: if one needs to be checked, the number need only be established (quoted by the enquirer, or looked up in the customer account perhaps) and can be easily found. This is known as a **numerical-sequential** system.

Numerical classification is very **flexible**. Unlike the alphabetical method, you do not have to decide how much filing space to allocate to each letter, wasting space if you are too generous and having to shuffle the whole system along if you are too 'mean'. With numerical order, you simply give a new file the next number and position in the system.

On the other hand, numbers may not be very meaningful in isolation. A strict **alphabetical index** also has to be kept, and also a **numerical file list** or **accession register**, in order to establish the file number to look for. It also means that there is little room for subdivisions for easier identification and retrieval, although blocks of numbers can be allotted to different departments, say.

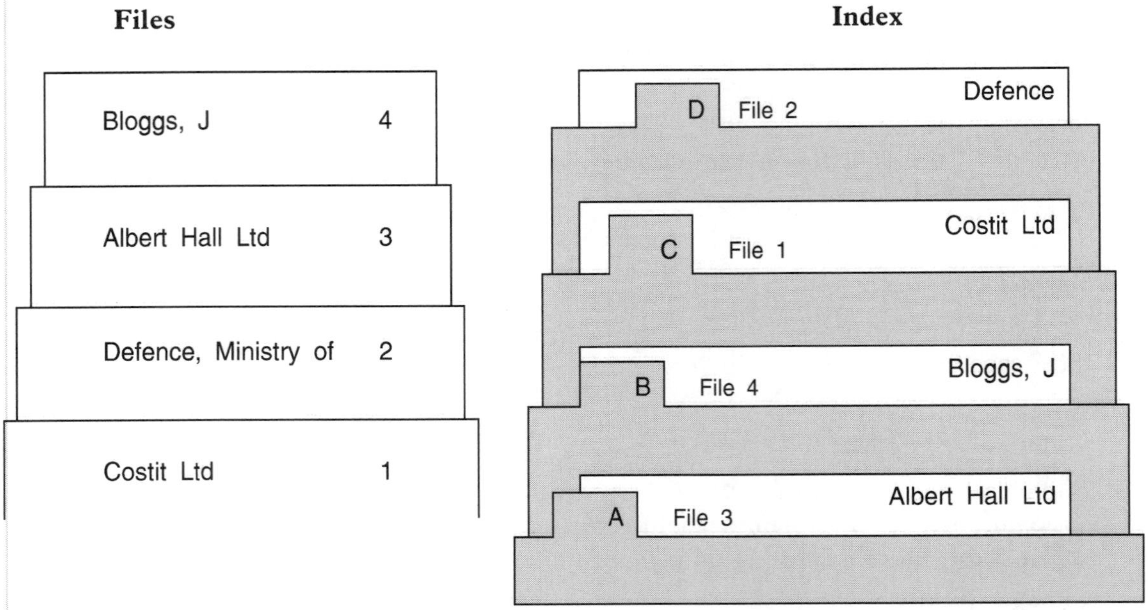

EXAMPLE: FILING

Numbers can be given a meaning to a limited extent. For example one of the leading UK Building Societies has account numbers constructed from three parts. A number in the form 7 - 666 - 55555 would indicate that this customer has a type 7 account (which pays such and such per cent interest and allows withdrawals with 60 days notice, say), that the account was opened at branch 666 (perhaps branches in the 600 range are in the Manchester region), and that it was account number 55555 opened at that branch, this being the number uniquely identifiable with a named customer. This type of coding is generally used in computer systems.

2.5 Alpha-numeric classification

In an **alpha-numeric system** files are given a reference consisting of **letters** and **numbers**. For example a letter received from Mr Blotson about the purchase of a flat in Mayfair might be given the reference BLO/8745/97/1. The system uses the first three letters of the correspondent's name and a number to distinguish him from anybody else called Blotson and/or to indicate that the subject matter is domestic property. The number 97 indicates that this correspondence began in 1997. The 1 shows that it is the first file which has anything to do with this subject. If Mr Blotson's property deal fell through but he then found another flat the correspondence relating to this would be kept in the separate but related file BLO/8745/97/2.

A system like this is most useful where there is a very large volume of correspondence on different but related topics. The Civil Service, for example, uses a system along these lines.

2.6 Other classifications

Using any of the above systems, bear in mind that you could group your files in any logical way. Common examples include:

(a) **Subject classification**, where all material relating to a particular subject (client, contract, project, product and so on) is kept together. (You just need to title your subjects thoughtfully, otherwise you end up with a lot of 'miscellaneous' items that do not fit your subject categories.)

(b) **Geographical classification**, which is useful for sales, import/export and similar activities that may be organised by region or territory.

Here is an example of geographical files, sub-classified by subject, in alphabetical order.

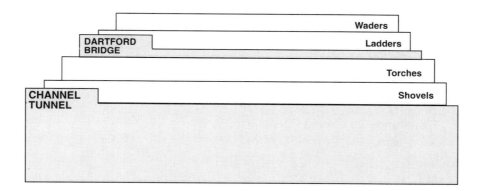

NOTES

Activity 3 **(30 minutes)**

Listed below are details of 30 people who have written to your organisation.

	Name and address	Account	Date
1	Cottrell J, 5 Heathview Avenue, Bromley	-	2.6.93
2	Holden R, 27 Exning Road, Bexley	-	13.7.92
3	Williams J, 29 Gray Gardens, Dartford	100276	5.4.94
4	Bidwell D, 176 High Road, Dartford	-	16.5.95
5	Bexley J, 25 Romney Road, Orpington	400452	17.5.95
6	Maclean T, 1 Pitt Road, Orpington	400721	7.12.95
7	54321 Discos, 107 Warren Road, Bexley	300924	19.4.96
8	Dr J Crown, 20 Wimfred Street, Woolwich	-	1.1.93
9	Locke D, 22 Davis Street, Crayford	-	14.8.95
10	Sainton E, 15 Filmwell Close, Bromley	200516	3.5.96
11	Argent-Smith M, 17a Waterson Road, Bexley	-	7.8.96
12	Britton T, 81 Ward Avenue, Crayford	-	27.8.94
13	McLaughlin D, 80 Brookhill Road, Orpington	200435	4.3.94
14	Williams J A, 148 Godstow Road, Woolwich	-	6.6.96
15	O'Grady E, 40 Holborne Road, Sidcup	300989	4.4.91
16	Saint Francis Pet Shop, 14 Glenesh Road, Dartford	-	7.9.93
17	Emly P, 8 Faraday Avenue, Orpington	-	18.4.96
18	Harry Holden Ltd, 5 Clare Way, Bexley	100284	9.7.93
19	BRJ Plumbing, 132 Lodge Lane, Crayford	200223	25.11.95
20	Gisling B, 18 Dickens Avenue, Woolwich	-	6.3.96
21	Argentson S, 20 Porson Court, Dartford	400542	5.2.92
22	Kelsey L C, 58 Cudham Lane, Bromley	-	8.1.95
23	ILD Services Ltd, 4 Cobden Road, Orpington	200221	3.2.96
24	Van Saintby A, 69 Brookhill Close, Bromley	400693	5.2.96
25	Williams, John, 10 Buff Close, Dartford	-	2.12.95
26	Page W, 11 Leewood Place, Crayford	400442	9.7.93
27	Harrison P, Robinwood Drive, Dartford	101301	16.4.95
28	Briton N, 3 Chalet Close, Bexley	-	7.2.92
29	Richmond A, 9 Denham Close, Crayford	-	4.1.96
30	St Olave's Church, Church Way, Bromley	400371	21.2.95

Required

(a) Referring to the documents by number (1-30), in what order would they appear if they were filed in date order?

(b) Rearrange the names in alphabetical order, noting the reference number in brackets after the name.

(c) In what order would those correspondents with accounts appear, if they were filed in account number order?

(d) Again referring to the documents by number, identify another sensible way of classifying them, and arrange them in this order.

2.6 Indexing

Direct access filing describes a filing system in which you should be able to insert or find a document in the files simply through knowledge of the system used, without reference to a separate index: information filed alphabetically according to name, subject or geography, for example. This sort of system is also known as **self-indexing**.

Indirect access filing is where you will have to consult a **separate index** before attempting to find your file, usually because information has been given a numerical code or label and put in numerical order: how do you know what the numbers refer to?

Definition

> An **index** is something which makes it easier to locate information or records: like your index finger, it is a 'pointer' to where a particular item may be found.

Most information needs to be indexed. For example, if you have got a lot of books in your office, say 500, how would you know where to find a certain book?

If you simply numbered all the books on your shelves from 1 to 500, how would you remember what number you had given to the particular one you then wanted to take out (short of going through all the books each time to remind yourself)? You would have to write the numbers down in an **index**, together with the books' titles and authors (perhaps listed alphabetically), which would give you a sufficient idea of where to find the information you wanted.

An index may also be a **record in itself**, containing sufficient information to make further reference unnecessary. You might keep revision cards as an index to your study notes and texts; they would each contain a résumé of the topic, as well as give references to appropriate pages of your study notes and to other index cards on related topics.

2.7 Cross-referencing information

Whatever system or combination of systems is used, there will always be items of information that could be filed in **more than one place**, or will be needed in connection with **more than one enquiry**. If the problem is simply that a piece of correspondence refers to more than one matter, the solution is to place a duplicate in each of the relevant files. Other problems may be more complex.

Definition

> **Cross-referencing** is a system of referring the reader of one item of information to other related or relevant items.

EXAMPLE: CROSS-REFERENCING

Dedd Boring Ltd, a company which produces various machinery for mining operations, has over the years fulfilled several contracts for drill bits and air vents for (among other companies) mining firm Olking Coal Ltd. There has also been further correspondence with Mr U Wing, Olking's Chairman, on general matters connected with the business.

In connection with this one relationship, Dedd Boring may keep files as follows.

Index cards

(a)	Air vents (production, sales etc)	X-ref: see also file (c),(f).
(b)	Drill bits (production, sales etc)	X-ref: see also file (d),(e).
(c)	Olking Coal Ltd Air vents contract (3/X4)	X-ref: see also file (a),(d),(g).
(d)	Olking Coal Ltd Drill bits contract (8/X2)	X-ref: see also file (a),(c),(g).
(e)	Olking Coal Ltd Drill bits contract (3/X6)	X-ref: see also file (b),(g).
(f)	Wing, U - correspondence	X-ref: see also file (c),(d),(e).
(g)	Other Company Ltd Air vents contract (6/X3)	X-ref: see also file (a).

A letter from Wing about maintenance services (for which there is no subject file) would go into (f), while one about the air vents and the latest drill bit contract would be duplicated and placed in files (c) and (e). The filing clerk meanwhile discovers that there is another contract file under 'Associated Olking Coal Ltd': this is actually the registered name of the company which has always been known (and refers to itself as) Olking Coal Ltd. He simply adds the appropriate cross-reference to the index cards.

In a real system the letters (a) to (g) would of course be replaced by the appropriate code, depending on the coding system that was in use.

You can also cross-reference documents within a file.

Learn as soon as possible to ensure that documents that you generate are properly cross-referenced to each other: this is often very important in accounting work. Cross referencing within files also gives you a useful sense of the **hierarchy** of information within files and the relationship between items of information: this is very useful for keeping **computer** file systems in order.

Activity 4 **(10 minutes)**

Suppose you are working on the section of a year-end accounts file that analyses fixed assets. The file is organised alpha-numerically so that each 'subject' (fixed assets, current assets, stock and so on) has its own letter of the alphabet. The letter for fixed assets is F. Fixed assets include the broad categories of land and buildings, plant and machinery, and fixtures and fittings. How might you cross reference the various items in this file?

3 STORING DOCUMENTS SECURELY

3.1 Keeping physical documents in good condition

It is vital that material containing information is stored in an appropriate location and that its condition does not deteriorate.

Documents containing information may be classified and indexed so that they are easily accessible, but unless they can be kept in **good condition**, with **economy of storage space and cost**, they will not fulfil our requirements for an effective and efficient filing system.

Most documents containing information will have to be placed in **folders** or **binders** before they can be housed in filing cabinets or other forms of storage. **Plastic folders** or

paper envelope (manila) folders are the most common and cheapest methods. For larger volumes of information, there are **lever arch files** and **box files**. If information is to be kept for a long time but not referred to very frequently, then box files are useful. If they are to be referred to and updated more often, ring binders or lever arch files would provide security (there would be no loose bits of paper flying about) but also accessibility.

Punching holes in a document so that it can be placed in some form of ring binder also needs to be carefully done so that vital numbers or words are not affected, either by the holes themselves or because they are placed in such a way that the information is hidden in the central binding, as it were.

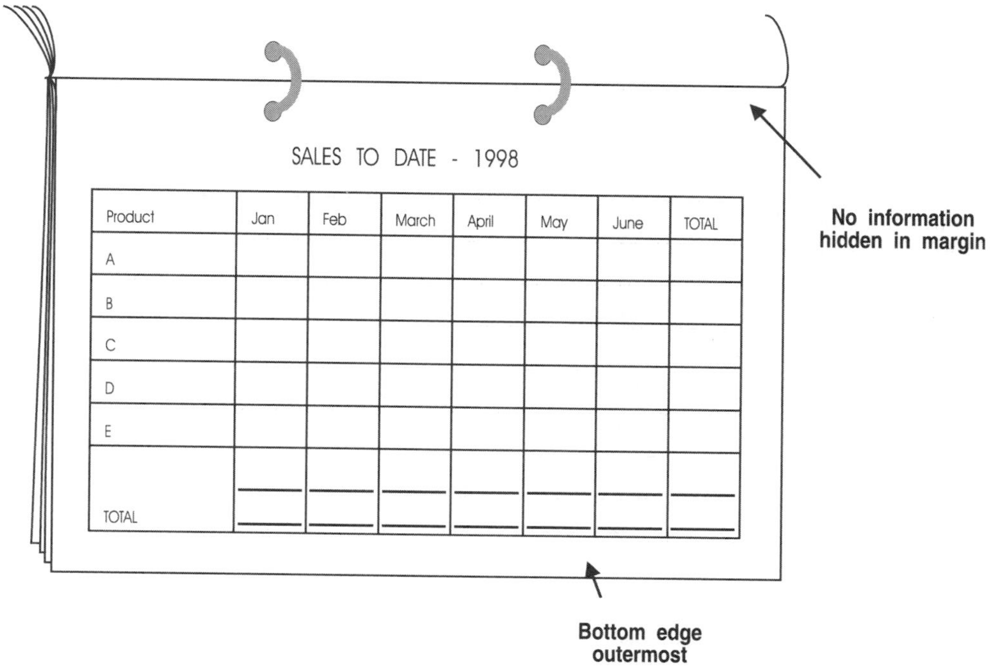

Paper can very easily get screwed up, torn, stained, or otherwise damaged. This can result in its contents becoming difficult to read or even getting lost. For example tearing off the edge of a misaligned print-out could easily result in the final column of figures being thrown away.

> **Activity 5** **(10 minutes)**
>
> Have a look around your office at work and look for examples of the different types of equipment that are used for storing and retrieving information.

3.2 Microfilm and microfiche

Microfilming is a particularly convenient means of information storage for saving space. Documents are photographed into a very much reduced ('micro') form. Microfilms are readable, but not to the unassisted naked eye, and a magnifying reading device (with a viewing screen) is needed by users. **Microfilm** is itself a **continuous strip** with images in frames along its length (like a photographic negative).

Micro film

Micro fiche

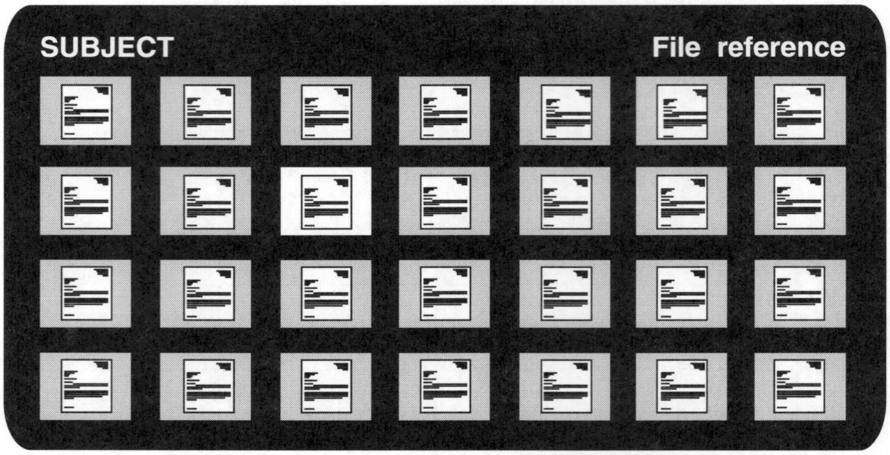

Microfiche consists of **separate sheets of film,** rather than a continuous strip. Microfiche is read by placing the fiche between two glass plates and moving a pointer (which is attached to the lens) across a grid.

Microfilm and microfiche need **special devices** in order to be read, updated or corrected. However, they do offer very space-saving, durable and secure information storage.

3.3 Document image processing (DIP)

DIP photographs documents onto a CD-ROM, and these photographs can be easily accessed.

3.4 File security and confidentiality

If files are **confidential** or **secret**, they will be '**classified**', which means that access will be limited to authorised people. A list of classified files will be required and a policy must be drawn up stipulating **conditions of access** (for example who keeps the keys to the security cabinet, and whether files may be copied or taken out of the filing room) and specifying who has clearance to consult classified material.

You may sometimes find it frustrating that you have to go through a system to get access to such files. It may be that the information that you need does not seem particularly confidential or secret to you, and it may indeed not be out of context. This is no excuse to buck the system, however. If you really think a file should be declassified, mention it to someone in authority: you may be right or, if not, you should at least receive an explanation as to why the documents are confidential.

Activity 6 **(25 minutes)**

Your manager is out of the office. He has phoned in and asked you to find a letter which is 'somewhere' on his desk and fax through a copy to him.

As you are searching for the letter you notice the following documents.

1 An electricity bill for £372.97 addressed to D Glover (your manager) at his home address.

2 A letter from a building society asking for a reference for one of your firm's clients.

3 A report entitled 'Potential Merger - Initial considerations'.

4 A mass of figures with your organisation's name at the head and the title 'Draft Budget'.

5 A staff appraisal report about you.

6 A thick sheaf of correspondence - the top sheet is signed 'Love, Nancy'.

7 A letter from P Glover asking for details about your organisation's services.

8 A *very* strongly worded letter of complaint from a Mrs Paribus.

9 A series of cuttings about your organisation from a trade journal.

10 A list of your organisation's directors with their addresses, telephone numbers and ages noted alongside.

Required

(a) Identify which, if any, of these documents you think should be filed away confidentially. Give reasons.

(b) Suppose that the letter that you had to fax was document 8 above. What would you do?

4 CREATING, UPDATING AND RETAINING FILES

4.1 Preparing documents for filing

When documents containing information have been received, acknowledged, acted upon or have otherwise fulfilled their immediate purpose, they are ready to be added to the storage system.

Procedures to be followed when adding new information to the organisation's storage system

(a) The document containing the information is **indicated as being ready for filing** - perhaps initialled by the recipient or supervisor. This is a signal to the filing clerk that it is OK to go ahead and file it.

(b) **Paper clips and binders are removed** leaving flat sheets for filing, and punched holes appropriate to the storage method are created so that documents can be inserted.

(c) Documents are placed at **random in a filing tray**, or kept in rough order in a **concertina file**.

(d) If the document is an internally generated one, it may have a **file reference** on it already (this will often be what the numbers and letters following 'Our reference ....' mean at the head of letters you receive). If not, a **reference number** will have to be determined.

(e) The **reference number**, or **name** or **subject** of the file into which the document is to be inserted should be shown on the document.

(f) Batches of documents can then be **sorted** (by each name, subject and so on) and put into the appropriate filing sequence (chronological, numerical or whatever).

(g) Documents are **inserted in the appropriate place** in appropriate files. This process should be carried out daily at a set time, to avoid pile-ups and disorganisation.

4.3 Opening a new file

If there is no file existing for a document (that is, to avoid needless duplication, if the filing clerk is sure there is no existing file), a **new file** will be opened.

(a) In a centralised filing system, a **request** and **authorisation** for a new file to be opened. This is to check for duplication or misnaming of files.

(b) **Appropriate housing** for the document - a **folder** or **binder**, noting size, colour and so on as necessary. An extra pocket may have to be inserted in sequence for suspended files.

(c) **Identification**. This will mean writing the number or name on files or suspension pockets or on a suitable tag or label. Colour coding may also be used.

(d) **Adding** the new file name/number to the index, file list, and cross-referencing system.

The procedure will be much the same as when a file cannot hold any more documents, and a **continuation file** is needed. Simply mark the cover of the original file 'Volume 1' and add the range of dates its subject matter covers. Then open a new file marked 'Volume 2'.

Activity 7 **(10 minutes)**

What matters should you take account of when you are considering opening a new file for some documents in your possession?

4.4 Retention policy

Files of data may be temporary, permanent, active, and non-active.

(a) **Master files** and **reference files** are usually **permanent**, which means that they are never thrown away or scrapped. They will be **updated** from time to time, and so the information on the file might change, but the file itself will continue to exist.

(b) A **temporary** or **transitory file** is one that is eventually scrapped. Many **transaction files** are held for a very short time, until the transaction records have been processed, but are then thrown away. Other transaction files are permanent (for example a cash book) or are held for a considerable length of time before being scrapped.

(c) An **active file** is one that is frequently used, for example, sales invoice files relating to the current financial year, or correspondence files relating to current customers and suppliers.

(d) A **non-active file** is one that is no longer used on a day-to-day basis. For example, files that contain information relating to customers and suppliers who are no longer current, and purchase invoices relating to previous financial periods. **Semi-active files** are those that contain information that is still active, but are on their way to becoming inactive, for example, as a contract nears completion, it will not be used so frequently, but should be kept on hand for reference if so needed.

When information contained within files is no longer needed on a daily basis, it is not automatically thrown away (as you may be forgiven for thinking). It is generally dealt with in one of the following ways.

(a) **Microfilmed or microfiched** (as discussed earlier) for long-term storage.

(b) Retained in its original form and stored elsewhere (this is generally known as **archiving**) for a certain period of time.

(c) **Securely destroyed**.

Imagine how distressed you would be if you needed to refer to a legal document that had been filed some years ago, and you found out that it had been thrown away by a filing clerk during the latest office spring-clean! (Alternatively, imagine trying to find an urgently needed current file, with *all* the paperwork of the organisation's history still in the active filing system!)

In order to streamline the system, information which is no longer current, but which may need to be referred to at some point in the future, should be given a revised **status**: no longer active, but semi-active; no longer semi-active, but non-active - in which case, a prime candidate for the **archive**!

Definition

> A **retention policy** sets down for how long different kinds of information are retained

Retention periods vary. Under **The Companies Acts**, documents concerned with the legal establishment of the organisation will have to be kept permanently, as will the annual accounts. Simple legal contracts will have to be kept for six years, and more important sealed ones for twelve. Other documents may be kept at the organisation's discretion but the principle overall is: if you think you might need it, for as long as you might need it - keep it!

Some recommended retention periods

Document	Years
Agreements	12
Balance sheets	30
Bank statements	6
Cheque counterfoils	1
Correspondence files	6
Credit notes	6
Customs and Excise VAT records	6
Delivery notes	1
Directors' reports	30
Expense claims	1
Insurance claims forms	6
Leases, expired	12
Licences for patents	30
Medical certificates	1
Patents, expired	12
Paying-in books	1
Powers of attorney	30
Prospectuses	30
Purchase orders	6
Quotations, out	6
Royalty ledgers	30
Sales invoices	6
Share applications	12
Specifications, product	6
Tax records	6

4.5 Deleting or destroying out-of-date information

Once information becomes **out-of-date,** it may be **deleted or destroyed**. Be aware that screwing up a piece of paper and throwing it in the bin is not destroying it. Even if information (particularly financial information) is out-of-date it may still be damaging if it falls into the wrong hands. Waste paper bins are the first place that the wrong eyes will look in!

Many organisations have **shredding devices** for such documents, or a system of disposal which involves **special confidential waste bags**. Find out what your organisation's system is and be sure to use it.

NOTES

5 RECORDING ITEM MOVEMENTS

Once you have located the information you require in the filing system, you need to **gain access** to it. Other people need to do the same - perhaps at the same time, so it is vital that when files containing information are moved, someone is keeping track of them.

5.1 Obtaining files

A typical procedure for **withdrawing a file from storage** is to fill out a **file requisition slip**.

1

To: Central Filing
Room 101

FILE REQUISITION SLIP

Please deliver the following file.

File reference: ☐☐☐ / ☐☐☐☐ / ☐☐ / ☐

Title: ....

Date required: ....

Deliver to: .... (Name)
.... (Department)
.... (Room number)

Signature: .... Date: ....

Authorisation: .... Date: ....

FILING DEPARTMENT USE

Reason for non-delivery

- ☐ File in use (see over)
- ☐ File destroyed
- ☐ Inadequate identification
- ☐ Slip not authorised
- ☐ Restricted access
- ☐ Other (see over)

This example is part 1 of a two part document – part 2 would be kept in the filing department, showing who had the file.

The system may vary in many ways. You may need to send the letter down to the filing department with a note saying 'File please', or just ring them up giving them the details and letting them do the rest. You may be able to fetch the file for yourself once you have found out the reference number. All the documents may be filed within reach in your own office. Make sure you familiarise yourself with whatever *your* system is.

5.2 Keeping track of files

When a file is taken out of storage on loan, a record must be kept identifying the **file**, the **borrower** and the **dates of borrowing** and **return**. Details can be entered in a book: loans are recorded in **chronological order**, and all in one place, so the clerk can see at a glance what files are out or overdue.

If a particular file is needed but is absent from its place, however, the whole book might have to be checked to find its whereabouts: in such cases, there is advantage in a system of **cards or slips which can be inserted in the filing system itself**, in place of the file which is absent.

In a larger filing system, the clerk may keep a series of 'out' cards with headings as follows.

File identification	*Date borrowed*	*By*	*Clerk*	*Date returned*
L 193 / x	7 / 9	E.A.M.	BL	

Any card can then be completed and inserted in place when a file is lent out.

In a smaller system, a card may be kept with each file, so that only the **borrower** and **date** need be noted: if very few people have access to files, it may be possible to have colour-coded cards for each likely borrower, which could be inserted with no further details.

If more than one person needs to use the information, a file may be passed from hand to hand without being returned to the file registry each time and the lending records will get hopelessly out of date. Files can still be kept track of, however, if the passer-on **sends a memo** or **fills in a file passing slip** to the clerk: his own name, the file name, the date and the new holder of the file are sufficient to allow the clerk to update the 'out' records.

NOTES

To: Central Filing
Room 101

FILE MOVEMENTS

File reference: ☐☐☐ / ☐☐☐☐ / ☐☐ / ☐

Title: ....

This file was passed from: | to:
Name: .... | Name: ....
Department: .... | Department: ....
Room no: .... | Room no: ....

Date: ....

If it is essential for a person to remove a document from a file, they will normally be expected to **photocopy and replace the original immediately**. If for some reason the document must be borrowed for a time, the same procedures apply as with an 'out' card. As well as borrower details, the document's identification details will be needed, including the **date, sender** and **subject of the document**. The **substitution note** is inserted into the file at the appropriate place, and should be signalled in some way, so that routine file checks will show when the file is still incomplete.

SUBSTITUTION NOTE

The following document has been
removed from the file

Document no./date: ....
Source: ....
Subject: ....

Reason for removal: ....
....

Name: ....
Date: ....

DOCUMENT REMOVED

5.3 Overdue files

Just as a public library sets a limit on the length of time you can keep a book you have borrowed (particularly if it is in high demand), so your organisation may only lend out files for a set period.

In any case, there will need to be a **follow-up system** to draw attention to files which have not been returned by the due date. Such a system may involve:

- A diary or calendar, in which due dates for the return of files are entered
- A diary file, with pockets for each day of the current month, in which pre-printed **follow-up slips** (filled in with the file and borrower details) are filed under their due date

When a file is identified as overdue, a **reminder** will be sent out, asking the borrower to return the file or to renew the lending period, if necessary.

6 COMPUTERISED SYSTEMS

Most of the principles of manual storage and retrieval of information still apply in a computerised context: it is still important to develop good habits, **to be tidy, to keep things in good condition** and so on. The computer does take some of the hard work out of such tasks, but it is also important to be careful, especially about keeping copies of your work.

We shall describe a typical PC-based system using Windows software. If the previous sentence sounds like a foreign language to you we suggest you spend half an hour or so in a High Street shop like Dixons looking at the PC displays (if any of the machines are turned on - they usually are) and perhaps getting someone to give you a demonstration of the word-processing and spreadsheet packages.

6.1 PC file organisation

In a PC system, information is organised in a clear hierarchy:

- Drives; which contain
- Directories; which contain
- Files; which contain
- Documents.

Most PCs access four 'drives'.

- The **C drive**, which contains the **non-removable hard disk**
- The **A drive**, into which **floppy disks** can be put interchangeably
- The **'D' drive** for CD-ROMs (you need special equipment to create, as opposed to see, files on a CD-ROM)
- The **'server'** where, in a network, data is held on a central server computer

Within each drive you can have as many **directories** as you need. You might have one directory for **spreadsheets** and another directory for **word-processed (WP) documents**. Within each of the WP directories you might have **sub-directories** for letters, memos and reports. You can call the directories whatever you like. With older systems the name you choose had to be no more than eight letters or digits (or a combination of letters and digits) long. This restriction does not apply with Windows 95 and subsequent Windows packages.

Your 'letters' sub-directory could be arranged into further **sub-sub-directories** for different types of correspondence. The PC itself can sort and re-sort the files within a directory or sub-directory in various ways as often as you wish, at the touch of a button.

(a) By **file name** (alphabetically or numerically)
(b) By **date created** or **last updated**
(c) By **size**

6.2 Storing data in PC files

When you open a new document 'page' in a PC system, the system will give it a working title like 'doc2.doc'. This means, quite simply, 'document number two', the second document that you have created during that working session. The three letters after the full stop are to tell the computer what type of document the file is: in this case, a word-processing document created with Microsoft Word software. Depending on the package you are using, a spreadsheet might have a three letter extension like 'xls' or 'wk4'. A diagram would have a different three letter extension again.

Names like doc2 are fine if you only have three or four files in total, but once it starts to grow, your collection of files will quickly become unmanageable unless you have a clearer method of identifying the specific file that you want. In the system we are describing the first part of the file name, before the full stop, can have up to eight letters or eight digits, or a combination of the two. In modern systems, the eight digit limit no longer applies, and a file can have a longer name.

You should follow the system of file-naming prescribed by your organisation if there is one. If not, try to give the file a name that would enable someone else to find it quickly, say, when you are on holiday.

Information can also be recorded on **back-up files**.

(a) Such files are very important, since if the files held on the PC are stolen or damaged in any way, the information contained in them will not be lost. It is usual to store back-up files in secure places, such as fire-proof safes.

(b) For this reason it is good practice to store work files, not on your PC's 'C' drive but on the server as this is likely to have backup copies taken daily.

6.3 Moving PC files

Like physical documents, electronic files can be moved or copied to other people and locations. However, this is a much quicker, easier and more efficient process on computer: copies can be made instantly and sent almost instantly to locations on the other side of the world (if necessary).

(a) A file can be **saved onto a floppy disk** and sent to the other user for insertion into his or her PC: the file can then be opened and/or saved onto his or her PC and used as required. **Beware viruses.**

(b) A file can be **'attached' to an e-mail message** and sent to the other user's inbox. He or she can download, open, save and use the file. This is a very efficient (although not yet entirely secure) way of sending files around the world. **Beware viruses.**

(c) PCs linked to each other in a **network** may be able to access the same files, whether they are stored **centrally on a server** or possibly on local PCs.

Like physical documents, electronic files should be clearly marked if they are:

- Classified for limited access
- 'Read only': that is, the data must not be changed by multiple users, to avoid confusion.

Electronic files can be 'locked' appropriately and access denied to users who do not have the password clearance, or who try to alter data on a 'read only' file.

Difficulties still exist where multiple copies of a file have been circulated and updated or amended by different users. Moved files should be saved under different names, so that the source file can be identified: even so, it may be difficult to keep track of exactly which version now has the most up-to-date information - or which copies have the most up-to-date version of any given item of information!

This problem is resolved by organising data in a **database**, as discussed below.

6.4 Deleting PC files

It is very easy to delete files from a disk or to write over files that you meant to save in their existing form. Most systems will ask you to **confirm** that you want to delete a file if you give the computer this instruction. If you have any doubt say no. If you want to free up space on your hard drive, **copy anything that you intend to delete onto a floppy disk** first, just in case you need it again later.

We shall not go into any further detail, partly because you really need to know more about computers first, but mainly because you should learn your organisation's own system. We are restricted here by the need to generalise.

However, as with manual filing systems, the golden rule is to get into good habits early on. Set some time aside to organise the files that you have created on disk each day. This is called '**housekeeping**'.

Activity 8 **(10 minutes)**

Identify the software used in your college or workplace.

(a) What procedures are followed for naming files?

(b) What procedures are in place for storing files (eg on tape or floppy disk, with daily backups)?

(c) How do you retrieve a file that is no longer stored on hard disk on one of your organisation's computers?

You will find it instructive to compare notes with colleagues or classmates who use different systems, or different procedures on the same system.

6.5 Databases

Definition

A **database** is a comprehensive, structured collection or file of data which can be accessed by different users for different applications.

In theory, a database is simply a coherent structure for the storage and use of data. It involves the centralised storage of information, which provides:

- **Common data** for all users to share
- Avoidance of **data duplication** in files kept by different users
- **Consistency** in the organisation's use of data, and in the accuracy and up-to dateness of data accessed by different users, because all records are centrally maintained and updated
- **Flexibility** in the way in which shared data can be queried, analysed and formatted by individual users for specific purposes, without altering the store of data itself

Such a structure could be fulfilled by a centralised file registry or library, or a self-contained data record like a master index card file. In practice, however, large scale databases are created and stored on *computer* systems, using **database application packages**, such as Microsoft Access.

6.6 Data storage

Computer database packages allow data to be stored in a coherent structure, in one place.

(a) **Data** are the raw components of information: names, dates, item descriptions, prices, colours, addresses and so on.

(b) **Fields** are the labels given to types of data. (the user-friendly manual, Access for Dummies refers to them as '*places for your data to live*'.) A customer database, for example, might include fields such as: title (data = Mr), first name (data = Joseph), last name (data = Bloggs), Company (data = Anon Ltd), Address, Phone Number, Fax Number, Contact Type (data = customer), interests (data = widgets) and so on.

(c) **Records** are the collections of fields relevant to one entry. ('Access for Dummies' suggests '*all the homes on one block*'.) So all the above data fields for a particular customer (Mr Bloggs) make up one customer record.

(d) **Tables** (or database files) are collections of records that describe similar data. ('*...all the blocks in one neighbourhood*'.) All the customer records for a particular region or product may be stored in such a file.

(e) **Databases** (or catalogues) are collections of all the tables (and other formats which can be created from them) relating to a particular set of information. ('*A community of neighbourhoods*'.) So your customer database may include tables for various regions' customers, product customers, customer contacts and so on, plus various reports and queries that you use to access different types of information.

There are two basic kinds of database.

(a) A **flat file** system lumps all the data into single table databases, like a phone directory where names, addresses, phone numbers and fax numbers are stored in the same file.

(b) A **relational database system** allows greater flexibility and storage efficiency by splitting the data up into a number of tables, which can nevertheless be linked and integrated together. For example, one table may contain customer names and addresses/contact details, while others track sales transactions by outlet or product, and another, customers' payment histories.

Flat systems are easy to build and maintain, and are quite adequate for applications such as mailing lists, or membership databases. **Relational systems** integrate a wider range of business functions, for invoicing, accounting, inventory, marketing analysis and so on: they are, however, complicated to develop and use.

6.7 Data manipulation

Basic features of database packages allow you to do these tasks.

(a) **Find particular records**, using any data item you know.

(b) **Sort records alphabetically**, numerically or by date, in ascending or descending order.

(c) **Filter records**, so that you 'pull out' and view a selection of records based on specified criteria (all addresses in a certain postcode, for example, or all purchasers of a particular product).

(d) **Interrogate records**, generating the selection of records based on a complex set of criteria, from one or more linked tables. (For example, you might specify that you want all customer records where the field 'City' equals 'London' or 'Birmingham' AND where the field 'Product' equals 'Widget' AND where the field 'Purchase Date' is between 'Jan 99' and 'Jan 00'. The query would generate a table consisting of customers in London and Birmingham who purchased Widgets in 1999.)

(e) **Calculate and count** data entries. (For example, if you wanted to find out how many customers had purchased each product, you could run a query that asked the database to *group* the data by the field 'Product' and then *count* by field 'Customer ID' or 'Last Name': it would count the number of customer ID numbers or names linked to each product. You could also ask to 'sum' or add up all the values in a field: total number of purchases, or total purchase value.)

(f) **Format** selected data for a variety of uses, such as reports, forms, mailing labels, charts diagrams and so on.

If you are working with a database, it will probably be one that has already been created for you, using a particular software package. It is up to you to get to know how to use it, what the protocols are, and how your organisation wants its data structured and formatted.

If you want to know more, talk to IT experts in your organisation, or borrow the handbook to one of the popular database packages.

Activity 9 **(30 minutes)**

Find out what type(s) of database your organisation (or college) uses, and for what applications. If possible, get access to the database and browse through the index, directory or switchboard to see what databases/catalogues contain what database files or tables, queries, reports and forms, with what fields. If you can't get access to a database at work, try the local library, where you may find that the 'index card' system has been computerised as a database. Or use an Internet search engine or browser to interrogate some on-line databases. This is not really something you can learn from books - have a go!

7 MANAGEMENT INFORMATION SYSTEMS

Core unit 7 of the HNC/HND qualification is devoted to Management Information Systems, and you should refer to that Course Book.

8 LEGISLATION

The storage and use of information is governed quite stringently by certain pieces of legislation. The most important aspects, data protection and copyright, are considered here.

9 DATA PROTECTION

9.1 General confidentiality

Information flows through the organisation - but to **whom**, precisely, should it flow? In deciding who is an '**appropriate person**' to receive any given piece of information, you will need to consider the following matters.

Matter to consider	Reason
Who has asked for it, and what their **authority** within the organisation is	If your supervisor asks for information, you will need a good reason *not* to give it to her - such as it being marked 'strictly private' or 'for the Managing Director's eyes only'. If the receptionist asks for information, you will want to consider whether it is relevant to his area of authority: say, affecting security or customer service procedures.
Whether the information is classified in any way	'Sensitive' information will often be clearly identified as being 'confidential' or 'private' or 'limited access' or 'for authorised individuals only'. (If you ever come across such files, take the opportunity to practise working out who the authorised recipients of the information would be.)
Whether the information is personal and private	Sharing it would infringe someone else's privacy (or your own).
Whether the information could be used for purposes detrimental to the organisation's business or personnel	We've already mentioned (in Chapter 4) the need not to disclose security procedures, legal dealings and new product plans, for example, but you might like to think about other categories of information that could be detrimental.

There may be established guidelines on any or all of the above in your organisation: now is the time to check! **Organisational policy** must be followed in this area.

NOTES

Activity 10 **(15 minutes)**

Would you give the following items of information to the following people, if asked to do so? (Briefly explain why you would or would not, or what you would do.)

(a) The company's security guard asks for details of the visitors expected by your department that week.

(b) The company's security guard (a 'casual' worker, whom you do not know) asks for the home addresses of several people in your department.

(c) The Human Resources Manager asks you for details of how many (a) sick days, (b) absences and (c) late arrivals have occurred in your department in the last month.

(d) Your supervisor asks you for details of the latest Research and Development expenditure on new products.

(e) A caller, saying she is a financial journalist, asks you for details of the latest Research and Development expenditure on new products.

(f) A trade union representative asks you for any projections on staff numbers for the following year, with particular reference to any changes in labour requirements.

9.2 The Data Protection Acts 1984 and 1998

Especially with the advent of computer records systems, fears have arisen with regard to:

- Access to personal information by unauthorised parties
- The likelihood that an individual could be harmed by the existence of computerised data about him or her which was inaccurate or misleading, and which could be transferred to unauthorised third parties at high speed and little cost
- The possibility that personal information could be used for purposes other than those for which it was requested and disclosed.

The Data Protection Acts 1984 and 1998 address these concerns.

The Acts are an attempt to afford some measure of protection to the individual. They cover data about **individuals** – not corporate bodies – and data which are processed **mechanically** (which includes any 'equipment operated automatically in response to the instructions given for that purpose', not just computers).

Definitions

Personal data are information about a living individual, including facts and expressions of opinion about him or her. Data about other organisations are not personal, unless they contain data about their members. The individual must be identifiable from the data, whether by name, or by code number (say, an employment number).

Data users are organisations or individuals who control the contents of files of personal data and the use of personal data which are processed (or intended to be processed) automatically.

Data users and computer bureaux have to register with the Data Protection Registrar. Data users must limit the use of personal data to the uses which are registered, and must abide by Data Protection Principles (discussed below).

The Acts establish the following rights for data subjects.

(a) A data subject may seek compensation through the courts for damage and any associated distress caused by:

(i) the loss, destruction or unauthorised disclosure of data about himself or herself; or by

(ii) inaccurate data about himself or herself.

(b) A data subject may apply to the courts or to the Registrar for inaccurate data to be put right or even wiped off the file.

(c) A data subject may obtain access to personal data of which he or she is the subject.

Data Protection Principles

Personal data held by data users

(1) The information to be contained in personal data shall be obtained, and personal data shall be processed, fairly and lawfully. Processing means amending, adding to, deleting or rearranging the data, or extracting the information that forms the data (eg printing out).

(2) Personal data shall be held only for one or more specified (registered) and lawful purposes.

(3) Personal data held for any purpose or purposes shall not be used or disclosed in any manner incompatible with that purpose or those purposes.

(4) Personal data held for any purpose or purposes shall be adequate, relevant and not excessive in relation to that purpose or those purposes.

(5) Personal data shall be accurate and, where necessary, kept up to date. 'Accurate' means correct and not misleading as to any matter of *fact*. An *opinion* cannot be challenged on the grounds of inaccuracy and breach of the fifth DP Principle.

(6) Personal data held for any purpose or purposes shall not be kept for longer than is necessary for that purpose or those purposes. Data users should therefore review their personal data regularly, and delete any data which no longer serve a purpose.

(7) An individual shall be entitled:

(a) at reasonable intervals, and without undue delay or expense:

(i) to be informed by any data user whether he/she holds personal data of which that individual is the subject; and

(ii) to have access to any such data held by a data user; and

(b) where appropriate, to have such data corrected or erased.

Personal data held by data users or in respect of which services are provided by persons carrying on computer bureaux

(8) Appropriate security measures shall be taken against unauthorised access to, or alteration, disclosure or destruction of, personal data and against accidental loss or destruction of personal data. The prime responsibility for creating and putting into practice a security policy rests with the data user.

9.3 Exemption from the Acts

There are some important **exemptions** from the Acts.

(a) **Unconditional exemptions**: personal data which are essential to national security, required to be made public by law, or concerned only with the data user's personal, family or household affairs;

(b) **Conditional exemptions**, including:

(i) personal data held for payroll and pensions;

(ii) data held by unincorporated members' clubs, relating only to club members; and

(iii) data held only for distribution of articles or information to the data subjects (say, for mailshot advertising) and consisting only of their names and addresses or other particulars necessary for the distribution.

(c) **Exemptions from the 'subject access' provisions only**, including: data held for the prevention or detection of crime, or assessment or collection of tax; data to which legal professional privilege could be claimed (for example, that held by a solicitor); data held solely for statistical or research purposes.

(d) A **special exemption for word processing operations** performed only for the purpose of preparing the text of documents. If a manager writes reports on his employees for disclosure to third parties using his computer as a word processor, he will not as a result become a data user. If, however, he intends to use the stored data as a source of information about the individual and can extract the information automatically, he must register as a data user.

9.4 Data Protection Co-ordinator

The organisation will need to appoint a Data Protection Co-ordinator. He/she will arrange registration and set up systems: to monitor compliance with the Principles; meet subject access requirements; and alert him/her to any changes in the organisation which may require amendment in the registered entry. The entry should be amended whenever there is a change in the nature or purpose of data being held and used. The organisation's staff should be informed of the Acts' implications and their rights as data subjects, as well as their duties as data users (if they work with computers).

Activity 11 **(15 minutes)**

Are the following examples permissible under the Acts, or not?

(a) You demand your right to access any personal data held by the Inland Revenue on your tax affairs.

(b) Your personnel file contains an appraisal report by your supervisor which states: 'In my opinion, [your name] appears to display a negative attitude towards supervision, which may account for recent disciplinary proceedings?' You do not, in fact, have a negative attitude towards supervision: the disciplinary proceedings were caused by factors outside your control. You demand compensation for loss caused to you (since you were not promoted, as expected, following appraisal) as a result of this inaccurate data.

(c) You discover that your employee record contains a mention of a conviction for drink-driving – which you have never had. You had wondered why you were always refused access to the 'pool' car at work. You claim compensation for the loss caused as a result of this inaccurate data, and ask for it to be wiped from the file.

(d) The Accounts Manager has compiled a recruitment file on a candidate for the position of his assistant. He hired a private investigation agency to search her home, access her bank records and tap her phone (all without her knowledge) in an effort to vet her character and circumstances, in the interest of the firm's security. The report is held on your database.

9.5 The Criminal Justice and Public Order Act 1994

This Act created new offences in the field of data protection by amending Section 5 of the Data Protection Act 1984. The new offences created were:

- Procuring the disclosure of computer-held information
- Selling computer-held information
- Offering to sell computer-held information.

This is relevant to accounts, because personal financial/taxation information could be quite valuable to other organisations for the purposes of credit control, product marketing and so on.

10 COPYRIGHT

10.1 What is copyright law?

Copyright law is a highly specialised subject. In this section we shall therefore have a brief look at those parts which are of general interest, and any parts which could be considered useful knowledge in your day-to-day office work.

Definition

The basic idea of **copyright** is that **the individual has an exclusive right to use his own work, and also has a right to stop others from exploiting that work.**

The Copyright, Designs and Patents Act 1988 covers the following types of 'work'.

- Original 'literary' works, which means books of all kinds (including this one that you are reading at the moment), short stories, poems, words of songs, articles and letters
- Dramatic works (plays, operas, etc)
- Musical works
- Artistic works such as paintings, drawings, photographs, pottery
- Sound recordings, films, broadcasts and cable programmes
- Computer programs

Copyright generally applies for a period of **70 years**.

Copyright protection covers the form of an idea, not the idea itself. For example, if you go on a course and pick up some new ideas from the lecturer about organising yourself at work, the lecturer cannot sue you for repeating those ideas to your colleagues. However, if the lecturer writes his/her ideas down in a book, the written version is protected by copyright and cannot be copied without his/her permission.

There is no need to register copyright with any third party agency (unlike patents). Where there is a strong likelihood that other people will try to exploit your work it is usual to mark it with the **international copyright symbol** © (see page (ii) of this book). This symbol warns other people that you are aware of your rights, that you will seek to protect them and that your permission is required for any commercial use of your work.

10.2 Photocopying

You can normally photocopy a few pages of someone else's work for **research** (either commercial or non-commercial) or **private study**. This is subject to the notion of '**fair dealing**'. It is not considered fair, for example, to make a copy of a *whole* book, or to copy extracts from a book to circulate to every member of a class of pupils. The use of photocopying for educational purposes is limited to 1% of a work in every three months, unless a licensing agreement has been entered into.

The author of this book, for example, photocopied a few pages of her colleague's copy of Kluwer's *Business Law Handbook* as an information source for this section. This was not an infringement of copyright because it was done for the purpose of commercial research.

10.3 Letters and other works written by you

If you write a **private** letter, you own the copyright in it. The person you send the letter to is not entitled to publish it without your permission (unless you write to somebody that normally publishes reader's letters, like a newspaper).

If you write a letter, a memo, a report or whatever in the course of your job you have created the letter for your employer, and **your employer owns the copyright**. The same applies to anything else you produce at work, unless you have an agreement to the contrary.

Chapter roundup

- A **file** is a collection of data records with similar characteristics.
- Characteristics of a '**good**' filing system are as follows.
  - It should contain all the information you may need
  - The information should be found easily
  - It should be of a convenient size
  - It should be capable of expansion
  - It should be easily accessible
  - It should be stored under suitable conditions so that it won't get damaged or lose its information
- An **index** is something which makes it easier to locate information or records.
- **Cross-referencing** information is commonly carried out when items of information could be filed in more than one place, or could be needed in connection with more than one enquiry.
- The three main systems for **classifying information** are **alphabetical**, **numerical** and **alpha-numerical**.
- **Adding new information** to an information storage system involves the following.
  - Indicating that the information is ready for filing
  - Removing any paperclips or binders
  - Placing information in a filing tray or concertina file
  - Allocating a reference number if there is not already a file reference
  - Sorting batches of documents containing information
  - Inserting the documents into the appropriate place in appropriate files
- Information is usually **destroyed** by using shredding devices or by placing in confidential wastebags.
- In general, when information is no longer needed on a daily basis, it is retained in its original form and stored elsewhere; this is known as **archiving**.
- A **retention policy** is the amount of time decided on by an organisation for the holding of various types of information.
- Most of the principles of manual storage information systems also apply in **computerised systems**.
- A database is a comprehensive, structured collection of data which can be accessed by different users for different applications.
- Information flow in an organisation includes:
  - Records of past and current transactions
  - Information about past trends and current operations
  - Routine transaction information
  - Information about performance/results

Chapter roundup (cont'd)

- Three basic types of documentation to be handled include:
  - Incoming correspondence
  - Outgoing correspondence
  - Financial records
- Care must be taken to ensure the confidentiality and security of information, and compliance with the Data Protection Acts and Criminal Justice and Public Order Act.
- Copyright law protects the rights of ownership of authors/creators of literary and dramatic works, musical and artistic works, broadcasts and computer programmes. There are constraints on what material can legally be reproduced without permission.

Quick quiz

1. What is a file?
2. List four systems used for arranging files.
3. How is information that is no longer needed on a regular basis dealt with?
4. What are classified files?
5. In organisations where there are a large number of files, how are file movements monitored and recorded correctly?
6. Why is it necessary to store back-up files?
7. What is the hierarchy of information in a database?
8. What external agencies are entitled to information from the organisation?
9. What should you consider when deciding whether it is appropriate to pass on information?
10. What rights do data subjects have under the Data Protection Act 1984?
11. What is the copyright symbol, and what warning does it carry?

Answers to quick quiz

1. A collection of data records with similar characteristics. (See para 1.3)
2. Alphabetical order, numerical order, alpha-numerical, chronological order. (See para 2.2)
3. - Microfilmed or microfiched
   - Archived
   - Destroyed. (See paras 3.2 and 4.4)
4. Confidential or secret. (See para 3.4)
5. The use of out cards which record the file reference, the date file was borrowed, who borrowed it, the name of the clerk who released the file and the date that the file was returned. (See para 5.2)
6. Information is stored in computer files, and if the computer is destroyed or stolen, the information is lost. It is therefore necessary to record this information on back-up files and to store such files in a secure place. (See para 6.2)

NOTES

7 Databases contain tables, which contain records, which contain fields, which contain data. (See para 6.6)

8 Other parties to transactions; parties interested in the financial performance of the organisation; outside agencies requiring information for their own activities; regulatory bodies. (See para 9.3)

9 Their authority to ask for and receive it; the classification or confidentiality of the information; the privacy of the subject of the information; the interests of the organisation's business and personnel. (See para 9.1)

10 Right to compensation for damages and distress caused by loss or inaccurate data; right to have inaccurate data corrected or removed; access to personal data. (See para 9.2)

11 ©. You are aware of your rights and will seek to protect them, and your permission must be sought for any commercial use of your work. (See para 10.1)

Answers to activities

1 Here are just a few of the items that might cross your desk

- Letters, memos, telegrams, telexes, emails.
- Notes of phone calls and meetings.
- Reports.
- Advertising material and press cuttings.
- Mailing lists.
- Important/routine addresses and phone numbers.
- Machinery documents such as guarantees or service logs.
- Legal documents such as contracts, property deeds or insurance policies.

2 You should have noted the following details.

Our (Lightfoot & Co's) reference:	Z/0335/MJD
Department:	Purchasing
Supplier name:	Sandimans Ltd
Previous correspondence:	11 April 2001
Recent correspondence:	4 May 2001
Subject:	Stationery (invoice 147829)

It is most unlikely that details like the geographical source of the letter or the name of its writer would be needed for filing purposes.

The accounts department should be sent a copy so that they can chase up the cheque that has not been received.

3 (a) The order would be: 15, 21, 28, 2, 8, 1, 18 and 26, 16, 13, 3, 12, 22, 30, 27, 4, 5, 9, 19, 25, 6, 29, 23, 24, 20, 17, 7, 10, 14, 11.

A good approach would have been to highlight all the documents of the same year in the same colour, thereby breaking down the task into more manageable portions.

(b) 54321 Discos (7)
Argent-Smith M (11)
Argentson S (21)
Bexley J (5)
Bidwell D (4)
Briton N (28)
Britton T (12)

BRJ Plumbing (19)
Cottrell J (1)
Crown Dr J (8)
Emly P (17)
Gisling B (20)
Harrison P (27)
Harry Holden Ltd (18)
Holden R (2)
ILD Services Ltd (23)
Kelsey L C (22)
Locke D (9)
McLaughlin D (13)
Maclean T (6)
O'Grady E (15)
Page W (26)
Richmond A (29)
Saint Francis Pet Shop (16)
Sainton E (10)
St Olave's Church (30)
Van Saintby A (24)
Williams J (3)
Williams J A (14)
Williams John (25)

(**Note**. Slight variations are possible, for example with the treatment of numbers and initials, depending upon the policy of the organisation.)

(c) The order would be: 3, 18, 27, 23, 19, 13, 10, 7, 15, 30, 26, 5, 21, 24, 6.

(d) Geographical classification by towns gives the following results.

Bexley:	2, 7, 11, 18, 28
Bromley:	1, 10, 22, 24, 30
Crayford:	9, 12, 19, 26, 29
Dartford:	3, 4, 16, 21, 25, 27
Orpington:	5, 6, 13, 17, 23
Sidcup:	15
Woolwich:	8, 14, 20

4 At the front of section F you could have a document F1 that summarises fixed assets by broad category - land and buildings, plant and machinery, fixtures and fittings, say. Each figure on this front sheet could then be cross-referenced to a later sheet that contained a more detailed breakdown of how the figure was made up: F2 for land and buildings, say, F3 for plant and machinery, F4 for fixtures and fittings. Figures on the sheet numbered F2 might be broken down further on other sheets numbered F2(a) or F2(1) and so on.

5 You were asked for relevant examples from your own workplace. Consider in-trays and pigeon-holes, computers, message boards etc as well as various forms of filing boxes, cabinets etc.

6 (a) There is room for some flexibility in answers here - what follows is very much a suggestion.

1 The bill is not confidential if Mr Glover chooses not to keep it so. It is nothing to do with your organisation anyway.

2 Not confidential. The reference that was given might be, but this is not mentioned.

3 This is probably very confidential: public knowledge of merger proposals could affect the outcome of the negotiations.

4 This may or may not be confidential depending upon your own organisation's policy. The general view is that budgeting should be done with the involvement of staff, so we are inclined to say that this is not, on the face of it, a confidential document.

5 This is obviously a highly personal document: it should be filed away in your personnel file.

6 This is probably not confidential. The familiarity of the signature is most likely to be due to the length of time your manager and 'Nancy' have been dealing with each other. If not, your manager is not ashamed of it and what business is it of yours anyway?

7 There is nothing confidential about this: the surname is irrelevant.

8 Mrs Paribus's letter is probably not particularly confidential although the nature of her complaint might make it so. To preserve the reputation of your organisation it might be better to shut it away in a file to stop cleaners, caterers or other external parties reading it.

9 This material is published: it is clearly not confidential.

10 There is no reason why personal details of directors should be confidential. If the list or an item on it had a heading or note such as 'Do not disclose to anyone below the level of Senior Manager', however, your manager should be ensuring that it does not fall into the wrong hands.

To summarise, documents 3 and 5 are definitely confidential, and documents 2, 7 and 9 are definitely not. The remainder may or may not be confidential depending on the circumstances, and whose point of view you are considering the matter from.

(b) The danger here is that your fax will be collected by someone other than your manager. Its contents seem as if they might be damaging to your organisation in the wrong hands. You should therefore ring your manager and discuss the problem with him. The best solution is probably for him to stand over the receiving fax machine until your fax is received.

7 A good deal of thought needs to go into the opening of new files.

(a) Is there already a file for this purpose?

(b) What other files are related to this purpose? In other words, what cross-referencing needs to be done?

(c) Are the documents to be filed of an unusual size or material, requiring special storage facilities?

(d) Are the documents confidential?

(e) Will the documents be needed by you frequently, so that a personal or departmental file would be more appropriate than a central one?

(f) What title should be given to the file to make it clear to all potential users what it contains?

(g) How should documents be arranged within the file?

You may have thought of other points in addition to the above. Point (a) is the most important.

8 & 9 You were asked to explore your *own* most relevant computerised filing system and database.

10 (a) Yes: this is information necessary to the security of the premises (although the 'details' given would not include personal information).

(b) No: home addresses might be used for purposes detrimental to the employees (for example, robbery or kidnap), especially since the guard is a casual and unknown worker. If he persists in his enquiry, it may be advisable to report the matter.

(c) Yes: this is a legitimate request backed by organisational authority. (Note that you were asked for numbers, not personal details, so you need have no doubts about privacy or 'whistleblowing' on absentee colleagues.)

(d) Yes: this is another legitimate request from someone in a position of authority (provided that the R&D information was not flagged as 'classified', in which case authorisation may be required).

(e) No: this is likely to be sensitive information integral to the organisation's competitive advantage. Even if the caller *is* a journalist (and you have no way of knowing: she may be a competitor's R&D manager ...), she has no right to this information, and should be politely refused.

(f) No: although trade unions will have to be informed in due course of proposed changes which affect their members' employment, it is not up to individual (junior) members of the organisation to precipitate this process! This is another type of information that may be detrimental to the organisation (its bargaining position in regard to redundancies, for instance).

11 (a) No: this is an exemption from the 'subject access' provisions.
(b) No: an opinion cannot be challenged on these grounds.
(c) Yes: this is your right.
(d) No: data must be obtained 'fairly and lawfully'.

Chapter 15 :
DISSEMINATION OF INFORMATION

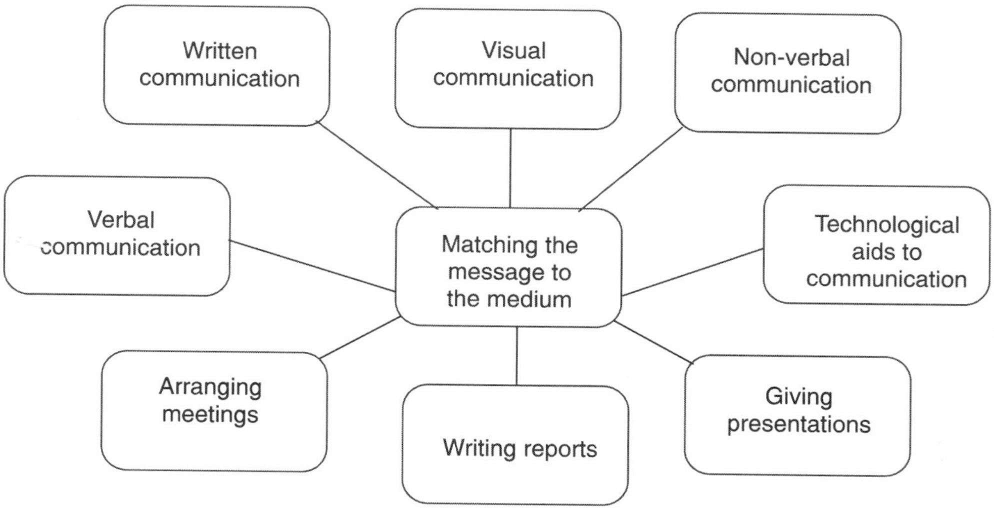

Introduction

There are generally accepted to be four main media of communication:

(a) Oral/verbal
(b) Written
(c) Visual
(d) Non verbal

We shall consider each of these in turn, highlighting the advantages, disadvantages, skills required and any environmental factors which may have an impact on their effectiveness.

Your objectives

In this chapter you will learn about the following.

(a) The various communication media

(b) Selection of appropriate media according to the purpose of communication

(c) How to produce an example of effective written communication

(d) Arranging a meeting

(e) Making a presentation

(f) Appreciate the impact of technology on communication, both generally and within organisations

1 VERBAL COMMUNICATION

Verbal communication can be face-to-face or long-distance. Long-distance communication through such technological media as the telephone is considered later. In this section we shall consider only face-to-face verbal communication.

1.1 Advantages

Verbal communication has the following advantages.

(a) **Speed**. Verbal communication can be the fastest way to impart information.

(b) **Clarity**. Verbally it is a simple task to ask for clarification, to ensure understanding of the message being transmitted. Even if clarification is not asked for, the communicator can receive the most instantaneous feedback.

(c) **Flexibility**. New information can be quickly assimilated and used as part of communication. For example, what began as an enquiry regarding lateness may become a reprimand when the manager hears the response to their enquiry.

(d) **Sensitivity**. Delicate or personal matters can be dealt with more empathy and responsiveness verbally than with any other communication media.

(e) **Interactivity**. When carried out face-to-face, verbal communication can be supplemented by non-verbal cues. The reinforcement or denigration of the verbal message by these cues enables the sensitivity, flexibility and clarity of the communication can be heightened.

1.2 Disadvantages

Verbal communication has the following disadvantages.

(a) **Articulation** Verbal communication requires both participants to be articulate. They also need to share the same language or have an interpreter present. Whilst the problems associated with sharing the same language may be the most obvious problems, problems of pronunciation, dialect and use of jargon can be just as destructive to effective communications.

(b) **Speed** We have already stated that speed is an advantage; however, it can also be a distinct disadvantage. Little time is available for planning the form the message will take.

(c) **Reliability** Although in law verbal contracts may be valid, the maxim that 'verbal contracts are not worth the paper they are written on' carries some merit. Certain circumstances dictate that verbal communication is not the most effective medium.

(d) **Logistics** it would be difficult, if not impossible for all the fans at a premier league football match to hold a conversation. Similarly, if information is to be passed by word of mouth through a large number of people the message tends to get changed (as anyone who plays Chinese whispers will know). The following example, allegedly from the first World War, illustrates this point.

EXAMPLE: DISADVANTAGES OF VERBAL COMMUNICATION

The soldiers at the front line needed to get a message to the company commander; the only means available was word of mouth. The message was passed from man to man in the trenches across a long distance. It finally reached the company commander, who was baffled by the request: 'Send three and fourpence, we're going to a dance'. So bemused was he, that he mounted his horse and set off find the source of the message. On arriving at the front line, he was greeted by the sergeant with 'Are you the only one, Sir?'. 'Only one of what?' he replied. The sergeant shook his head in disbelief. 'We asked for reinforcements, we're going to advance'.

Activity 1 **(30 minutes)**

You are negotiating with a supplier to overcome quality problems you have had with a product. Taking into consideration the advantages and disadvantages of verbal communication and the elements that make up the process of communication, write a short scenario to show how the proceedings may evolve.

Now identify the one component (which has not yet been mentioned) that is likely to increase the chances of your negotiations reaching a successful outcome.

(Tip: think though the scenario, focusing on what each person does at each stage).

1.3 Skills required

Listening

The **key skill** required for verbal communication is that of listening. It is commonly believed that listening is an innate skill; however the importance it holds for effective verbal communication means that its development merits special attention. Effective listening helps to avoid many of the disadvantages of verbal communication.

(a) Concentrating on listening focuses the attention and reduces the effect of noise.

(b) Effective listening facilitates clarity of understanding

(c) Effective listening encourages feedback.

Articulation

As we have already stated, verbal communication requires both participants to be articulate and to share the same language or have an interpreter present.

1.4 Environmental factors

Culture

In the modern business world, language and culture are important factors. Language can be aided by use of interpreters, but culture must be understood if effective communications are to take place.

EXAMPLE: VERBAL COMMUNICATION AND CULTURE

The Japanese have strict cultural and social rules regarding the nature of verbal exchanges. Failure to adhere to any of these may prevent the knowledge being imparted from being considered seriously, in the light of what may be seen by the Japanese as ineptitude at social skills.

The behaviour of women in business is of particular relevance to Japan, as their social standing is not considered to be equal to that of men. Aggressive negotiating will therefore not be taken seriously if it comes from a woman.

Activity 2 **(15 minutes)**

You wish to pass on some highly sensitive information to your Managing Director. His secretary gives you five alternative times when you might catch him. Rate these possible meetings in order of preference, using your knowledge of the communication process and the advantages and disadvantages of verbal communications as the basis for your choice. Give reasons for each of your ratings.

Option	Meeting	Rating	Reasons
1	5pm Friday – en route to his car		
2	11 am Saturday – on the golf course		
3	3.30pm Thursday – in his office (10 minute appointment)		
4	10am Monday – at the office meeting		
5	8pm Friday at the company Christmas dinner		

Verbal communications are used both formally and informally in organisations. They take the form of meetings, briefings and the 'grapevine'.

If we wish to refer back to what we have said, we must create some record of it. The written word is the most common medium for doing this.

2 WRITTEN COMMUNICATION

Within organisations great emphasis is placed upon written communications. This medium is used for recording information for future use, eliciting information from others, enabling more than one person to do a job by having 'silent' communications and 'talking' to others, on paper (letters and memo).

NOTES

2.1 Advantages

Written communication has the following advantages:

(a) It is a **lasting record of the communication**. The permanence of the information given in writing allows it to be referred to at a later date (does not make sense)

(b) **Clarity**. There is a general belief that written information prevents ambiguity.

2.2 Disadvantages

(a) **Loss or damage.** Documents can go astray or be mislaid; documents produced on a computer must be 'backed up' to prevent loss if the system fails.

(b) **Ambiguity.** The written word, if not produced with care, can still be ambiguous. For important documents, such as reports or contracts, specific training should be undertaken to improve skills.

(c) **Time.** Documents take time to prepare and pass onto the intended recipient. This problem is being addressed in some measure by the new technology which we shall consider later.

2.3 Skills required

Writing

This may seem an obvious requirement for written communications, but it would be wrong to assume that if an individual can write, they can communicate effectively in writing. Different written skills are required for differing types of communications.

Activity 3 **(45 minutes)**

Prepare a short piece of written work (no more than 200 words) for an employment agency, using the title 'My ideal job'.

Now re-write the piece as if you were telling a friend about the kind of job you would like.

Now list the differences between these two pieces of work, highlighting differing language, phraseology and content.

Activity 4 **(15 minutes)**

List at least five forms of written communications used by organisations.

We use our eyes to read the written word but there are other ways of communicating through visual aids.

3 VISUAL COMMUNICATION

This relates to charts, graphs and tabulated data, and also to colour, design and symbols.

3.1 Advantages

Visual communication has the following two main advantages:

(a) **Quantity of information**. Appropriately used, a well designed graph can impart more information, with greater clarity, than several pages of text or several minutes of verbal description.

(b) **Impact** The use of symbols can act as a short cut to understanding. When driving it would be impossible to assimilate all the information given if it were in the form of words. A symbol, once learned, will trigger understanding in the human brain.

3.2 Disadvantages

Visual communication has the following disadvantage.

Ambiguity Symbols and the use of colours must be learned before they are understood. Children are not born knowing that a red light signifies stop or that a green light signifies go; they must learn these meanings. Different cultures use different symbols. For example, a symbol used to warn workers in a food factory of the dangers of dust build up would have little meaning to a new employee or visitor. Thus symbols and coding must be used with care.

Activity 5 **(30 minutes)**

The pictures below show two examples of symbols. What does each one communicate to you? Write down the meanings of each.

Draw or find pictures of five other symbols in common usage (use no more than two road signs). Write down their meanings.

Now show these symbols to five of your colleagues and write down their understanding of the meaning.

(a)

(b)

Communication is not always just what we write or say. There are levels of communication that hover below the conscious level, not entirely subconscious, but almost.

4 NON VERBAL COMMUNICATION

Non-verbal communication relates to the non-verbal aspect of personal interactions. It can be divided into four areas:

(a) physical appearance;
(b) paralinguistic (tone and speed of voice);
(c) kinetic (movements, gestures, facial expression and eye contact);
(d) proxemic (body proximity, orientation and posture).

Each of these areas can reinforce the message being passed, so long as they are appropriate to the verbal communication. If they are inappropriate, the message may be confused or ambiguous. Non-verbal communication is considered to be the aspect of communication over which an individual has least control; however, it is possible to become aware of the meaning of certain gestures etc. By doing so, verbal communication skills can be reinforced and so understanding can be enhanced.

Non-verbal communication has a strong cultural aspect to it. Certain bodily movements in particular are unacceptable in various parts of the world. For example, it is considered a gross insult to give the thumbs up sign in South America, and in Arab countries it is unacceptable to point the soles of your feet in another person's direction. What we consider usual may not be acceptable elsewhere; many a business has run into difficulties as a result of lack of preparation before venturing abroad.

4.1 Advantages

Being aware of non-verbal communication brings the following advantage.

Competitive advantage Understanding and being aware of the non-verbal signals being communicated from another person can help you ask the right questions or give the correct responses. The use of your own body language can reinforce the message you want to convey, and this can be used by adopting a 'listening' pose. All good sales people know that customers buy from individuals they like or identify with; this fact can be used to advantage by those in control of their own body language.

4.2 Disadvantages

There are two main disadvantages associated with non-verbal communication.

(a) **Concentration** Just as control of one's own body language, and an understanding of the body language of others, can be an advantage, it requires a high degree of concentration and training. A lapse in concentration during an important meeting could be unfortunate, if one is using controlled body language to reinforce a point that is not genuine.

(b) **Ambiguity** You will have seen photographs of celebrities, where the caption has been added by the publication editor. Usually designed to be amusing, the captions fit words to the body postures of the celebrity. No-one expects the caption to reflect exactly what was said, but the results are often believable. This illustrates the possible ambiguity that can be attributed to non-verbal communication.

NOTES

FOR DISCUSSION

In seminar groups discuss the following statement:

'Non-verbal communication exists only in the minds of those who believe it to be true'.

Remember that all great actors not only say their lines convincingly, but alter the body movements, postures and facial expressions to create the illusion of another person.

5 TECHNOLOGICAL AIDS TO COMMUNICATIONS

5.1 The telephone

The telephone is probably the oldest commonly used technology. We are so used to it that we consider a telephone conversation virtually as good as a conversation face-to-face.

Advantages

The telephone has three main advantages.

(a) **Speed** Communicating verbally with someone who is at a geographic distance can be time consuming in terms of travel. The telephone has made long-distance communication possible.

(b) **Convenience** Most people, and certainly all organisations, in the industrialised world are able to be contacted by phone. The advent of the mobile phone has made it even easier to contact people, but the contribution to effective communications is debatable.

(c) **Participation** Conference calls are now a reality, and therefore calls are no longer restricted to two participants only.

Disadvantages

The telephone has the following disadvantages.

(a) **Association** The benefits that come from associating verbal and non-verbal communication are not available; although if video phones become more widespread this may change.

(b) **Distraction** There are potential problems of distraction for the participants in a telephone conversation.

5.2 Facsimile machines

The facsimile machine (fax) has made it possible to send hard copies (that is, on paper) through telephone communications. In this way documents such as contracts can be passed on for perusal faster than through the post or even by courier.

5.3 Electronic mail (e-mail)

The use of electronic mail has had a profound effect on cutting down the time lapse inevitable with written communications. All participants in the communication must have access to a computer and be able to link their computer into whatever network is to be used.

E-mail can be both formal and informal. Letters and other documents can be posted to the recipient's 'mailbox' to be read at their leisure, or conversations in written form can be conducted in real time.

Voice mail is an extension of electronic mail, it enables recorded messages to be left to be picked up at a later time.

The impact of the IT revolution, and especially that of e-mail, is covered in detail in Core Unit 7, *Management Information Systems.*

5.4 Inter-organisation computer networks

Computer networks within organisations have been possible, although expensive, for some years now, but the most recent development has been the ability of related companies to link up part of their computer system with each other. This has particular implications for strategic alliances and partnership arrangements. Without this kind of system the co-operation of so many countries in the Airbus project, for example, would have been very much more complicated and difficult to achieve.

5.5 Internet

The Internet is the most recent addition to the technological communications tool kit. The medium can be used in two ways: firstly as an interactive communications channel and secondly as a form of notice board where information can be displayed. It is fast becoming a world wide form of communications, although the problems of differing language and culture still exist.

5.6 Television and video

Whilst these are not commonly seen as communication media used in organisations, they are playing an increasingly important part in the marketing function. The music business is the best example. Once songs were sold purely as sheet music, to be played by those who had mastered an instrument. Then came the various recording devices, allowing music to be enjoyed by even those with no musical ability. Now, for a song to be popular enough to be worth money, a video is needed as part of the promotion.

Similarly, television has become probably the most important advertising medium, having access as it does to millions of people at once. Its outward appearance is of a medium that fits with our 'one way' communication model. However, one could regard the purchase of advertised products as a form of feedback. The message has got across and been understood: 'Buy BPP's other HND books, they're great!' Whether the consumer believes the message or not is irrelevant, they bought the product. Thus television and video can be considered to be true two-way communications (and are likely to be even more interactive in the future)'.

Within organisations the use of videos for training (either produced 'in house' or bought in) and facilities for video conferencing are becoming more common.

Activity 6 **(15 minutes)**

List all the methods you can think of for finding out the day's news – local, national and international. Identify each medium and show which methods facilitate feedback.

NOTES

With such a vast array of different media to choose from, how do we know which to choose?

6 MATCHING THE MESSAGE TO THE MEDIUM

Activity 7 **(10 minutes)**

You are marketing manager for a major retailer; you wish to tell your customers of an amazing offer. What media would you use?

Would you use the same media if you wished to warn your customers of a wet floor in your store? Write down a list of alternatives.

The choice of medium depends upon a variety of factors including the following:

(a) **Urgency** Some media, by their nature, take longer than others. The time span available must be considered. A request for the fire brigade to attend a fire at your office would not be effective if done by letter!

(b) **Permanency** Some pieces of information are required to be repeatedly proven. Your qualification from this course might not be of much use to you if it existed only in verbal form. Other pieces of information may need to be referred to over and over again to ensure accuracy.

(c) **Complexity** Detailed information regarding last year's sales would be too complex to impart over the phone. On the other hand, you would not consider it appropriate to use an internal memo to inform your secretary that you take sugar in your coffee.

(d) **Sensitivity** This can be in the emotional sense or in the sense of secrecy. You would not post strategic marketing plans on the Internet, for fear that your competitors would see them. Nor would a purely verbal plan be appropriate, as there are issues of complexity and permanence.

(e) **Cost** Lengthy analysis and formal report production can be an expensive business. (If similar information is to be gathered from many sources then *forms* may be an inexpensive and appropriate method).

None of these factors can be considered in isolation. Often several factors need to be considered when deciding upon the best medium, each factor having a varying degree of importance to the specific decision.

In your career as a student and in business you will be asked to focus on one medium in particular: the written word, specifically written reports. We shall now consider how to make your reports communicate effectively.

7 WRITING REPORTS

Report writing is the most intricate form of written communication and requires a high degree of skill. As a business student you will be required to produce reports in preparation for your entry into the world of organisations. This section contains guidelines to help you ensure that your reports are effective in imparting the information you wish to impart.

7.1 Planning

Before putting pen to paper you should consider the following.

(a) Who is the report for? (who is the user?)
(b) What information is required?
(c) For what purpose is the information to be used?
(d) Are recommendations required?
(e) What time span and budget are available to produce the report?

A basic report format is given below:

Title page	Title/subject of report, author, recipient and date	The title should be descriptive of the contents, not poetic or ambiguous.
Contents page	List of contents with page and paragraph numbers	This must be clear and concise, the aim is to enable sections to be found quickly.
Terms of reference	Purpose of the report and scope of the investigation made.	Terms of reference will sometimes be given, but on occasion it is up to the author to define the parameters. Methodology can be included here in academic pieces of work, or can be a separate section. (It is not usual in commercial reports to detail methodology in this way.) Detailed findings may be included as an appendix.
Executive summary	Brief description of the key issues and/or recommendations	When you write this consider the needs of a busy executive who wishes to 'skim' the main points before reading the full report.
Introduction	Background information	Only include that which is *necessary* in order to make sense of the rest of the report. Begin to tell a story (though not in the poetic sense).
Main body	Concise analysis of the subject.	Key words here are *concise* and *analysis*. Do not be descriptive or include redundant information. More detail can be included in the appendices.
Conclusion	Round up of key points to this stage.	Do not introduce any *new* information. Reiterate the key points which lead onto the recommendations.
Recommen-dations	If this is within the terms of reference, recommend changes, improvements etc.	All recommendations must be backed up by solid reasoning and evaluated for their feasibility, suitability and acceptability.
Appendices	Detailed information gathered and analysed in the process of writing the report.	May contain financial analysis, tables and graphs. Used as supporting information should the reader wish to read them. Of paramount importance when undertaking reports for academic purposes.

7.2 General aspects of report writing

Analysis

It is usually best to make your analysis objective. It is sometimes necessary to make subjective judgements; if so, you should make sure that you clearly indicate where this is the case. For example, you might use informal interviews to gain information; this is a valid method of data collection. However, when you come to interpret what has been said, you should indicate that your conclusions are inevitably subject to your own values and beliefs.

Writing style

Each individual has his or her own writing style. Style can include the way sentences are structured and the phraseology used. Some writing styles are more effective in reports than others. General points to remember about good report writing style include the following.

(a) Short sentences are easier to understand; they reduce the potential for ambiguity and make reading easier.

(b) It is best to avoid emotional and value judgements.

(c) You should avoid colloquialisms and abbreviated forms of language (which may seem inappropriately informal).

(d) Only use technical jargon if the report is intended for use within an organisation where this jargon is in common usage.

(e) It is usual to de-personalise language and avoid the use of 'I' or 'we'.

Layout

Reports are presented in a formal layout. Ensure that key points are highlighted by the use of emboldening, italics, type size, spacing or underlining. Section paragraphs should be numbered. This helps users to find specific sections and makes it easier for a group of people to discuss the contents. Sections should be clearly headed and the use of sub-section headings is recommended.

8 MEETINGS

8.1 The purpose of meetings

As we noted earlier in the text, meetings are used in different contexts in an organisation. Because they can be held for a wide range of purposes, it is important that the purpose of the meeting is made clear to the participants in advance. If this is done, the meeting is more likely to be a success. The most common reasons for holding a meeting are the following.

- To give or obtain information
- To address a problem, grievance or complaint for resolution
- To make a series of specific decisions about an issue
- To generate creative ideas for development outside the meeting
- To present a proposal for discussion and approval
- To secure certain attitudes

8.2 Arrangements for meetings

Arrangements for meetings can be split into three stages and the following points are common to all meetings whatever their purpose or form and will help ensure that the meeting is effective and useful.

(a) **Preparation** – establish a valid purpose for the meeting and consider whether this could not be achieved by other means.

Consider on which day the meeting should be held.

Determine who should attend – ensure quorum for decisions.

Book room with due regard for ventilation, noise, refreshment, seating and security.

Prepare agenda.

Inform participants well in advance (if possible), giving details of the time, venue and purpose of the meeting.

(b) **Conducting the meeting (as chairperson)** – start on time.

Put members at their ease and focus minds on purpose of meeting.

Outline procedure to be followed (if irregular) and define technical terms.

Direct a general or specific question to get meeting started.

Ensure fair play – link speakers and deter verbosity.

Summarise at appropriate times and at end but do not impose your own views.

Try to finish on time – if impossible get agreement to continue but never drift.

Thank those present for attending.

(c) **After the meeting** – have memo or minutes prepared by secretary and approved by chairman. These form the basis of the next meeting. Follow up decisions taken.

8.3 Managing meetings

Some meetings achieve very little. Hindrances to productive meetings are shown in the following table.

Hindrance	**How to avoid**
Participants are unclear about the purpose of the meeting	Agree goals in advance.
Attendees have conflicting aims.	The goals agreed provide a common aim. Use negotiation skills.
The meeting lacks focus and direction.	Prepare a focused agenda and ensure people stick to it.
'Action points' agreed on in the meeting are not performed.	Name the person responsible for completing each action point, and assign a completion date. Include all actions required and the assigned dates in the minutes.

NOTES

8.4 Running a meeting

The chairperson aims to ensure the successful completion of business. The chair should maintain control of the meeting without talking excessively. A group mentality should be encouraged where all feel willing and able to contribute.

Several techniques can be used by the chair to encourage the best utilisation of the skill-set present at the meeting.

Technique	Desired result
Make opening statements	Clarify the scope and objectives of the meeting.
Ask 'opening questions'	These should relate to the opening statements and stimulate the thoughts of the group as a whole.
Ask a specific question to a specific participant	Can be used to encourage 'shy' attendees to participate and/or to ensure those with specialist knowledge contribute when appropriate.
Use summaries	Consolidate points agreed on as a basis for moving on.

8.5 Handling undesirable behaviour

The participants at a meeting may be drawn from wide-ranging backgrounds, with their own (undisclosed) 'agendas'. As with any group of people, different personalities and attitudes can be expected. Undesirable behaviour is anything that could prevent the meeting achieving its objectives in the most efficient manner. The chair has a range of options available to deal with participants displaying undesirable behaviour.

Undesirable behaviour	'Typical' personality	Chair tactic to modify behaviour
Dismissive of others' ideas	'Know-it-all'	Ask for their views early in the discussion and tactfully point out areas where others may be able to suggest improvements.
Contributes regularly, but rarely relevantly	'Unfocused'	Stress the agenda and objectives.
Looks disinterested. Yawns	'Bored'	Ask a direct question. Should encourage them to pay attention in future.
Talks too much, shouts others down	'Aggressor'	Re-direct their comments back to them ('reverse' questioning) or to the group ('relay' questioning). A warning may be required, with the ultimate sanction of expulsion.
Attempts to catch the chair or participants out	'Devious'	Re-direct their comments back to them ('reverse' questioning), eg 'Fair enough. Do you have a better suggestion?'
Unenthusiastic, 'seen it all before' attitude	'Cynic'	Emphasise the authority the group has to act on decisions taken. Encourage positive contributions through questioning.
Plays no part in proceedings	'Timid'	Ask a direct question you are reasonably sure they know the answer to. This should build confidence.

8.6 Handling difficult situations

The chair may be presented with a difficult situation such as those outlined below.

Difficult situation	Suggested approach
Bad news (eg redundancies) needs to be communicated	Prepare well to gain a thorough knowledge of the issues. Ignorance is likely to be interpreted as not caring.
Personal tension between participants	Select the group carefully. Use the seating plan to reduce the possibility of confrontation.
Lack of enthusiasm/interest	Only those who need to be at the meeting should be invited. If a topic is particularly uninteresting stress the need to reach a decision/cover ground quickly, so the meeting can move on. Suggest taking a break.
Too much digression	Allow digression to continue for a short time to allow the issues to be explored. If participants don't 'right' themselves use frequent summaries to refocus the discussion.

Meetings are time-consuming, costly events. The major cost is to some extent hidden – participants' time. As the saying goes, 'time is money'.

If a meeting is proposed ensure that:

- It is really needed
- Only those that need to be there are invited
- The aims and agenda are clear to all
- A good chair with the required skills is appointed

9 PRODUCING A PRESENTATION

Definition

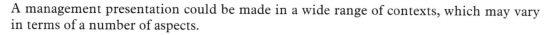

> A **presentation** is the act of making something (eg information) available to an audience. Presentations are usually planned acts of communication.

A management presentation could be made in a wide range of contexts, which may vary in terms of a number of aspects.

(a) The size and composition of the audience. This could range from a single manager to a small group of decision-makers or a large conference. The audience may be known to you or be complete strangers. They may have prior knowledge of the area you are speaking about or be complete 'laymen'. All these factors will affect the audience's ability to accept your message.

(b) The purpose and approach of the presentation. You may be offering:

- Technical information
- Instruction
- A comparison
- A recommendation
- Persuasion

(c) The complexity of the subject matter.

(d) The level of formally. A staff briefing may be informal while a presentation to senior management is likely to be formal.

(e) The time available. The purpose of the presentation should be a guide as to time required, but time available may be different, placing constraints on your content and style.

9.1 Purpose

As a starting point in your preparation you should devise clear objectives for your presentation. If your objectives are going to help you plan your presentation they need to be specific and measurable. Your objectives should be stated in terms of what the audience will do, or how they will be changed, at the end of the presentation, for example they will believe, be persuaded, agreed, be motivated, do, understand, be able – or something similar.

Start with your primary objective, then move on to secondary objectives you will need to achieve along the way. This hierarchy of objectives provides a useful aid to planning the content and structure of your presentation.

You are likely to have a fair idea of the audience composition - from senior decision-makers to trainees. The audience's motivations and expectations will influence their perceptions of you and your message. Why might they be at your presentation?

(a) They are required to be there – attendance may be compulsory. Unless interest can be stimulated by the presentation, compulsory attendance may create resistance to the message. Attendance may be recommended by a superior. Participants may be motivated because they perceive it to be in their own interest to do so.

(b) They are interested in the topic of the presentation. This often means there is a fine line to tread between telling the audience what they already know, and losing them by assuming more knowledge than they possess.

(c) They need specific information. An audience, which is deliberately seeking information, and intending to use it to further their own objectives, is highly motivated.

Taking into account audience needs and expectations, your message needs to have the following qualities.

(a) Relevance. It should be relevant to the audience's needs and interests, eg making a difficult decision easier, or satisfying a need.

(b) Credibility. It should be consistent in itself, and with known facts; apparently objective; and from a source perceived to be trustworthy.

(c) Accessibility. This means both:

  (i) Audible and visible. Do you need to be closer to the audience? Do you need a microphone? Enlarged visual aids?

  (ii) Understandable. What is the audience's level of knowledge of the topic? What technical terms or 'jargon' will need to be avoided or explained?

9.2 The presentation

Introduction

You only get once chance to make a good first impression!

- Establish your credibility on the subject
- Gain the audience's interest
- Establish a rapport with the audience
- Prepare the audience for the content and structure of your presentation
- Set the scene, introduce the topic and state your 'theme'

The body of the presentation

Your structured notes and outline should contain cues that clarify the shape and progression of your information or argument. This will help keep you 'on track' and enable the audience to:

(a) Maintain a sense of purpose and motivation
(b) Follow your argument, so that they arrive with you at the conclusion

Logical cues indicate the links between one topic or statement and the next. Here are some examples.

- You can simply begin each point with *linking words or phrases* like:

  This has led to ...

  Therefore (conclusion, result or effect, arising from previous point)

  So ...

  As a result ...

  However ...

  But ... (contradiction or alternative to previous point)

  On the other hand ...

  Similarly ... (confirmation or additional example of previous point)

  Again ...

  Moreover ... (building on the previous point)

- You can set up a framework for the whole argument, giving the audience an overview and then filling in the detail. For example:

  'There are three main reasons why ... Firstly ... Secondly ... Thirdly ...'

  Of course, this isn't a perfect solution. It has the advantages of ... But there are also disadvantages, in that ...'

  'You might like to think of communication in terms of the 5Cs. That's: concise, clear, correct, complete and courteous. Let's look at each of these in turn.'

  You can use devices that summarise or repeat the previous point and lead the audience to the next. These have the advantage of giving you, and the listener, a 'breather' in which to gather your thoughts.

Other ways in which content can be used to clarify the message include the following.

(a) Examples and illustrations – showing how an idea works in practice.

(b) Anecdotes – inviting the audience to relate an idea to a real-life situation.

(c) Questions – rhetorical or requiring the audience to answer, raising particular points that may need clarification.

(d) Explanation – showing how or why something has happened.

(e) Description – helping the audience to visualise the setting you are describing.

(f) Definition – explaining the precise meaning of terms that may not be understood.

(g) The use of facts, quotations or statistics – to 'prove' your point.

Your vocabulary and style should contribute to the clarity of the message. Use short, simple sentences. Avoid jargon, unexplained acronyms, colloquialisms, double meanings and vague expressions.

9.3 Adding emphasis

Emphasis is the 'weight', importance or impact given to particular words or ideas. This can be achieved through delivery – the tone and volume of your voice, eye contact and gestures. Emphasis can also be provided through the following techniques.

Technique	Comment
Repetition	'If accuracy in income estimation is vital to our investment decisions, then accurate income estimation techniques must be developed'
Rhetorical questions	'Do you know how many of our departmental heads are unhappy with the management information provided? Fifty percent. Do you think that's acceptable?'
Quotation	'Information overload is the number one issue in the information we are producing. That's the conclusion of our survey'
Statistics	'One in two of our internal customers have complained this year: that's 20% more complaints than last year. If the trend continues, we will soon have more complainers than satisfied customers!'
Exaggeration	'We have to look at our quality control system, because if the current trend continues, we are going to end up without any customers at all'

9.4 Adding interest

Simple, clear information may only be interesting to those already motivated by the subject. You should strike a balance between the need for clarity and the need to make the message vivid, attention-grabbing and memorable.

Here are some further suggestions.

(a) Analogy – comparing something to something else, which is in itself more colourful or interesting.

(b) Anecdote or narrative – telling a story that illustrates the point, using suspense, humour or a more human context.

(c) Curiosity or surprise – for example, 'If you put all the widgets we've sold this year end to end, they would stretch twice around the equator.'

(d) Humour – used well this will add entertainment value and serve as a useful 'breather' for listeners. Be careful, humour may not travel well. The audience may not be on the speaker's wavelength. Use with caution!

(e) Emotion – you may wish to appeal to the audience's emotions. As with humour you have to be sure of your audience before you attempt this. Your appeal may come across as patronising, manipulative or just irrelevant. Emotion does add human interest, and can be used to stress the humanity and involvement of the speaker.

9.5 Visual aids

Visual aids use a visual image to aid communication. The purpose of visual aids is not to look good for their own sake, but to support the message. Michael Stevens (*Improving your presentation skills*) notes:

'The proper use of aids is to achieve something in your presentation that you cannot do as effectively with words alone. They are only a means to an end, for instance to clarify an idea, or prove a point. A good aid is one that does this efficiently.'

Visual aids include:

- Slides (used with an overhead projector or PC and projector) – may include photographs, texts, diagrams and other images projected onto a screen or other surface.
- Flipcharts – where the presenter intends to write notes or draw diagrams in the course of the presentation.
- Handouts – may include notes or diagrams referred to during the presentation, or additional supporting information.
- Props and demonstrations – objects and processes can be displayed or demonstrated to the audience. This gives credibility to the message. Demonstrations are particularly effective to illustrate how efficient a process is, or how easy a device is to operate. For example, a demonstration is common before a new software package is purchased.

9.6 The effective use of visual aids

(a) Ensure that the aid is:

(i) Appropriate to your message, in content and 'style' or mood.
(ii) Easy to see and understanding.
(iii) Only used when there is support to be gained from it.

(b) Ensure that all equipment and materials are available and working and that you can operate them efficiently and confidently.

(c) Ensure that the aid does not become a distraction.

(i) Show each image long enough to be absorbed and noted, but not so long as to merge with the following idea.

(ii) Maintain voice and eye contact with your audience, so they know that it is you who are the communicator, not the machine.

(iii) Introduce your aids and what they are for, placing the focus on the verbal presentation.

(iv) Hand out supporting material either well before the presentation (to allow reading beforehand) or at the relevant point. If you hand out material just before starting it will distract the audience from your presentation.

(v) If you need to write or draw during the presentation, do so as quickly and efficiently as possible (given the need for legibility and neatness).

9.7 Concluding the presentation

The conclusion should be used to:

(a) Clarify and draw together the points you have made. Use an example, anecdote, review, summary or conclusion but do not introduce any new ideas at this stage.

(b) State, reinforce or imply what you expect your audience to do, know, believe, feel or agree to. You should leave the audience with the seed of response to action in their minds.

(c) Reinforce the content and the audience response expected. You may use repetition, a joke or anecdote, quotation or surprising statistic to make your main message memorable.

Inviting or accepting questions can be a helpful – if slightly nerve-wracking – part of a presentation. Questions provide an opportunity to:

(a) Clarify any misunderstandings the audience may have perceived.
(b) Address specific doubts or resistance the audience may have.

Ignorance or excessive hesitation in the face of a (relevant) question may cast doubt on your credibility. As this is usually the last stage of the presentation, your response to questions will leave a lasting impression.

The way to tackle questions effectively is to anticipate them. Put yourself in your audience's shoes, what questions might they ask and why? When questions arise, listen to them carefully, assess the questioner's manner, and draw the questioner out if necessary, in order to ascertain exactly what is being asked, and why. People might ask questions:

(a) To seek additional information of particular interest to them.

(b) To seek clarification of a point that is not clear.

(c) To add information of their own, which may be relevant, helpful and accurate – or not!

(d) To undermine the speaker's authority.

Incorporate the answers to expected questions into your outline notes. The important points about answering questions are as follows.

(a) You may seek limited feedback throughout your presentation. It is common to invite the audience to let you know if anything is unclear, but you should encourage more involved questions to be held until the end of your presentation. Questions should not be allowed to disrupt your message to the audience as a whole.

(b) You should add or clarify information if required to achieve your purpose. An honest query deserves a co-operative answer.

(c) To maintain your credibility and authority strong tactics may be required, without in any way ridiculing or 'putting down' the questioner.

(i) If a question is based on a false premise or incorrect information, correct it. An answer may, or may not, then be required.

(ii) If a question is rambling, clarify what the question is and answer it. If it is completely irrelevant, say politely that it is outside the scope of the presentation.

10 TYPES OF NETWORK

With the development of *team centred* working, the dynamics of communications within groups become of relevance, as they affect the structures of these teams. Five main types of communications networks have been identified through research into group interactions:

(a) the star configuration;
(b) the circle configuration;
(c) the Y configuration;
(d) the chain configuration;
(e) the all channel configuration.

10.1 The star configuration

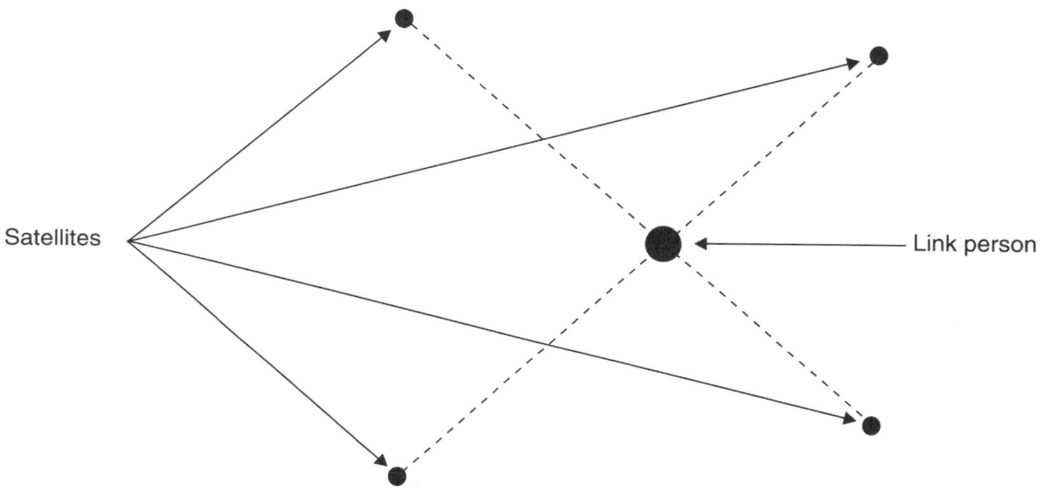

Definition

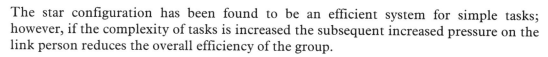

Star configuration: also known as the 'wheel configuration', the star is the most centralised of the communications networks. It includes a 'link' person through whom all communications must travel. The 'satellite' individuals communicate only with the 'link' person (or department) and not with each other.

The star configuration has been found to be an efficient system for simple tasks; however, if the complexity of tasks is increased the subsequent increased pressure on the link person reduces the overall efficiency of the group.

This is a group with a clear leader. The level of satisfaction and motivation is highest for the group leader, with the other members gaining very little satisfaction. Star networks can evolve through the interrelationships within the group if there is one dominant individual. Star networks may be specifically implemented where contact between the various satellites is not desirable.

NOTES

Activity 8 **(10 minutes)**

Identify and draw two examples of star networks from your own experience: one from a work or educational setting and one from your social life. Which was the easiest to identify? What do these two examples have in common?

Star networks have a strong leader. Next we consider the type of network which has no leader.

10.2 The circle configuration

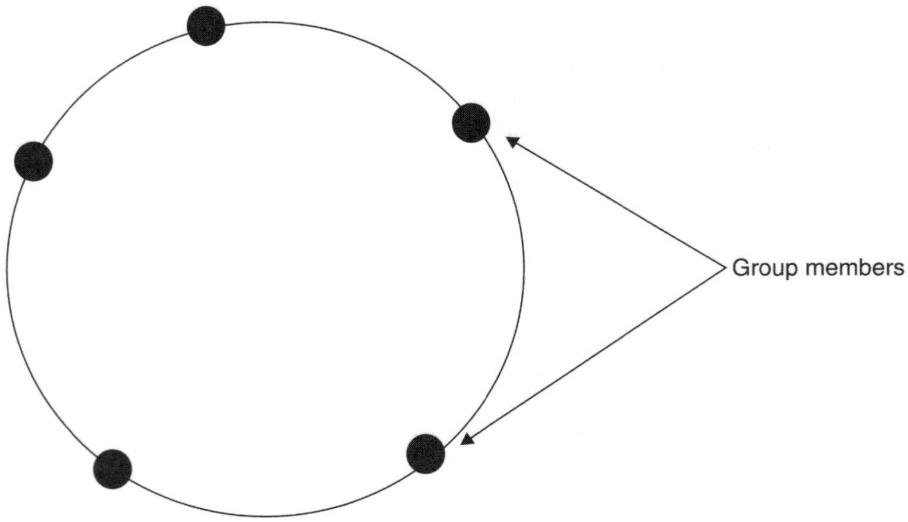

Definition

Circle configuration: in this configuration the group has no defined leader. All members communicate with their immediate neighbours only.

The result of the circle configuration is an unorganised group, which tends to be slow and erratic in problem solving. However, with complex problems, this type of network does have a greater efficiency than a star, with its reliance upon a single individual. Group members within a circle network gain satisfaction and motivation through perceived participation.

10.3 The Y and chain configurations

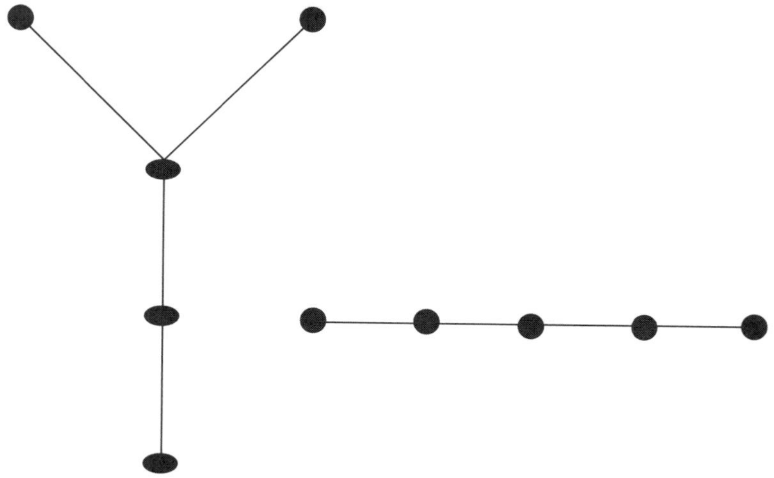

Both these types of communications network are commonly found in large organisations, although this does not preclude their use in organisations of all types and sizes.

Definitions

> **Y configuration:** in this network there is a key person at the linkage of the three arms of communication, but this does not result in clear leadership of the kind found in the star configuration.
>
> **Chain configuration:** with this network the situation is much the same as with the circle, with individuals only communicating with their immediate chain neighbours.

These configurations are often artificially produced. The purpose of their production is related to the structure of the organisation and the way in which the culture has been developed to achieve the corporate objectives.

> **Activity 9** **(30 minutes)**
>
> Consider a large multi-departmental organisation, with centralised purchasing and supply function. All requests for inputs into the company – from raw materials to toilet paper for the lavatories – are required to go through this department. New suppliers have no access to the engineering, research and development or other departments, only to purchasing.
>
> Write a few paragraphs on the advantages and disadvantages of this situation. Ensure that you substantiate your arguments.

10.4 The all channel configuration

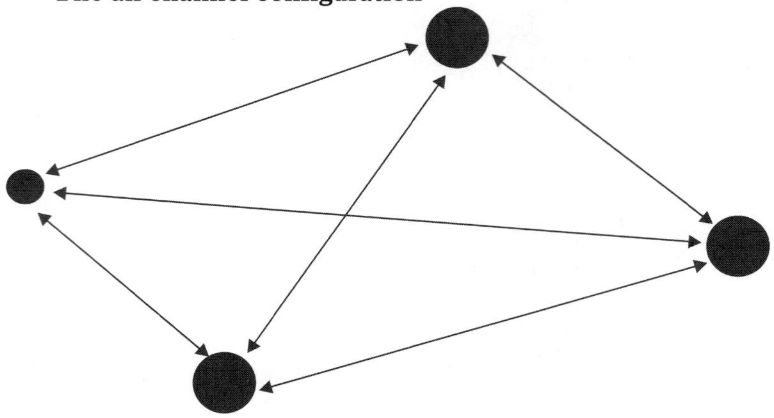

Definition

> **All channel configuration:** all members of the group can freely communicate with other members.

This has been found to be the most effective network for complex problems. The participatory style leads to this being the chosen network for project teams in most organisations.

11 NETWORKS AND ORGANISATIONAL STRUCTURES

11.1 Which networks suit which organisational structures?

All networks suit all organisational structures to a greater or lesser degree. As a heuristic, the shorter the scalar chain, the more opportunity there is for all channel communication networks to develop.

Many organisations today are changing their structures to allow for increased empowerment of employees at all levels. This has been most evident at 'shop floor' level.

Definition

> **Shop floor level:** all those at the lower end of the scalar chain, not only those in the manufacturing industries.

In an effort to increase flexibility and the ability to react towards changing markets, structural changes are needed to speed up communications. As we have seen, the more rigid and inflexible the communications network, the slower it is to react to external change.

Nowhere has this been more evident than in the UK motor car manufacturing industry. The time taken from inception to production has been cut by half in recent years. Not only is this due to the formation of easily adaptable production techniques, it is also due to the involvement of and communication between all departments from a very early stage. For example, production of a new car model used to be driven mainly by the advancing technology of the time. How the product would be marketed was seen as a process to be considered well after the design stage, as was the sourcing of materials. Now production of a new model is very much consumer led, with marketing having input in the early stages as to the type of product that would suit the market. Similarly, sourcing of materials during the design stage highlights potential problems before manufacturing is imminent.

The increase in all channel communication has been communicated by the formation of design and project teams that cover all aspects of the organisation that have a bearing on the product at any stage of its life cycle.

However, increasing the use of all channel communication networks is not without its problems. Interdepartmental rivalry, which may have developed over many years, is hard to break down, and the resulting attitudes and behaviour can act as noise, preventing the accurate exchange of information. The reasons for and implications of this kind of noise are complex, involving the *culture* of the organisation. This is a subject we shall return to in later chapters.

FOR DISCUSSION

In order to improve communication within an organisation, does the structure need to be changed first? Or should the culture be changed first?

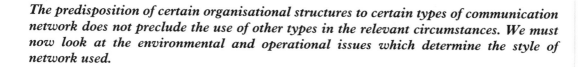

The predisposition of certain organisational structures to certain types of communication network does not preclude the use of other types in the relevant circumstances. We must now look at the environmental and operational issues which determine the style of network used.

12 THE IMPACT OF TECHNOLOGY

12.1 Contact versus Communication

One might assume that, with the recent surges in information technology, the need for face-to-face communication would have been greatly reduced. This is, in fact, what has been projected to happen. Technology will allow us to work from home with minimal direct contact with our employers and with communication being conducted through computers and telephone lines. However, the undoubted growth in communication through technological means has not been as swift as anticipated.

It is certainly true that it is very easy for contact to be made between individuals and organisations worldwide. Note the use of the word 'contact': these technological aids facilitate communication by allowing us contact with one another; they do not ensure the effectiveness of that communication.

One sphere where technology has improved communications is in remote geographic areas.

12.2 Geographic isolation

Technology has improved, and is likely to continue to improve, opportunities for paid employment in areas of less dense population. The financial services industry has been quick to take advantage of this opportunity. Although this use of technology is mostly in evidence in the western world at present, the ability to provide communication links anywhere in the world is now a reality.

12.3 The global organisation

The concept of a global organisation would not be possible without the advances that have been made in information technology. The ability to communicate regularly, and at will, with the core organisation, enables the entity to act as one, whilst allowing room for different branches to act independently, as local conditions dictate.

12.4 Power and control

The best example of a technology-related increase in power and control can be seen with what used to be known as 'travelling salesmen.' Just as technology has improved the speed and distance of travel, it has enabled the individual to be contacted at almost any time. Earlier technologies, such as the telephone, enabled the individual to contact the organisation, but not visa versa. The mobile telephone has changed this. The widespread use of computers and modems now allows sales data to be downloaded to an organisation's computer from vast distances, and the facsimile machine has facilitated the transmission of documents, bearing legitimate signatures. Pagers and message services mean that it is possible to keep track of employees in the field with much more accuracy, appointments can be centrally booked and changes to a schedule made at short notice.

Employees working away from the office in this way now have little need to spend any time at the organisation's base. This has the effect of further isolating them from their working colleagues and so makes management control of the individual easier.

Activity 10 **(20 minutes)**

You are the Sales Director of a large corporation. List the technological means you could employ to keep in touch with your sales staff who are distributed nationwide.

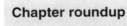

Chapter roundup

- Communication can be conducted through four main types of media: written, verbal, visual and non-verbal.
- Each medium has its own distinct advantages and disadvantages.
- Each medium requires different skills.
- Some media are affected by environmental factors, such as culture.
- Non-verbal communications can reinforce or confuse verbal communications.
- Technology has expanded the media available for communication, particularly the verbal and written forms.
- Reports play an important part in organisational life. If written with care they can provide easily accessible information.
- Networks represent the way in which communication points are connected.
- Each network type has purposes for which it is best suited; there is no one best type of network.

NOTES

Chapter roundup (cont'd)

- Some types of network occur with more frequency than others in specific organisational types.
- All channel communication networks allow free communications between all and any levels in an organisation.
- Faster communications lead to flexibility for the organisation.
- Networks do not necessarily follow the lines of authority.
- Technology has made communications easier and faster than ever before.
- Without the advances in technology that have been made over recent decades, the global organisation would be impossible to control.
- Improvements in communications technology have brought employment to areas of geographic isolation.

Quick Quiz

1 What are the four main media of communications?

2 List three methods of written communication used in organisations.

3 What is the Internet?

4 Name two disadvantages of verbal communication.

5 How do we know that red means stop or danger?

6 In verbal communication, what can you do to facilitate feedback?

7 Name three types of communication network.

8 Which networks are more suited to a participatory style of management?

9 Choose one network and state how its structure influences the motivation of the participants.

10 List three ways in which technology has affected the working environment.

Answers to Quick Quiz

1 Verbal, non-verbal, written and visual. Technology aids the use of these media. (See introduction)

2 Letters, memoranda, reports, forms, leaflets, posters, payslips and many more. (See para 2)

3 The Internet is an international web of communication links. It can be accessed by any computer owner, through the use of telephone satellite links and a modem. It can be used for either active or passive communication. (See para 5.5)

4 It can not be relied upon for future reference and allows little time for planning one's message. (See para 1.2)

5 We know that red means stop or danger because we were taught this as a child. It is not inborn knowledge. (See para 3.2)

6 Listen. (See para 1.1)

7 You could have named the star, circle, Y, chain or all channel networks. (See para 8)

NOTES

8 All channel networks, because all members of the network have the same rights of access to all other members. (See para 8.4)

9 The use of the all channel network can increase feelings of commitment in staff towards the organisation in which they work. (See para 3.4)

10 Technology has influenced the working environment by: (a) increasing the ability to contact people; (b) allowing outworking to take place; (c) increasing the number of global organisations. (See para 10)

Answers to activities

1 Your scenario should highlight the 'to and fro' nature of conversation, with one party appearing passive while the other is active and then roles reversing. You should have recognised that the passive party *must* be listening to the active party for the communication to be effective and an amicable result to be negotiated.

2 The following shows the best and worst scenarios; those in between may vary depending on your relationship with the MD.

Option	Rating	Reasons
1		
2		
3	1	Privacy, chance of distraction low, feedback facilitated
4		
5	5	Distraction from many forms, lack of privacy, feedback inhibited

3 The piece written for the employment agency will be more formal in style, the language will be more correct and the description of the job will be what you think they would like to hear. To a friend you are likely to be more honest, the phraseology will be more relaxed and the expression of ambition may be less realistic, but more enthusiastic.

4 Your list could include the following: reports, memoranda, leaflets, posters, notices, payslips, signs, letters, handbooks/manuals, mail shots, forms.

5 Figure 7.2 (a) indicates 'disabled facilities available; Figure 7.2 (b) indicates 'no smoking'. You may have found many other symbols, some easy for everyone to understand and others that are more obscure.

NOTES

6

Medium	Feedback
Local papers	Some possible but slow
Local radio	Some possible but slow
National papers	Some possible but slow
National radio	Some possible but slow
National television	Some possible but slow
Internet	Yes
Teletext	No
Other people	Yes

(This is not a comprehensive list, there are many more.)

7 You could tell people about the offer by using written media (posters, leaflets, signs) or verbal communications (radio advertising, costermongering (market traders)). You could warn about the wet floor by using written media or by telling people verbally.

8 In a university, for example, a star network exists between students from various colleges within the university, tutors and external examiners.

You may have found it difficult to identify a star network from your personal life unless you have a dominant personality in your circle of friends or family. This type of network is more common in families with a strong 'figurehead' culture.

9 You could have stated the following advantages.

(a) The purchasing department has specialist expertise in negotiating with suppliers.

(b) Other departments are not disrupted by reps calling.

(c) There is less opportunity for suppliers to influence the organisation's purchasing by using incentives and inducements.

(d) All departments will receive standard supplies. Costs can be more easily controlled.

(e) Economies of scale can be achieved.

You could have stated the following disadvantages.

(a) Departmental managers have no autonomy over the supplies they require and receive.

(b) Internal paperwork will slow the supply process.

(c) High cost and low cost items will receive the same scrutiny, or more likely neither will.

(d) Specification must be detailed in order to receive suitable products.

(e) Departments will be slow to become aware of new products or technological developments.

10 You could have suggested the following: (a) land-based telephone; (b) mobile telephone; (c) pagers; (d) conference calls; (e) video phones; (f) email (to laptop computers); (g) internet bulletin boards (again using a modem and a laptop computer).

PART D: UNIT 16

MANAGING SELF

Chapter 16 :
MANAGING SELF

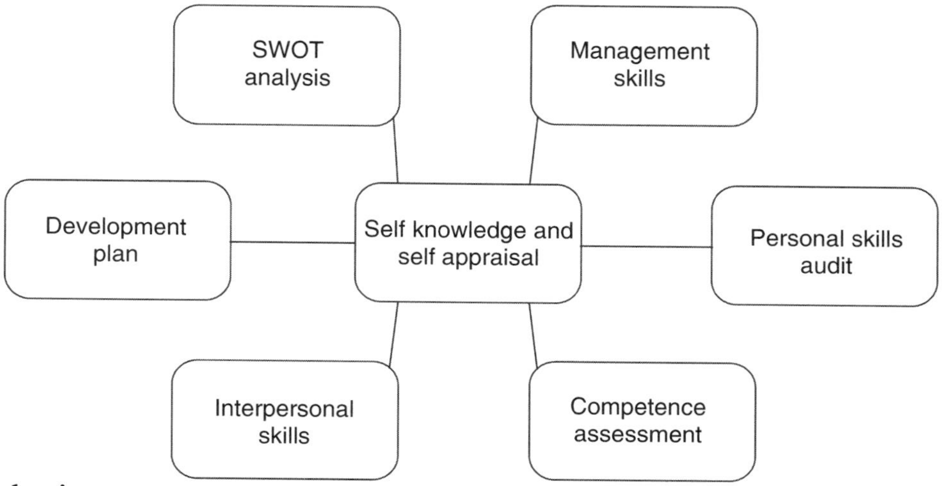

Introduction

Unit 16 is unusual, not just in the context of the HND and HNC qualification but in the context of all exam syllabuses, as it requires you to carry out a fairly detailed self-analysis. The four activities which you are required to carry out in order to achieve this Unit are:

- Carry out a personal skills audit and self-appraisal
- Prepare and agree a personal development plan with your line manager
- Review and monitor your progress in achieving learning objectives and personal targets
- Evaluate progress and achievement of personal development and learning targets and re-set objectives.

As the introduction to the Unit says, 'the emphasis is on the needs of the individual' and the Unit is concerned with personal development and enables you, the student, to build on existing skills to enhance current performance and develop new skills for future personal and career development.

The Unit is therefore highly personal to you, and although this Course book can make suggestions, it is up to you to tackle the Unit honestly.

Your objectives

In this chapter you will learn about the following.

(a) Assessing your strengths and weaknesses, opportunities and threats

(b) Management skills

(c) Planing your own time management programme

(d) Interpersonal skills

(e) Assessing your competences

(f) Preparing a personal skills audit

(g) Drawing up a development plan

1 ASSESSMENT OF THE UNIT

The Edexcel guidelines for this Unit suggest that it could be assessed via a personal journal or skills log which you compile throughout the programme. It should be based on your own personal and career aims and needs.

You should maintain the journal through various different parts of your studies, so that you can keep track of areas where you think there is room for improvement, and those areas where you feel that you have improved.

2 SELF KNOWLEDGE AND SELF APPRAISAL

2.1 Reasons

Every manager needs clear images of his or her personal skills and characteristics for the following reasons.

(a) **Interacting with other people and developing interpersonal skills.** People's perceptions of themselves and others, and the roles they play, are crucial in the process of communication and relationship-building. A supervisor will be better able to identify and solve problems with teamworking and leadership, if he is able to be objective about his own perceptions, role and behaviour.

(b) **Goal-planning and self-development.** An individual will be more able to take control of his future development if he has a realistic picture of his aspirations, capabilities, and potential at a certain point in time. There would be no point planning to take professional exams and become an assistant supervisor in five years, if you did not have the ambition, capacity for hard work or leadership qualities required. On the other hand, many people have a low opinion of themselves and do not attempt to plan a positive course for their careers and lives - which an objective appraisal of their strengths and weaknesses might indicate.

(c) **Motivation and performance**. If you do not know what you are capable of, you may not be motivated to fulfil your potential to perform at a higher level. If you are not performing well, it is too easy to shift the blame on to 'fate', 'the system' or other people. You could be aware of weaknesses in yourself that contribute to the problem - and overcome them.

The organisation obviously has an interest in assessing its employees' skills and characteristics as well: for selection, training, promotion planning and pay awards. We discussed formal performance appraisal in an earlier chapter, and you should be aware that the process can be used to further self-knowledge and is therefore of value to the individual as well as to the organisation.

(a) An appraisal report, for example, may require the employee's assessor to grade him on a number of personal characteristics and skills, to assess particular strengths and weaknesses which affect his job performance and to recommend areas for development. If the employee accepts the assessment (and he should have opportunity to discuss it in an interview or counselling session), he can add the information to his own picture of himself.

(b) Potential assessment techniques are designed to gauge:

   (i) the employee's strengths and weaknesses in existing skills and qualities;

   (ii) potential for improvement, correction and development; and

(iii) the goals, aspirations and attitudes of the appraisee, with regard to career advancement and the acceptance of responsibility.

Various techniques can be used, including written tests, simulated desk-top tasks or case studies, interviews and personality tests.

(c) Group assessment and training techniques are particularly useful to help supervisors and managers to gain an accurate picture of how they relate to other people, and how people react to them. Role-play exercises allow people to participate in situations requiring negotiating or influencing skills, conflict resolution or team leadership, with subsequent feedback from the trainer and other group members: participants are made aware of their own patterns of behaviour and how these affect others, how they are perceived and what responses they get.

(d) **Assessment centres**. An assessment centre is a place where a person's behaviour and performance in job-related tasks and activities can be conveniently evaluated. Candidates are brought to a central location such as an hotel for a period and are tested and observed by a panel of assessors: exercises include leaderless group discussion, role play and business games. They are used in recruiting outsiders and assessing existing employees for advancement.

There are ways, however, in which an individual can engage informally in the same process of developing self awareness, which may involve two broad activities:

(a) compiling a personal dossier in order to build up an accurate self-image;
(b) carrying out a strengths and weaknesses analysis.

2.2 Building an accurate self-image

Humans are self-conscious creatures: we behave partly in accordance with the image or concept that we have of ourselves. That self-image is something we mainly learn from interacting with other people; a reflection of their behaviour and attitudes towards us. It is formed by experience over time and is constantly adjusted. For example, repeated failure or criticism at work might tend to create a low self-image spreading into other areas of the individual's life, where it may be completely unjustified. Every individual has a self-image, but very few people attempt to confirm, refute or change their self-image in any systematic or objective fashion. In other words, they are not self-aware.

2.3 Developing self-awareness

In order to become more self-aware, you might try out the ideas below.

(a) Acquire knowledge about human beings and their behaviour in general. Your own studies of motivation, people in groups, interpersonal skills etc will help you to observe and understand what is going on when you act or interact with other people.

(b) Gather the opinions of trusted individuals who know you well. On the basis that, in dealing with other people, 'you are what they think you are', this is a practical way of finding out about yourself. For example, even if you have low self-confidence, you may appear to others to be aggressive and overbearing, perhaps because you try to cover up your lack of confidence.

(i) In this process, you are using other people as a mirror which reflects your image back to you. You see yourself as others see you. This can be quite a daunting prospect, so you would need to talk to someone whom you could trust to be honest but supportive: bolstering - or crushing - your ego is not only unhelpful, but downright dangerous, since your self-image will get further distorted. The other person also needs to trust you: they will not be honest with a criticism if they think you will never speak to them again!

(ii) A friend or partner, relative or colleague might be consulted. They would be in a position to help you with those aspects of your personality and behaviour that are displayed in contact with other people in various situations ('you tend to snap at people when you are under pressure'; 'you're not a good listener in meetings'; 'you're a good person to have around in a crisis').

(c) Compare yourself to role models in your life. All individuals consciously or unconsciously select models or ideals for themselves, for the various roles that are relevant to their lives. Parents, school teachers, colleagues or superiors at work are often influential in giving the individual a picture of what he should aspire to be like at different stages in his life. You may choose your model because of your view of his or her charisma, knowledge or expertise (the appeal of the teacher or more experienced colleague); success (as with a hero or celebrity or tycoon); or dominating personality. Festinger suggested that most people seek to evaluate their own performance through comparison with other individuals rather than by using absolute standards. So having a role model to measure yourself against helps to formulate your self-image and your aspirations to change and grow.

(d) Take tests - independently, or as part of the appraisal or training processes of the organisation. You might take an IQ test, or aptitude test (for particular skills). If you wanted to know more about your personality, there are various kinds of test for that too - although it is uncertain how scientifically accurate and objective some of them really are.

(e) Analyse incidents at work or outside work. A particular problem with the work group, for example, may give you insight into your own behaviour in that situation. A new challenge might bring out in you a quality you had not displayed before.

Activity 1 **(30 minutes)**

Whom do you look up to - at work or outside work, whether you know them personally or not? Do you want to be like them - and if so how? Compare yourself to this 'role model': what areas of yourself would you have to change in order to be more like them - and how could you go about it?

Does your employer have a system of mentoring? If you do not have, or are not yourself, a mentor, ask your superior whether there is mentoring at more senior levels. If there is, what is the mentor expected to do? How useful is it in practice?

It is a good idea to compile the findings from such an investigation into a written self profile. You could start with information from your discussions with others, and your own observations. Take Rodger's 'Seven Point Plan' personnel specification, which includes such features as aptitude, disposition, interests and physical attributes - or consider what aspects are likely to be important to you in your own life: your impact on other people, your motivation, your confidence level, whether you are introvert or extrovert and so on. Test results and copies of assessment reports can be added to the file as they are acquired, along with any changes, for instance, if you gain some further insight from a particular incident, or you get training in some area which enhances your skills or attributes.

2.3 Self appraisal: strengths and weaknesses analysis

Strengths and **weaknesses** analysis is a technique used for corporate appraisal - the self-awareness exercise for a whole organisation. It is sometimes added to an analysis of the **opportunities** and **threats** facing the organisation: hence the abbreviation SWOT. A personal SWOT is equally valuable for individuals.

(a) Identify your **strengths**, and your **positive assets:** physical, mental, behavioural and emotional. You may dress well, have a good memory, be good with the telephone, be honest, calm under pressure, a good listener and so on.

(b) Identify your **weaknesses**, or **liabilities**. You may have no head for numbers, have a tendency to fidget, be subject to stress, or impatient with other people.

This is a useful exercise. You may gain confidence and set higher goals for yourself as a result of appraising your strengths. You may need to find more realistic goals, or plan to practise/train to minimise your weaknesses. You may decide that you are not in the job - or are not doing enough outside work - to make the most of your strengths. You may identify in your weaknesses the root of certain problems you have had, say, with passing exams or leading a group.

Activity 2 **(20 minutes)**

Draw up a two-columned chart and list some of:

(a) your strengths; and
(b) your weaknesses,

that are relevant to your present job, or studies.

Do the strengths outweigh the weaknesses? Can you identify ways in which your weaknesses can be overcome or at least minimised

There are a number of dimensions to this analysis for individuals.

(a) Do you have the skills necessary to do the job **today?** (You should have - but if not, training is essential.)

(b) Do you have the skills to do the job **tomorrow?** (This may be because of a change in the environment or an expansion of the department - if not, pro-active training should be planned to ensure you are prepared.)

(c) Do you have the skills to do **tomorrow's job?** (Will you be promoted? If so, what new skills and knowledge will be needed? This is development and would be a pro-active approach to succession planning, or a personal strategy to increase the chances of promotion.)

(d) Do you have the skills for a different job tomorrow? (What will be the alternative employment options in the future and what skills and qualifications will be needed? This is the personal career development planning and investment for which many managers are today taking personal responsibility.)

NOTES

Activity 3 **(30 minutes)**

You have already undertaken a personal strengths and weaknesses analysis of your current management competences. You can add to that an **opportunities** *and* **threats** assessment which will encourage you to think about career prospects and future opportunities. This external analysis of your own personal job market should help you to extend and prioritise the areas of skill development you want to focus on.

You are already undertaking your HND or HNC qualification so are clearly committed to personal development. Your study time can have considerable added value if you use it to develop additional and specific management skills.

Select four skill areas you want to work on or your boss suggests might be beneficial.

(a) These may be areas of weakness like time management or presentation skills.

(b) They may be areas of strength like analysis and problem solving which you want to develop further.

Using the grid below identify each area, set a **quantified** objective for the next 6 months and give some thought to how (your strategy) to achieve this improvement. The next section of this chapter has ideas on training and development which may stimulate some thoughts on strategy. Here is our example:

Area	Objectives	Strategy
Time management	• To hit at least 90% of deadlines set over the last 6 months • To find at least 6 hours per week for HND/HNC studies	• To spend time every morning planning my time • Agreeing a study plan and sticking to it • Taking measures to reduce timewasting

	Objective	Objectives	Strategy
1			
2			
3			
4			
5			
6			
7			

Review Dates 1..................... 2..................... 3.....................

This should not be simply an academic exercise. It is a specific requirement of this Unit.

BPP PUBLISHING

3 MANAGEMENT SKILLS

3.1 Self development

An important part of the process of improving the performance of managers is self-development. Part of being an effective manager is the responsibility to further one's own development. A significant factor affecting the success of self-development is the extent to which individual managers take advantage of development opportunities around them. This demands that the manager must be able to identify clearly real development needs and goals, to take responsibility for actions to reach these goals and recognise opportunities for learning. Self-development has to be self-initiated but if this is to be a realistic aim, it requires an organisational climate that will encourage managers to develop themselves and the active support of top management.

3.2 Skills required

It is difficult to list the skills that you will personally need in your job but at least some from the following list of skills will be necessary. The first six on the list are the main management skills, whilst the other skills are ones that you might like to include in your skills audit.

(a) **Planning** – setting goals, deciding on the means by which the goals will be achieved and scheduling. Forecasting means looking into the future, while planning means making decisions on what course of action should be adopted to meet the challenge of the future. Planning implies having precise aims or objectives and working out how to achieve them.

(b) **Organising** is the next stage after planning. It can be broken down into three parts.

(i) working out the actual jobs needed to be done to fulfil the plans agreed upon

(ii) grouping activities into a pattern or structure

(iii) giving specific people in the organisation particular jobs to achieve the objectives of the plans agreed upon

(c) **Motivating** – there are three basic types of behaviour essential for an organisation to function effectively:

(i) people must be induced to enter and remain within the organisation (labour and absenteeism can be costly) but obviously mere physical attendance is not enough

(ii) people must do their appointed jobs in a dependable way. Organisations have to rely on a continuous, fairly stable pattern of relationships over time

(iii) people must, on occasion, be innovative and exhibit spontaneous activity to achieve organisational objectives that go beyond what is expected of them

(d) **Communicating** is necessary to achieve co-ordination. It may take the form of:

(i) giving instructions
(ii) receiving instructions
(iii) exchanging ideas
(iv) announcing plans or strategies

(v) comparing actual results against a plan
(vi) laying down rules or procedures

(e) **Controlling** is the essential process of ensuring that what was planned to happen actually does happen. Controlling involves the following activities:

(i) setting objectives or standards of work
(ii) devising ways of measuring actual performance
(iii) measuring actual performance against the objectives or standards
(iv) evaluating whether and why deviations from the planned results exist
(v) taking corrective action where this is possible to restore the position

(f) **Creating**. Using your imagination in problem solving. Creativity can include innovation, synthesis and development. Innovation is where you find a completely new way of thinking about, or doing something. If you can improvise quickly at work, eg use an alternative material for a job in an emergency, find a quicker way around a job or work out a new procedure, then you are being innovative or creative. Synthesis is where you take ideas from different sources and combine them. For example, you can receive advice from many people at work, a bit of help from a course tutor or friend and the essential contribution from yourself can provide a useful and satisfactory solution to a problem. Development occurs when you take a basic idea and extend it.

(g) Working with people.

(h) Identifying and tackling problems.

(i) Numeracy.

(j) Gathering and analysing data.

(k) Being objective.

(l) Selling/persuading.

4 TIME MANAGEMENT

4.1 The importance of time management

Time management (TM) implies planning the best use of time, including cutting down on time wasted, devoting more time to the really important issues or jobs on hand, and completing more in the time available. Failure to manage your time can leave you so short of it that you have a 'last minute rush' to get a really important job done. Inevitably, something gets overlooked, causing yet another crisis which, in turn, takes yet more time to put right.

An essential objective of looking at time management is to enable you to save at least some of the time you presently waste in one way or another at work, and to use this time better in tackling jobs which really require your undivided attention and effort. It is of course unlikely that you will never waste time in the future, but even a 10% saving in the first year could give you up to four hours a week extra productive time.

You always have the choice: let time manage you, or manage your own time. Which is it to be?

4.2 The consequences of poor time management

The following are possible consequences of poor TM.

(a) *Activity mania.* Because every day begins without a proper plan, jobs become fragmented, are left unfinished, and have to be picked up again and again. In the end you are left rushing from one crisis to another, without a moment left for thought and reflection. The law of diminishing returns begins to operate, and yet more activity is required to keep things going.

(b) *Reacting to, and not controlling, events.* Instead of being able to take the initiative, having plans to meet emergencies (so that they are dealt with in the way that you prefer), you spend much of your time fending off customers and superiors, or dealing with telephone calls from all and sundry. In what time you have left, you try to cope with the problems which have emerged.

(c) *Living in the present, rather than the future.* Charles Handy (*Understanding organisations*) points out that the manager is above all responsible for the future. This means you need to devote time to anticipating and planning for the future: marshalling resources, creating the best possible working environment, recruiting, training and developing staff. Living in the present means the future is neglected and more potential problems remain undetected.

(d) *Becoming less effective.* A manager with poor TM skills is seen to be inefficient by senior management so advancement and promotion become less likely.

(e) *Work overload.* Being pressed for time as a result of poor TM generally leads to an ever-increasing list of jobs yet to be tackled. Too often, the only perceived way out is to work overtime.

(f) *Less leisure time.* The more time spent at work the less is available for sport, leisure activities or for home and family. Interpersonal relationships can be threatened and job satisfaction limited.

(g) *Stress.* All the above consequences of poor TM can lead to stress. This has implications for you, the work team, the organisation at large, as well as family and friends.

4.3 What happens to the time?

Given the consequences that we have just outlined it is a useful exercise for you to consider what happens during time available for work. All activities are time consumers but many, often too many, are time wasters. Here are some of the time wasters which can take big slices of time if you do not control them properly.

(a) *Lack of forward planning.* As you have already seen, this can result in 'crisis management' – rushing from one fire-fighting situation to the next.

(b) *The telephone.* OK, if your telephone rings it has to be answered. But many people let conversations go on far too long. On the other hand, when making calls it is easy for you to prolong conversations or 'hang on' for long periods. This shows poor telephone technique.

(c) *Visitors.* These can be from within the organisation as well as from without. As with telephone calls, visitors can take up valuable time if they are handled badly and encouraged to stay too long.

(d) *Paperwork.* It is all too easy to dawdle over dealing with routine forms and correspondence, especially when the alternative is to deal with a more demanding job.

NOTES

(e) *Deadlines.* These are usually set by other people and you may get to know about them well in advance. Even so, it is all too easy to leave things to the last minute. The later you initiate action to meet a deadline the more critical any unforeseen delay becomes, and the more time may have to be taken to ensure it is met.

(f) *Doing it yourself (DIY)* takes several forms: failing to delegate is the worst. Doing jobs that subordinates could do equally well is generally inexcusable; taking on jobs voluntarily from others could be a recipe for overwork. Don't be one of those who can't say 'no'.

(g) *Taking on too much work.* A variation on DIY, this is particularly difficult to avoid for those who are not very assertive or those who want to please or impress. The worst version of this is offering to take on extra jobs which realistically can't be finished in the time available.

(h) *Taking work home.* If you go home with a bulging briefcase or a carrier-bag full of paperwork, it is a sure sign of poor TM. When you do get home there are bound to be many other legitimate activities for you to carry out: how said it is to go back to work next day with the work taken home largely untouched.

(i) *Meetings* should be a tool that help things to get done efficiently and in good time. Frequently, meetings are badly run and what you put into them is not matched by the outcomes. A lot depends upon how much preparation people are prepared to make before a meeting starts; and the amount of participation individuals are willing to undertake during meetings (including listening to what others have to say).

(j) *Communication problems.* Failures abound in most organisations. Time is wasted in clarifying obscure messages, checking on missing facts, chasing overdue statistics or reports. Poor filing systems or inefficient documentation preparation and transmission systems assist in yet more time wasting within the organisation.

(k) *Lack of self-discipline.* Most people find some jobs more attractive than others. It is much more difficult to motivate yourself to tackle the less interesting tasks or those demanding much efforts, for example making out complicated returns. The choice often made is to 'put things off', especially where no immediate deadlines are involved. The inevitable consequence yet again is uncompleted work piles up creating problems for the future.

(l) *Not assessing priorities.* Generally a result of not sitting back, sorting through and thinking about what work is on hand. Instead of the really important tasks being completed the ones on the top of the pile, or those someone makes a fuss about, are tackled first.

Few of us could truthfully claim not to have committed at least one of the errors mentioned above.

Activity 4 **(30 minutes)**

Check carefully what you did (or did not do) at work recently against the list and ask yourself how many errors you made. If you score five or more then you have a real TM problem. Even a score of one indicates a need to examine your TM behaviour carefully.

NOTES

4.4 Assessing your own time management behaviour

Time spent on considering the following twenty questions will help you develop ways of improving your TM. Only by answering truthfully can you begin to appreciate where skills need developing.

Question	Regularly	Sometimes	Rarely	Never
Do you make 'to do today' lists every working day and use them?				
Do you put the most important items first in your lists?				
Is your desk tidy and organised?				
Have you a place for everything?				
Do you deal effectively with callers and visitors?				
Can you easily find papers and documents you need?				
Do you deal with paperwork quickly?				
Do you deal with unpleasant jobs as soon as they need to be done?				
Do you begin and finish jobs on time?				
Do people know the best times to see you?				
Do you meet deadlines with time to spare?				
Do you delegate when appropriate?				
Do you allow yourself 'free' or quiet time during the day when you can work undisturbed?				
Do you try to prevent problems arising rather than solve them after they crop up?				
Do you get to work/meetings/events on time?				
Do you find it easy to say 'no' to requests from others?				
Do you prepare properly for meetings?				
Do you avoid taking work home?				
Do you review the way you spend your time at work?				
Do you tackle the most demanding tasks at your 'peak energy' times?				

Scoring: Never = 0, Rarely = 2, Sometimes = 2, Regularly = 3

Interpretation

0-10	You do very little or no conscious TM and are at the mercy of events. A fresh start is needed.
11-20	You do some TM but you do need to review your weak areas in a planned fashion one at a time.
21-40	You have generally good TM behaviour but there is still some room for improvement where you have low-rated scores.
41-60	Well done. You seem to have very good TM skills but keep looking critically at any low-rated answer.

These questions do not cover all of TM behaviour but are sufficiently representative to take account of its more important aspects.

BPP PUBLISHING

4.5 Improving your time management

What follows is a list of practical suggestions and hints to help you improve your time management.

(a) **Cost your time**. Take your annual salary and divide it by the number of working days in a calendar year to give a daily rate. Add about 20% for administrative and other overheads then divide by the number of working hours in the day (say 7½). The resultant figure is the hourly cost of your time to your employers. Every occasion when you 'save' an hour, or put it to better use, you become more cost-effective.

(b) **Identify significant job elements**. Examine your job description. (If necessary, draw one up for yourself and get it checked out by a superior or a colleague.) Select from it three or four key activities or significant job elements. These could be, for example:

 (i) allocate work to teams and individuals agreeing objectives and work plans

 (ii) manage work activities to achieve organisational goals

 (iii) recording or storing information

 (iv) developing and maintaining a healthy and safe working environment. (All outcomes that are part of this course)

 List the tasks and duties falling under each significant job element then estimate the time taken each month to complete the task and duties under each significant job element and cost this time. Assess the corresponding 'payback' to you and the organisation of the time spent on each significant job element. After reviewing the figures you may decide to increase or decrease this amount of time.

(c) **Assess your long-term priorities**. There are two kinds of priorities you will need to take into account: long-term priorities and short-term priorities. Long-term priorities are clearly recognised by those organisations that have corporate plans, company objectives, mission statements and the like. Long-term priorities are much less often set for individual employees. Even more rarely do individual employees sit down and assess their *own* long-term plans and objectives in detail. However, having them clarified helps you with your priorities.

 This applies to all long-term priorities, except that in an emergency you can postpone a long-term priority for a day or so. However, if no action is taken to further a long-term priority over a period of time then you will be faced with having to pull out all the stops to catch up.

(d) **Consider your short-term priorities**. These have the advantage of being newer, easier to remember, easier to achieve. The big temptation is to spend more time and effort on the short-term priorities. What is required is for you to strike a *balance* between the two, on any given day.

(e) **Use a planning aid**. You may well have gathered by now that you will need a planning aid of some sort (a time/appointments diary, a work-planner or daily schedule form) to assist in planning the day's activities. Only by using such a device will you be able to plan ahead successfully, allocate time and keep an overall check on what you are doing.

(f) **Prioritise**. If you do decide to use a planing aid like a daily work schedule, facing you at the start of any one day will be a mixture of activities to sort out. Some will be long-term priorities, some short-term priorities and yet more will have much lower priorities still.

Additionally, some activities will be imposed upon you by others, eg meetings and visitors. These will obviously go into your schedule from the start.

The question now is what to do first out of the items under your control. A simple guide is to follow the 'MOP', or the 'Must, Ought and Prefer' principle. This involves listing all the tasks, duties and activities you need to do within a given day and assessing (a) the approximate time each is likely to take, and (b) to which one of the MOP categories to allocate each task.

M is a 'must' task, one which simply has to be completed in whole or part on that day (and probably by a particular time, too). These jobs are best tackled first in any given day when you have sufficient discretion over your time. When you are under time constraints imposed by others M jobs should be done at the earliest opportunity.

O or 'ought' tasks are those which you decide are highly desirable to be completed during the day but as a last resort could be delayed. These need to be attempted after the M tasks are underway.

P or 'preferred' tasks are those jobs you like doing because you find them pleasurable and satisfying. Additionally, such jobs will normally contribute to the good of the organisation, provided you do not spend too much time on them. However, by the very nature of P tasks, the tendency is to spend time on them to the detriment of Ms and Os unless you have carried out the approximate time assessment mentioned above (an M task!) and kept to it.

After working out all the tasks and jobs to be done during a day you may want to add 'cushion time', a further period of time to cover for unscheduled interruptions, and breaks for tea, coffee and lunch. Now you may find the total time available is insufficient to do every job listed. Several strategies might help here.

One way out is to start work earlier (but to do this regularly goes against good TM). Another is to enter only the Ms and Os into the schedule, then reassess the Ps. Perhaps some can wait; others can be delegated sideways, downwards or upwards. Yet others will just not get done at all. Don't think you are inefficient if you cannot complete in a day every job you can think of: you will be effective if you do all the Ms and Os well, and just some of the Ps.

(g) **Work through the day in an orderly way**. Now you have a plan for the day: the jobs and tasks to be done have been established and the order in which they are to be done. You have made sufficient time available to accomplish the work. You can now focus on one job at a time, giving your whole attention to the task in hand. Avoid lots of short work periods whenever you can. Spend say two hours with M jobs, two with Os and the rest of the time with fixed appointments (eg regular meetings), interruptions and P tasks.

The advantage of this type of approach is that, provided the tasks determined by others do not come too often in the early part of the day, the 'must' ones are done when you are fresh and more able to cope with demanding activities. At the end of the day when your energy level is lower it is easier for you to have to deal with the preferred tasks.

(h) **Distinguish between the urgent and the important.** This is a classic dilemma: choosing between doing jobs that are *urgent* (to be done within a given time in the near future) and those that are *important* (significant or critical to the organisation in the long term). Too often the urgent and unimportant jobs get done to the detriment of the important. One way of resolving the dilemma is to use the urgent versus important matrix, shown below. Tasks that are both important and urgent should get top priority (A). The ones that are urgent but not very important (B) need to be done soon but spend as little time as possible on each. Important but not urgent tasks (C) should be started as soon as possible as they have *disaster potential*, ie they could suddenly become both important and urgent. Tasks that are neither important nor urgent (D) go to the back of the queue.

		Important High	**Important** Low
Urgent	High	A	B
	Low	C	D

(i) **Review each day's work**. At the end of each day take five minutes to review what you have done and how successful the day has been. Make a note of anything not achieved or which still needs completion. Put it on the list for tomorrow. Clear your desk before you leave.

(j) **Make yourself unavailable**. When you have a task on hand that is both urgent and important use any subterfuge to prevent interruptions.

(k) **Learn to speed read**. Much time is spent reading forms, returns, reports, memos or other paperwork. Savings can be made if you learn to read faster. Read whole phrases or even whole lines at a time rather than individual words. Skim quickly through the conventional or routine parts of the document. The average person reads about 300 words a minute – you could aim for 400 and save 15 seconds for every 300 words.

(l) **Learn to delegate**. Each task you do should be critically evaluated from time to time. Many of your preferred tasks could be candidates for delegation. Let a member of your team enjoy doing them; it saves your time and develops and motivates subordinates.

(m) **Stop procrastinating**. Find out what it is that causes you to put off doing something and remedy it. Maybe it is a feeling of inadequacy due to lack of information, lack of a particular skill or lack of training.

5 INTERPERSONAL SKILLS AND WORKING RELATIONSHIPS

Interpersonal behaviour includes:

- Interaction between people – a two-way process such as communication, delegating, negotiating, resolving conflict, persuading, selling, using and responding to authority.
- An individual's behaviour in relationship to other people.

The way you behave in response to other people includes:

- how you perceive other people
- listening to and understanding other people
- behaving in a way that builds on this understanding

NOTES

5.1 Interpersonal skills

Interpersonal skills involve inspiring, motivating, leading and controlling people to achieve goals which are often poorly defined. They are needed by an individual in order to:

(a) understand and manage the roles, relationships, attitudes and perceptions operating in any situation in which two or more people are involved

(b) communicate clearly and effectively

(c) achieve his or her aims from an interpersonal encounter (ideally allowing the other parties to emerge satisfied too)

Issues to consider in interpersonal communication and work relationships

Issue	Comment
Goal	What does the other person want from the process? What do you want from the process? What will both parties need and be trying to do to achieve their aims? Can both parties emerge satisfied?
Perceptions	What, if any, are likely to be the factors causing 'distortion' of the way both parties see the issues and each other? (Attitudes, feelings, expectations?)
Roles	What 'roles' are the parties playing? (Superior/subordinate, customer/server, complainer/soother) What expectations does this create of the way they will behave?
Resistances	What may the other person be 'afraid of'? What may he or she be trying to protect? (His or her self-image/ego, attitudes?)
Attitudes	What sources of difference, conflict or lack of understanding might there be, arising from attitudes and other factors that shape them (sex, race, specialism, hierarchy)?
Relationships	What are the relative positions of the parties and the nature of the relationship between them? (Superior/subordinate? Formal/informal? Work/non-work?)
Environment	What factors in the immediate and situational environment might affect the issues and the people? (eg competitive environment: customer care; pressures of disciplinary situation: nervousness; physical surroundings: formality/informality)

5.2 Communication skills

In addition, a range of communication skills will be deployed. The following checklist identifies and classifies communication skills.

Oral	Written	Visual/non-verbal
Clear pronunciation	Correct spelling	Understanding of control over body language and facial expressions
Suitable vocabulary	Suitable vocabulary	Drawing ability
Correct grammar/syntax	Correct grammar/syntax	
Fluency	Good writing or typing	
Expressive delivery	Suitable style	

BPP PUBLISHING

Skills in sending messages include the following.

(a) Selecting and organising your material – marshalling your thoughts and constructing your sentences, arguments etc

(b) Judging the effect of your message on the particular recipient in that particular situation

(c) Choosing language and media accordingly

(d) Adapting your communication style accordingly – putting people at their ease, smoothing over difficulties (tact) or being comforting/challenging/informal/formal as the situation and relationship demand

(e) Using non-verbal signals to reinforce (or at least not to undermine) your spoken message

(f) Seeking and interpreting feedback

Skills in receiving messages include the following.

(a) Reading attentively and actively making sure you understand the content, looking up unfamiliar words and doubtful facts if necessary and evaluating the information given: is it logical? correct? objective?

(b) Extracting relevant information from the message and filtering out the non-essentials.

(c) Listening attentively and actively – concentrating on the message and not on what you are going to say next; questioning and evaluating what you are hearing.

(d) Interpreting the message's underlying meaning, if any, and evaluating your own reactions. Are you reading into the message more or less than what is really there?

(e) Asking questions in a way that will elicit the information you want to obtain.

(f) Interpreting non-verbal signals and how they confirm or contradict the spoken message.

(g) Giving helpful feedback if the medium is appropriate (eg poor telephone line) or the message is unclear, insufficient etc.

5.3 The importance of good working relationships and good interpersonal skills

Good working relationships and good interpersonal skills can assist in the following areas.

Area	**Comment**
Motivation	Work can satisfy people's social needs because it provides relationships
Communication	Poor interpersonal relationships can cause a barrier to communicating effectively –messages will be misinterpreted
Team working and team-building	Good working relationships and good interpersonal skills can develop a climate in which people can communicate openly and honestly
Customer care	Good interpersonal skills are recognised as being increasingly important when dealing with customers

Area	Comment
Career development	Good interpersonal skills are increasingly necessary to get promotion
Managerial roles	Many of the managerial roles require interpersonal skills
Power and persuasion	Interpersonal skills can be a source of personal power in an organisation and can make a manager more effective
Team management	Interpersonal skills are required for the manager's tasks of appraisal, interviewing etc

5.4 Effective negotiation skills

Negotiating is an activity that seeks to reach agreement between two or more starting positions.

The skills of a negotiator can be summarised under three main headings.

(a) Interpersonal skills – the use of good communicating techniques, the user of power and influence, and the ability to impress a personal style on the tactics of negotiation

(b) Analytical skills – the ability to analyse information, diagnose problems, to plan and set objectives, and the exercise of good judgement in interpreting results

(c) Technical skills – attention to detail and thorough case preparation

There are behaviours that are typical of successful negotiations and distinguish them from the less successful.

Successful negotiators	Less successful negotiators
Skilled negotiators avoid criticising or attacking the other person and concentrate instead on 'attacking' the problem in a no nonsense but constructive way.	Less skilled negotiators are more likely to get locked into an attacking spiral where one side attacks the other, which provokes a counter attack and so on.
Skilled negotiators ask many more questions than the less skilled. The skilled negotiator asks questions not only to gain more information and understanding but also as an alternative to disagreeing bluntly, and as a means of putting forward suggestions.	The less skilled tend to assume that they understand the other person's point of view and that the other person has the same basic information. This makes asking questions redundant.
The skilled negotiator summarises and tests understanding, knowing that being explicit aids common understanding and leads to quality agreement that is more likely to stick.	
Skilled negotiatiors keep the emotional temperature down by sticking to the facts.	Less skilled negotiators are inclined to exaggeration, using expressions such as 'an offer you can't refuse' and 'mutually beneficial'.
The skilled negotiator is more likely to say things that reveal what he or she is thinking, intending and feeling than the less skilled.	The less skilled negotiator feels vulnerable to losing the argument and is more likely to 'keep his cards close to his chest'.

Successful negotiators	Less successful negotiators
Disagreements are inevitable during the course of a negotiation. The skilled negotiator gives the explanation first and rounds off the explanation by saying that they were in disagreement. This has a more constructive effect because the explanation becomes the focus for the other person's reaction rather than the fact of a disagreement.	Less skilled negotiators disagree first and then go on to give reasons. This often provokes a negative reaction from the other person who bridles at the explicit disagreement and therefore fails to listen to the reasons.

6 COMPETENCE ASSESSMENT

6.1 What are competences?

Competences are the critical skills, knowledge and attitudes that a job-holder must have to perform effectively. They are expressed in visible, behavioural terms and reflect the skills, knowledge and attitude (the main components of any job), which must be demonstrated to an agreed standard and must contribute to the overall aims of the organisation. The term is open to various interpretations because there are a number of competence-based systems and concepts of competence. As a general definition, a competent individual can perform a work role in a wide range of settings over an extended period of time.

Some competence-based systems are development-led – they focus on the development of competence and are linked to training and development programmes to develop people to a level of performance expected at work. Other systems are achievement-led – they focus on assessment of competent performance – what people do and how well they do it.

This is an important distinction when considering competence-based systems as the system may include many components, each linked to a different aspect of human resource activity within an organisation.

6.2 Process

For any competence based system the process is the same.

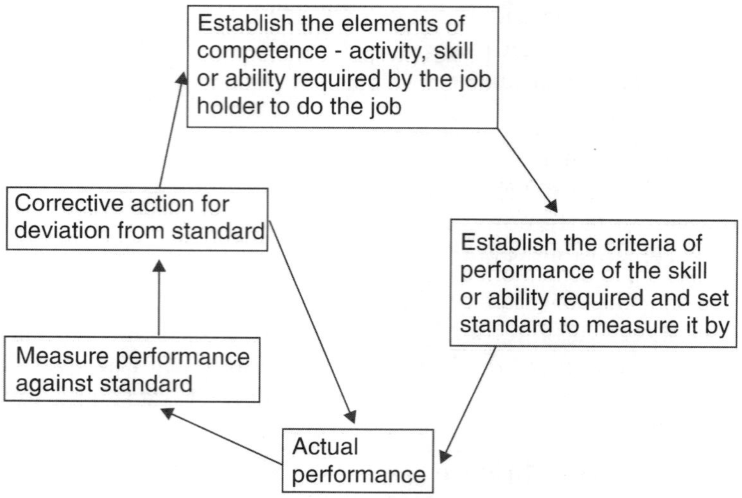

Although it is not a work-based activity, think of the process of passing a driving test. It is an observable skill which is measured against set standards. In the case of failure a list which outlines the failed areas is given to the learner driver and is used to form the basis of any corrective action needed before re-applying for the test.

6.3 Standards of competence

Highly qualified representatives from different occupational and professional groups get involved in setting standards. They analyse jobs in specific areas to provide units of competence. These are written as statements incorporating:

(a) the elements of competence – the specific activities a job holder should be able to perform

(b) performance criteria – how well it should be performed

(c) a range statement – in what context and conditions, and

(d) the knowledge and understanding which underpins the competence

7 PERSONAL SKILLS AUDIT AND SELF-APPRAISAL

The personal skills audit and self-appraisal requires you to identify, review and assess your own performance of current management skills.

EXAMPLE: MANAGEMENT SKILLS

Look at the following list of skills which we have considered in this text. For each identify why it is important or relevant for the business manager:

Skill		*Importance*
1	Time Management	
2	Prioritisation	
3	Delegation	
4	Communication	
5	Negotiation	
6	Leadership	
7	Motivation	
8	Team Building	

ANSWER

1 **Time management**. Fewer managers means more responsibility for those in the business. Time management is essential to avoid stress and to get everything done.

2 **Prioritisation** is an integral part of time management. In marketing, managers may have to prioritise markets or customers and need to understand the process and criteria by which priorities can be established.

3 **Delegation** is essential:

(a) in ensuring that tactical details of activities are attended to;

(b) to give younger managers and staff experience and chance to develop their skills;

(c) to act as a motivator.

4 **Communication**. The essence of the manager's job is communicating, both sending messages and listening to them. It must be done professionally both inside and outside the organisation.

5 **Negotiation** with clients and staff is a key aspect of bringing buyers and sellers, employees and the organisation together in a way which satisfies everyone's needs.

6 **Leadership**. The business manager is often a figurehead and must share the organisation's vision in order to communicate it effectively to others. Managers are in the business of leading the business down the path of customer orientation.

7 **Motivation**. Management roles can be very isolated and motivation has to be clear and effective to get the best out of those working at the customer interface.

8 **Team building**. Management is about co-ordination. Satisfying customers has to be a team effort. Managers have to be able to build teams even when they have no line authority, for example teams with advertising agencies and distributors as well as with operations and distribution.

7.1 Self-appraisal

Take each of the headings listed in the exercise above, and consider to what degree you have each of the skills. You should spend at least five minutes on each one, and jot down your thoughts on a separate sheet of paper for each one. Consider these factors about each one:

- Is it relevant to you in your current job? If it is not relevant now, is it likely to be in the future?
- If it is a skill which is relevant now, how well do you think that you exercise it?
- Think of specific examples of ways in which you have used that skill
- Could you use the skill better than you do at the moment, or differently?
- Would it improve your ability to do your job if you improved your use of that skill?
- What impact would it have on your management skills generally if you exercised this skill better
- In summary, do you use that skill effectively or is there room for improvement?
- Do you use or have any other management skills which are not included in our list? Think of the nature of your own job, and consider whether you carry out any tasks which are unique to your own role.

You may find it helpful to take a short break after each one so that you tackle the next one with a refreshed mind.

It is vital that you are honest in assessing your skills! You will only be deluding yourself and wasting your time if you are not honest.

Once you have thought through each of the skill headings, and made rough notes, make a more formal record of your deliberations. This will be useful for two reasons:

- It will form a key part of journal or skills log and provide important evidence which can be assessed as part of the Unit
- It may form the basis of the personal development plan which you will need to draw up with your line manager as part of this Unit.

You could draw up a chart like this:

NOTES

Area for development	Level of skill before (1-5)	Activities completed	Level of skill now	Comments on the process	New Goals
1.					
2.					
3.					
4.					
5.					

This will enable you to record progress as you go along.

If you are committed to personal progress and development, you should take time now to set goals for the next six months. Develop a plan for each skill and add review dates to your diary now.

7.4 Conclude

Reach a conclusion as to your abilities as far as each of these skills is concerned.

8 PREPARATION OF A DEVELOPMENT PLAN

You are required to produce this with your line manager. If you are not employed, consider whether you could produce it with your college tutor or supervisor.

Bear in mind that the development plan can include a wide range of targets, not just improvements in the management skills identified in the self-appraisal covered earlier in this chapter. The Edexcel guidelines refer to 'personal development targets' and devising a 'personal development plan'. The emphasis on the word 'personal' indicates that this area of the Unit will be very specifically geared towards you as an individual. You may find that the production of the development plan provides you with the ideal opportunity to think seriously about your current situation and future plans. You should regard it as an opportunity which could pay considerable personal dividends, and not a chore.

8.1 Set, prioritise and agree targets

Targets establish what you are aiming for. They can be short, medium or long term. If you can set and then meet a target, you are demonstrating that you have acquired the skill of managing yourself, the main theme of this Unit.

8.2 Targets

Decide what you would like to achieve over a specified time, for example one year. This book cannot tell you exactly what targets you should set for yourself, because they are intensely personal to you and to your own particular set of circumstances, but we can make suggestions.

Some of these may be relevant:

- Complete Unit 16 of the HND/HNC qualification by a certain date. What date? Perhaps it should be by a forthcoming holiday or by Christmas or within a fixed number of weeks.
- Complete the entire HND/HNC qualification by a certain date, for example this time next year or the end of 2002.
- Gain promotion at work, for example by your next birthday
- Improve your standard of French or another foreign language
- Acquire additional computer skills, for example learn a new package, or how to do something that you cannot do at the moment, such as draw tables
- Try to delegate more
- Go on a course on presentation skills

8.3 Prioritise

Once you have established a list of targets, allocate numbers to them to indicate how important they are, with 1 as the highest, 2 as the next highest and so on.

You may find it difficult to decide which order they should go in. The targets could be prioritised in terms of

- Importance to your job
- Importance to you as an individual
- How much you want to achieve them
- How quickly you need to achieve them
- Cost to you or your employer
- Enjoyability and potential satisfaction arising
- How realistic it is that you will achieve them

This is an aspect which you should perhaps discuss with your manager: remember that your personal development plan is to be devised with him or her.

The order in which you put your targets may change a number of times before it is finalised. You may want to prioritise improving your command of French, but if you do not use the language at work it would not be regarded as a high business priority. However, if it is something which you personally have a burning desire to do, it should not necessarily be consigned to the bottom of the heap, as it would pay dividends in terms of personal satisfaction and sense of achievement.

Similarly, you may well want to be promoted or given the chance to work in a different department before a certain date, but that may not be realistic from a business planning point of view. Alternatively, your promotion may depend on your passing exams and gaining qualifications, or on someone ahead of you being promoted themselves, so that the matter is not entirely under your control.

8.4 Short and long term learning objectives

Note that the Edexcel guidelines require you to think in terms of learning both in the short and the long term.

Your short tem learning objectives probably include completing this and other HND/HNC Units, but your long term learning objectives could encompass more or less anything, for example qualifying as an accountant or with the Chartered Institute of Marketing or Institute of Personnel Management. The only limit really is that you must be realistic in terms of timing and your own abilities.

9 RESPONDING TO FEEDBACK

Many people find it very difficult to respond to feedback and make the best use of it, because it is usually viewed as a form of criticism. This is especially so when the feedback relates to the attainment of personal goals and targets.

9.1 Feedback from your line manager

Remember that it is part of the role of the line manager to question you on the work done.

You should try to accept his or her comments in that very positive light, and take the view that they are helping you to achieve your ultimate goal, which is to progress through your HND studies and attain your other targets.

If your manager gives you constructive criticism, he or she is not saying that you are wrong in what you have said, or that your ideas are no good. The criticism is designed to help you to improve your skills and thus improve your job satisfaction and promotion prospects overall.

9.2 Feedback from your work colleagues

The emphasis within the feedback from your work colleagues is likely to be different from that received from your manager. Your colleagues do not have a specific responsibility to report on your work. To put it at its most basic, your colleagues are giving you feedback because you will be giving it to them.

When receiving colleague feedback, bear in mind that they are learning from the process too, as you will learn from providing feedback to them.

10 EVALUATING PROGRESS

When establishing your original development plan, you should set deadlines, or target dates by which you intend to achieve particular targets. In setting these target dates, you should be realistic and only set as a target what you know to be feasible, given time constraints and other demands on your time.

10.1 Conducting a review

Draw up a schedule of your targets and the relevant dates, or note them in your diary.

When the dates are reached, you should carry out a review, and construct a revised plan if necessary.

At the review, consider these issues:

- Have you achieved the target?
- If so, have you achieved it well? Do you feel really pleased and satisfied with what you have achieved?
- If you have not achieved the target, identify in what respect you have missed it. Is it a case purely of timing, or did you fail to obtain all the information you needed?
- If you did not have all necessary information, try to consider why not. Did you put enough effort into trying to obtain the information or carry out the task? Have you been held up because information was delayed in reaching you? Have you been delayed because of circumstances beyond your control?
- If timing was an issue, consider why? Was your original deadline unrealistic, for example did you think that you would carry out HND assignments more quickly than you actually have, or did you under-estimate the amount of time needed for your studies?

10.2 Re-setting aims, objectives and targets

Do not take the view that because you have failed to meet your targets you have failed in some way. That is de-motivating and depressing, and is likely to weaken your resolve to continue.

Once you have established, by means of the review discussed above, **why** problems have arisen, you are better placed to resolve them. Once you re-state your aims and objectives in a more manageable form, you will be more motivated to achieve them. It is always easier for you to attain something which is positively attainable.

Perhaps you should resolve to complete your HNC/HND studies within a longer period than you had originally planned, meaning that you are under less time pressure. Perhaps you should decide to take fewer units together, so that you can do yourself justice in the ones that you take.

Do not be afraid to discuss these issues with your line manager or your work colleagues and fellow students. Their feedback in the discussion process will be invaluable, and may give you an insight into your strengths and weaknesses which you had not previously appreciated.

Chapter roundup

- Different personal skills are required for interacting with other people, goal-planning, self-development, motivation and performance. To appraise yourself you need to make a start by building an accurate self-image and developing self-awareness.
- A SWOT analysis helps to identify your personal strengths and weaknesses and the opportunities and threats that affect your career opportunities and future prospects.
- The main management skills include planning, organising, motivating, communicating, controlling and creating. There are also other skills that are important, eg working with others, identifying and tackling problems and persuading.
- Time management implies planning the best use of time. It enables you to save at least some of the time you presently waste in one way or another in work and to use this time better in tackling jobs that really require your undivided attention and effort.
- Interpersonal skills involve inspiring, motivating, leading and controlling people to achieve organisational goals that are poorly defined. They are necessary for effective communication and achieving your aims from an interpersonal encounter.
- Competences are the critical skills, knowledge and attitudes that you must have to perform effectively. They are expressed in visible, behavioural terms and reflect the skills, knowledge and attitudes (the main components of any job) which must be demonstrated to an agreed standard and must contribute to the overall aims of the organisation.
- A personal skills audit and self-appraisal requires you to identify, review and assess your own performance of current management skills.
- In your development plan you must establish targets that you are aiming for. They can be short, medium or long-term targets. You can develop this alongside your time planning aid which will help you to prioritise the tasks that you have set yourself.
- Remember that all good plans must be monitored and evaluated. By establishing target dates for completion of certain aspects of your skills audit or development plan, you will need to carry out a review and, if necessary, construct a revised plan.

This chapter does not end with a Quick Quiz or an assignment as the subject matter has not comprised technical issues with specific answers.

The entire chapter has been a process of self-evaluation.

ASSIGNMENTS

NOTES

UNIT 13

Assignment 1 **(2 hours)**

Take an organisation that you know, or on which you can get the basic information required.

1 Draw an organisation chart for the organisation.

2 Explain the structure shown in the chart with reference to:

(a) the organisation's mission;
(b) its products;
(c) its markets;
(d) its method of production;
(e) any particular external influence.

Write up a list of your findings in the form of a list of bullet points for a presentation to be made to new recruits to the organisation.

Assignment 2 **(1½ hours)**

Duntoiling Nursing Homes

You are the personnel officer for Duntoiling Nursing and Retirement Homes PLC, a chain of residential complexes for senior citizens in the West Midlands region. Recently, Gareth Cheeseman, the bullish, entrepreneurial director, sent a brief memorandum to all staff informing them that all premises now constitute 'No Smoking' areas for patients, visitors and staff alike. Notices to this effect have gone up all round the homes. Duntoiling is also declaring its 'No Smoking' policy in recruitment advertisements.

The abruptness with which Cheeseman introduced this policy is now causing problems. It seems that some staff are continuing to smoke 'behind closed doors', and visitors and patients are flouting the ban in the corridors and toilets. Staff rebuking them have been subject to verbal abuse. Some staff also complain of suffering from stress because they cannot give up the craving.

The crunch came last week, when one supervisor issued a formal oral warning to a member of his staff caught 'red-handed' smoking in her office, and stated that if she repeated the offence she would be dismissed. The employee in question resigned in a fit of pique and is now claiming constructive dismissal, with union support.

Cheeseman has asked you to brief him on what action needs to be taken:

(a) to deal with the disciplinary case; and
(b) to ensure that the policy is complied with in the future.

What advice will you give? Present your answer in the form of a memorandum to Gareth Cheeseman.

UNIT 14

Assignment 3 **(1 hour)**

Broadside Retail Services

Broadside Retail Services of Leeds has a vacancy for an assistant accountant. The post is located in the financial accounting section of the company's large finance department which, among other things, is responsible for the preparation of interim and published accounts and the maintenance of the computerised nominal ledger records from which these accounts are compiled. The person appointed to the post is responsible for updating these records and this entails the supervision of a number of clerks. For these reasons the Chief Accountant is seeking to recruit a certified accounting technician.

(a) Prepare a draft of an appropriate advertisement for the post and indicate what you consider would be the most appropriate media of communication to prospective applicants.

(b) Define 'job description'.

(c) Specify the types of information that you consider should be incorporated into the job description for the post.

Assignment 4 **(1½ hours)**

Biotherm PLC

You are the Personnel Director for Biotherm PLC, a detergent and washing powder manufacturer based in Bootle, Merseyside. You have a staff of nine reporting to you, from junior clerks to senior managers, and you are just preparing for the annual round of appraisal interviews. One of your senior personnel officers, Alan Heath, has become a real problem child of late. You have never particularly warmed to this individual; he never really seems part of the team, his attendance record is poor and he never works beyond contracted hours. You know that Alan is not especially fit and healthy, but you rather feel he is playing on his physical condition.

You would describe yourself as a 'person-oriented' leader, although you acknowledge that with difficult staff you tend to become *laissez faire.* This has been the case with Alan: you have never tackled him on his absence record (29 days sickness in the past year) nor on his desire to work to contract. Apart from yourself, he is the only person with extensive and detailed knowledge of employment law, which is valuable in your organisational environment. You secretly admit that this is the main reason for your reticence in handling him: in spite of his difficult demeanour you would be lost without him.

However, you must now grasp the nettle and deal with the situation at his appraisal interview. Prepare a plan for the interview which not only reviews his past performance but also proposes a set of acceptable objectives for the forthcoming year. Remember that your meeting should not, if possible, degenerate into a disciplinary case! Your plan should be organised according to the following headings:

- assessment of performance
- how to improve current performance
- how to motivate Alan Heath
- how to assess him for promotability
- how to tackle unsatisfactory performance areas

Throughout this plan, you should anticipate questions, issues and objectives which he will raise, and resolve how to deal with them.

NOTES

UNIT 15

Assignment 5 **(1 hour)**

Managers need to assess the **quality** and **value** of information provided to them.

What attributes might they consider when they are doing this?

Assignment 6 Part 1 **(30 minutes)**

Read the following case study. As you read, make notes of any important information about the company (for example, size, type of organisation). Take particular note of any information regarding the forms of communications within this organisation. Try to structure your notes into issues that arise and actions which you think should be taken. (You will need these notes for this chapter's assignment).

John Gibb, the owner of Gibbs Motors, a small second-hand car garage, needed to invest in more stock. John usually obtained his cars from Wally's Car Auctions, a local auctioneers, but although John never had any problems with the cars he bought, rumour had it that some of the cars Wally's sold were of dubious ownership. He decided to look around for a more reputable car auctioneer.

After visiting many car auctions, John came across Quality, a car auctioneer selling second-hand cars of extremely high quality. John told Peter Gold, the owner, that he was interested in obtaining cars and said he would phone them the next day to confirm his order and specify which cars he wanted.

John spent a couple of days deciding which cars he wanted to buy. Before he could contact Quality, Peter Gold rang to ask John whether he still wanted to place an order. John specified the models he wanted and told Peter his price limit was two thousand pounds for each car, There was a lot of interference on the phone lines that day and the parties found it difficult to understand each other. John told Peter that he would fax through a confirmed order in writing. Before leaving the office that day, John left a note for his secretary to confirm the order.

Within the week five cars were delivered to John's garage. John was delighted with the quality of these cars and thought them good value for money. He advertised them in the local paper the next evening. Before the paper came out, the invoice for the cars arrived. To John's amazement the invoice was for £15,000. Thinking that there must be some mistake, John rang Peter Gold and asked why the bill was for £15,000 when it should have been for a maximum of £10,000. Peter said that once the vehicles were delivered to their new owner, whether it was a member of the public or another garage, they could not be returned and must be paid for. John sought legal advice, and found that, as he had confirmed the order in writing, Quality would either have to charge him the agreed price or accept the cars back. When John spoke to his secretary she denied all knowledge of his note and said she had not confirmed the order at all. John realised that short of being able to prove a verbal contact over the agreed price, he was stuck with five cars he could barely afford to pay for.

Part 2 **(1½ hours)**

From your notes above, write a report for John identifying the communication problems within his company. Make recommendations as to how communications could be improved to prevent a similar situation in the future.

ANSWERS TO ASSIGNMENTS

Answer to assignment 1

An example is Jones Brothers Department Store

It is organised in sales departments and support departments such as accounts and warehouse.

1 The mission is to be the best department store in town providing high quality goods and services to our customers.

2 Products are household goods and furniture, clothes, gardening goods, electrical and kitchen goods, hairdressing and haberdashery.

3 The market is the area around the town.

4 Purchase from original manufacturers and contract making of clothing.

5 The retail park ten miles away.

Answer to Assignment 2

Duntoiling Nursing Homes

To deal with this difficult situation effectively you need to do the following:

(a) introduce a disciplinary procedure if none currently exists;

(b) consider the Health and Safety at Work legislation, particularly the employer's obligations of duty and care towards staff;

(c) define constructive dismissal (this means where an organisation has changed terms and conditions of employment to such an extent that the employees feel they have no other option but to resign);

(d) consider the wisdom of unilateral changes in terms and conditions without notice (ie Cheeseman imposing these changes without any consultation);

(e) consider reinstating the employee with possible concessions (eg counselling to give up smoking);

(f) prepare your ideal and 'fall-back' positions when negotiating;

(g) question why the policy was introduced in the first place;

(h) ask why there was no involvement from the personnel function in implementing the smoking policy;

(i) develop a 'best practice' model showing how to introduce a smoking policy and do it again (remember the employer's duty to protect employees from the effects of passive smoking). The model should include:

    (i) a consultation period (say 3 months);
    (ii) establishing a consultative committee;
    (iii) conducting a staff attitude survey;
    (iv) making provision for special cases;
    (v) make formal changes to terms and conditions;
    (vi) retrain line managers in disciplinary matters;
    (vii) review and monitor the policy.

Again remember that the question asks for your answer to be in the form of a brief to Mr Cheeseman.

Answer to Assignment 3

Broadside Retail Services

Helping hand

For (a) include all the essential items you would expect to see in an advertisement.

For (b), a simple definition is all you need. Listing the key features of what a job description sets out would be a suitable approach.

For (c), use your answer to (b) as a list of the contents of a job description and then think about how to apply them to the situation in the question.

(a)

Guidance

You are asked to draft an advertisement for a job vacancy, and in examination conditions, you cannot be expected to devise a 'perfect' advertisement. However, you will be expected to include all the essential data items, and it is worth listing what these are before you start to write your advertisement.

1 Who is offering the job?

2 What, as a 'headline' for the ad, is the job?

3 What is the salary? Are there any other 'perks' with the job?

4 What are the qualifications needed for the job?

5 What does the job consist of?

6 Are there good career prospects?

7 How to apply for the job.

BROADSIDE RETAIL SERVICES

(Company logo)

ASSISTANT ACCOUNTANT

Salary £xxxx

Broadside Retail Services, a fast-growing company based in Leeds, needs an Assistant Accountant to join its large accounts department and to be responsible for maintaining the company's computerised nominal ledger records and for the preparation of interim and published accounts.

The successful applicant will be a certified accounting technician with some previous experience of working with computerised financial accounting systems. Experience in the supervision of staff would be an advantage.

Career prospects for hard-working and well-motivated accountants are outstanding, and conditions of employment are all that you would expect from a successful company.

For further information about the job, or for an application form, please telephone or write to

John Smith

Personnel Manager

Broadside Retail Services

(address)

(telephone number)

The media used to advertise the job vacancy should reach the 'target audience' of certified accounting technicians, probably in the Leeds area only.

Two media

(i) An advertisement in a professional accountancy magazine, such as Accountancy Age might be considered useful,

(ii) A 'space' advertisement in one or more local newspapers in the Leeds area, which will be read by local residents, including accounting technicians.

(b) A job description is a document or record which sets out in a standardised format:

(i) the job title and the purpose of the job;

(ii) details about the scope and contents of the job and the tasks performed;

(iii) the responsibilities involved;

(iv) the skills, training and/or qualifications required;

(v) the organisational relationships between the duties of the job and other jobs.

(c)

Guidance

Do not forget that the question is not asking about what, in general terms, are the contents of a job description. You are being asked to specify the type of information that should go into the job description for the assistant accountant at Broadside Retail Services. Try to specify the main duties of the job in some detail - about five duties would probably be sufficient. The format of a job description can vary, but should contain somewhere at least most of the information given in the suggested answer.

Job title: Assistant accountant

Department: Accounts department

Job Code Number: 1234

Responsible to: Senior accountant

Job summary:

The job holder is responsible for the preparation of the company's interim and published accounts and for the maintenance of the computerised nominal ledger records from which these accounts are compiled.

The computer system consists of a multi-user system of [type of computer] using [type of software].

Main duties:

(1) Maintain up-to-date nominal ledger records.

(2) Provide for the security of the nominal ledger accounts by maintaining suitable back-up files.

(3) Supervise the work of the three input clerks.

(4) Provide the management accountant with data for budgetary control.

(5) Assist the senior accountant in the preparation of the interim and published accounts.

Responsible for:

(1) The budget for the nominal ledger section of the accounts department.

(2) Three input clerks in the nominal ledger system.

(3) Liasing with IT suppliers.

Co-operative relationships: with the management accountant for budgetary control.

Reporting to: senior accountant

Experience required for the job:

(1) Working experience with financial accounting microcomputer systems.

(2) Professional qualification as an accounting technician.

Job description:

Prepared by	J Smith, senior accountant
Agreed by	W Brown, chief accountant
Date of preparation	....

Answer to Assignment 4

Biotherm PLC

The overall purpose of the appraisal interview should be to encourage Alan Heath to become more a part of the personnel team (after all he has specialist knowledge which cannot be replaced). You cannot ignore his sickness record because it impacts on performance. However, you should attempt to understand the reasons behind his poor attendance rather than tackling it at this stage (this is best left for a separate occasion). You should ensure at all costs that the appraisal interview does not become a disciplinary one.

Your plan should include the following:

(a) discussion on achievement of past objectives;

(b) reasons behind failure to achieve objectives;

(c) problems and successes in current performance (you should have consulted in advance with the main people Alan interacts with, eg line managers, colleagues, external clients);

(d) attempts to understand Alan's personal needs (he may be motivated by his 'expertise' for example, rather than any additional pay award);

(e) a discussion of Alan's job aspirations; this will follow on from the previous point but you should have done your homework in advance on the requirements of the job immediately senior to his;

(f) a commitment not to duck difficult issues but to explore; you may find out some very good reasons behind his refusal to work beyond contracted hours, for example;

(g) an attempt to agree a set of SMART objectives.

Your approach to this interview should be 'problem-solving', rather than 'tell and sell' or 'tell and listen'.

Answer to Assignment 5

Quality

A manager should weigh up the quality of information he or she receives against certain theoretical qualities of 'good information'. These include [*five of*] the following.

(a) **Relevance**

Information must be relevant to the purpose for which a manager wants to use it. Far too many reports fail to 'keep to the point' and contain purposeless, irritating paragraphs which only serve to vex the managers reading them.

(b) **Completeness**

An information user should have all the information he needs to do his job properly. If he does not have a complete picture of the situation, he might well make bad decisions.

(c) **Accuracy**

Information should obviously be accurate because using incorrect information could have serious and damaging consequences. However, information should only be accurate enough for its purpose and there is no need to go into unnecessary detail for pointless accuracy.

(d) **Clarity**

Information must be clear to the user. If the user does not understand it properly he cannot use it properly. Lack of clarity is one of the causes of a breakdown in communication, which is referred to in information system theory as 'noise'.

(e) **Consistency**

An important quality of information (especially in accounting) is that it is prepared consistently, for instance so that it is valid to compare reports from two different periods.

(f) **Reliability**

Information must be trusted by the managers who are expected to use it. Information sources will not be used if they have proved unreliable in the past. Information relating to the future or to the external environment is uncertain.

(g) **Communication**

Information that is needed might be communicated to a person who does not have the authority to act on it, or who is not responsible for the matter and so does not see any need to act on it. Sometimes one method of communication is better than another, for instance a telephone call as compared with a letter.

(h) **Conciseness**

There are physical and mental limitations to what a person can read, absorb and understand properly before taking action. An enormous mountain of information, even if it is all relevant, cannot be handled. Reports to management must therefore be clear and concise and in many systems, control action works basically on the 'exception' principle. This is especially true of tactical information for management control.

(i) **Timeliness**

Information, to be of any use, must be produced when it is needed. Information which is not available until after a decision is made will be useful only for comparisons and longer-term control, and may serve no purpose even then.

(j) **Costs and benefits are dealt with below.**

Value

The **value** of information can also be assessed by reference to certain theoretical ideas.

Basically, information is only worth collecting if the **benefits** obtainable from it exceed the **costs** of collection. There are many ways in which information might give value. For example, it might lead to a **decision to take action** which results in reducing costs, eliminating losses or increasing sales - or it might lead to a **better utilisation** of **resources**, or **prevent fraud**.

As the value of information lies in the action taken as a result of receiving it, an assessment of value may be reached by asking the following questions:

(a) **what** information is provided?

(b) what is it **used** for?

(c) **who** uses it?

(d) **how often** is it used?

(e) does the frequency with which it is used coincide with the frequency with which it is provided?

(f) what is **achieved** by using it?

(g) what **other** relevant information is available which could be **used instead**?

An assessment of the value of information can be derived in this way, and the cost of obtaining it should then be compared against this value. On the basis of this comparison, it can be decided whether certain items of information are worth having.

Answer to Assignment 6

Part 1

Your notes could include the following points.

- Gibbs Motors seem to be a small company; there is an owner and a secretary, but no one else is mentioned.
- Gibbs has used a local supplier and never had any problems.
- John Gibb listens to rumours.
- John Gibb has time to visit many auctioneers.
- John Gibb is not in a hurry for new stock.
- John Gibb placed the order when prompted.
- John Gibb did not confirm his own order.
- John Gibb communicated by a note to his secretary.

- The cars were of good quality.
- John Gibb is in a hurry to sell them.
- Is his secretary telling the truth?
- Gibbs Motors has low cash flow.
- Communications – John Gibb does not seem to like written communications.

Part 2

Check your report against the following guidance:

The Terms of reference are given in the questions:

(a) identify communication problems;
(b) make recommendations for the future.

Your Introduction should not retell the story, but should outline the salient points: the size and nature of the organisation, the individuals, and the circumstances.

In the Main body of your report, you should highlight any problems, such as:

(a) the owner of Gibbs Motors listens to rumours and ignores his own experience

(b) there is an over reliance on verbal communication

(c) there is a reluctance on the part of the owner to enter into written communication with his supplier

(d) the owner of Gibbs Motors does not encourage feedback from suppliers or staff. (You may also identify other problems.)

You may have decided that some of these problems are symptoms of a deeper problem. You should draw all this together into your Conclusion.

In your Recommendations you should have included the need to:

(a) identify appropriate media for the message;
(b) use written communications where records are needed;
(c) encourage and listen to feedback;
(d) ensure that the message actually reaches its intended recipient.

Your recommendations should be detailed and focused on the case. They must be backed up by reasoned argument.

INDEX

NOTES

BPP PUBLISHING

NOTES

BPP PUBLISHING

NOTES

BPP PUBLISHING

NOTES

ORDER FORM

Any books from our HNC/HND range can be ordered in one of the following ways:

- Telephone us on **020 8740 2211**
- Send this page to our **Freepost** address
- Fax this page on **020 8740 1184**
- Email us at **publishing@bpp.com**
- Go to our website: **www.bpp.com**

We aim to deliver to all UK addresses inside 5 working days. Orders to all EU addresses should be delivered within 6 working days. All other orders to overseas addresses should be delivered within 8 working days.

BPP Publishing Ltd
Aldine House
Aldine Place
London W12 8AW
Tel: 020 8740 2211
Fax: 020 8740 1184
Email: publishing@bpp.com

Full name: ______________________________

Day-time delivery address: ______________________________

____

______________________________ Postcode ______________

Day-time telephone (for queries only): ______________________________

BPP PUBLISHING

Please send me the following quantities of books:

Core

		No. of copies	Price	Total
Unit 1	Marketing (8/00)		£7.95	
Unit 2	Managing Financial Resources (8/00)		£7.95	
Unit 3	Organisations and Behaviour (8/00)		£7.95	
Unit 4	Organisations, Competition and Environment (8/00)		£7.95	
Unit 5	Quantitative Techniques for Business (8/00)		£7.95	
Unit 6	Legal and Regulatory Framework (8/00)		£7.95	
Unit 7	Management Information Systems (8/00)		£7.95	
Unit 8	Business Strategy (8/00)		£7.95	

Option

Units 9-12	Business & Finance (1/2001)		£10.95	
Units 13-16	Business & Management (1/2001)		£10.95	
Units 17-20	Business & Marketing (1/2001)		£10.95	
Unit 21-24	Business & Personnel (1/2001)		£10.95	

Other Material

	Workbook (3/00)		£9.95	

Sub Total	£

Postage & Packaging

UK : Course book £3.00 for first plus £2.00 for each extra, Workbook £2.00 for first plus £1.00 for each	£
Europe : (inc. ROI) Course book £5.00 for first plus £4.00 for each extra, Workbook £2.50 for first plus £1.00 for each	£
Rest of the world : Course book £20.00 for first plus £10.00 for each extra, Workbook £2.50 for first plus £1.00 for each	£

Grand Total	£

I enclose a cheque for £______________ (cheque to BPP Publishing Ltd) or charge to Access/VISA/Switch

Card number: ☐☐☐☐☐☐☐☐☐☐☐☐☐☐☐☐☐☐☐

Issues number (Switch only): ______________________________

Start date: ____________________ Expiry date: ____________________

Signature ____

BPP PUBLISHING

REVIEW FORM & FREE PRIZE DRAW

We are constantly reviewing, updating and improving our Course Books. We would be grateful for any comments or thoughts you have on this Course Book. Cut out and send this page to our Freepost address and you will be automatically entered in a £50 prize draw.

Jed Cope
HNC/HND Range Manager
BPP Publishing Ltd, FREEPOST, London W12 8BR

Full name: ______________________________

Address: ______________________________

____

______________________________ Postcode ______________

Where are you studying?

Where did you find out about BPP range books?

Why did you decide to buy this Course Book?

Have you used our texts for the other units in your HNC/HND studies?

What thoughts do you have on our:

- Introductory pages
- Topic coverage
- Summary diagrams, icons, chapter roundups and quick quizzes
- Discussion topics, activities and assignments

The other side of this form is left blank for any further comments you wish to make.

Please give any further comments and suggestions (with page number if necessary) below.

FREE PRIZE DRAW RULES

1. Closing date for 31 January 2001 draw is 31 December 2000. Closing date for 31 July 2001 draw is 30 June 2001.
2. Restricted to entries with UK and Eire addresses only. BPP employees, their families and business associates are excluded.
3. No purchase necessary. Entry forms are available upon request from BPP Publishing. No more than one entry per title, per person. Draw restricted to persons aged 16 and over.
4. Winners will be notified by post and receive their cheques not later than 6 weeks after the relevant draw date.
5. The decision of the promoter in all matters is final and binding. No correspondence will be entered into.

BPP PUBLISHING